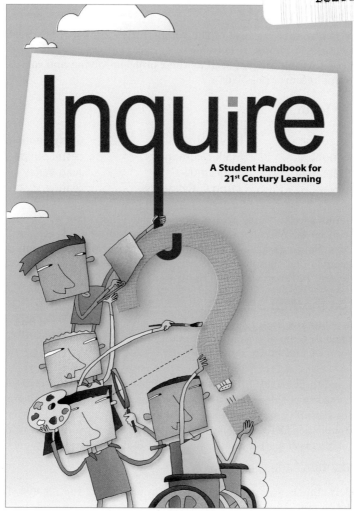

Inquire

A Student Handbook for 21st Century Learning

Robert King, Christopher Erickson, and Janae Sebranek

Created by

Thoughtful Learning

Distributed exclusively by

ZB **Zaner-Bloser**

Acknowledgments

Inquire is a reality because of the collaborative efforts of our hardworking team of educators, students, researchers, writers, editors, and designers. Their critical and creative thinking, as well as their problem-solving and communication skills, made this resource possible.

The *Inquire* Team

Steven J. Augustyn	Lois Krenzke	Cindy Smith
Colleen Belmont	Mark Lalumondier	Lester Smith
Mariellen Hanrahan	April Lindau	Jean Varley
Tim Kemper	Jason C. Reynolds	Jeanne Yost

A special thanks goes to Cindy Smith, project-based instructor at Karcher Middle School in Burlington, Wisconsin. In addition to providing guidance and feedback on *Inquire*, Mrs. Smith graciously allowed the team to field-test the material in her class. Her insights and those of her 32 seventh- and eighth-grade students greatly improved *Inquire*. To them, we say "Thank you!"

Inquire on the Web

This book is just the beginning! Log on to thoughtfullearning.com to find dozens of downloadable templates and forms, additional models and projects, links to great resources, and much, much more.

Trademarks and trade names are shown in this book strictly for illustrative purposes and are the property of their respective owners. The authors' references herein should not be regarded as affecting their validity. Wikipedia is a registered trademark of the Wikimedia Foundation. Microsoft and PowerPoint are either trademarks or registered trademarks of Microsoft Corporation in the United States and/or other countries.

Copyright © by Thoughtful Learning

Distributed in the U.S.A. exclusively by Zaner-Bloser, Inc., 1-800-421-3018, www.zaner-bloser.com.

No part of this work may be reproduced or transmitted in any form or by any means, electronic or mechanical, including photocopying and recording, or by any information storage or retrieval system without the prior written permission of Thoughtful Learning unless such copying is expressly permitted by federal copyright law. Address inquiries to Permissions, Thoughtful Learning, PO Box 460, Burlington, Wisconsin 53105.

ISBN (softcover) 978-1-932436-34-1
6 7 8 9 10 13880 16 15 14 13

ISBN (hardcover) 978-1-932436-35-8
3 4 5 6 7 8 9 10 13880 16 15 14 13 12

ISBN (online) 978-1-932436-38-9

Printed in the U.S.A.

SUSTAINABLE FORESTRY INITIATIVE

Certified Chain of Custody
Promoting Sustainable Forestry

www.sfiprogram.org
SFI-01171

This SFI label applies to the text paper.

About *Inquire*

Inquire is your personal learning guide. It will help you become a better thinker, problem solver, speaker, team player, planner, and researcher in all of your classes. This guide is divided into three parts.

Part I: Building 21st Century Skills

The first part helps you develop the skills you need to succeed in school, in life, and later in the world of work. It covers everything from critical thinking and building strong arguments to using social media and studying for tests.

Part II: Using the Inquiry Process

The second part provides an overview of the inquiry process, including conducting research and presenting what you have learned. To inquire means "to question," and the process of asking questions and searching for answers leads to authentic learning.

Part III: Developing Projects

The third part helps you create all sorts of exciting and meaningful projects—from writing news reports to creating podcasts, from developing brochures to building scale models.

Electronic Aids

The **e-book version** of *Inquire* contains links to make it easy to search for information from part to part. And the *Inquire* Web site contains downloadable planning sheets, additional models, activities, and projects to try! (Go to thoughtfullearning.com.)

Using *Inquire*

The special design of *Inquire* makes it easy to find information from part to part and within each part. With practice, you will know the best way to turn to the guidelines, models, and tips that you need.

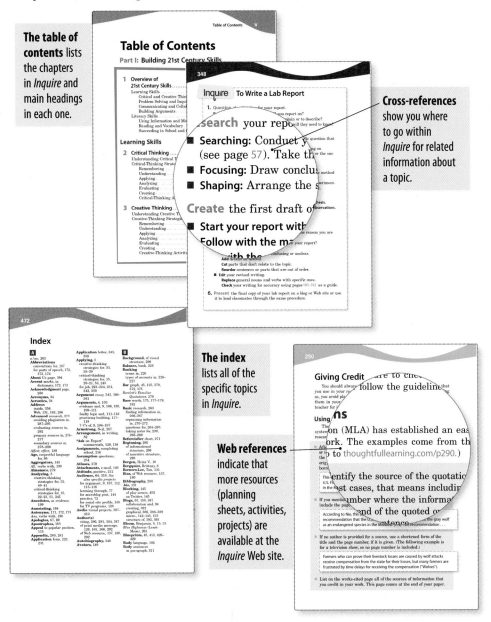

The table of contents lists the chapters in *Inquire* and main headings in each one.

Cross-references show you where to go within *Inquire* for related information about a topic.

The index lists all of the specific topics in *Inquire*.

Web references indicate that more resources (planning sheets, activities, projects) are available at the *Inquire* Web site.

Table of Contents

Part I: Building 21st Century Skills

Learning Skills

Literacy Skills

Part II: Using the Inquiry Process

Part III: Developing Projects

Photos

Arnold Zucker: 433 (Burglar Alarm)

Corbis: 299, 313, 314

Cory Militzer: 413, 433, 436 (Rube Goldberg Machines)

iStockPhoto: xiv, 7, 16 (Marie Curie Stamp), 17 (Westward Expansion), 20, 45 (Diorama), 53 (Airboat), 79, 90, 113, 115, 175, 205, 331, 365, 425 (Diorama Plants)

Jennie King: 439, 454 (Play Photos)

Public Domain: 363, 416 (Political Cartoon)

ShutterStock: vii, viii, x, xii, 4, 5, 9, 11, 16 (Ford's Theater and Abacus), 17 (Justice Statue and Martin Luther King Jr. Stamp), 18, 19, 28, 34, 36, 37, 40, 41, 42, 44, 45 (Blueprint, Future City, and Video Camera), 46, 50, 53 (Speed Boat Illustration), 55, 57, 62, 65, 68, 73, 75, 88, 92, 94, 95, 96, 98, 100, 104, 111, 112, 118, 120, 122, 124, 126, 132, 133, 135, 136, 138, 141, 142, 143, 144, 145, 146, 147, 151, 152, 153, 154, 159, 161, 162, 170, 172, 173, 180, 186, 189, 192, 196, 199, 201, 206, 215, 218, 220, 221, 222, 225, 227, 228, 230, 232, 239, 240, 242, 246, 251, 256, 258, 262, 264, 266, 267, 268, 269, 270, 276, 278, 283, 285, 288, 295, 297, 302, 304, 305, 308, 318, 319, 321, 325, 327, 329, 330, 333, 335, 336, 337, 339, 342, 343, 345, 347, 349, 350, 351, 353, 355, 359, 360, 361, 367, 368, 380, 386, 387, 388, 389, 391 (all except Persian Windmill), 393, 396, 398, 399 (Computer Screen), 403, 409 (Video Camera), 412 (all except Cartoon), 413 (all except Rube Goldberg Machine), 417 (Photo Cartoons), 419, 421, 423, 425 (Ambulance and Army Dioramas), 429, 431, 438, 439 (Horse), 441, 443, 447, 449, 453, 456, 457, 460, 465, 467, 469, 471

Why *Inquire*?

What do artists, engineers, scientists, doctors, and students like you have in common? All of you have to ask questions, conduct research, communicate, and collaborate to do your best work. In fact, skills like these are at the core of real learning.

A Handbook for 21st Century Skills

Inquire will help you learn about and practice all of the key learning skills. Here are the main skills covered in the first part of the book:

- Critical and creative thinking
- Collaborating and communicating
- Problem solving and building arguments
- Understanding and using media
- Studying and taking tests

A Handbook for Inquiry and Projects

Inquire also helps you use the inquiry process to solve problems and develop great projects. Here are some of the inquiry-based skills and projects covered in the next two parts of the book:

- Asking questions and planning research
- Creating and presenting projects
- Developing writing and Web projects
- Building audio-visual and graphic projects
- Preparing community and performing projects

A Handbook for All of Your Classes

You can use *Inquire* in all of your classes, in your extracurricular activities, and in life itself. *Inquire* will help you succeed right now and prepare you to learn and succeed for years to come!

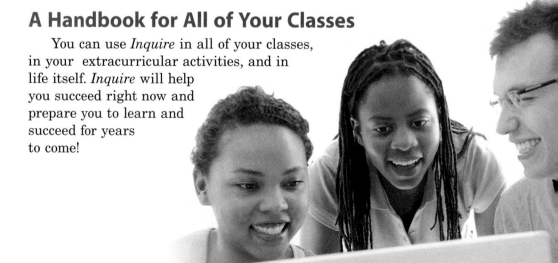

Part I: Building 21st Century Skills

Part I: Building 21st Century Skills

This section covers all of the important 21st century skills—and more. If you follow the strategies in each chapter, you will become a better thinker and learner now and for years to come. These skills will also help you use the inquiry process and create great projects in Parts II and III.

Chapters in This Section

1. Overview of 21st Century Skills
2. Critical Thinking
3. Creative Thinking
4. Problem Solving
5. Communicating
6. Collaborating
7. Building Arguments
8. Understanding Media
9. Using Social Media
10. Reading to Learn
11. Improving Vocabulary
12. Following Basic Conventions
13. Improving Study Skills
14. Succeeding in School
15. Succeeding in the Workplace

Chapter 1
Overview of 21st Century Skills

Take a thin strip of paper, lay it flat, and you've made a straight line. Then connect the ends, and you've made a circle—simple enough.

Next, take that same strip of paper, twist it once, and then connect the ends. You've made a new shape, called a Möbius (mō-bē-ŭs) strip, which forms a continuous curve with only one surface. An ant crawling along this strip could cover every part of it without crossing an edge.

We want you to think of learning as a continuous curve, a process that never stops. It's like looking out over a vast landscape. There is always more ground to cover, and more to learn.

You will learn . . .

- Critical and Creative Thinking
- Problem Solving and Inquiry
- Communicating and Collaborating
- Building Arguments
- Using Information and Media
- Succeeding in School and the Workplace

Becoming a Better Learner

You are riding the great wave of technology right along with everyone else, including your teachers. This wave is determining the way you learn, socialize, and live. And since it is getting bigger and stronger, you must build a new set of skills, often called "21st century skills," to help you control and enjoy the ride. These skills include . . .

- **Critical and creative thinking**
- **Problem solving and inquiry**
- **Communicating and collaborating**
- **Building arguments**

But you need to strengthen your basic reading and study skills, too, including the following:

- **Using information and media**
- **Reading and vocabulary**
- **Note taking**
- **Managing your time**
- **Preparing for tests**

> **One thing is certain: In today's world, everyone must be a strong learner, now and in the future.**

Your Turn

Which of these skills do you already use, and which are completely new to you? Which ones do you really need to work on? Jot down your thoughts in a short paragraph or two.

Learning in Context

The best way to learn these skills is in context, while you are involved in a project or a unit of study. Knowing about creative thinking, for example, won't do you much good until you put your creativity to use.

Remember: Learning is not a straight line, starting here and stopping there. Instead, learning is continuous—involving the subjects you are studying and the skills that help you learn. They are all part of your personal Möbius strip.

Creative Thinking Collaboration Note Taking Managing Your Time Preparing for Tests Critical Thinking

Learning Skills

The next five pages review the skills that have become especially important in today's world, starting with critical and creative thinking. Each of these skills is also covered in its own chapter.

Critical and Creative Thinking

You think creatively to gather new possibilities, and you think critically to examine ideas and discard the ones that don't work. Just as breathing requires inhaling and exhaling, thinking requires inspiration and examination.

Critical thinking is looking closely at something and using reason to explore it. When you think critically, you do the following:

- identify
- reason
- diagram
- measure
- rate
- organize

Creative thinking is reaching out to capture new ideas and possibilities. When you think creatively, you do the following:

- wonder
- imagine
- brainstorm
- connect
- reimagine
- invent

Your Turn

Freewrite for 5 minutes about critical and creative thinking. Which type of thinking is like breathing in, and which type is like breathing out? Why?

Deepening Your Thinking

To be a really effective thinker, you need to deepen your thinking. A researcher named Benjamin Bloom identified ever-deeper levels of critical and creative thinking.

Remembering is recalling facts.

Understanding is knowing what facts mean.

Applying is using your knowledge.

Analyzing is breaking something apart.

Evaluating is judging the worth of something.

Creating is making something new.

Problem Solving and Inquiry

When you face a problem or challenge, you need your best critical and creative thinking skills. To solve a complicated problem, you may need to work through a series of steps called the inquiry process. You'll learn much more about problem solving and inquiry later in this book, but here is a quick overview.

Problem-Solving Steps

- **Questioning** involves identifying the problem, analyzing its causes and effects, brainstorming ways to solve it, and evaluating your ideas.

- **Planning** involves choosing a solution, setting goals and objectives, and deciding what time, tools, and talent you will use to solve the problem.

- **Researching** means gathering the information and resources that you need to be able to make your solution a reality.

- **Creating** is putting your solution together, making something new, and applying it to fix the problem.

- **Improving** means evaluating what you have created, seeing what works and what could work better, and then making changes to make it better.

- **Presenting** is implementing the solution, putting it into practice with the hope of solving the problem.

Your Turn

Think of a problem you face and imagine using the process above to solve it. Start by identifying the problem, analyzing its causes, and brainstorming solutions. What would you do then?

Communicating

You are part of a communications revolution, and you have technology to thank for it. Everyone is talking and texting and blogging. Let's look at some of the electronic communication opportunities for a typical student on a typical day.

A Day in the Life of a Student

Nahla woke up and started her day with a text message to her friend.

In social studies, she e-mailed a student in another school to exchange ideas.

In English class, Nahla wrote a book review and posted it on the classroom blog.

Later, in the evening, she checked her RSS feed for ideas for a current-events paper.

Then she chatted with friends on an instant messenger before going to bed.

What You Need to Know

In today's world, becoming a skilled communicator is very important. And each new digital advance seems to make communicating that much more important. You may be fine with communicating socially (texting), but what about communicating in formal school settings? Can you write strong essays and make oral presentations? Can you compose clear e-mails and express yourself in class discussions? In this digital age, you need strong writing and speaking skills.

A Closer Look

Writer William Zinsser says, "Writing and learning and thinking are all the same process." We'd like to add "speaking" to the list. Every type of communication helps you to think and learn as you share your ideas with others.

Your Turn

In a brief paragraph, list the kinds of writing and speaking you do in school. (Consider all of your communicating experiences.)

Collaborating

LeBron James and Drew Brees are star athletes, and their individual skills may amaze you. But when stars like these are interviewed, they say they couldn't have achieved success without their teammates.

Collaborating, which means "working together as a team," helps all kinds of people do all kinds of great things. If you have been part of a strong team, you already know about the value of collaborating.

Playing as a Team

A team succeeds on the strength of each of its members. A strong team member . . .

- knows how to listen,
- contributes as needed,
- shares the stage,
- offers compliments,
- gives constructive criticism,
- avoids put-downs,
- helps reach decisions, and
- works toward the team goal.

> **"Coming together is a beginning. Keeping together is progress. Working together is success."**
> —Henry Ford

What You Need to Know

Developing effective group skills will help you in school, especially since learning is becoming more and more collaborative. You will be a member of many learning teams, asking and answering important questions and working on interesting projects. Group work, by the way, is common in almost all careers and professions.

In Focus

Brittany Bergquist, with the assistance of her classmates and teacher, helped soldiers in our armed services pay their cell phone bills for calls to their families. They started with bake sales to pay for one soldier's bill; then the phone company canceled the bill after hearing about the sale. Next, Brittany's team earned money by collecting and recycling old cell phones. Before long, "Cell Phones for Soldiers" was born, providing free phone time for soldiers. *Lesson:* Look for opportunities to collaborate and make a difference.

Your Turn

In a brief paragraph, answer this question: What has been your best experience with a team or group? (Consider what the group accomplished, your role in the group, and the roles of other group members.)

Building Arguments

Your best thinking and communicating skills come together when you build an argument. An argument is a line of reasoning that provides strong evidence to prove a specific point. You can use the 7 C's to build an argument.

The 7 C's of Argumentation

1. **Consider the situation.** Begin by thinking about your topic, your audience, and your purpose. Then create a beginning position statement.

2. **Clarify your thinking.** Look at both sides of the issue. In addition to gathering support for your own position, consider what the opposition thinks.

3. **Construct a claim.** Go back to your position statement and see if you still agree. Then rewrite the statement, giving not just a position but also a reason.

4. **Collect evidence.** Research the topic in depth, looking for facts, statistics, examples, quotations, and other details to support your position.

5. **Counter or concede objections.** Think about the arguments of the opposition, and come up with ways to answer the arguments.

6. **Convince your audience.** Build your argument, appealing to the audience's sense of fairness and logic.

7. **Conclude your argument.** Draw together your best thoughts in a memorable way and call the audience to take action.

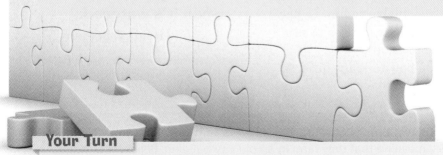

Your Turn

Think of an argument you recently made, whether supporting an idea or opposing it. Which of these 7 C's did you use? Was your argument convincing?

Literacy Skills

In this information age, your ability to find and evaluate information is crucial. Literacy skills will help you succeed in school and in life.

Using Information and Media

You are surrounded by information: Web sites, commercials, magazine articles, contests, TV shows, games . . . Managing information is a modern survival skill. You have to know what to pay attention to, what information is accurate and unbiased, and how you can find what you need.

And you aren't just a consumer of information. You also produce it. You can create multimedia presentations, videos, live news shows, podcasts, and many other types of media. Just as you evaluate the information that you receive, you need to evaluate the information that you send out.

Your Turn

On a scale of 1, meaning "not experienced," to 10, meaning "very experienced," how would you rate your online searching skills? Explain your rating in a brief paragraph.

Digital Learning and Sharing

The Internet is the ultimate learning tool. A skilled online learner . . .

- finds appropriate information on the Internet,
- evaluates the information for accuracy and reliability,
- understands all of the digital tools available to him or her,
- takes risks and tries to use these tools, and
- knows how to judge different media choices.

> **"Information is the seed for an idea and only grows when it's watered."**
> —Heinz V. Bergen

In Focus

Joe Heineman and Johanna Hearron-Heineman have become vertical farmers, meaning that they farm in an old city building. Believe it or not, they grow butter lettuce and tilapia (fish) in their farm. They are a green business and got their start by doing research on the Internet. *Lesson:* Gathering and using information creatively is an important lifelong skill.

Reading and Vocabulary

Reading is a *gateway skill* because it opens up so many learning opportunities. As you read more skillfully, your vocabulary will naturally grow, which, in turn, will improve your ability to think and to communicate.

Reading to Learn / Learning to Read

Reading every day will help you develop your talents and interests to their fullest. An effective reader . . .

- reads for enjoyment and reads to learn,
- understands the value of different types of reading material,
- uses study-reading strategies,
- writes and speaks about reading material, and
- uses vocabulary-building strategies.

In Focus

Reading opens doors. Lois Lowry, author of *The Giver,* learned to read when she was three. And her mother continued to read out loud to her long after she could read on her own. Lowry's introduction to reading at such an early age prepared her for the writing career she pursued later in life. *Lesson:* Make reading an important part of your life, and it will benefit you in more ways than you can imagine.

Your Turn

Share with a partner or small group of students the title of a favorite novel, nonfiction book, or article you have read recently. Explain your choice.

Succeeding in School

Effective learners take control of their learning. They actively engage in class by

- valuing all learning opportunities,
- managing time wisely,
- taking clear notes,
- summarizing important information, and
- using effective test-taking strategies.

Unless you have a positive attitude about learning, you are unlikely to do well. So be determined to be a strong student in all of your classes. You will learn a lot—and have fun doing it.

Your Turn

On a scale of 1, meaning "ineffective," to 10, meaning "very effective," rate your study skills. Explain your rating in a brief paragraph.

Succeeding in the Workplace

Of course, all of these traditional and 21st century skills are also meant to help you succeed in your career. As you will see in a later chapter, success in the workplace is a matter of respect.

You need to respect your . . .

- **organization,** understanding the company's goals and working to achieve them.
- **boss,** knowing what this person expects and following her or his directions.
- **coworkers,** treating them well and working together with them.
- **customers,** providing them the best products and services you can.
- **self,** dressing appropriately, conducting yourself professionally, and taking pride in what you do.
- **job,** following the schedule, arriving on time, and working hard.
- **career,** proving your value and taking on new challenges.

Your Turn

Imagine your dream job. What would it be? Freewrite for 5 minutes about the job and describe how respect will help you excel.

Chapter 2
Critical Thinking

Critical thinking is careful thinking, measured and exact—the kind of thinking that someone like Albert Einstein did. And your brain is wired to think critically, too. Every day you must remember, analyze, and evaluate information both in and out of school.

This chapter will show you how to strengthen your critical-thinking skills, preparing you not only to accomplish everyday tasks but also to take on complicated assignments. As Albert Einstein once said, "The whole of science is nothing more than a refinement of everyday thinking."

You will learn . . .

- Critical-Thinking Strategies
- Remembering
- Understanding
- Applying
- Analyzing
- Evaluating
- Creating

Understanding Critical Thinking

Critical thinking involves looking very closely at something and using reason to thoroughly understand it. On the next few pages, you'll find a series of strategies that will help you think critically. With these critical-thinking strategies, you can learn just about anything and solve almost any problem.

A Critical State of Mind

When you have a problem to solve or an important question to answer, you'll be at your critical best if you work in the following ways.

Be patient. Many problems or questions can be complex. If solutions or answers don't come to you immediately, keep thinking.

Be open. Be open to surprises—enjoy them, value them. Ask "Why?" and "What if?" just like little brothers and sisters do.

Be focused. Make it your goal to concentrate on your task (*finding a solution, answering a question*). Try to block out distractions.

Be observant. Find evidence to support your decisions. Adjust your thinking if a new idea changes your point of view.

Be critical. Ask yourself questions such as, "Is this information up to date?" "Does it match up with the thoughts of others?" "Can I trust this person's ideas?"

Be flexible. Understand that you can't neatly answer every question or resolve every problem. Some problems, for example, may have two reasonable solutions that are quite different.

Your Turn

Review the list above. Which habits of critical thinking do you naturally have? Which habits do you need to learn?

Critical-Thinking Strategies

A researcher named Benjamin Bloom created a list of thinking skills, moving from simpler, surface thinking to deeper thinking. The newest version of this list is shown below. On the following pages, you'll learn critical-thinking strategies to use in many situations to think more deeply.

Bloom's Thinking Skills

Remembering

is recalling basic information.

You'll learn strategies for identifying and remembering the key details about a topic (pages 16–17).

Understanding

is knowing what the information means.

You'll learn strategies for thinking deductively and inductively about a topic (pages 18–19).

Applying

is putting the information to use.

You'll learn strategies for planning a project and setting goals (pages 20–21).

Analyzing

is looking at the parts of something and figuring out how they fit together.

You'll learn strategies for comparing, contrasting, classifying, and sequencing ideas, as well as exploring causes and effects (pages 22–23).

Evaluating

is determining the value or worth of something.

You'll learn strategies for rating something and using a rubric to evaluate it (pages 24–25).

Creating

is putting ideas together in new ways to make something.

You'll learn strategies for creating a three-part structure and organizing ideas (pages 26–28).

Remembering

Critical thinking begins with remembering the basic information about a topic. To discover the basic information about a topic, ask yourself the questions in each category below.

Person

Name? Marie Curie
Life Span? 1867-1934
Nationality? French/Polish
Occupation? Physicist and chemist
Accomplishments? Discovered polonium
                 Discovered radium

Place

Name? Ford's Theater
Location? 511 Tenth Street, NW
          Washington, D.C.
Importance? Theater where Lincoln was
            assassinated by Booth
Description? This fully renovated 19th-century theater is run by the
             national parks service. It includes a museum about
             Lincoln and the Civil War.

Thing

Name? Abacus
Color? Black/brown
Shape? Rectangular
Size? Small
Material? Wood
Age? Old
Use? Calculation

Your Turn

Identify a person, place, or thing that you are studying by answering the questions listed above about it. Come up with other questions you could answer about the topic. Then answer them.

Idea

Name? Justice
Definition? Providing what is due to all
Synonyms? Fairness, correctness
Antonyms? Discrimination, unfairness
Example? Equal opportunity employment
Quotation? "Injustice anywhere is a threat to
   justice everywhere." —Dr. Martin Luther King, Jr.

Event

Name? Westward expansion
Who? European settlers
What? Headed west
Where? On the Oregon Trail
When? From the 1830s to the 1890s
Why? To homestead
How? They rode in wagon trains

Your Turn

Choose a person, a place, a thing, an idea, or an event that you are currently studying, and write down answers for each question about the topic. Then give your list of questions and answers to a partner and have the person quiz you aloud about the topic. Here's an example:

Questions and Answers

Name? March on Washington
Who? Martin Luther King, Jr.
What? Gave his "I Have a Dream" speech
Where? At the Lincoln Memorial in Washington, D.C.
When? August 28, 1963
Why? To push for civil rights
How? By speaking persuasively to an audience

Partner Quiz Questions

What is the event named?
Who was the key participant?
What did the person do?
Where did it take place?
When did it take place?
Why did it happen?
How did he do it?

Understanding

When you understand something, you know what it means. You've puzzled it out using your reasoning skills. You can reason in two different directions—deductively or inductively.

Reasoning Deductively

When you reason deductively, you begin with a general idea and work toward specific details. Most paragraphs and essays are written this way, starting with a topic sentence or thesis statement and then providing details that support the statement. The following paragraph uses a deductive pattern.

Deductive Paragraph

Main point or thesis

If you want to improve the quality of the air that you breathe, start by looking inside your own home. Daily, we use home products without realizing that they are air polluters. Products such as air fresheners, cooking gas, and cleaning fluids pollute the air. Then people themselves pollute the inside air. We all emit bioeffluents, or contaminants such as perspiration and carbon dioxide. However, the biggest reason why in-home air is so polluted is the lack of air circulation. As we try to make our houses airtight, we trap air inside the house. We then recirculate this air behind airtight windows and doors until it becomes stale, dust filled, and unclean. The most *immediate way* to fight this type of pollution is simple: open a window.

Supporting details

Your Turn

In a textbook, search for a paragraph that is arranged deductively. What is the topic sentence of the paragraph? What details support the sentence? Explain how this organization affects your understanding of the paragraph's main point.

Reasoning Inductively

When you reason inductively, you start with the specific details and work your way toward a general conclusion. Often when you are researching a project, you will work inductively—first gathering lots of information before sorting through it all to decide what it means. (See page 59.) The following paragraph is organized inductively.

Inductive Paragraph

Specific examples

Schools are expected to provide one and sometimes two meals to each and every student. They are expected to provide counseling for any student who needs advice and guidance. They are expected to provide health care for those individuals who require medical attention. They are expected to provide programs to meet the special needs of students. They are expected to provide a variety of extracurricular activities. And, above all else, they are expected to provide quality instruction for all. Clearly,

General conclusion

schools in the 21st century are asked to do many things to meet the needs of their students.

Your Turn

Write an inductive paragraph describing the place you are in right now. Use this formula to build the paragraph.
1. Write a sentence that describes a touch sensation in this location.
2. Write a sentence that describes something you can hear.
3. Write a sentence that describes something you can smell.
4. Write a sentence that describes something you can see.
5. Write a sentence that names the location.

Applying

Critical thinking deepens when you take some of your ideas and apply them. When you apply an idea, you connect it to a real situation and use it in a purposeful way. The 5 W's and H can help you apply an idea.

Applying Ideas

Name: _Josiah Clark_   Date: _April 7_

Idea: _There should be a Web site that tracks misinformation in_
political advertising.

Who could use this idea? _Voters could use it mostly, but also_
candidates could refer to it if there's false information.

What would it be used for? _Voters would check it to find out the_
facts being addressed in politics.

Where would it be used? _People could check the site from_
anywhere. They could also report misinformation to it.

When would it be used? _It would be used mostly during political_
campaigns.

Why would it be used? _It would point out misinformation and_
would keep politicians honest.

How could it be used? _The site would post any political_
inaccuracies each week and then list facts from
reliable sources.

Your Turn

Choose an idea that you have recently thought of in one of your classes or activities. Answer the 5 W's and H about the idea, imagining ways to apply your idea to a situation.

Creating a Goal

After finding ways to apply an idea, you should take the next step and come up with goals and objectives for making your idea a reality. This page shows you how. A goal matches your idea with an opportunity or a situation. Use the following formula to form your goal:

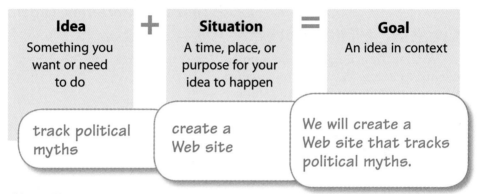

Idea	+	Situation	=	Goal
Something you want or need to do		A time, place, or purpose for your idea to happen		An idea in context

track political myths

create a Web site

We will create a Web site that tracks political myths.

Your Turn

Use the formula above to create a goal by connecting an idea to an opportunity.

Defining Objectives

After setting your overall goal, you can create subgoals, or objectives, by answering the 5 W's and H.

Objectives

Who?   My friends in civics class and I
What?   Make a Web site to track political misinformation
Where?   We can host it on Mrs. Jenkin's class site.
When?   We'll build it over the next two weeks, and we'll keep it going throughout the election.
Why?   To show what is true and false in political ads
How?   We'll watch ads, check out their claims, and report inaccuracies.

Your Turn

Answer the 5 W's and H to create objectives to accomplish your goal.

Analyzing

Analyzing a topic means separating it into parts and looking closely at those parts. Analysis also involves exploring how the parts fit and work together. Here are four graphic organizers that help you analyze a topic.

Creating a Time Line

A time line helps you sequence events, putting them in time order. When you create a time line, follow these steps:

1. Research the topic and note important dates and events.
2. Arrange the events in the order that they occurred.
3. List the date on one side and the event on the other.

Time Line: Track Time Order

Marie Curie's Career

1898	Paper on radioactivity Discovered polonium and radium
1903	Received DSc degree Nobel Prize in Physics
1906	Lost husband/partner
1910	Isolated radium metal
1911	Nobel Prize in Chemistry
1921	U.S. tour to support research
1929	Second U.S. tour
1932	Radium Institute founded
1934	Died of aplastic anemia

Creating a Cause-Effect Chart

A cause-effect chart helps you analyze the conditions that led up to a specific topic or event and the conditions that resulted from it. When you create a cause-effect chart, follow these steps:

1. Research your topic, noting causes and effects.
2. Draw a cause-effect chart.
3. Include the topic name. ("Fire" is the topic below.)
4. Label the left side "Causes" and the right side "Effects."
5. List causes and effects.

Cause-Effect Chart: Track Causal Relationships

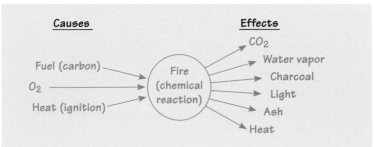

Causes — Effects

Fuel (carbon)
O_2
Heat (ignition)

Fire (chemical reaction)

CO_2
Water vapor
Charcoal
Light
Ash
Heat

Creating a Venn Diagram

A Venn diagram helps you analyze the similarities and differences between two topics. When you create a Venn diagram, follow these steps:

1. Research two topics that have some similarities and some differences.
2. Draw two overlapping circles.
3. Label one circle for one topic and the other circle for the other topic.
4. Write similarities between the topics in the overlapping space.
5. Write the differences in the parts that do not overlap.

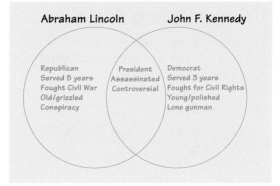

Venn Diagram: Compare and Contrast

Abraham Lincoln   John F. Kennedy

Republican   President   Democrat
Served 5 years   Assassinated   Served 3 years
Fought Civil War   Controversial Fought for Civil Rights
Old/grizzled   Young/polished
Conspiracy   Lone gunman

Creating a Line Diagram

A line diagram helps you analyze the parts of a structure, a group, or an organization. When you create a line diagram, follow these steps:

1. Research your topic, noting the parts of it and how each connects to the whole or to each other.
2. Write the topic name at the top of the page.
3. List the major parts in boxes in the first row.
4. List subparts in the next row, sub-subparts in the next, and so on. (Each new part adds more specific detail.)
5. Connect the parts to show their relationship.

Line Diagram: Show the Parts

The U.S. Federal Government

Legislative   Executive   Judicial
(Make Laws)   (Enforce Laws)   (Interpret Laws)

House   Senate   President   Supreme Court

Vice President   Cabinet   U.S. Courts of Appeals

U.S. District Courts

Your Turn

Think of a topic you are currently studying. Analyze the topic by creating a time line, cause-effect chart, Venn diagram, or line diagram.

Evaluating

"Evaluating" means placing a value on something, telling whether it is useful, helpful, meaningful—or not. Here are two strategies for evaluating.

Using a Rating Scale

A rating scale lets you quantify the quality of something. First, you define what you are rating and what scale you are using. Then you give your rating and explain it.

Book Rating Scale

Poor	Fair	Good	Excellent
★	★★	★★★	★★★★

The Outsiders by S. E. Hinton ★★★★ I give this novel four stars because it has great characters like Ponyboy, the plot is exciting, and it feels tragic. At first when I found out it was about a Greaser gang in the 1950s, I thought it would be out of date, but this book is still really great.

Survey Rating Scale

12. How often do you use your virtual locker?

Never	Rarely	Sometimes	Often	Always
1	2	③	4	5

Explain: Most of our work is done on paper and handed in that way. The virtual locker helps with longer writing assignments, though.

Richter Scale (Earthquakes)

Micro	Minor	Light	Moderate	Strong	Major	Great	Epic
1.0	2.0-3.0	4.0	5.0	6.0	7.0-8.0	9.0	10.0

The Haiti earthquake of 2010 measured 7.0 on the Richter scale and killed 230,000 people. The Sumatra earthquake of 2004 registered 9.2 on the Richter scale and (with the resulting tsunami) killed nearly 230,000 people.

Your Turn

Create a rating scale to evaluate an event or a topic you are studying. Give the concept a rating, and then explain the reason for your rating.

Using a Rubric

A rubric allows you to evaluate a number of traits at once. This rubric is based on the goals and objectives for a student project.

Name: Sharissa Smith   **Project:** Pharaoh's Burial Chamber

Goal:	Evaluation	Rating			Score
We will build a diorama that shows the burial chamber of a pharaoh.	The diorama looks terrific, with hieroglyphics, too!	Beat (60)	Met 40	Didn't 20	60
Objectives: 1 My table partners and I will build it.	Most of the work was done by Ryan and me.	Beat 10	Met 6	Didn't (2)	2
2 We'll make a diorama of a burial chamber.		Beat (10)	Met 6	Didn't 2	10
3 We'll do most of the work at home.		Beat 10	Met (6)	Didn't 2	6
4 We'll schedule two work sessions for the next two weekends.	The two sessions had just Ryan and me.	Beat 10	Met 6	Didn't (2)	2
5 We'll show how the chamber was arranged.		Beat 10	Met (6)	Didn't 2	6
6 We'll use cardboard, construction paper, clay, pipe cleaners, and paint.	Instead of clay, we used Sculpy and baked it!	Beat (10)	Met 6	Didn't 2	10

TOTAL: 96

Your Turn

Assess a project you've done recently. Write down the goal and objectives, and assess how well each was achieved. Then rate the project and total the score. (Go to thoughtfullearning.com/p25.)

Creating

"Creating" means putting ideas together in a new way. You need to organize parts in a logical way to create an overall structure.

Organizing Ideas

Here are the basic organizational styles.

Organizational Style	Transition Words	Graphic Organizer
Time Order: Placing details in the order that they happen (chronological order)	after, as soon as, before, during, finally, first, later, meanwhile, next, second, soon, then, third	Time Line (See page 22.)
Place Order: Placing details in the order that they appear in space (order of location)	above, along, among, around, behind, beneath, by, inside, near, off, onto, throughout, under	Diagram (See pages 378–379.)
Categories: Placing details according to the groups or parts of a topic (classification)	another type, on the one hand, on the other hand, a second variety, one kind, the final version	Line Diagram (See page 23.)
Cause-Effect: Examining the causes of a topic and then looking at the effects	as a result, as a by-product, because, due to the fact that, since, therefore	Cause-Effect Chart (See page 22.)
Logical Order **Deductive:** Reasoning from general to specific **Inductive:** Reasoning from specific to general	also, and, another, as well, besides, for example, for instance, for this reason, in addition, in conclusion, likewise, next, therefore	Outline (See page 272.)
Comparison-Contrast **Similarities-Differences:** Treating all similarities and then all differences **Subject-by-Subject:** Treating one subject and then the other subject **Point-by-Point:** Looking at one point for both subjects before going to the next	**Comparing:** again, along with, also, as, both, likewise, just as, in the same way, like, similarly, too **Contrasting:** although, but, by contrast, or, even though, however, on the one hand, on the other hand, otherwise, still, yet	Venn Diagram (See page 23.)

Your Turn

Think of a topic that you are currently studying. If you were to write an essay about the topic, which style of organization would you choose? Why?

Creating a Three-Part Structure

Things that are meant to be experienced over time have a three-part structure. Paragraphs, essays, novels, e-mails, phone calls, meals, concerts, holidays, expeditions—all have this structure. (See page 295.)

Beginning

Successful beginnings often . . .

- greet the person.
- introduce other people or ideas.
- provide background information and ground rules.
- focus on a specific topic for a specific purpose.

Middle

Successful middle parts often . . .

- give details and ideas that support the topic and purpose.
- lead the person through an important process.
- provide an experience that the person seeks.
- provide a product or service that the person needs.
- connect people to ideas and to each other.

Ending

Successful endings often . . .

recap the ideas in the middle.
revisit the topic and purpose from the beginning.
highlight a specific important idea.
provide a final memorable thought or experience.
encourage the person to take action.

Your Turn

List things that are experienced over time. Choose one thing from the list and write down what happens in the beginning, middle, and ending of the experience. How does it match up to the ideas shown above?

Creating Other Structures

Some things are not experienced over time. They have a different structure depending on their function. Note the following structures.

Building Structure

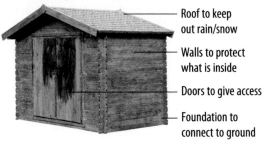

— Roof to keep out rain/snow

— Walls to protect what is inside

— Doors to give access

— Foundation to connect to ground

Pen Structure

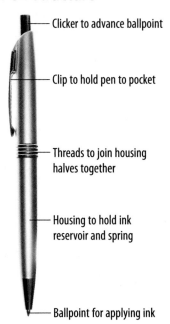

— Clicker to advance ballpoint

— Clip to hold pen to pocket

— Threads to join housing halves together

— Housing to hold ink reservoir and spring

— Ballpoint for applying ink

Tool Structure

Motor to turn bit

Bit to drill holes —

Trigger to start drill —

Handle to grip tool —

Battery to power tool —

Vehicle Structure

Seat for passenger —

Frame to join parts —

Steering to control direction

Wheels to roll on the ground

Propulsion to provide thrust

Your Turn

Name the parts and function of two other structures. (See pages 422–436.)

Critical-Thinking Activities

The activities listed below will help you work on your critical-thinking skills and become a more thoughtful learner.

Writing to Think

Write in a notebook about the subjects you are studying. When your thoughts run dry, turn your last point into a question and answer it.

> What are "significant figures?" When I do a math problem in science, I'm supposed to show only the significant figures. But my calculator shows five or six numbers after the decimal point. Why are they insignificant? Is it because the original numbers weren't that specific? I guess it is all about keeping track of how precise information is.

Our best advice: Write regularly about your learning in order to make personal connections with new ideas.

Your Turn

For a week, write about your work in one class. Explore your thoughts after each class period. At the end of the week, assess how well it helped you connect with the material.

Asking *Why?* and *So What?* and *Who Says?*

Researcher Michael W. Smith suggests that you ask these three questions—*Why? So what?* and *Who says?*—about subjects that you are studying in your classes. Doing so will help you think critically about your course work.

Our best advice: Write these three questions at the top of each page in your notebook when you take notes. This will remind you to try to answer these questions when you encounter new concepts and subjects.

Your Turn

Use this strategy for a week in one of your classes. Make sure that you answer the three questions for each set of notes you take. Evaluate the helpfulness of this strategy at the end of the week.

Debating the Issue

Make it a point to debate important issues. A debate is a discussion in which you and your classmates defend opposing points of view about the issues. As each side argues for a particular point of view, a lot of good thinking will occur.

To conduct a debate, write down a proposed change. Then assign one person or team to argue for the proposal and another team to argue against it.

Proposal: School start time should be moved back by 1 hour.

Your Turn

Stage a debate. Brainstorm changes that could make life at your school better. Choose one change and write it as a proposal. Then assign one person (or team) to argue the "pro" position, and the other to argue the "con" position. (For more, see pages 103–118, 450–451.)

Thinking Graphically

Using graphic organizers is an effective way to gather and organize your best thoughts about topics you are studying. This Venn diagram compares and contrasts two alternative sources of power.

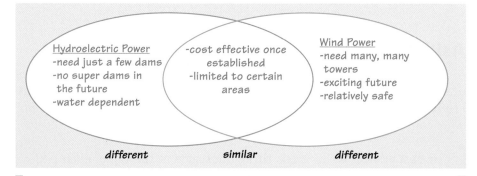

Hydroelectric Power
-need just a few dams
-no super dams in
  the future
-water dependent

-cost effective once
  established
-limited to certain
  areas

Wind Power
-need many, many
  towers
-exciting future
-relatively safe

different   similar   different

Our best advice: Use graphic organizers as thinking and learning tools, especially when you are studying challenging ideas and information.

Your Turn

Create your own Venn diagram, showing the similarities and differences between two things.

Chapter 3
Creative Thinking

It would be nice if all you had to do was pull a switch for creative thinking to begin. But it takes effort to see things in a new way, to make connections that nobody else has—to wonder, explore, discover, and invent. Creativity is more than an impulse.

This chapter provides specific, practical strategies for awakening and engaging your creative brain. Creative thinking will help you in your classes, at home, and wherever you go.

You will learn . . .

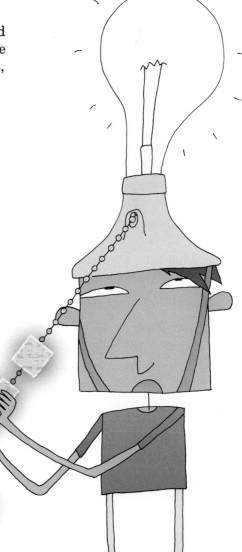

- Creative-Thinking Strategies
- Remembering
- Understanding
- Applying
- Analyzing
- Evaluating
- Creating

Understanding Creative Thinking

Creative thinking allows you to discover possibilities. While critical thinking narrows your focus, creative thinking broadens it, bringing in ideas and potential. The following pages contain many strategies for creative thinking. With these strategies, you'll discover diverse and original ideas.

In Focus

Creative thinking is defined as the process of moving from where you are to where you want to be via a unique route.

Creative State of Mind

You'll be at your creative best if you think in the following ways.

Observe. Looking is one thing; observing is another. Get into the habit of studying something until it tells you about itself.

Receive. Be open to all types of thoughts and ideas. Experiment. Take risks. You need to be open to new ideas.

Wait. Sometimes your best ideas, the most creative ones, will occur to you when you least expect them.

Accelerate. Take advantage of creativity when it hits. Get to work and see what you can create.

Accept. While developing a creative idea, be prepared for new and unexpected thoughts and write them down.

Manage. Don't expect creativity to be a straightforward process. Expect to face detours and unexpected side trips.

Your Turn

Rate your own creativity by considering how often you think in the following ways. How could you improve your thinking in the future?

	Never	Sometimes	Often	Always
Observing	1	2	3	4
Receiving	1	2	3	4
Waiting	1	2	3	4
Accelerating	1	2	3	4
Accepting	1	2	3	4
Managing	1	2	3	4

Creative-Thinking Strategies

As you saw in chapter 2, Benjamin Bloom outlined deeper and deeper levels of thinking. You can use creative-thinking strategies at each level, as you will see below and on the following pages. Here's the latest version of Bloom's thinking skills.

Bloom's Thinking Skills

Remembering ——————
is recalling basic information.

You'll learn strategies for using memory aids to recall the key details about a topic (pages 34–35).

Understanding ——————
is knowing what the information means.

You'll learn strategies for thinking metaphorically to deepen your understanding of a topic (pages 36–37).

Applying ——————
is putting the information to use.

You'll learn strategies for brainstorming, listing, freewriting, and drawing to discover ways to apply ideas (pages 38–39).

Analyzing ——————
is looking at the parts of something and figuring out how they fit together.

You'll learn strategies for creating problem-solution charts and square pegging to discover new connections between ideas (pages 40–41).

Evaluating ——————
is determining the value or worth of something.

You'll learn strategies for creating pro-con charts and listing traits to evaluate a topic and discover ways to improve it (pages 42–43).

Creating ——————
is putting ideas together in new ways to make something.

You'll learn strategies for building, growing, and exploring projects as well as presenting them (pages 44–46).

Note: During most tasks, you will jump up and down this scale of thinking.

Remembering

The following creative-thinking strategies can help you remember key details about a topic. They are called *mnemonics*, or memory aids.

Acronyms are words that are spelled from the first letter in a set of other words. Use acronyms to help you remember a set of things.

Colors in the Rainbow	**Great Lakes**
ROY G. BIV	HOMES
Red	Huron
Orange	Ontario
Yellow	Michigan
Green	Erie
Blue	Superior
Indigo	
Violet	

Acrostics use funny sentences to help you remember the first letters of a group of words.

Biological Classification

Kings play chess on folding glass sheets.

- Kingdom
- Phylum
- Class
- Order
- Family
- Genus
- Species

Categories allow you to organize many ideas and details under a few memorable groups. They give you a handle to grab onto.

Musical Instruments

Winds	Strings	Percussion
Flutes	Violins	Drums
Oboes	Violas	Cymbals
Clarinets	Cellos	Xylophones
Saxophones	Bass	Pianos
Brass		

Rhymes, raps, chants, and songs use rhythm to help you remember key information. You probably learned your A-B-C's by singing them to "Twinkle, Twinkle Little Star." You also might have learned the "Fifty Nifty United States" song by Ray Charles. Here are some additional rhymes, raps, and chants—and you can also make up your own.

The Civil War

In Eighteen Hundred and Sixty-One,
The Civil War had just begun.

Days of the Months

Thirty days hath September,
April, June, and November;
All the rest have thirty-one,
Except February, my dear son.
It has 28, and that is fine,
But in Leap Year it has 29.

Stages of Cell Division

Interphase
Prophase
Metaphase
Anaphase
Telophase
Cytokinesis

Visuals help you connect words to images, storing the ideas in more than one place in your brain.

Tightening a Screw

Righty-tighty
Lefty-loosey

Spelling with *E* and *I*

I before *e*, except after *c*,
Or if sounding like *a*
As in *neighbor* or *weigh*.
But *weird* is just weird.

Multiples of 5

5, 10, 15, 20,
25, 30, 35, 40,
45, 50, 55, 60,
65, 70, 75, 80,
85, 90, 95, 100!

Greater-Than/Less-Than

Think of the sign as the open mouth of a fish. The fish always swims toward the bigger number to gobble it up.

Your Turn

Think about a difficult concept you are learning in a class. Create a memory aid like one of those shown on these two pages to help you remember the concept.

Understanding

Creative thinking can help you understand an idea more deeply. These pages show how you can think metaphorically and use personification. Both ways of thinking involve comparing two things in an interesting or creative way. (See also page 252.)

Thinking Metaphorically

You can think metaphorically by asking a question that contains a simile or metaphor and then answering it many times.

Simile Question

How is electricity like water?

Both have flow.
Both have current.
Both have waves.
Both look bluish.
Both run through walls.
Both can be stored.
Thunderstorms produce both.
Water can conduct electricity.
Both are important for living.
Both come into houses from the outside.
Both prefer to keep moving when given a chance.
Friction in clouds (water vapor) makes lightning (electricity).
Both play a big part in the atmosphere.
Hydroelectric dams make electricity from water movement.
Water and electricity are both important parts of weather.

Your Turn

Ask a simile question about your topic. Use the following formula. Then answer the question in as many ways as you can. Review your list, looking for new ideas and connections.

How is _____ like _____ ?
            (your topic)   (something else)

Using Personification

Personification is a specific type of metaphorical thinking. Personification gives an object or animal the qualities of a person. Ask yourself a personification question about your topic and then answer it in as many ways as you can.

Personification Questions

How is lightning like a mad scientist?

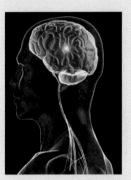

It is powerful.
It is unpredictable.
It is bristly.
It is loud.
It is bright.
It is scary.
It is cracked.
It is hard to escape.
It has scraggly hair.

Who is lightning like and why?

It is like a dancer because it twists and leaps.
It is like a rock star because it takes center stage.
It is like a boxer because it comes out swinging.
It is like a glassblower because it melts sand into glass.
It is like a politician because it is loud and powerful.
It is like a scientist because it probes the ground below.

Your Turn

Ask yourself a personification question about your topic, using one of the following formulas. Then answer the question in as many ways as you can. Review your list, looking for new ideas and connections.

How is _____ like _____ ?
    (your topic)   (person)

Who is _____ like and why?
    (your topic)

Applying

Creative thinking helps you to apply ideas to real-world contexts. The strategies on these pages show ways to generate ideas for alternative energy.

Listing

1. Write the topic at the top of the list.
2. Write down items in the list.
3. List as many possibilities as you can.
4. Don't stop to edit or evaluate.

Clustering

1. Write the topic in the middle of a page and circle it.
2. Around it, write ideas as they come to mind.
3. Draw lines to connect ideas, creating an idea web.

Listing

Plant Energy Sources

Photosynthesis
Sap/Rosin
Ethanol/Oil
Corn Cobs—Burning
Composting (Methane)
Wood Burning
Algae (Is it a plant?)

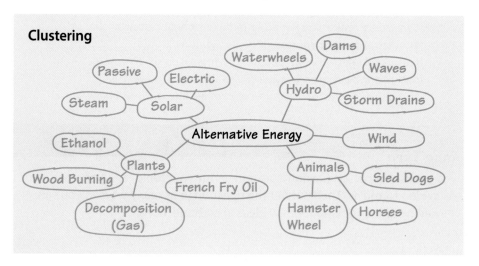

Clustering

Dams
Waterwheels
Passive
Electric
Waves
Steam
Hydro
Storm Drains
Solar
Alternative Energy
Wind
Ethanol
Plants
Animals
Wood Burning
French Fry Oil
Sled Dogs
Decomposition (Gas)
Hamster Wheel
Horses

Your Turn

Brainstorm about a topic, either listing your ideas or creating a cluster of them. Produce as many ideas as possible. Write everything down without evaluating or editing. (See also page 247.)

Freewriting

1. Write about your topic for 5 to 10 minutes without stopping.
2. If you get stuck, repeat a word or phrase until you can go on.
3. Write as many words as possible.
4. Don't edit or evaluate—just write.

> **Freewriting**
>
> The problem with burning things is that they produce CO_2, which is a greenhouse gas. But human beings have been burning things ever since somebody discovered fire. We can't give up fire! That's like giving up thousands of years of advance. Are we supposed to live in caves? Maybe we could hook up people's treadmills and stationary bikes and they could make electricity. What about a video game that gets energy from the people moving around in front of it? What about making a floor that gets energy from people walking on it? Or how about revolving doors that have turbines on them? That could be huge! They save heating and cooling anyway, and if every place had turbine doors, people would get energy . . .

Your Turn

Freewrite for 5 to 10 minutes nonstop about a topic that you are studying. Pour out as many words as you can, and watch the ideas come with them. (See also page 247.)

Drawing

1. Think about your topic and begin to sketch.
2. Don't worry about artistic quality—just get ideas down.
3. Keep going and see where the drawing leads you.

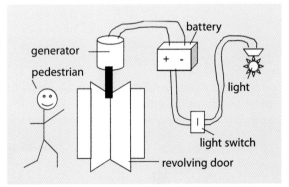

Your Turn

Draw an idea to think creatively about it. It's fine to use stick figures, to doodle, to draw whatever comes to mind about the idea.

Analyzing

Creative thinking can strengthen any analysis. These two pages provide creative-thinking strategies that can reveal new possibilities.

Using a Problem-Solution Chart

A problem-solution chart helps you understand and solve a problem. These charts are key to problem solving in all your classes, from math to science to social studies. In the chart below, both the problem and the solution are analyzed. When you create a problem-solution chart, follow these steps:

1. Research the problem, looking at all of its causes.
2. Label the chart by naming the problem.
3. List causes in the left-hand column.
4. List possible solutions in the right-hand column.

Problem-Solution Chart: Solve Problems

Problem: Depleted Fossil Fuels

Causes of the Problem	Possible Solutions
limited supply	conserve fuels
150 years of industry	open new wells
U.S. consumption	use renewable ethanol
rise of China/India	use alternative energy
increased demand	

Your Turn

Create a problem-solution chart to analyze a problem that you have studied or heard about recently.

Square Pegging

Square pegging something simply means using it in a way that it was never intended to be used. The term comes from the old expression, "putting a square peg in a round hole." The exercise requires you to think in new ways about the thing or idea. You can square-peg something by asking how it could be used in a new way and answering the question in as many ways as possible. (It's okay if an answer seems ridiculous.)

Square-Peg Question

__How can you use a flashlight to keep a boat from sinking?__

Use the flashlight to find the leak and stand on it.
Jam the flashlight in the hole in the boat.
Use the flashlight to find the boat-patching kit.
Wave the flashlight to get help.
Spell out S.O.S. in Morse code.
Use the flashlight to attract friendly dolphins.
Shine the flashlight to find a sandbar to land on.
Use the empty flashlight to bail.
Use the empty flashlight to row the boat to shore.
Use the empty flashlight for flotation.
Trade the flashlight for a better boat.

Your Turn

Answer one of the following square-peg questions in as many ways as possible.

How can you use an electric fan to disperse a crowd?
How can you use a song to dig a hole?
How can you use a bad idea to pave a road?
How can you use an onion to make a movie?

Your Turn

Create your own square-peg question by using the following formula. Then answer the question in as many ways as possible.

How can you use ＿＿＿＿＿＿＿＿＿＿＿＿＿ to ＿＿＿＿＿＿＿＿＿＿＿＿＿ ?
　　　　　　　　　　(topic)　　　　　　　　　　　　(action)

Evaluating

When you evaluate something, you assign it a value, telling its worth. The following creative-thinking strategies can help you evaluate a topic.

Creating a Pro-Con Chart

Use a pro-con chart to list the positives (pros) and negatives (cons) about an idea. Complete the chart by yourself or in a group. When you create a pro-con chart, follow these steps:

1. Research the topic, noting the positives and negatives about it.
2. Label the chart by naming the topic.
3. List the positive points under "Pro" in the left-hand column.
4. List the negative points under "Con" in the right-hand column.

Pro-Con Chart: Evaluating Topics

The Westward Expansion

Pro	Con
New opportunity for settlers	Lands taken forcefully
Great Plains/rich farmland	Trail of Tears tragedy
Resources discovered	Nez Perce conflict
United States coast to coast	Buffalo killed for fun
Transcontinental Railroad	Resources exploited
Gold in California	U.S.-Mexican War
New American spirit	Little Bighorn

Your Turn

Create a pro-con chart of your own about a topic that you are studying. List the positives and negatives of the topic and evaluate it.

Evaluating Traits

Evaluating traits helps you improve each part of a topic. Start by creating a three-column table. In the first column, write traits of the topic—parts, qualities, or functions. In the second column, rate each trait. Then, in the third column, write ideas for improving the trait. Here is a chart for a charity fund-raiser:

Class Charity Competition: Every class has a large plastic jar for gathering coins and bills to donate to the food pantry and shelter. Each class is competing to contribute the most.

Traits	Evaluation	Improvements
Money goes to the food pantry and shelter.	This is a very good charity.	
Homeroom classes compete to contribute most.	The competition element doesn't seem strong.	What if silver coins count against the total, so students are encouraged to put them in other classes' jars?
Students put in money.	Most students just give pocket change once or twice.	Having only pennies and bills count for the total would make it a game.
The drive is school-wide.	All of the home-room teachers are participating.	
The drive finishes up before the holidays.	The food pantry gets a lot of help this time of year, but not from January to March.	Next year, the drive should be in February to give more support when it is needed.

Your Turn

Pick a project or an event that you are involved with and evaluate the traits. List traits of the project in the left column, rate each trait in the middle column, and brainstorm improvements on the right.

Creating

Creative thinking is most powerful when you make something new. Here are three basic approaches to creating something.

Building

This approach to creating focuses on careful planning followed by patient and precise work. When you build something, you think everything through before launching into the process.

Best Use: Use this approach when materials are expensive and precise outcomes are critical.

Growing

This approach to creating is more flexible, including some planning but also some experimentation. When you grow something, you know what you are trying to accomplish, but you should not be surprised by unexpected detours along the way.

Best Use: Use this approach when you have some time to fiddle and the outcomes are not precisely planned.

Exploring

This approach to creating is free-form with little advanced planning and a lot of experimentation. When you explore, you venture out with a sense of discovery, not knowing where you will end up.

Best Use: Use this approach when you have plenty of time and resources and are trying to create something completely new.

Your Turn

Consider a recent project you have finished. Which approach did you use—building, growing, or exploring? Why?

Previewing Projects

Inquire provides many project ideas. Here is a quick sampling of the kinds you will find.

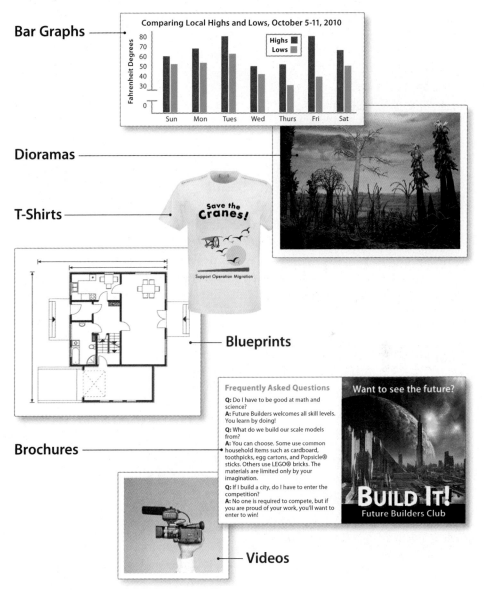

Bar Graphs

Dioramas

T-Shirts

Blueprints

Brochures

Videos

Your Turn

Turn to pages 315–470 of this book and flip through the pages. What kind of project would you most like to work on? Why?

Presenting

After you have created something, take the next step of sharing it with others. Here are strategies for presenting.

Publish It

If your project is written, publish it in the best venue—whether a school or local newspaper, a magazine, or even a contest. You can also publish essays and fiction online. Go to thoughtfullearning.com/p46 to find publishing opportunities.

Present It

If your project is a speech, a diorama, a model, a shirt, an event, or some other visual project, present it in person or on video. See pages 66–72 for suggestions on connecting to your audience.

Post It

If your project is a podcast, a video, a Web page, a Web site, an infographic, or any other type of digital project, find a place to post it online. Go to thoughtfullearning.com/p46 to find online venues for posting projects.

Perform It

If your project is a sketch, play, song, dance, or some other performance project, then gather an audience and perform it. See pages 437–454 for more on performing.

Your Turn

Choose a way to network your creation, connecting it to a real audience in the real world.

Creative-Thinking Activities

Keeping your body in shape makes good sense. So does keeping your mind in shape for creative thinking. How? By bending, stretching, and turning ideas inside out. The strategies listed below suggest ways to practice your creativity.

Writing Freely

Writing freely in a notebook or journal puts you in the best zone for unlocking your most creative thoughts.

> *On the way to my friend's house, I noticed something odd. In front of an old, run-down house, I saw a red geranium planted in a rusty coffee can. I never knew anyone even lived there, maybe no one does. So who put the flower there and why? That one flower is like a sign of life. Maybe tomorrow I'll see another sign. . . .*

[**Our best advice:** Get into a regular writing routine and stick to it. Write to improve your fluency or endurance.]

Your Turn

For 5 minutes, write freely about something strange that you noticed this week. Do not stop. Keep pouring out words for the full 5 minutes, and take note of any creative thoughts that come to mind. (See page 39.)

Speaking Freely

Talking about ideas is becoming a lost art. Sure, you may talk about a new movie or how a new video game works. But you also need to talk about other things—not just entertainment—on a regular basis.

[**Our best advice:** Share your ideas with a variety of audiences. All of this talk will do wonders for your confidence . . . and for your creativity.]

Your Turn

For 5 minutes, carry on a conversation with a classmate, sticking to one subject. Decide on a subject together, and then start the clock. Offer an idea, and then listen to the other person. Build on each other's thoughts, noting the creative ideas that come to mind.

Pushing Yourself

An important element of creativity is elaboration, the ability to describe, explain, or illustrate with plenty of rich details. A creative thinker is never satisfied until he or she has generated many ideas from multiple points of view.

> **Our best advice:** Always push yourself to think of as many details as possible, no matter if you are freewriting, listing, speaking, clustering, or drawing. The next thought that comes to mind may be your most creative one.

Your Turn

Spend at least 10 minutes using one of the strategies on pages 38–39 to explore a topic of interest. Keep going no matter what, seeing how many great ideas you can dig up. Share your results.

Creating Clusters or Maps

Work on your flexibility—your ability to push out ideas—by developing clusters or mind maps. Each new idea you add to a cluster will trigger additional ideas.

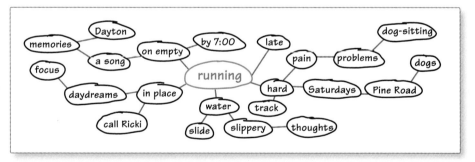

> **Our best advice:** If visual connections help you, give clustering a try. Use it whenever you need to explore a topic for a project, a debate, or a discussion.

Your Turn

Write a topic of interest in the middle of a piece of paper and circle it. Then write related ideas around the topic, circling them and connecting them as you create the cluster. Continue for at least 5 minutes to discover a number of unexpected connections and new ideas.

Chapter 4
Problem Solving

You may never have to figure out how to get across a deep gorge, but other problems are bound to come your way. Learning how to manage and solve those problems is the secret to success in school, at home, and in the workplace.

This chapter will give you the strategies you need to become a solution maker. It is an important process that you are capable of learning. Soon you will be making solutions for all kinds of problems, from simple issues to long-term projects.

You will learn . . .

- Problem Solving
- Problem Solving and Inquiry
- Inquiry and the Scientific Method
- Problem Solving in Math

Understanding Problem Solving

Problem solving involves both critical and creative thinking skills. Here is the general process for problem solving. The pages that follow show how this process was applied to a real-world problem.

Critical Thinking

Creative Thinking

Question the problem.
- Answer basic questions about the problem.
- Explore causes and effects.

Plan a solution.
- Brainstorm solutions and pick one.
- Set a goal and plan the tasks and time.

Gather information.
- Look for resources and conduct research.
- Arrange teams and collect tools.

Create the solution.
- Put your solution together in a first form.
- Try it out and see if it works.

Evaluate the solution.
- Check the solution against your plan.
- Decide how you can improve your solution.

Present the solution.
- Put your solution to work, solving the problem.

Your Turn

Imagine that you are in the center of a hedge maze, like the one in the picture. Your problem is that you don't know the way out. Use the steps to solving a problem above, beginning by examining the problem. How will you find your way out? Will you just wander until you stumble upon the exit, or will you use some more systematic method? How many ways can you think of to solve the problem of the maze?

Problem Solving in Action

The following pages explain the problem-solving process used to tackle a real-world problem faced by school children on an island in Lake Superior.

Examining the Problem

The 5 W and H questions identify the main parts of a problem.

The Problem:

Who?   Students on Madeline Island
What?   Cannot get to school for one month out of the year
Where?   Between Madeline Island and Bayfield in Lake Superior
When?   At the beginning and the ending of winter
Why?   Ferries can't run; the ice road hasn't formed
How?   Unpredictable weather

Your Turn

Identify a problem in your school or community. Then answer the 5 W's and H about it.

Analyzing the Problem

A cause-effect chart helps analyze the problem.

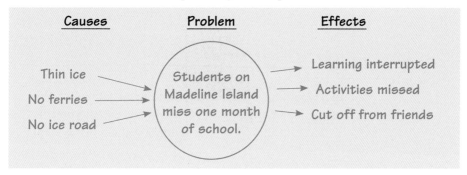

Causes	Problem	Effects
Thin ice	Students on Madeline Island miss one month of school.	Learning interrupted
No ferries		Activities missed
No ice road		Cut off from friends

Your Turn

Create a cause-effect chart like the one above for the problem you've identified.

Brainstorming Ideas

This cluster shows initial brainstorming.

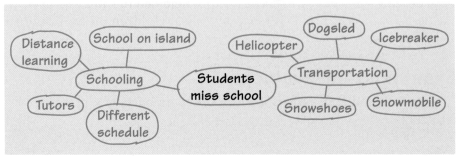

Create a cluster to brainstorm solutions to your problem. Don't evaluate ideas yet; just write down every possibility that occurs to you.

Evaluating Ideas

The following chart helps evaluate and improve ideas.

Solutions	Evaluation	Improvements
Change school schedule	This won't work because we never know when the lake will be impassible.	
Tutors	This would be expensive.	Perhaps parents could volunteer to teach students.
Icebreaker	This would keep the ice road from ever forming.	
Helicopter	It would be expensive and would have to make many, many trips.	We could use a boat with wind propulsion, like they do in the everglades. We could call it a wind sled.

Create a chart like the one above to evaluate ideas. Write ideas in the left column, evaluate each in the middle, and suggest possible improvements in the right column.

Planning the Solution

The 5 W's and H help to create goals and objectives, applying ideas to a specific situation.

Goal: Build a wind sled.

Who?	The people of Madeline Island
What?	Design the wind sled
Where?	In a boat-building shop
When?	As soon as possible
Why?	To provide transport over the partly frozen lake
How?	Using a boat hull and airboat propeller

Your Turn

Write a goal and objectives for your solution. Answer the 5 W's and H to create objectives.

Applying the Solution

Stating the idea first in words and then in pictures gets the point across.

Idea: Use an airboat fan plus a powerboat with a flattened hull and a cover. The wind sled can slide on ice, but it if breaks through, it can still float.

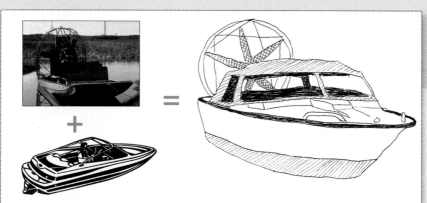

Your Turn

Use your goal and objectives to guide you as you apply your solution to the specific situation.

Evaluating the Solution

This rubric rates the project based on goals and objectives.

Project Rubric

	Evaluation	Rating			Score
Goal Build a wind sled.	The wind sled is even faster than the ferry.	Beat 60	Met (40)	Didn't 20	40
Objectives 1. Get community behind it.	A small group did the actual work, but we got community help.	Beat 10	Met (6)	Didn't 2	6
2. Design the wind sled.	With a six-person capacity, the boat has to make four trips for students.	Beat 10	Met 6	Didn't (2)	2
3. Find a boat-building shop.	It was good of Terry to let us use his shop.	Beat 10	Met (6)	Didn't 2	6
4. Complete the sled as soon as possible.	We hoped to have it last season, but at least it's done.	Beat 10	Met (6)	Didn't 2	6
5. To provide transport over the partly frozen lake	The residents want it, too. We need a bigger sled!	Beat 10	Met 6	Didn't (2)	2
6. Use a boat hull and airboat propeller.	The design works perfectly. Now to upscale it.	Beat (10)	Met 6	Didn't 2	10
				TOTAL:	72

Your Turn

Create a rubric using the goal and objectives you wrote on page 53. (Go to thoughtfullearning.com/p54 to download a digital version.) Assess your project and score it. (For more help, see pages 302–305.)

Making Improvements and Presenting the Solution

The evaluation showed that the original idea worked well for six people, but the community needed a larger craft to be able to carry more students at one time. While the first wind sled operated, the group began building a much larger version. Here is a sketch of the larger craft, which has twin propellers and can accommodate twenty-two people and cargo.

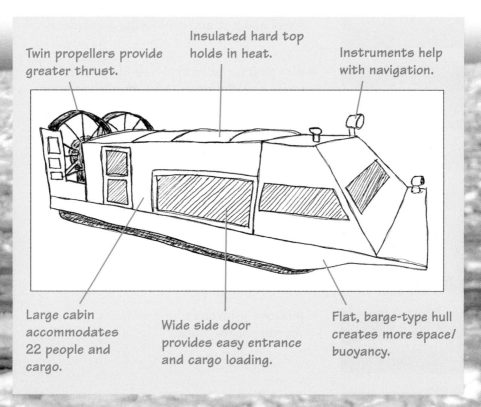

Twin propellers provide greater thrust.

Insulated hard top holds in heat.

Instruments help with navigation.

Large cabin accommodates 22 people and cargo.

Wide side door provides easy entrance and cargo loading.

Flat, barge-type hull creates more space/ buoyancy.

Your Turn

Based on your rubric (page 54), make a plan to improve your project. (For a sample improvement plan, see pages 306–307.) Then make the changes.

Problem Solving and Inquiry

The process you witnessed on the last five pages is called inquiry. It's a thoughtful approach to understanding and solving problems, discovering and applying new ideas, and making the world a better place. You'll explore inquiry in depth in chapters 16–23, but here is a quick overview.

1 Questioning

■ **Questioning** includes identifying and analyzing the topic as well as brainstorming ideas about it and evaluating your ideas.

2 Planning

■ **Planning** includes applying ideas, creating goals and objectives, and scheduling your project.

3 Researching

■ **Researching** involves gathering resources that you need in order to put your project together.

4 Creating

■ **Creating** is the same as inventing—putting your ideas together to make something new.

5 Improving

■ **Improving** involves an evaluation and a revision of the work.

6 Presenting

■ **Presenting** means putting your solution into practice and sharing your work with others.

Your Turn

Consider the work you did in the "Your Turn" activities on the past five pages. Pinpoint the places where the different steps of the inquiry process explained above played a role.

Inquiry and the Scientific Method

One specific version of the inquiry process is the scientific method. You may have used the scientific method to complete an experiment or a project in one of your science classes. Here are the basic steps:

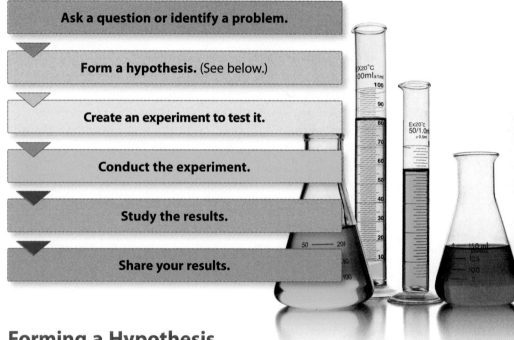

Ask a question or identify a problem.

Form a hypothesis. (See below.)

Create an experiment to test it.

Conduct the experiment.

Study the results.

Share your results.

Forming a Hypothesis

A **hypothesis** is a temporary explanation for a scientific question or problem. A statement such as *Consuming a lot of caffeine may cause anxiety* is an example hypothesis. Stated formally, the hypothesis could read as follows:

*If anxiety is related to the amount of caffeine consumed, **then** people who drink a lot of caffeinated soda will more likely experience anxiety.*

An "If . . . then . . ." statement like this provides the basis for an experiment to test the hypothesis.

Your Turn

Share with your classmates at least one experience that you have had using the scientific method. Then discuss why scientists follow this method of inquiry.

Thinking Deductively

Scientists often begin with a general idea (the hypothesis) and then test it by gathering evidence to prove or disprove it, or by conducting an experiment. They think deductively, from general to specific.

Lab Report

Name: Latonya Williams   Date: Dec. 10

Title: Earthquake Magnitude and Frequency
Purpose: To understand how magnitude and frequency of quakes
                are related
Hypothesis: Having many small earthquakes can prevent larger
                earthquakes.
Materials: The U.S. Geological Survey Web site
Procedure: Gather earthquake data from the USGS Web site to see
                if years with more small earthquakes have fewer large
                earthquakes.

Data:

Year	Below 5.0	Above 5.0
2005	3,560	52
2006	2,712	58
2007	2,687	82
2008	3,504	94
2009	4,187	63
2010	7,249	67
Total	23,899	416
Average	3,983	69

Analysis:

Year	Below 5.0	Above 5.0
2005	< average	< average
2006	< average	< average
2007	< average	> average
2008	< average	> average
2009	> average	< average
2010	> average	< average

> = greater than; < = less than

Conclusion: For four of the six years, more small quakes meant fewer big quakes, or vice versa. The hypothesis has some support. But overall frequency of quakes varies widely year to year.

Your Turn

Turn to pages 348–351, which explain how to create a lab report. Then discuss with a partner how lab reports exhibit a deductive structure.

Thinking Inductively

Scientists may also begin with specific details and work toward general conclusions. Often, scientists will spend many weeks, months, or even years gathering information and analyzing it. They are looking for patterns, relationships, and trends and will reach a general conclusion at the end of the process. In other words, they are working inductively, from specific to general.

Earthquake Tracking Sheet

Name: _Latonya Williams_   Date: _Dec. 3_

Directions: Monitor the USGS Web site and record all earthquakes this week that measure 5.0 or above on the Richter scale. After gathering data, write any trends you see.

Date	Magnitude	Location
Sunday, Nov. 28:	5.0	New Zealand
Monday, Nov. 29:	6.9	Japan
Wednesday Dec. 1:	5.4	Indonesia
Thursday, Dec. 2:	6.9	Papau New Guinea
Thursday, Dec. 2	5.9	Sumatra
Thursday, Dec. 2	6.1	Fiji

Conclusion:

All of these earthquakes happened on the western side of the Ring of Fire. There were smaller earthquakes in California and near Reno, Nevada. There was even a 3.9 quake in New York City, but the big quakes were all out in the western Pacific. The Pacific Plate must be moving this week since all these fault lines are active.

Your Turn

Turn to pages 346–347, which explain how to create an observation report—a form of inductive thinking. What topic would you like to write about in an observation report? Why?

Problem Solving in Math

Mathematicians also use a version of the inquiry process to solve problems. Here is an example math problem and the process for solving it:

What pattern do you see in the numbers below? Describe the pattern and then write the next three numbers.

4, 12, 36, 108, _____, _____, _____ . . .

| Question the problem. | What is the pattern? How much larger is 12 than 4? How much larger is 36 than 12? Is the increase by addition, multiplication, or another function? |

| Plan a solution. | Each number is 3 times the number before it, so the three missing numbers can be found by multiplying 108 by 3, and the result by 3, and the result by 3. |

| Create a solution. | Here are the calculations: |

4 X 3 = 12   108 X 3 = 324
12 X 3 = 36   324 X 3 = 972
36 X 3 = 108   972 X 3 = 2,916

| Check the solution. | Check the answers by dividing each number by the preceding number. The answer each time should be 3. |

2,916 ÷ 972 = 3   108 ÷ 36 = 3
972 ÷ 324 = 3   36 ÷ 12 = 3
324 ÷ 108 = 3   12 ÷ 4 = 3

| Present the solution. | Each number is 3 times the number before it. The next three numbers are 324, 972, and 2,916. |

Your Turn

Use this problem-solving method to solve the following problem:
What pattern do you see in the figures below? Describe the pattern and sketch the next three figures.

Solving Word Problems

A word problem presents a real-world situation that requires a mathematical solution. You can use the same problem-solving approach to solve word problems.

The displacement of a boat tells how much water it pushes aside (the volume). Find the total displacement (volume in cubic feet) of this hull.

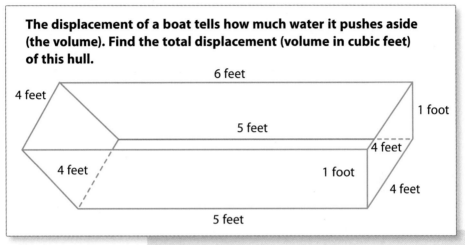

| Question the problem. | How do I figure the volume of a geometrical shape? What is the height, width, and depth of the hull? How can I figure the volume for the sloping part in front? |

| Plan a solution. | If the hull were rectangular, I could figure the volume by multiplying height, width, and depth. To find this shape, I could calculate the volume for a 6-foot-long rectangular hull, then for a 5-foot-long one, then average them. |

| Create a solution. | Here are the calculations:
6-foot hull: 6 ft X 1 ft X 4 ft = 24 cubic feet
5-foot hull: 5 ft X 1 ft X 4 ft = 20 cubic feet
Hull above: $(24\ ft^3 + 20\ ft^3) \div 2 = 22$ cubic feet |

| Check the solution. | Check the answers by reviewing the plan and checking the math. |

| Present the solution. | The displacement of the hull is 22 cubic feet. |

Problem-Solving Activities

Use this activity to practice problem solving. And of course, be sure to apply your problem-solving skills whenever the need arises.

School Improvements

You spend a lot of time in school, so you should know what works well—and what doesn't. Maybe your computer lab is great, but the band room is too small. This activity will help you examine and solve problems at your school.

Your Turn

Think of problems in your school or community. What one thing would you change if you could? Choose one problem and use it to practice your problem-solving skills by completing one or more of the following activities.

1. **Examine** the problem by answering the 5 W and H questions about it. (See page 51.)

2. **Analyze** the problem by creating a cause-effect chart about it. (See page 51.)

3. **Brainstorm** ideas. (See page 52.)

4. **Evaluate** the ideas. (See page 52.)

5. **Plan** a solution for the problem. (See page 53.)

6. **Apply** the solution to the problem. (See page 53.)

7. **Evaluate** the solution and its application. (See page 54.)

8. **Improve** your solution. (See page 55.)

9. **Present** your solution. (See page 55.)

Chapter 5
Communicating

Communicating has been part of your life since you were born and let out your first cry. Now you're growing up, and so must your communication skills—in person, on paper, and online.

Some forms of communicating are easy, like texting a friend. Other forms take practice, like speaking in front of your classmates or writing a report. Because 21st century jobs require them, it is important for you to develop strong communication skills now. This chapter will help.

You will learn . . .

- Speaking One-on-One
- Speaking in a Small Group
- Speaking to a Large Group
- Listening Actively
- Writing Effectively
- Communicating with Technology
- Using Levels of Language

Understanding Communication

Each communicating situation has a specific *purpose, topic, audience,* and *form*.

Shannon wants to tell a friend about her play audition. Here are the basics of this simple exchange.

> **Purpose:** to share
> **Topic:** how the audition went
> **Audience:** Alyssa, a good friend
> **Form:** texting conversation

Roy has written and recorded a song for a local contest. Here are the basics of this type of communication.

> **Purpose:** to entertain
> **Topic:** small-town living
> **Audience:** contest judges
> **Form:** song

Anna is writing a campaign speech for a classmate. These basics will guide her work.

> **Purpose:** to persuade
> **Topic:** Jon Snyder, running for student council president
> **Audience:** Parkview students
> **Form:** three-minute speech

Kristos has created a public service announcement (PSA) for the morning announcements. Here are the basics of this situation.

> **Purpose:** to inform/encourage
> **Topic:** Saturday's walkathon
> **Audience:** Dover School staff and students
> **Form:** PSA

Speaking and Writing

There are many types of communication. The following graphic shows many of them, organized according to their level of difficulty and formality.

Types of Communicating

Casual and simple	
	friendly talk
	quick notes
	texting
	personal e-mails
	blogs
	class notes
	class discussions
	business e-mails
	business letters
	interviews
	informational speeches
	stories/songs
	podcasts
	essays/reports
	persuasive speeches
Formal and complex	project presentations

Your Turn

Which of these types of communication have you done? What other types of writing and speaking have you done? Where would they fit in this list? Share your ideas with a partner.

Speaking

As the chart on the previous page shows, the easiest type of communication is the friendly conversation. More formal types, such as talking with a counselor or participating in group discussions, are not so easy. This may be the case because you don't have much experience with them. Some experts call formal speaking a "lost art" because it is so seldom practiced.

Speaking One-on-One

Speaking with a guidance counselor or conducting an interview requires planning and preparation. The following guidelines will help you carry out formal conversations.

Before . . .

Analyze the situation. Understand the purpose, audience, topic, and form of the conversation. Then decide what details about the topic you need to address. In an interview, for example, deciding what you need to know will help you prepare a list of questions. (See page 446.)

Learn about the person you will be talking with. Know (1) how to pronounce the person's name and (2) how to address him or her properly: Mr. Brown, Captain Riley, Mayor Karas. (See page 86 for help.)

During . . .

Make eye contact. Also show your interest in the person's ideas by nodding your head, using facial expressions, and so on.

Express yourself clearly and sincerely so the other person can easily follow your ideas.

Try to remain calm and relaxed, but do not slouch in your chair or lean against a wall.

Stay on task. Remember your purpose. Also be sure that the conversation doesn't become one-sided. When you are finished, thank the person for her or his time.

After . . .

Reflect on the experience. Did you get the information that you needed? Did you give the information your audience needed? Were you polite and sincere? Did you thank the person?

A Closer Look at Formal Conversations

The following tips will help you carry out conversations in formal situations (when speaking with authorities).

■ **When introducing yourself . . .**

>   **Do Say:** "Thank you for meeting with me, Ms. Jones." (or) "It's nice to meet you, Ms. Jones."
> **Don't Say:** "How's it going?" (or) "What's up?"

■ **When completing a conversation . . .**

>   **Do Say:** "Thank you for your time, Ms. Jones."
> **Don't Say:** "Hey, thanks." or "I'm out of here."

■ **When asking for help . . .**

>   **Do Say:** "Mr. Berkman, could you please help me with this?"
> **Don't Say:** "Give me some help."

■ **When apologizing . . .**

>   **Do Say:** "Ms. Johnson, I'm sorry for what I said yesterday."
> **Don't Say:** "Forget the whole thing." or "Just forget yesterday."

■ **When asking for an explanation . . .**

>   **Do Say:** "Could you please explain that for me?"
> **Don't Say:** "Whoa, what are you talking about?"

■ **When clarifying something . . .**

>   **Do Say:** "Mr. Richter, that's interesting, but I really think . . . "
> **Don't Say:** "I think . . ." or "Listen to this . . ."

■ **When disagreeing with an idea . . .**

>   **Do Say:** "Ms. Arnold, I'm not sure I accept that."
> **Don't Say:** "What are you talking about?"

Your Turn

Think about one of your last conversations with a teacher, counselor, principal, or coach. How many of the "Do Say" examples did you follow? Which ones will you use next time?

Speaking in a Small Group

Responding to your classmates' writing, discussing a class project, planning a team's fund-raiser, working on a group project—these are situations that involve small-group discussions. The guidelines that follow will help you carry out effective discussions. (See pages 90–93.)

Before . . .

Analyze the situation. Understand the purpose and topic of the discussion. Then plan for it by reviewing the topic and, if necessary, preparing handouts.

Consider the group members. Know people's names and use them as you discuss the topic. (Say, "Julie, what do you think?" rather than "So what do you think?")

During . . .

Make eye contact as you speak and listen. And show interest in each speaker's ideas.

Politely ask and answer questions of other group members, but wait for a good time to speak.

Avoid any nervous actions, such as tapping a pen or pencil. Also sit up in your chair rather than slouch over.

Stay on task. Remember your purpose. Don't allow one group member (including yourself) to dominate the talk.

After . . .

Revisit the situation. Did the group accomplish what it needed to? What worked well and not so well?

Your Turn

In a brief paragraph, describe a recent group discussion. In your description, consider whether the discussion followed the guidelines above.

A Closer Look at Group Discussions

"What a crazy idea!" "Get real!" "I don't think so!" Responses like these don't lead to productive group discussions. Instead, respond with tact. Using tact means "responding with understanding and care." Everyone ought to feel that his or her ideas are appreciated and valued. The following tips will help you respond with tact.

- **Keep comments positive and helpful:** "I like how our project is coming together."
- **Begin your responses with "I," not "You":** "I wonder if we are going to finish all of our work on time."
- **Offer a compliment or a thank-you for work well done:** "Gerald, those illustrations are perfect."
- **Apologize if you make a mistake or if you treat someone in a hurtful way:** "Sorry, I thought you said something else. I need to listen more carefully."
- **Focus your responses on a group member's ideas or work rather than on the person:** "I like the presentation, but I wonder if the final slide is strong enough."
- **Make responses that help everyone feel like an important part of the team:** "Sonja, I think that you and Josie could work together to improve the final slide."

In Focus

How should you respond if someone interrupts you? You might say, "Please, I'm not quite finished" or "I'm almost done." Be as courteous as possible in your comment; then get on with your remarks. There's no need to overreact to an occasional interruption.

Your Turn

In a small group, discuss the following statement made by Orson Rega Card, grandfather of Orson Scott Card: "Among my most prized possessions are words that I have never spoken." What is he trying to say? How does it apply to group work? Do you agree with him?

Speaking to a Large Group

As soon as you stand up and face the entire class, speaking suddenly becomes very difficult, doesn't it? Use the following guidelines to make this type of speaking easier. (See also pages 440–445.)

Before . . .

Analyze the situation. Understand the purpose, the audience, the topic, and form of the presentation or speech. Then carefully plan it. Write your presentation out word for word, or list key points on note cards. Also prepare any "extras," such as electronic images and sound.

Practice your speech. Rehearse out loud in front of a mirror until you can give your presentation smoothly and clearly. (Memorizing the speech is also an option.) As you practice, think about the pace (speed) of your delivery, your posture, and so on.

During . . .

Make eye contact. Even if you are reading your presentation, you should regularly scan your audience.

Express your thoughts clearly and sincerely. And show that you are interested in what you have to say. At the end, ask for and answer questions from the audience.

Try to appear calm and relaxed, but not too relaxed. Also avoid any nervous actions, such as shuffling your feet or tapping your fingers.

Monitor your delivery. Slow down if you feel that you are going too fast, and speed things up if your presentation is dragging.

After . . .

Revisit the experience. Use a checklist to evaluate the experience (see page 74) or write freely about the experience in your notebook. Answer questions like these: Did your speech go as planned? How so? What will you do differently next time?

Your Turn

On a scale of 1 to 10, with 1 representing "needs practice" and 10 representing "very strong," rate your presentation skills. Then explain your rating in a brief paragraph.

A Closer Look at Types of Speeches

There are many different types of speeches, and each one requires a special type of preparation and presentation.

- An **informative speech** shares important information about an interesting topic. To develop an effective informative speech, learn as much as you can about your topic. Here are example topics:

  Social Studies: A little-known historical site in your area
  Science: High-speed rail
  Math: The origins or history of algebra
  The Arts: A high-tech form of art

- A **persuasive speech** offers an opinion about an important topic. To be convincing, provide strong, logical support for your opinion. (See also pages 440–441.) Here are example topics:

  Social Studies: Community-service requirements
  Science: Fertilizer-free lawn care
  Math: Computing devices for tests
  The Arts: Open-mike poetry nights

- A **demonstration speech** shows how to do something or how something works. To develop an effective demonstration speech, gather the necessary materials and clearly show each step in the process. (See also pages 444–445.) Here are example topics:

  Social Studies: The citizenship process
  Science: Hydroponics (growing plants in mineral-rich water)
  Math: Using an abacas (an ancient computing device)
  The Arts: Jazz drumming

- An **entertainment speech** engages the reader with a personal story, a reading, a monologue, and so on. To be entertaining, select an appealing topic and polish your delivery. Here are examples:

  Social Studies: Become a past athlete and share your wisdom.
  Science: Read an essay from an environmentalist.
  Math: Present a day-in-the-life monologue of a math student.
  The Arts: Discuss and perform original songs.

Overcoming Stage Fright

Stage fright is a nervous, panicky feeling that many people have before they speak or perform before an audience. It is something that everyone feels, even experienced speakers and performers. The tips below will help you reduce, or at least manage, those nervous feelings that come with speaking or performing before a large group.

Know your topic.

Knowing a lot about your topic should reduce your nervous feelings and build your confidence. Knowledge is power.

Practice often.

Rehearse your speech or presentation on your own and before "practice" audiences. If possible, have someone record one of your practice runs to help you identify parts you need to improve.

Feel ready to speak.

To ease the tension, exercise the day of your speech. Dress comfortably, but appropriately (no T-shirts and shorts for a formal speech). As part of your preparation, imagine yourself giving the speech. Then right before you begin, take a few deep breaths.

Get through the first part.

Sailing smoothly through the beginning part will help you settle in and deliver a strong speech. Remember this when you rehearse.

Focus on your message.

Concentrate on effectively communicating your thoughts and ideas. This is your goal. Wondering if the audience will "like" you will simply weaken your spirit. Giving a speech is not a popularity contest.

In Focus

That nervous feeling—"butterflies in your stomach"—is because of adrenaline. Your body is preparing a fight-or-flight response. Don't flee. Instead, switch into "fight mode" by stepping up boldly and speaking loudly and clearly. When you face down your fear, it will melt away.

Your Turn

Discuss the tips above with a partner. Which ones have you used before? Which ones seem especially important? Then try to come up with an additional tip. Afterward, share your thoughts with your classmates.

Communicating to Everyone

When you give a presentation, speak slowly, loudly, and clearly. Doing so will help everyone hear what you have to say. Remember that some people are hard of hearing and may need to read your lips. Face your audience as you speak to make sure that they can. Also, use visuals such as a slide show to help all people follow along.

Using Sign Language

Often during a speech, a person who knows sign language is available to sign for those who have hearing impairments. Here are the signs for the letters of the alphabet. (For more on sign language, go to thoughtfullearning.com/p73.)

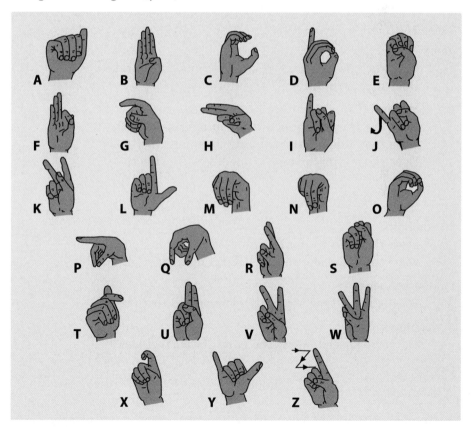

Your Turn

Learn to spell your full name in sign language. Time yourself, seeing how fast you can correctly spell it.

Evaluating an Oral Presentation

Use a checklist like the one below to evaluate your own or your classmates' speeches.

Speech Checklist

Speaker: _____ Date: _____

Speaker
____ Does the speaker seem well prepared?
____ Does she or he seem interested in the topic?
____ Does the speaker make eye contact and appear relaxed?

Speech

Ideas
____ Does the speech focus on a timely and important topic?
____ Does it contain interesting information?

Organization
____ Does the beginning get attention and identify the topic?
____ Does the middle part support or explain the topic?
____ Does the ending bring the speech to an effective close?

Voice
____ Is the speech delivered loudly and clearly?

Word Choice
____ Does the speech contain interesting words and phrases?
____ Does the speaker use any helpful metaphors or similes?

Sentence Fluency
____ Do the ideas flow smoothly from one to the next?

Conventions
____ Does the speech follow the rules for correctness?

Design
____ Do visuals (if used) enhance the speech?

Your Turn

Use a copy of this checklist from thoughtfullearning.com/p74 to evaluate formal speeches presented in your class.

Parts of an Oral Presentation

The note cards that follow are from a presentation given in a science class. The student compiled a slide show to coordinate with the speech.

The **first card** includes the complete introduction.

Introduction (show first slide)

This animal is quite an acrobat, considering it can weigh up to 40 tons. One of its stunts is exploding from the water until its huge body is almost completely airborne; another stunt is thrusting its massive fluke or tail straight out of the water. This amazing animal, the humpback whale, has been entertaining whale watchers for years.

The
Humpback
Whale

The **middle cards** list main points.

Wonderful singers (show second slide)
— may last 7 to 30 minutes
— singer will float with head pointing down
  (show photograph)
— may be a means of communicating

Migrating mammals (show third slide)
— go in a specific order
— journey may cover 2,000 miles
— takes two months

The **final card** includes the complete closing.

Closing (show last slide)

We can't turn to zoos to save the humpback whale if it were to become an endangered species. So it is good news that the population is once again healthy. But we must do whatever we can to protect the humpback's natural habitat so this amazing mammal can remain free to play and sing and entertain us with its antics.

Listening Actively

Communicating is a two-way process: One person speaks and one or more other people listen. Then the roles reverse, with the first speaker listening and someone else speaking. Back and forth the process continues. So far, this chapter has focused on speaking. The information that follows concentrates on listening.

Pilots and Copilots

Compare a speaker to a pilot and a listener to a copilot. The pilot controls the speed and direction of the words and ideas, and the copilot must follow along, ready to take the controls, no matter how fast or slow the pilot is flying the plane. The guidelines that follow will help you become a good copilot, or listener.

Before . . .
- **Be positive,** expecting to listen and to learn during each conversation or group discussion.

During . . .
- **Make eye contact** with the speaker and note his or her facial expressions and hand movements. The speaker's gestures may help you follow his or her words.
- **Listen for signal words** like *as a result, next,* and *finally.* These words help you follow the speaker from one point to the next.
- **Think about what is being said.** What do the words mean?
- **Take brief notes,** if necessary. But do more listening than writing so you don't miss anything.
- **Write down questions** you would like to ask the speaker, but ask them only at an appropriate time.

After . . .
- **Review the speaker's message** afterward to make sure that you understand it.
- **Avoid poor listening habits** such as daydreaming or giving up on a speaker's ideas.

Your Turn

On a scale of 1 to 10, with 1 representing "very poor" and 10 representing "very good," how would you rate your listening skills? Explain your rating to a partner.

A Closer Look at Learning and Listening

Listening is one of your most important learning tools. But to ensure that you remember the main points of a presentation or discussion, use the information as soon as you can, and as often as you can. Here are some ways to do this.

Learning Through Listening

- **Write in a learning log or blog.** Explore your thoughts and feelings about the topic of the presentation or discussion. Push yourself to write freely for at least 5 minutes. (See pages 198–199.)
- **Think critically about the topic** by analyzing it. This means comparing it to similar ideas, describing it step-by-step, deciding if it is a problem or a solution, and so on. (See pages 13–30.)
- **Think creatively about the topic** by asking and answering creative questions about it: What piece of clothing is this topic like? What type of food does it enjoy? What type of personality does it have? (See pages 243–254 for more ideas.)
- **Use the information in your class work**—during discussions, in assignments, and in projects. Using new information helps you remember it.
- **Expand your understanding of the topic** by conducting research online or by talking about it with an authority. The more you learn about it, the better. (See pages 263–292.)
- **Talk about the topic with different audiences**—friends, family members, younger kids, and so on. This will force you to explain the information several times, in different ways, which will help you remember it.
- **Review the material regularly.** Read over your notes and learning-log entries every week or two to help you remember the information.

Your Turn

Someone once said, "Everyone can hear. Even a duck can hear. But it takes effort to listen." What does this quotation say about the difference between listening and hearing? Do you believe that there is a difference between the two? Discuss the quotation with a partner or small group of classmates.

Writing Effectively

In school, you write paragraphs, essays, and reports. At your job, you might take phone messages, fill out forms and write reports. On your own, you may keep a journal or notebook and write poems and stories. Online, you communicate on a social networking site. Writing, in fact, is a very important part of your life.

Completing Assigned Writing

For your writing assignments, you should follow the steps in the writing process to do your best work. (See the graphic on the next page.) The basic guidelines below will help you complete your assignments using this important process.

Before . . .

Analyze the situation. Identify the purpose, topic, audience, and form of the assignment so you know what is expected of you.

During . . .

Prewriting: Select a specific topic for your writing. Then collect ideas and plan how you will organize them.

Writing: Create a first draft, using your prewriting plan as a general guide.

Revising: Review your writing and then change parts that need work. At this point, focus on improving the ideas in your writing. (Correct errors during the next step.)

Editing: Check your revised writing for grammar, spelling, punctuation, and capitalization errors.

Publishing: Prepare a final copy of your writing to share.

After . . .

Revisit the situation. Evaluate your finished product using a checklist like the one on page 80. You may also explore your feelings about your work in a three-minute freewriting. Ask yourself what worked well and what you need to improve upon.

In Focus

Writing is a key skill in school and in the workplace, and each assignment is an opportunity to learn and grow as a writer. The effort you put into your writing now will pay off in the future.

A Closer Look at Writing

This graphic shows how you move back and forth between the steps in the writing process. For example, after starting a first draft, you may decide to collect more details (prewriting) before you go on.

The Writing Process

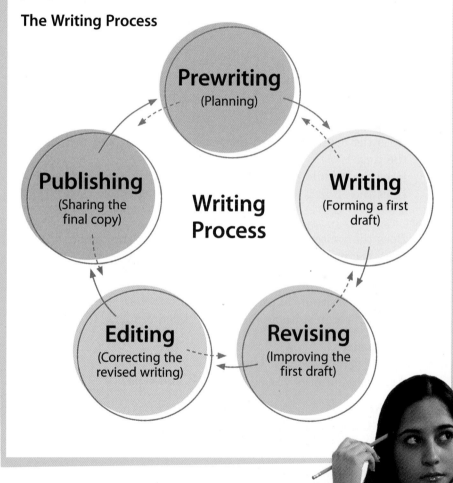

Writing Process

Prewriting (Planning)

Writing (Forming a first draft)

Revising (Improving the first draft)

Editing (Correcting the revised writing)

Publishing (Sharing the final copy)

Your Turn

On a scale of 1 to 10, with 1 representing "not familiar at all" and 10 representing "very familiar," how would you rate your knowledge of the writing process? Explain your choice.

Evaluating Writing

Use a checklist like the one below to evaluate your own writing as well as your classmates' writing. (See also pages 183–194.)

Writing Checklist

Writer: _____ Date: _____

Ideas
____ Does the writing focus on an interesting topic?
____ Does it contain plenty of supporting facts and details?

Organization
____ Does the beginning gain the reader's interest and introduce the topic?
____ Does the middle part support or explain the topic?
____ Does the ending bring the writing to an effective close?

Voice
____ Does the writer seem knowledgeable about the topic?
____ Does the writer sound interested in the topic?

Word Choice
____ Does the writing contain specific rather than general words?
____ Are the words suitable for the intended readers?

Sentence Fluency
____ Do the sentences flow smoothly?
____ Are the sentences varied in length and type?

Conventions
____ Does the writing follow the rules of the language?

Design
____ Does the writing follow the guidelines for final copies?

Your Turn

Use a copy of this checklist to evaluate the report on the next page. (Go to thoughtfullearning.com/p80 to download a copy of this checklist.)

Parts of a Written Report

A student included this report about the history of roller coasters along with his project on thrill rides. (Not all of the middle paragraphs are shown here.)

The Ultimate Thrill Ride

In the **beginning**, the topic is introduced, and its origins are discussed.

The roller coaster as we know it today was actually born on ice. More exactly, its ancestor was the ice slide used for centuries as public amusement in Russia. In the late 1700s, the idea was transferred from Russia to Paris, but the ice slide was impractical in the warmer climate. As a result, a ramp of rollers was built for toboggans to slide down. For many years after, well into the 1800s, toboggans on rollers were all that were available to thrill seekers.

In the United States, a mining company in Pennsylvania constructed a long downhill track to transport coal from the mine to the freight lines. By the 1850s the company saw another way to make money with the track by offering cart rides down the track for 50 cents a ride. They provided a rough ride by our standards, but at the time, it was the best thing available to thrill seekers.

The **middle** part of the report continues the history of roller coasters.

In 1878 Richard Knutsen of Brooklyn took out the first American patent for a roller coaster on wheels; unfortunately, he never built the ride. It was La Marcus Thompson who built the first American roller coaster on wheels at Coney Island in 1884. It was called Thompson's Gravity Pleasure Railway and was a huge hit. Two couples sat facing each other in a cart that was raised by an elevator up to a tower. The cart then sped down a track, came to a stop, and was raised by an elevator for the next ride. . . .

The **ending** provides an interesting final thought.

The roller coaster quickly became one of the main attractions at most amusement parks, and the designs of new roller coasters kept improving to meet the demands of riders. Each new design provided bigger and better rides— much to the delight of everyone. Believe it or not, a few of the early roller coasters still exist today. However, these old-time rides don't really meet the needs of today's thrill seekers, who, like past thrill seekers, want rides that push the envelope.

Glossary for Speaking and Writing

Your teachers might use these terms in class discussions about speaking and writing.

Speech Terms

The following terms are often used when developing, discussing, and evaluating speeches. (See also pages 440–445.)

Cadence: The rhythm or flow of a speech

Emphasis: Giving special attention or stress to different words or phrases

Enunciation: The act of pronouncing words and phrases

Gesture: Motion used to emphasize a point

Inflection: The rising and falling in the pitch of a voice

Monotone: A voice that does not change in pitch; considered dull

Pace: The rate of speed or movement in a speech

Pitch: The high, middle, or low tones of the voice

Projection: Directing the voice so it can be heard at a distance

Script: The written copy of a speech

Stage fright: The nervousness a speaker feels before and during the speech

Tone: The feeling or attitude the speaker reveals about the topic.

Writing Terms

The following terms are often used when developing, discussing, and analyzing writing. (See also pages 317–368.)

Arrangement: The order of details in writing

Coherence: The logical arrangement of ideas

Description: Writing that creates a mental picture of a person, place, or thing

Details: Words and ideas used to describe, persuade, and explain

Essay: A multiparagraph composition that develops or explains a main idea (thesis)

Exposition: Writing that explains

Focus: A specific part of a topic that is emphasized in writing, also called the *thesis*

Limiting the subject: Narrowing a topic so it will work for a writing assignment

Narration: Writing that shares a story

Objective: Sharing information without adding personal feelings or opinions

Persuasion: Writing that supports an opinion, meant to change a reader's mind

Point of view: The position a writer takes

Subjective: Sharing information with personal feelings or opinions

Theme: The message in a piece of writing

Thesis statement: A statement of the main idea or focus of an essay

Tone: The writer's attitude about his or her topic

Transitions: Words or phrases that connect ideas in writing

Unity: The way writing holds together; how effectively the ideas are ordered and related to the topic

Communicating with Technology

In your personal life, you may write status updates on Facebook or post stories on a fan fiction site. In your social life, you may text your friends or network in other ways. In school, you may create digital stories or develop multimedia reports. In other words, technology offers a variety of communicating opportunities.

Technology allows you to combine your speaking and writing in creative ways. Voice, visuals, music, print—they are all available to you. You may start with something simple, combining a piece of writing with a few visuals, but there is so much more you can do.

Electronic Communication Options

The list that follows identifies many exciting communication options available to you because of technology. Your school may have access to many of them. (See also pages 139–156.)

Blogs are online journals that you can add to and readers can comment on.

Comic-book software lets you arrange photographs or drawings in comic-book style and add speech bubbles.

Fan-fiction sites allow users to share their stories. Often these stories are interactive, with one writer starting a story and others continuing it.

Music-mixing programs let you record and edit your own songs on a computer.

Online word processors allow you to create and edit documents on the Web with other people.

Photo-sharing sites let users post photos to the Web for other people to view. Some of the sites share photos only with the poster's friends and family. Other sites make photos available for anyone to view and use.

Podcasting sites let people post audio files for others to listen to. Podcasts may include music, lessons, commentary, or even audiobooks.

Slideshow software allows users to create and display multimedia presentations. Classrooms and businesses alike use these programs to present reports to an audience.

Social-network sites let people view text and photos posted by friends and family. They also may list recommended books, movies, and music, and provide games and quizzes.

Video-editing software lets you import recorded video into your computer, edit it, and post it to sharing sites.

Wikis are projects written and edited by a community of people. Your class might create a Wiki about your town's history, for example.

Your Turn

With a partner or small group of students, discuss which of these options you have used (or would like to use). What are the strengths and limitations of the ones you have used?

Using Levels of Language

Knowing about the different levels of language allows you to communicate appropriately. For most of your school communication, informal or formal English is required.

Using Informal English

Use **informal English** when you write personal stories and articles for your classmates, engage in classroom blogs, and participate in group discussions or relaxed one-on-one conversations. People feel comfortable with informal English.

Informal English usually contains personal references (*I, you, he, she*), simple words, short sentences, and expressions of personal feelings ("It was awesome!"). Overall, it sounds friendly and real.

Music just doesn't sound as good without drums. Just think of a rock band without a drummer, or a hip-hop track without a beat. They'd be so boring! Drums are the backbone of a band. They create the beat that makes you bob your head and tap your feet. Watch a good drummer at work, and you'll see that drums do more than make loud noises that your mom loves to hate.

Using Formal English

Use **formal English** for business letters, most informational and persuasive essays, and assigned speeches and presentations. People expect formal English to be used in serious communication.

Formal English pays careful attention to word choice; it includes longer, complex sentences; and it focuses on facts and ideas rather than on feelings.

Drums play an important role in music. Rock, pop, jazz, and R&B music rely on drums to maintain a steady beat. Drums are considered percussion instruments because a person must strike them to create the vibrations that produce sound. In basic drum kits, cymbals accompany a collection of different-sized drums such as toms, snares, and bass. When they are struck with different levels of force, they create a pattern of thumps, tings, and booms.

Using Standard English

Standard English (SE) is the dialect that should be used in all formal speaking and writing situations. Learning how to use SE is a vital part of your schooling since any career you enter in the future will require that you use it.

The chart below shows the most common grammatical differences between SE and other common dialects. Whenever you have a question about using SE, refer to this chart for help. (See also pages 183–194.)

Differences in . . .	Other Dialects	Standard English
1. Expressing plurals after numbers	10 mile	10 miles
2. Expressing recurring action	He always be early.	He always is early.
3. Expressing ownership	My friend car . . .	My friend's car . . .
4. Expressing the third-person singular verb	The customer ask . . .	The customer asks . . .
5. Expressing negatives	They don't never . . .	They don't ever . . .
6. Using reflexive pronouns	He sees hisself . . .	He sees himself . . .
7. Using demonstrative pronouns	Them are . . .	Those are . . .
8. Using forms of *do*	He done it.	He did it.
9. Avoiding double subjects	My manager he . . .	My manager . . .
10. Using *a* or *an*	I need new laptop. She had angry caller.	I need a new laptop. She had an angry caller.
11. Using the past tense of verbs	Carl finish his . . .	Carl finished his . . .
12. Using *isn't* or *aren't* versus using *ain't*	The company ain't . . .	The company isn't . . .

Using Fair Language

The information below shows how to identify people and groups according to their differences. Always use language that treats everyone with respect.

When referring to race, say
American Indians, Native Americans or specific tribes *(Hopi, Stockbridge, Inuit)*
Asian Americans (rather than Orientals) or specific nationalities *(Japanese Americans)*
Hispanic or Latino or specific nationalities *(Mexican Americans)*
African American, *though black is preferred by some individuals*

When referring to age, say
Older adults, older people (not elderly) *when referring to people 70 or older*
Women, men, adults *when referring to people 30 or older*
Young adults *when referring to late teens and 20's*
Young people, adolescents *when referring to people between 13 and 19*
Girls, boys *when referring to people 12 or younger*

When referring to adults, say
Mr. Nelson *when referring to an adult man*
Ms. Brand *when referring to an adult woman without noting her marriage status*
Mrs. Larson *when referring to a married woman*
Miss Long *when referring to a single woman*

When referring to adults with titles, say	
■ President Obama	■ Mullah Abdul
■ Rabbi Gould	■ Dr. Monk

When referring to disabilities, say	Don't say
disabled	*handicapped*
a person with autism	*an autistic*

When referring to inclusive gender, say	Don't say
police officer	*policeman*
chair	*chairman*
postal worker	*postman*
he or she	*he*

Communication Activities

Use these activities to help you practice speaking and writing in school and in your personal life.

Breaking the Ice

To become more comfortable with speaking in front of people, try reading to your classmates. Share brief news articles, the lyrics from favorite songs, stories about interesting people, and favorite poems.

> **Our best advice:** The first time that you do this activity, share your selection with a small group (two or three students). Over time, increase the size of your audience. Sharing what others have written is a good way to gain experience and begin to feel comfortable with speaking in front of others.

Your Turn

Select something that is interesting to you and that you would enjoy sharing. You may also prepare a brief introduction (explaining the reason for your choice). Use the guidelines on pages 68–72 to help you prepare for and present your selection.

Writing for Yourself

Write every day at a set time—in the morning, during study hall, or after school. Write whenever and wherever it feels comfortable to you. Explore your experiences, your schoolwork, and your hopes and dreams. The important thing is to get into a writing routine and stick to it.

> **Our best advice:** Regular writing will help you become more fluent and comfortable with writing. As your writing fluency improves, so will your ability to express yourself.

Your Turn

Reserve a notebook or create a computer file for your personal writing. To get started, write as freely and rapidly as you can to unlock your best ideas. Try to write nonstop for at least 5 to 8 minutes. (Count the number of words that you write during each session to see how fluent you become.)

Changing Voices

To expand your speaking and writing abilities, try communicating in different voices. Write or speak first as yourself, then as a second grader, and finally as a scientist or doctor. This exercise helps you understand more about word choice, sentence structure, and different levels of language.

Our best advice: Make this activity a regular part of your communicating routine. You'll learn a lot about your speaking and writing abilities and gain an appreciation of the wonderful language you are working with.

Your Turn

Write a journal entry in a casual voice. Review the entry and rewrite it using a formal voice. Read both entries aloud to hear the difference.

Communicating with Someone New

Pick someone new—a classmate who isn't a close friend, a member of your extended family, and so on. Then interact with this person on an online site sponsored by your school or one that your family uses.

Our best advice: Communicate occasionally with a new person via a blog, an e-mail, a chat room, or another social medium. This activity makes you more alert to what you say and how you say it.

Your Turn

With the help of a teacher or parent, find a person to interact with online. Then decide on a form for your communication (blog, chat room) and start talking. As time goes on, consider adding other people to the conversation.

Chapter 6
Collaborating

Right before a game, teams often huddle up, join hands, and yell "Teamwork!" Working together, or collaborating, is important everywhere—on sports teams, in clubs, in organizations, and in group projects.

Collaboration puts the group first. In a music studio, for example, that can mean playing an instrument in a way that enhances rather than overpowers the vocalist, or fine-tuning equipment so that all the musicians sound their best.

The pages that follow will teach you how to work with others, from collaborating online to solving problems.

You will learn . . .

- Collaboration
- Appreciating Diversity
- Collaborating Online
- Conducting Meetings
- Group Brainstorming
- Group Problem Solving
- Resolving Conflicts

Understanding Collaboration

You have been practicing group skills ever since you began school. Early on, you learned about taking turns, being nice, and playing together. Now it is time to expand on those skills. The information that follows will get you started.

Being Active

Being active in group work means being involved and contributing your ideas and abilities. Here's how you can get actively involved.

- **Listen carefully** to others and keep an open mind about their ideas. Think about what is being said and take notes if necessary.

- **Offer your own ideas** at the right time, perhaps during a pause in the discussion. If your idea is related to someone else's, say so: "After Ravi said, . . . I thought that . . ." Always show respect for other group members.

- **Focus on ideas** not personalities. Instead of saying, "You're wrong!" say, "I'm not sure about that plan . . ." And don't be surprised when someone questions one of your ideas. Working in a group is a give-and-take situation.

- **Make decisions** after all group members have shared their thoughts.

Your Turn

Rate how active you are when you collaborate. Note ways that you are actively involved, and think about ways that you can improve.

How often do you ...	Never	Rarely	Sometimes	Often	Always
1. listen carefully	1	2	3	4	5
2. offer ideas	1	2	3	4	5
3. focus on ideas	1	2	3	4	5
4. make decisions	1	2	3	4	5

Being Respectful

A group's success depends on its ability to be encouraging and cooperative. A positive group works in the following ways.

- **Create trust.** Trust is created by respecting each other. Each member should know that her or his contributions will be valued.
- **Involve everyone.** Don't let any one person control a discussion, and try to get everyone to participate.
- **Maintain good relations.** But don't ignore problems, either. Address disruptive comments with statements such as "Jerry, we're starting to make some progress. We need to stay focused" or "We're getting off track. Let's go back to Mia's idea."
- **Offer to contribute.** Once the group decides on the next step, volunteer to help with the work.

Focus

Coaches, teachers, and business leaders often post teamwork reminders on bulletin boards. Here are a few examples: "There is no 'I' in 'team,' " "A successful team beats with one heart," and "Teamwork: It is less *me* and more *we*."

Being Helpful

Each group member has an important role to play. Here are three key roles to consider, especially if you are working in a small group of four to six members.

- A **leader** manages the flow of a team, keeping everyone on task, contributing ideas, and dealing with problems.
- The **other group members** offer ideas, ask questions, and work together. (See page 254.)
- A **note taker** writes down important questions, decisions, and next steps—in addition to contributing ideas.

Your Turn

Discuss the following questions with a partner: Would you rather lead or serve as a player in a group? Why? What strengths and abilities can you offer a group or team?

Appreciating Diversity

Your school may have a diverse student population. (Diverse means "differing from one another.") Classmates may come from different backgrounds, have special customs, and practice unique learning styles. Keep the following points in mind when you work with diverse groups of students.

Appreciate different cultures.

Befriend students from other countries or backgrounds and learn about their cultures.

Recognize different perspectives.

People of varying backgrounds approach learning in different ways. For example, some feel very comfortable with sharing their thoughts and feelings, while others are careful about what they say.

Work toward common goals.

Inform everyone plainly about the purpose of the group's work, his or her role in it, and the important deadlines and outcomes. (See also page 225.)

Maintain a friendly, helpful attitude.

Remain positive, supportive, and open-minded when problems occur. Work together to find solutions. (See page 99.)

In Focus

One year, six students from five different countries—Malaysia, Singapore, the Netherlands, Egypt, and the United States—created an award-winning Web site for a contest. Their Web site educated people about the SARS virus. (SARS stands for severe acute respiratory syndrome.) Even though the students came from diverse backgrounds, their strong group skills led them to success.

Your Turn

Working with a partner, identify at least three ways you would use technology to work with students from other countries. Also discuss any questions or concerns you have about working with students from varying cultures. Afterward, share your thoughts and feelings with the rest of your class.

Carrying Out Group Work

Sports teams succeed when they are organized and prepared. The same holds true for the groups that you form in your classes. At the start of a project, you need to answer the following questions to be clear about what your group is trying to accomplish.

Identifying the Basics

Why are you working together? (*Project*)	To create a historical reenactment in social studies class
What is your goal? (*Purpose*)	To inform and entertain
Who is involved? (*People*)	Angela Brown, Jack Dawkins, Molly Lee, Roger Smith, and Alex Karas
Where will you do the work? (*Place*)	In class and during study halls
When must it be ready? (*Performance*)	Four weeks from now, on March 12

Understanding the Project

Long-Term Projects: For a long-term project such as a reenactment (see above), you would have to decide on a topic, research it, plan tasks, set deadlines, gather materials, write a script, create the costumes and props, and rehearse. Chapters 24–31 explain step-by-step how to develop long-term projects.

Short-Term Projects: Other projects are more limited in scope. You may have a problem to solve, a conflict to resolve, or a decision to make—tasks that a group can accomplish in one or two class periods. See pages 99–100 to help you solve problems and resolve conflicts.

> **Your Turn**
>
> Think of a long- or short-term project that you have worked on in the recent past. Prepare to explain what the group accomplished, what your role was, and what the experience taught you about group work. Share your thoughts with your classmates.

Collaborating Online

The Internet makes it possible to collaborate with students both near and far away. Check with your teacher for online collaborating opportunities approved by your school.

Ways to Collaborate Online

Collaborating online allows groups to share new knowledge, bounce ideas back and forth, comment on each other's work, and team up to create exciting new content. Here are some Web resources that you can use to collaborate electronically.

- **Wikis** are Web pages that allow multiple users to write, edit, and save texts. Anyone visiting the wiki page can edit or add to the texts. (See pages 152–153 and 392.)
- **Blogs** are online personal journals or informational sites where you can write new content, share links to other blogs or Web sites, and post videos and music. Blogs allow readers to comment on entries, offer suggestions, and share links. (See page 150.)
- **Chat** services let you communicate with one or more people, but in real time.
- **E-mail** is a sure way to communicate with group members all around the world. (See pages 140 and 324–325.)
- **VOIP (Voice Over Internet Protocol)** allows you to connect with students in other schools via voice and video calls. With VOIP you can send files, participate in conference calls, and share screens. Check with your teacher about the availability of VOIP at your school. (See page 154.)
- **Online Forums,** or message boards, offer opportunities to discuss topics of common interest by posting messages on threads. A thread is a group of comments about a single, specific topic. You can find online forums on just about any subject. (See page 151.)

Your Turn

Discuss these questions with a partner: In what ways have you already collaborated online? What other ways would you like to try? Why?

Understanding Netiquette

Netiquette refers to proper conduct online. The guidelines that follow offer some best practices for online group projects.

- **Respect others.** Remember, you are communicating with another person, not a computer screen. Be respectful at all times and avoid actions or messages that could be interpreted as hurtful.
- **Respect privacy.** Avoid giving out any passwords or personal information online, except for information agreed upon by group members and your teacher.
- **Respect cultural differences.** Be respectful of other cultures and religions, especially if you are collaborating with a student or peer from a different country.
- **Discuss changes.** Online projects often allow users to add to or edit each other's work. Talk with your fellow group members before making any major changes.
- **Beware of copy/paste.** If you use information from another Web site, summarize it in your own words and include a link to the site. If you use a picture or graphic from another Web site, give credit to the photographer or designer. (See pages 287–290.)

Your Turn

Have you ever encountered poor netiquette? If so, discuss it with your partner or with the whole class.

"Respect your fellow human beings, treat them fairly, work together for a common goal, and help one another achieve it."

—Bill Bradley

Conducting Meetings

Here's a familiar scenario: A group of elementary students is playing kickball, and suddenly an argument erupts. One player claims he is safe while the other side says he is out; someone says her kick is fair while others say it went foul. There is never, ever an orderly discussion of problems like these.

Just think if meetings were conducted like this. There would seldom be agreement about anything. Meetings must be orderly and conducted according to the following guidelines.

Meeting Guidelines

1. As a leader, announce the meeting ahead of time so that people can plan to attend.

2. Create and follow an agenda, a listing of ideas and possible actions you want to consider. (See page 97.)

3. Establish a basic time schedule to stay on course.

4. If you are the leader, or chairperson, call the meeting to order. If you are the secretary, or recorder, read the minutes of the previous meeting. (Minutes record the actions of a meeting. See page 97.)

5. Address any old business before discussing new business.

6. Use a set of rules, such as Robert's Rules of Order, to conduct discussions. Here are the basics:
   - The leader introduces each new point of discussion.
   - The leader also recognizes each new speaker before the person speaks. This prevents everyone from speaking at once.
   - Once a discussion reaches a logical ending point, the leader asks for a vote to approve or deny an action or postpone a decision for another time.

7. If you are the leader, end the meeting, making sure that everyone is clear about any next steps.

Minutes

The minutes that follow record the actions at a student council meeting. Notice how they follow the guidelines on page 96.

Bell City Student Council Meeting Minutes

Tuesday, March 8, 2011: Library Meeting Room

The **beginning** identifies the time and place and the students at the meeting.

Present: Thea Karas, president; Dashane Baker, vice president; Anne Henderson, secretary; Nathan Winn, Lari Bankley, Jan Stoud, and Nara Wilson, class reps; Ms. Arnold, faculty rep

11:119 Thea called the meeting to order. The agenda was approved.

Old Business

In the **middle**, each topic is identified with the year (2011) and item number.

11:120 The secretary read the minutes of the March 1 meeting. They were accepted without change.

11:121 The council revisited motion 11:102 and voted to have a March 11 bake sale. Jan Stoud and Nara Wilson will coordinate.

New Business

11:122 Nathan proposed that the school should join in the city's spring cleanup project (April 2 and 9). These were his reasons:

1. The event would help students contribute to the community.
2. The event would make students more aware of the city's litter problem.

The motion to join this event passed.

Details will be discussed in two weeks.

Next Meeting

In the **ending**, actions for the next meeting are identified.

11:123 The study-hall policy will be discussed.

11:124 The next meeting will be on March 15 at 12:30 p.m. (Library Meeting Room).

Submitted by Anna Henderson, secretary

Group Brainstorming

Brainstorming is a group information-gathering strategy. The goal is to generate many options and ideas—the more the better. Being careful and selective may be important when taking a test, but it is not important when brainstorming.

Brainstorming Guidelines

1. **Start** a brainstorming session with a specific goal in mind. For example, you may be looking for fund-raiser ideas or for a solution to a problem.

2. **Select** someone to start the brainstorming and someone to record ideas as they are offered.

3. **Record** all ideas offered in good faith. If everyone talks at once, ask for order so good ideas are not lost.

4. **List** ideas in a place where everyone can see them. Seeing the list helps everyone think of even more ideas.

5. **Keep** brainstorming for as long as possible. The best idea may be the next one.

Sample Brainstorming

Here is a list of fund-raising ideas produced in one brainstorming session.

Ideas for Fund-Raisers

bake sale	softball game	3-on-3 tournament
faculty bb game	fashion show	car wash
dog-sitting	senior-living visits	city cleanup
talent show	dance	table-tennis tournament

Your Turn

With a partner, begin brainstorming ideas for a Learning Fair project. List the ideas on your own paper and share them with your classmates.

Group Problem Solving

Let's say your school has announced the cancellation of this year's musical production because of budget cuts. The musical is a popular event, so this is a serious problem.

You could establish a committee to solve the problem. The guidelines below would help. (See also pages 49–62.)

Problem-Solving Guidelines

1. **Examine the problem** by identifying the 5 W's and H about it (who? what? where? when? why? and how?).

2. **Analyze the problem** by looking at its causes and effects. In this case, the cause of the cancellation is budget cuts. The effects are far reaching, denying students the chance to perform in and attend the production.

3. **Brainstorm ideas** for ways of solving the problem. Ideas might include fund-raisers, charging a fee for participation, finding a sponsor, or starting a booster club.

4. **Evaluate ideas** to decide which solutions are the most promising. Of the offered ideas, the best one would eliminate the causes and effects of the musical's cancellation.

5. **Plan the solution** by defining your goal and objectives and organizing resources. Scheduling would be crucial to save the musical before time runs out.

6. **Apply your solution** to the situation, sharing it with the people who are involved. In this case, it would be crucial to work with the musical director and administration.

7. **Evaluate the solution,** deciding what is working and what is not. The director and administration would help with this process.

8. **Make improvements,** changing any parts that are not as strong as they need to be. Improving the solution makes success more certain.

9. **Present the solution,** making it work in the real world. In this case, the solution should result in a student musical production.

Your Turn

With the help of a partner, identify a problem in your school. Then follow steps 1–5 in the guidelines above to find a solution to this problem. Afterward, share your work with the rest of the class.

Resolving Conflicts

All groups have days when members aren't working well as a team. Conflicts that do not resolve naturally must be dealt with directly.

Suppose four students—Jon, James, Miguel, and Hari—are discussing how to present the results of their science project. Jon feels that a PowerPoint presentation is the best way to go. But James and Miguel want to do a demonstration speech instead. Hari is not sure what they should do. The boys are getting impatient and upset with one another.

To resolve this conflict, the students must (1) practice good group skills (listening, offering ideas, and asking questions), (2) focus on the conflict rather than on the group members, (3) explore the situation or options, and (4) agree on a solution.

In Focus

If the members of a group can't get along, they won't accomplish much. So maintaining positive feelings has to be a priority.

Finding the Solution

Here are four options for finding the solution to a group conflict.

- **Negotiate:** The individuals can try to work out the problem themselves by practicing good group skills.
- **Direct:** A director, most likely a teacher or an adviser, can simply tell the members how to resolve the conflict.
- **Mediate:** The group can ask a teacher or some other trusted person to mediate for them. The mediator works with the group to discuss the conflict and come to a solution.
- **Arbitrate:** An outsider can manage the discussion and select a solution.

Your Turn

Team up with a partner to resolve the conflict explained above. Discuss the problem, consider the options, and propose a solution.

Collaboration Activities

The four activities that follow will prepare you to work in groups. Once you try these exercises, think of others for practicing group skills.

One on One

Team up with a classmate and interview each other, following the guidelines on page 446. Afterward, use the information you gathered to introduce your partner to a group of classmates or to the entire class.

[
Our best advice: Work with partners as often as you can. It is good preparation for working in small groups of three or more classmates.
]

Your Turn

Interview a partner and introduce her or him to the class. This will help everyone to get to know each other better.

Chain Reaction

Team up with a small group of classmates (four to six people). Have one group member write down two sentences of a story or scenario, without showing the paper to the others. He or she then whispers the story to the next group member, that person whispers it to the next group member, and so on. The last person says out loud what was whispered to him or her. Compare this "final" story with the one that was written down.

[
Our best advice: Complete activities like this chain-reaction game to improve your group-communicating skills.
]

Your Turn

Try this activity whenever you feel ready to transition from working with a partner to working in a small group. You will discover that speaking and listening in a group requires concentration and focus.

Two and One

Team up with a small group of classmates (three to five people). To get started, have team members privately list two things that actually happened to them, and one thing that didn't. Then as a group, each member reads her or his list, and the other members try to identify the event that is made up.

Our best advice: Use this activity in a group as a way to get to know each other. It will reinforce good listening skills and help to prepare you for working together.

Your Turn

When you make your two-and-one list, include two surprising and interesting things that have actually happened to you and one made-up event that is also interesting, but not obviously fictitious. Also, share your ideas in a random order with a steady tone of voice.

Nonverbally Speaking

Team up with a small group of classmates (three to five people) and discuss the importance of nonverbal communication in group work. Make a list of positive and negative facial expressions as well as examples of positive and negative body language. Afterward, share your list with other groups in your class.

Our best advice: After your class discussion, make a master list of nonverbal do's and don'ts to post in your classroom. Refer to the list during group work to maintain friendly, positive communications.

Your Turn

When you make your list of positive and negative communication practices, choose a leader to keep the conversation moving and a recorder to clearly list the group's ideas.

Chapter 7
Building Arguments

Often, you need to convince others to agree with you. You need to urge, budge, and turn them toward your way of thinking. This is the case whether you are asking for votes in a student-council campaign, or getting permission to go to the movies.

To develop a strong, tight argument that will change minds and convince others to accept your point of view, you need to be clear, thorough, and logical. Appeal to your audience's moral sense rather than to emotions. And use your best critical-thinking skills. This chapter will show you how.

You will learn . . .

- The 7 C's of Argumentation
- Separating Opinions from Facts
- Using Effective Evidence
- Avoiding Faulty Logic

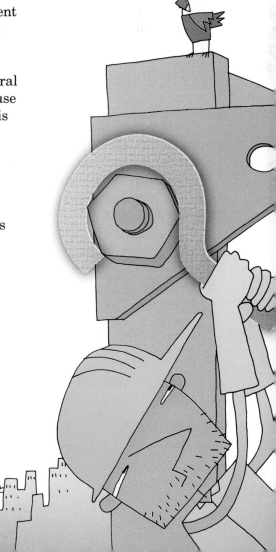

Following an Effective Plan

To build a strong argument, follow a good plan, one that covers all the bases. The plan listed below identifies the 7 C's of putting together an argument. If you follow these steps, you will be able to convince others to accept your line of thinking.

The 7 C's of Argumentation

1. Consider the situation.
2. Clarify your thinking.
3. Construct a claim.
4. Collect evidence.
5. Consider key objections.
6. Craft your argument.
7. Confirm your main point.

1. Consider the situation.

The first step in the process is to consider the situation. Ask yourself these questions: What is my topic? What is my purpose? Who is my audience? What action do I want my audience to take?

You need to have answers to each of these questions before you can begin. It's a good idea to write your answers down in a clear, concise position statement.

Topic:	The school board policy of charging for involvement in sports
Purpose:	To convince people that this policy is wrong
Audience:	Classmates
Action:	I want classmates to e-mail school board members.
Position:	The new policy of charging for involvement in sports is wrong, and students should e-mail school board members to tell them so.

Your Turn

List changes you would like to see in your school. Choose one change that you feel strongly about. Then consider the situation and fill in a chart like the one above. Summarize your position in a clear, concise statement.

2. Clarify your thinking.

Before you can convince others, you must be clear in your own mind about your position. What are you trying to prove? Why do you feel the way you do? What kind of proof do you have? Who will be affected by this?

In addition, it's a good idea to consider both sides of the issue before you begin writing. To do this, set up a pro-con chart like the one shown here.

Pro	Con
The new policy . . . • does not cut teachers. • saves taxpayers money.	The new policy . . . • will cost students more money. • will hurt school spirit. • will deny some students the chance to participate in sports.

Your Turn

Create a pro-con chart, arguing for and against your position.

3. Construct a claim.

Once you have clarified your point of view, you need to construct a *claim*. Your *claim* is your position statement, or the key point of your argument. Use the following formula:

Position	+	Reason	=	Claim
The new policy requiring students to pay to be in sports is wrong.		It denies participation to some and hurts school spirit.		The new policy requiring students to pay to be in sports is wrong because it denies participation to some and hurts school spirit.

Your Turn

Construct a claim that names your position and your reason(s) for it. Consider using a qualifying word (*almost, usually, may, many, often, in most cases, too much*) to make your claim more reasonable and easier to prove.

4. Collect evidence.

Next, you need to gather plenty of facts and details to support your claim. Use examples, statistics, graphics, and illustrations to make your argument clear and easy to follow. The bottom line is this: The stronger your evidence, the stronger your argument. (See "Using Effective Evidence" on page 109.)

Your Turn

Gather different types of evidence to support your claim. Check your evidence to make sure that you have avoided faulty thinking. (See pages 111–116.)

5. Consider key objections.

After you've collected your evidence, you need to consider other points of view, or objections to your position. Once you understand these objections, you should be able to counter (disprove) them or concede (admit) the point.

To counter an objection, you need to point out its flaw or weakness. Don't belittle the people who make the objection, but focus on the reasoning behind it. Keep your tone positive.

Supporters of the policy say it saves money for taxpayers, but it costs students more and prevents some from participating.

To concede an objection, recognize the value of another viewpoint. Making a concession does not necessarily weaken your argument, especially if your argument is strong to begin with.

I admit that the plan prevents teacher cuts, which is a good thing; but it hurts students in other ways.

Concession Starters		
I admit that	Even though	Certainly
It is true that	Perhaps	I accept
Of course	I agree that	I realize that

Your Turn

List objections to your position. Choose the two strongest objections, and then counter them or concede that they are valid.

6. Craft your argument.

The best way to convince your audience to accept your claim is to support it with solid evidence. But you also need to appeal to what the reader wants or needs. Appealing to someone's sense of fairness or common sense, for example, can be more convincing than a list of facts and figures alone. But avoid appeals to fear or ignorance. (See pages 111–116.)

Fact:	Six other local schools offer soccer programs.
Fairness appeal:	Shouldn't we have one, too?
Commonsense appeal:	Without a free soccer program, we'll struggle to compete with these schools.

Also be sure to deal with the main objections to your argument. (See the previous page.) You can do this early on or later in your argument, depending on what seems best to you.

Your Turn

Develop the important facts, consider an appeal to fairness or common sense, and address the main objections to your position. (See page 106.)

7. Confirm your main point.

Finish your argument by drawing your best thoughts together into a logical conclusion. To do this, make a final appeal to your audience and call them to act on your main point. Use a command verb to make your call to action as clear and compelling as possible: *Go . . . Write . . . Donate . . . Join . . . Call . . . E-mail.*

Final appeal:	This new policy of paying for sport participation will do more harm than good. We need to ask the school board to reconsider.
Call to action:	Please e-mail your concerns to members of the school board. Tell them that the new policy will harm students and school spirit.
Final word:	Together, we can make a real difference.

Your Turn

Provide a final appeal and call your reader to act, using a command verb.

Separating Opinions from Facts

To build a strong argument, you need to understand the difference between opinions and facts.

Opinions

■ An **opinion** is a personal view or belief. An opinion may be supported by facts, but it is not a fact itself.

> The appearance of green algae is ruining Pine Lake for many vacationers. *(a personal view that can be supported)*

Keep in mind: Opinions that include words like *all* and *every* may be hard to support.

> Green algae affects everything on Pine Lake. *(a personal view that would be hard to support)*

Facts

■ A **fact** is knowledge or information that can be checked for accuracy. Facts are used to support opinions.

> As the algae decays, it creates a putrid odor. *(a reasonable, provable statement providing strong support)*

Keep in mind: Facts must be accurate and used in reasonable ways. The following statement distorts the truth.

> The only cause of the algae is the fertilizer runoff from Jon Grayson's farm. *(an unreasonable statement, providing no real support)*

Your Turn

Decide which statements below are opinions and which are facts. Then rewrite the opinion statements to make them easier to support.

1. Being president of the United States is the hardest job in the world.
2. The president is head of the executive branch.
3. The president appoints a cabinet of secretaries.
4. The cabinet members are the smartest people in the country.

Using Effective Evidence

Your argument will be strong if—and only if—you use reliable and logical evidence. This list includes some of the most important types of evidence you can use to support your opinion or argument.

■ **Facts** are provable statements, and **statistics** are facts that contain numbers.

> The lake floor affects the occurrence of algae *(fact)*; according to one study, there will be greater than 80 percent coverage of algae when there is a mucky bottom *(statistic)*.

■ **Examples** show how something works or what happens.

> Wind causes algae to wash up on beaches. *(main point)*
> When the wind blows east to west, we get a lot of algae at Half Moon Beach on Pine Lake. *(example)*

■ **Anecdotes** are stories that help explain a point.

> My grandfather has had a cottage on Pine Lake for 30 years. He can remember a time when no algae appeared on the surface of the water or on the beaches. He began noticing it about 10 years ago, and it just seemed to get worse and worse.

■ **Quotations** are the specific words spoken or written by experts.

> Sarah Follet, a state water resource official, stated, "There are many causes of the algae, including farm runoff, poor septic systems, and lawn fertilizers."

■ **Definitions** explain new words or concepts.

> Blue-green algae produces *endotoxins*, which are chemicals that affect the skin, the eyes, and the throat.

■ **Reasons** tell why something is the case.

> The invasion of zebra mussels is the major cause of blue-green algae on Pine Lake.

■ **Reflections** include the speaker's or writer's own thoughts.

> I wonder if Pine Lake could ever be what it once was, a lake that just invited people to swim and to fish. Maybe science can come up with a reasonable solution.

Your Turn

List the types of evidence that you have used in your presentations and reports. What is one other type that you would like to use in your next project? Why? Share your work with your classmates.

Using Levels of Evidence

As you build an argument, use different levels of evidence or details. For example, you may support a main point with an important fact or example. Then, to be even more convincing, you may add another related detail, reason, or reflection. Here's how the levels of evidence can work:

Main point:	Wind causes algae to wash up on the beaches.
Level 1 (example):	When the wind blows east to west, we get a lot of algae at Half Moon Bay.
Level 2 (reason):	Algae is common because of the mucky bottom.

In Focus

You may include three or even four levels of detail to support a main point. In the example above, for instance, a statistic about 80 percent or more of a mucky lake floor being covered by algae could serve as a third-level detail.

Your Turn

With the help of a partner, write down a passage from *Inquire* or one of your textbooks that contains a main point followed by at least two levels of supporting evidence. Share the passage with your classmates.

Using Quotations

Quotations from experts can add authority to your argument. But keep these points in mind:

- Include quotations only when they support your ideas.
- Identify the source of the quotation.
- Work quotations smoothly into your argument.
- Add your own thoughts after the quotation, as in the following passage:

The sources of the algae problem are fairly predictable, resulting from poor environmental practices by people living around lakes. Sarah Follet, a state water resource official, stated, "There are many causes of the algae, including farm runoff, poor septic systems, and lawn fertilizers." In the case of Pine Lake, farm runoff is the central problem.

Avoiding Faulty Logic

Using effective evidence makes it much easier for you to explain your point or prove your argument. The opposite of effective evidence is evidence that is fuzzy, exaggerated, illogical, or dishonest. You find this type of slanted evidence in advertisements, political ads, and radio and television programs that are biased. By carefully studying the following examples, you can avoid faulty thinking in your own arguments, recognize when it is used by others, and improve your critical thinking skills. (Consider also the persuasive methods on page 129.)

Distorting the Issue

The following examples of faulty thinking occur when someone twists the facts in order to mislead the reader or listener.

Exaggerating the Facts

> Drinking soda can cause all different kinds of diseases, even if you only drink one can of it a day.

This statement is an exaggeration. While drinking soda can cause health issues, it is an exaggeration to say that drinking one can a day will cause illness. Make sure the facts you use, read, or hear are not exaggerated.

> Ask yourself, "Is everything that is being said true and accurate, or is this claim exaggerating things a bit?"

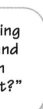

Your Turn

Watch a commercial break during a favorite show. Each time you hear an exaggeration, write it down. How many did you find during one commercial break? How many during the breaks in a half-hour show? How many during an hour show?

Distracting the Reader

> Soda is not only bad for your health, but it also costs a lot of money and adds to the problem of littering.

Very often, people who are trying to convince others will try to distract them from the real issue. In the example above, the real issue is how drinking soda can affect your health, not what it costs or how many soda containers are left lying around.

Ask yourself, "Is this person dealing with the real issue, or is he or she trying to distract the reader away from it?"

Your Turn

Listen to an argument between friends. Do both friends stick to the subject? How often does one friend try to distract the other?

Offering Two Extremes

> Either we give up drinking soda, or we are going to face incredible increases in health-care costs.

Sometimes people try to reduce an argument to just two choices. Either we do what they suggest, or we are going to be in serious trouble. What this argument ignores is that people may be able to drink diet soda or a limited amount of sugared soda and still be healthy.

Ask yourself, "Are these the only two choices, or are there other possibilities that should be considered?"

Your Turn

Listen to a political debate. Whenever a candidate offers two extremes, write down what is said. How often do you hear this type of argument in a half-hour debate? In an hour debate?

Drawing False Conclusions

The following examples of faulty thinking are used to get the reader or listener to come to the wrong conclusion.

Making a Broad Generalization

> Today's students don't spend enough time checking the sources they use in their schoolwork, especially when they use the Internet.

This statement suggests that *all* students are guilty of not checking their sources, when in fact, only *some* students may be guilty of this. It's never a good idea to make a broad generalization about a group of people. Use qualifiers such as *some, many,* or *most.*

> Ask yourself, "Is this claim true for *all* of the people being discussed, or just for *some*?"

Using a False Cause

> Ever since students have started using the Internet to do their assignments, the number of discipline problems at school have increased. Students should stop using the Internet for schoolwork.

In this case, the claim makes a direct connection between the use of the Internet and discipline problems at school. Though use of the Internet and discipline problems have risen at the same time, there is no proof that the Internet is causing the problems.

> Ask yourself, "Is it fair to assume that the cause of the problem is exactly what the writer says, or might there be completely different causes?"

Your Turn

Watch a commercial for a weight-loss product or service. Note what the product or service is supposed to do. Then note all of the other associated results the commercial shows (beautiful hair, clear skin, lots of friends). Is the advertised product or service able to deliver these other benefits? What about the main benefit? Explain.

Going Down a Slippery Slope

> If we allow students to use school computers to do their homework, they will begin using them for all kinds of other things, too.

In the example above, the writer suggests that if one thing happens, other things will also happen. When someone insists that a single step will start an unstoppable chain of events, you need to consider just how likely this is to happen.

> Ask yourself, "What is the evidence that allowing this first step will cause the other things to happen?"

Misusing Evidence

The examples of faulty thinking below misuse evidence and often lead people to the wrong conclusion.

Telling Only Part of the Truth

> The new sports-fee schedule is a good idea because it will lower taxes for all the residents in the school district.

One of the most misleading forms of faulty thinking is telling only half or part of the truth. In this example, it may be true that the new fee schedule will save taxpayers money, but it's also true that it will cost the students and their parents more money—and it could result in some students not being able to participate in sports.

> Ask yourself, "Is this the full story—the whole truth—or is there another side to it that is not being told?"

Your Turn

Listen to your friends argue. How often does one person tell only part of the truth? How does this faulty thinking affect the person's persuasiveness?

Appealing to a Popular Position

> It's clear that the new sports policy is a good idea because a majority of the people at the meeting voted for it.

This form of faulty thinking is often used to convince people that because others like it, you will too. Advertisers do this when they report that more people use their product than any other. The problem is that these claims suggest that all people think alike or have the same needs. Of course, that's not true.

Ask yourself, "Does it really matter that lots of other people feel this way, or is it more important that I think for myself and use my own best judgment?"

Using "If Only" Thinking

> If only the school board had asked the students first, they wouldn't have passed their new policy.

A very common form of faulty thinking is the "if only" argument. The problem with this argument is that it cannot be tested. You can't test for something that never happened.

Ask yourself, "How does the writer know that this would have happened? Is there other evidence, or is it simply an 'if only' argument?"

Your Turn

Listen to sports fans discussing the outcome of a game. How many times do you hear "if only" arguments? How often do you hear such arguments when the favorite team loses instead of wins?

Misusing Language

Even though all forms of faulty thinking result in the misuse of language, the following examples purposely use misleading or threatening words to support an argument.

Using Name Calling

Many students are lazy and irresponsible, so why should we care about what kind of sports programs they have at their schools?

People who use name calling usually do not have enough evidence to prove their point. They purposely draw attention away from the real issue and turn it onto the character of the individuals involved.

Ask yourself, "Does the name calling or personal attack have anything to do with the real issue being argued?"

Using Threatening Language

If this policy isn't changed, there will be big trouble in our school.

One of the worst ways to misuse language is to threaten the reader or listener. Using threatening language is wrong. If there is a serious problem, solid evidence and logical thinking are needed more than ever.

Ask yourself, "What kind of trouble is the writer talking about, and what actual evidence supports this claim?"

Your Turn

Watch political attack ads. How often does one candidate use name calling or threatening language? How does this sort of faulty thinking affect your opinion of the candidate?

Argumentation Activities

Use these activities to practice building arguments. (See also the guidelines and model for an argument essay on pages 360–361.)

Is that reasonable?

A claim establishes the position that is developed in an argument. The best claims are reasonable but thought provoking, and they often contain a qualifying word such as *usually* or *normally*. (See page 105.)

Your Turn

Identify each of the following claims as either *effective* or *ineffective*. Remember that an effective claim is reasonable and provable whereas an ineffective claim is not. Afterward, share your thoughts with your classmates.

- A later starting time for school makes no sense.
- In all fairness, Jefferson School should offer boy's volleyball.
- Funding after-school tutors is well worth the expense.
- Television violence always causes violent behavior in viewers.
- Nuclear power may be the best source of energy available.
- No more farmland should be turned into housing developments.

It's all in the planning.

Pages 104–107 list the steps for building an argument, from thinking clearly about your position to considering other viewpoints to ending your argument. It is an involved process, not a quick and easy one.

Our best advice: There are seven steps (the 7 C's) in the argument-building process. Always set aside plenty of time for careful planning.

Your Turn

Team up with two or three classmates to build an argument. In your plan, identify a reasonable claim about an important topic, two or three examples of strong support, and at least one objection (opposing point of view) to address. Your topic can be related to school life (*Should school start later?*), to an important global issue (*Should all food be organic?*), or to a subject you are studying. Afterward, share your plan with the rest of the class.

Find the Evidence

Your arguments will be convincing if you have strong, trustworthy evidence to back them up. Strong evidence is provable, believable, and logical. (See page 108–110.)

> **Our best advice:** Learning about strong supporting evidence—facts, statistics, quotations—will help you build convincing arguments. As you read or review arguments, always evaluate the evidence for its trustworthiness.

Your Turn

With the help of a partner, search in *Inquire* for one example for each type of evidence shown on page 109. Afterward, share your findings with the rest of the class.

That doesn't make sense!

You may already know faulty thinking when you read it or hear it: *Buy these athletic shoes and you'll jump higher. A vote for me is a vote for full employment.* Statements like these make false promises, so don't be swayed or influenced by them.

> **Our best advice:** Recognizing and understanding faulty thinking is especially important when you are evaluating and developing arguments in your classes. Study and understand the different types of faulty thinking discussed on pages 111–116.

Your Turn

Write a new example for three or four of the types of faulty thinking listed on pages 111–116. Then team up with a small group of classmates to share and discuss your work. Other group members must identify the type of faulty thinking represented by each of the shared examples. Take turns.

Chapter 8
Understanding Media

People have used media to share their thoughts since prehistoric times. Consider Stone Age cave paintings and clay tablets with Babylonian cuneiform. Egyptians began writing hieroglyphs on papyrus, and the invention of paper led to printing presses in the fifteenth century.

We're experiencing just such a media explosion now because of the Internet. On it, text, photos, video, and sound are all available—including those prehistoric cave paintings. To understand your world now and in the future, you need to understand media.

You will learn . . .

- The Purpose of Media
- Evaluating Messages
- Appreciating Print Media
- Listening to the Radio
- Viewing Television
- Viewing Movies
- Understanding the Internet
- Using the Internet

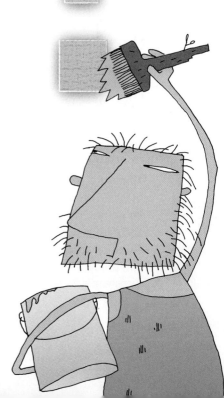

Understanding the Purpose of Media

The media are powerful because they can reach so many people. Books speak across centuries, radio broadcasts cross national borders, music and movies connect audiences to other cultures. Media are used to educate, entertain, and persuade, so it is important to recognize the purpose of each type of media message you encounter.

To Educate

Whenever you read the news, watch it on TV, listen to it on the radio, or find it online, you're learning something. You learn from documentaries and from online video tutorials. You even learn from historical movies (if they're faithful to the facts) and from science-fiction stories (if the science is accurate).

To Entertain

Much of what we see or listen to every day is designed to entertain. Think of the music you hear, the comic strips you read, the TV shows you watch. And how do the media pay for this entertainment? Usually, the answer is "commercial advertisements," which leads us directly to the final purpose of media communications—persuasion.

To Persuade

Your parents, your teachers, and your coaches often try to persuade you to do what is right, best, or good for you. However, when it comes to media messages, especially commercials, they are often meant for someone else's good, not necessarily yours.

Your Turn

1. Think of a movie or book that taught you something new—some fact or piece of information. Write down what you learned. Now check an encyclopedia or other trusted source to see if what you learned is accurate and complete.
2. Think of your favorite advertisement. Write a paragraph explaining why you enjoy it so much. Do you buy the product advertised?

Evaluating Messages

You need to evaluate the messages that you encounter before deciding how to use the information—if you use it at all. One way to do this is to complete a message evaluation sheet like the one below. In this example, a student evaluates an ad he read about a new diet.

Message Evaluation Sheet

Message

What is the topic? **+** What is the focus? **=** What is the message (thesis)?

| the Veggie 1st Diet | eat a lot and lose a lot | The new Veggie 1st Diet lets you eat a lot and lose a lot. |

What supports the message? The ad shows a chart that compares weight loss on four popular diets, with the Veggie 1st Diet showing the most weight loss. In the corner, there is a quotation by a famous actress. A seal says, "Approved by Dietitians."

Purpose

Who is behind the message? A man named Charles Lietner

What does the person/group want you to do or think? Why?
He wants me to buy the Veggie 1st Cookbook for three monthly installments of $25.95 plus shipping and handling. He wants to make money and be famous.

Problems

What problems does this message have? Some people don't like vegetables. This diet makes you want to stuff yourself rather than use control. The chart doesn't give a source for the information. I'm sure this actress has always been thin, and who are the dieticians that the seal of approval refers to? Finally, cookbooks shouldn't cost $77.85 plus shipping and handling.

Your Turn

Find an ad in a newspaper or magazine and complete a message-evaluation sheet about it. (Download a blank sheet at thoughtfullearning.com/p121.)

Appreciating Print Media

Because print has been around for centuries, people have had plenty of time to master its use. Consider the different ways in which print is formatted and published.

Types of Print Media

Different types of print media have slightly different purposes.

- **Books:** Books preserve text in a long-lasting format especially suited for literature, law, history, and mathematics. But books on other topics can become outdated quickly.

- **Newspapers:** Newspapers supply short-lived information like daily news, local events, and advertisements with coupons. By law, some public announcements about things like incorporating a business, declaring bankruptcy, and estate sales must be printed in a local newspaper. Other public announcements like weddings, births, and deaths are commonly published there, too.

- **Magazines:** Like newspapers, magazines serve well for short-lived information, but with this difference. Magazines generally focus on a special topic, such as model trains, skateboarding, or sightseeing.

- **Ground mail:** Besides greeting cards and personal letters, ground mail is often used for bulk-mail business advertisements or political announcements.

Your Turn

Go to the library and look at the selection of magazines. Which ones interest you most and why? Then look at the newspapers. Which ones interest you most and why?

Elements of Print Media

The following layout techniques are used to present text in an interesting, reader-friendly way.

■ **Headings:** Headings predict the content of the material. Chapter titles are major headings, while subheadings within the chapters announce main and supporting points. Reading the headings first will help you understand the organization and predict the main ideas in a reading selection.

■ **Columns:** Columns keep lines of text short so that you can read more quickly. Textbooks often divide pages into two columns. Newspapers and magazines may use three or more columns.

■ **Lists:** Lists make a set of items memorable. Bulleted lists suggest items of equal importance, while numbered or lettered lists suggest a sequence of events or hierarchy of importance.

■ **Pop quotes:** Often a publisher will use a larger font to set off from the text an excerpt or a related quotation.

■ **White space:** Margins, space above and below headings, paragraph and list indentations, and even space around graphics help to break up the text. White space keeps a page from becoming a sea of gray.

■ **Graphics:** Charts, tables, drawings, and photos all help to convey information quickly.

Your Turn

Search your *Inquire* handbook for an example of each element listed above. (For more help reading print media, see pages 158–159, 162–166.)

Understanding Graphics

You may have heard that "a picture is worth a thousand words." A graphic can present lots of information all at once. (See pages 369–384.)

Photos

A photograph can reveal lots of detail about a setting or an event. However, a photographer can affect your perception in subtle ways— through lighting, angle, and other adjustments.

Your Turn

How does this photo make you feel about President Barack Obama? How would you feel if he were frowning?

Illustrations

Like photos, illustrations can quickly convey a setting. Unlike photos, however, that setting can be completely imaginary! An artist's style also affects a drawing's emotional impact.

Your Turn

Which drawing in this book is your favorite? What makes it your favorite?

Diagrams

Diagrams can help you quickly understand the way something is arranged. Consider this house floor plan.

Your Turn

In this floor plan, which bedroom would you want? Why?

Graphs

Graphs are a type of illustration that present facts and figures in a concise format. Different types of information call for different types of graphs.

Line Graph

A line graph shows how things change. The vertical line shows amount, and the horizontal line shows time.

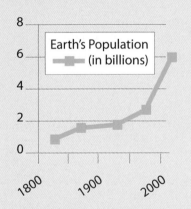

Bar Graph

A bar graph uses columns to compare things.

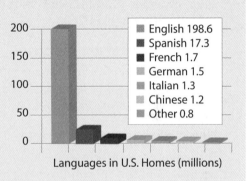

Languages in U.S. Homes (millions)

Stacked Bar Graph

A stacked bar graph divides each column to show further details.

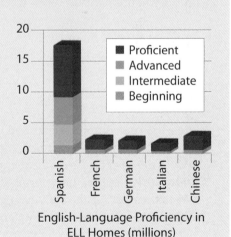

English-Language Proficiency in ELL Homes (millions)

Pie Graph

A pie graph shows how something is divided up or distributed.

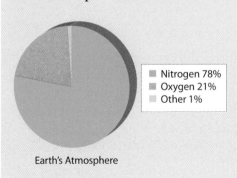

Earth's Atmosphere

Your Turn

Choose the type of graph you would use to show how you spend each hour of a Saturday—all 24 of them. Draw the graph and label each part with the appropriate information. (See pages 369–384 for more on graphing.)

Evaluating Print Media

Not all print media is reliable, so you must carefully evaluate the sources you use. To do so, ask the following questions.

Who created the source?

First consider the author. Is he or she an authority on the subject? Is this author well respected? Why did he or she write this material? Then consider the publisher. Is it a reputable house? Why did they publish this material?

What is the source's purpose?

Does the material inform or persuade? If it is persuasive in nature, does it address opposing viewpoints? Consider the author's intentions. Who would benefit from his or her ideas or proposals?

How accurate is the information?

If the material informs, check the facts that are presented. Are they accurate? Is the information complete? Does this resource mention and connect to other reputable resources, or does it stand alone?

How current is the source?

Check the publication date. Recognize that older publications about fields that are constantly changing, such as technology or science, would be out of date or inaccurate. However, older resources that deal with an event such as the Civil War could still be very useful.

Your Turn

Write a four-paragraph review of something you've read recently.
1. **Overview:** Introduce the text and tell your reader enough to understand what the selection is about, without "giving away the ending."
2. **Strengths:** Tell the best things about the text.
3. **Weaknesses:** Tell the weakest things about the text.
4. **Verdict:** Sum up your recommendation about the text. Should your friends read it? What will they gain from it?

Listening to the Radio

There are many reasons to listen to the radio. Some people tune in to hear their favorite music. Others listen to catch an important game or to hear the news. No matter why you are listening, you should evaluate what you hear.

Evaluating Radio Messages

You can evaluate radio messages by completing a message-evaluation sheet. (Go to thoughtfullearning.com/p127 to download a blank form.) Here are specific issues to consider:

Talk Radio

Talk radio focuses on current issues. Some talk radio shows provide balanced discussions with people on all sides of an issue. Others, however, provide the opinion of one person. Evaluate whether the opinions being presented are balanced or one-sided.

News Radio

News radio shares the most newsworthy stories of the day. Five factors make a story newsworthy. To evaluate a specific story, consider the following points.

- **Timing:** Is it current?
- **Proximity:** Is it close to home?
- **Significance:** Does it impact many people?
- **Prominence:** Does it impact famous people?
- **Human interest:** Does it connect to the listener?

Sports Radio

Sports announcers provide scores, facts, and discussions about sports. They help listeners visualize the action of a game. Often, one commentator does the play-by-play, and another does the "color commentary." The first is presenting facts and the second opinions. Commentators may be biased when talking about hometown teams.

Music Radio

Music radio stations play specific types of music to target a specific audience. That means advertisers can target the audience as well. Don't allow your favorite songs to sell you something you don't need.

Viewing Television

Television can inform, entertain, and educate, but it can also distract you, keep you inactive, and sell you things you don't need. When you do tune in, remember to evaluate what you watch.

Evaluating TV Programs

To become a more active, in-control viewer, answer the following questions about the TV shows you watch.

Who is the show's intended audience?

Considering the target audience for a show will help you better understand the program.

What is the show's purpose?

A TV show may be intended to entertain, to educate, or to persuade.

What do the producers want from the viewers?

The people who create the show may simply want you to watch future episodes, but they may also want you to adopt a particular social or political perspective.

Who sponsors this show?

- **Public TV:** Some stations are funded by public donations. Note the list of donors at the beginning or end of a show, and ask yourself why they chose to fund this show.
- **Commercial TV:** Most commercial stations are funded by paid sponsors. Notice which advertisers sponsor which shows.
- **Paid TV:** Today, many networks are broadcast only by cable or satellite services purchased by the viewers themselves.

What do the sponsors want from the viewers?

A sponsor of public TV might simply want to benefit the public or be thanked for their generosity. Commercial sponsors want you to buy their products. (See page 129.) Cable and satellite providers want you to pay their subscription fees.

Your Turn

Watch a TV program and complete a message-evaluation sheet about it. (Go to thoughtfullearning.com/p128 for a download.)

Evaluating Commercials

TV commercials can sometimes be very entertaining. Always remember, however, that they are trying to convince you to buy something. Professional advertisement companies are hired to make you want those products. Here are five methods they often use.

Cult of Celebrity

When companies hire celebrities to recommend products, they know fans want to be like those celebrities. Remember, though, that these celebrities are paid and may not actually use the products.

Problem-Solution

A story is acted out, in which one person has a problem and another offers a product to solve it. Companies hope that the next time you face the problem, you'll think of their solution.

Ask an Expert

Many commercials have a doctor or other expert talk about why a company's brand is so good. Often these "experts" are just actors and the testimony offers just one side of the story.

Tip: When you hear, "Nothing works better than," it means lots of things could work just as well. (See pages 111–116.)

Part of the Gang

We all need to feel like we belong. Ad companies rely on this fact to sell you brand-name jeans, sneakers, and other things. Usually the brand-name version costs more than similar products. After all, the brand needs to make money to pay for those commercials!

Funny Bone

Many commercials are designed to make us laugh or feel good. That way, we remember the product in a positive way and may decide to buy it. Remember, though, that a funny commercial may tell you very little about the product's real worth.

Your Turn

The next time you see a TV commercial, ask yourself which of the five methods it uses. If it uses none of these, try to figure out the method it does use. (Consider the faulty logic demonstrated on pages 111–116.)

Viewing Movies

Like television shows, movies are a fairly passive form of entertainment. However, because they are longer, they require more concentration and are more challenging to evaluate.

Evaluating Movies

Most movies cost millions of dollars to produce. As you evaluate a movie, think about how a studio makes money on that investment.

Theaters

The movie studios rent films to movie theaters to show on their big screens. Studios make money through the rental fees and through ticket sales, usually getting a portion of each ticket sold.

Video Sales and Rentals

After a film's ticket sales decline, or when the next film comes along, the studio releases the older film on video media. Your purchase or rental pays the store, which in turn pays the studio.

TV Broadcasts

TV networks or stations may rent a film for broadcast. Besides cutting it to insert commercials, they may leave out parts.

Product Placements

Studios often get money or products from advertisers to use those products as props in their films. For example, one reason that wedding rings are commonly set with diamonds is that diamond producers encouraged their use in early romantic comedies. Nowadays, you may see a film's characters stop to drink a cola or park in front of a chain store. These are subtle advertisements.

Public Figures or Organizations

In some cases, an organization, a celebrity, or a movie journalist may produce a movie, using her or his own money. Be aware that these films are usually used to promote a specific message.

Your Turn

Watch a movie with a modern-day setting. Write down any products or establishments you recognize. How does their appearance affect you?

Understanding the Internet

- **The Internet** is a huge network of computers. It began in 1969 with a network of U.S. government computers, but now the Internet is a worldwide system. E-mail, cell phones, and satellites all access and use the Internet, as do people on the World Wide Web.

- **The World Wide Web** is an enormous group of Web sites on the Internet. It was started in 1989 by a British engineer named Tim Berners-Lee. He invented the hypertext transfer protocol (HTTP) that allows computers anywhere to share information.

- **A URL (uniform resource locator)** gives the Web address for each page available on the World Wide Web. The Web address for each page is just like the street address for a building—a unique set of letters and numbers for finding one specific page.

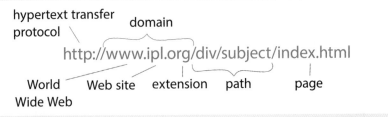

- **The domain name** is the part of the Web address that often starts with www and ends with an extension. The extension tells the type of domain. Here are some common extensions (new types are often added).

.**com** a commercial or business site
.**gov** a government site for federal, state, or local government
.**edu** an educational site
.**org** a site for an organization, often a nonprofit
.**net** a site for an organization that belongs to the Internet's infrastructure
.**mil** a military site
.**biz** a business site
.**info** an information site

Your Turn

Get on the Internet and go to a favorite Web page. Identify the different parts of the URL. What does the domain extension tell you about the type of site you are looking at?

Using the Internet

The Internet includes the World Wide Web, e-mail, online chat and text messaging, online file storage, cooperative project editing, and more.

Browsing the Web

A Web browser is like a vehicle that can take you nearly anywhere on the Internet. It can show text, images, video, and animations, as well as play audio. Hyperlinks in a Web site's menu, text, or images lead you from page to page. Links can also lead to downloadable files like PDF documents and software. To avoid damaging your computer, never download software without evaluating the Web site and getting a parent's or teacher's permission. (See also pages 160–161.)

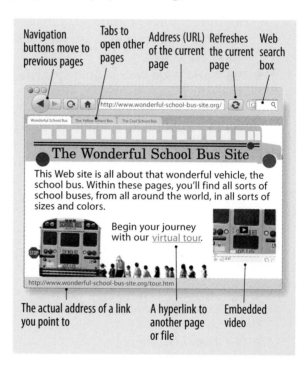

Navigation buttons move to previous pages

Tabs to open other pages

Address (URL) of the current page

Refreshes the current page

Web search box

The actual address of a link you point to

A hyperlink to another page or file

Embedded video

Staying Safe Online

The Net is an exciting place, but you must keep your computer, and yourself, safe when online.

- **Use trusted sites.** Sites with a national or worldwide reputation are safer than those less well known.
- **Protect your identity.** Don't reveal your home address or telephone number online.
- **Look before you click.** Not all links are what they seem. If you aren't sure, don't click.
- **Don't download anything questionable.** The surest way to get a computer virus is to download something you shouldn't. Always ask an adult before downloading.

Using Search Engines

Search engines are online sites that catalog the Web. Use the search box in your browser or on a search engine to find Web pages. (See also pages 284–285.)

Tips for Searching

- **Use search terms wisely.** Choose words and phrases related to your subject. If you aren't satisfied with the results, adjust your search terms. *Tip:* A phrase like *apple pie* will bring up results with *apple* alone, with *pie* alone, or with both. Put quotation marks around "*apple pie*" to make sure you get only pages that feature the dessert.
- **Recognize sponsored links.** Companies pay to have their links at the top of a search-results page. So before you click a search result, check to see if it's listed as a sponsored link.
- **Look beyond the first page of listings.** Most searches result in multiple pages of results. Sometimes what you need is on the second, third, fifth, or even tenth page of listings.
- **Try more than one search engine.** Not all search engines operate exactly the same. If you can't find what you need with one, try another. Your browser's search box may list more than one.

Saving What You Find

When you find a page with helpful information, print out a copy so you won't forget. Or bookmark the page so you can return to it.

Your Turn

Launch your browser and search for a topic you are currently studying. Refine your search, evaluate what you find, and save your information. Then discuss your findings with a classmate.

Using Information Sites

Many Web sites exist specifically to provide information to the public. That's true of government sites, public library sites, and others. Here are a few interesting sites to visit.

- **WhiteHouse.gov:** The White House has a rich Web site full of information, including an interactive tour, histories and images of former presidents, and topics of public interest.

- **NASA.gov:** The National Aeronautics and Space Administration (NASA) site is filled with images, text, and multimedia about the planet Earth and its many neighbors in outer space. Be sure to check the "For Students" tab near the top of the page.

- **CIA.gov:** The Central Intelligence Agency (CIA) site provides information about the many nations and cultures of our world. If you want to find out about the national anthem of Australia, countries with active volcanoes, or the agriculture of Belgium, the CIA's *World Factbook* is a great place to look.

- **LOC.gov:** The Library of Congress is the largest library in the world, and many of its materials are available through its Web site. This site is an especially good source of historical information. Check the "Kids & Families" link for a list of fascinating topics.

- **Public Library Sites:** Besides general search engines, your school library or local public library may have a site with searchable resources. The librarians are experts at finding information, so don't be afraid to ask them for help.

- **Other Public Sites:**

  IPL.org: The Internet Public Library is a public Web site developed by educators. Use the "For Kids" link to access homework help, online dictionaries, and encyclopedias.

  PBS.org: The Public Broadcasting Service is a nonprofit organization using radio, television, and the Web to provide information for the public. Use the "PBS Kids" link at the bottom of the home page to access games and videos.

Your Turn

Log on to three of the resources above and explore what each has to offer. Check out the information that is specifically labeled for students or "kids." Which of the sites is most interesting to you and why?

Using Online Map Search Sites

Map search sites allow you to search for an address and view a map of that location. Here are three main uses of a map search site.

- **Learn About a Location:** Type a ZIP code, a city name, or a full address into the search box, and you can view an interactive map of that location.

  Zoom in or out: Use the slider in the corner of the map to see more detail or a larger area. You can also click on the plus or minus or use the scroll wheel to do this.

  Drag the map: By clicking on part of the map and holding the mouse button down, you can drag the map in any direction.

  Use satellite view: Take a virtual tour of a location. Do you want to see what the Kremlin in Moscow looks like? Type it into the search box, choose satellite view, and zoom in.

  Use street view: Some map search sites even let you see an address as if you were in a car parked outside the building.

- **Get Directions:** By entering one address in the upper search box and another in the lower one, you can create a map with a route marked between the two.

- **Find Nearby Businesses:** Map sites also let you search for businesses near the location you have found.

Your Turn

Search for a familiar location using a map search site. Write down one new fact you discover about the location. Then search for a famous location. Write down one new fact you discover about that location.

Accessing Video, Podcasts, and Feeds

As you know, the Net is more than just pages of text and pictures. It also makes video, audio, and RSS feeds easily accessible.

Using Online Video

Many Web sites include video to help illustrate a point or to entertain. Math concepts, bicycle repair, guitar chords, and all sorts of other topics are demonstrated in videos.

- Remember that video files are larger than audio or text files, so they take longer to load, especially on slow Internet connections.
- Some sites give the option of downloading a large video instead of streaming it from the Net. For safety's sake, always ask a teacher or parent before downloading a file.

Using Podcasts

Like radio broadcasts, podcasts are audio programs. The difference is that you download podcast recordings instead of receiving them by radio waves. Many Web sites note that they have a podcast for download. Your computer's music program may have a podcast search option as well.

- Podcasts are available on all sorts of topics, both for entertainment and education.
- You can transfer podcasts to your portable audio player.

Using RSS Feeds

News sites, blogs, and other Web pages are often published as RSS feeds. (RSS stands for Really Simple Syndication.) You can use a "feed reader" to gather feeds you want to follow, sort of like building an online newspaper page just for you. Most people use an online feed reader like Google Reader or My Yahoo!, but smart phones have RSS apps too.

- As a student, you can use an RSS reader to stay up to date on current events.
- You can also use RSS during a research project to follow blogs and news sites about your topic.

Your Turn

Think of something you would like to learn to do. Then search first for a how-to video about the subject, and second for a how-to podcast about the subject. Compare what you find. (See also pages 400–401, 404–410.)

Evaluating Web Resources

Because it is very easy to publish to the Web, you should carefully evaluate any Web resources that you use. Think carefully about the following issues.

Author/Organization

On the Web, material often appears without a clear author or source. Do your best to figure out who created the material and also who is paying for the Web site. Is the person or organization reliable? Is contact information provided?

Balance or Bias

Because it's easy for people to publish to the Web, much information on the Web is one-sided. Is the material pushing one side of an argument? Is it trying to sell a product or service? Unless a Web resource links to other sites in a larger community, you may suspect that the material is biased.

Accuracy

Inaccuracy of information is another problem on the Web. When you find what appears to be unbiased information from a reliable source, make sure to check the information against other sources. Is the material correct? Is it current?

Quality

Another cue to the reliability of Web material is the quality of the presentation. Look for professional design, well-written text that is free of errors, and media (pictures, videos, audio, and so on) that work well. Be wary of resources that are poorly designed, have many grammatical errors, and are full of broken links and other problems.

Your Turn

Review page 136. Find a video or podcast and evaluate it by completing a message-evaluation sheet. (Go to thoughtfullearning.com/p137 for a download.) Consider the issues explained above as you complete the sheet.

Media Activities

Use Your Senses

Humans learn best when they use several senses during the process. In terms of the media, that could mean reading, listening, watching video, and taking notes.

Your Turn

Find a book, a magazine article, a Web page, a video, and a podcast about a zoo or your favorite animal. Write a letter to your grandparents to explain what you learned from each source.

Gauge the Message

Although commercials can be entertaining, their primary purpose is to persuade you to do something. Sometimes their message is for the public good, but often it's just to get you to spend your money.

Your Turn

Using cardboard and a paper fastener, make a gauge like the one pictured here. Whenever you see or hear a commercial, use the gauge to indicate the ad's persuasive method. In a notebook, list the methods and keep track of how many times each is used.

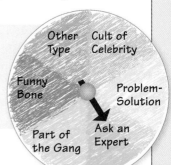

A View from Space

Map search sites use satellite photos to reveal information about the earth. In many places, those satellite photos are paired to photos taken from automobiles, so that you can actually see the building at an address or the intersections along a route.

Your Turn

Enter your own address into a map search site. Switch to satellite view and zoom in until you can see your own neighborhood. Do you see anything you hadn't noticed about your neighborhood before? Now do the same for your school. Finally, ask the site to suggest a route from your home to your school. Compare the suggested route to the one you normally take.

Chapter 9
Using Social Media

The Internet is more than just a place to go for information and entertainment. It's also a place where you can meet and interact with other Internet users.

Many applications connect people in all-new ways. People send messages to one another and chat by text, voice, or video. They gather in virtual spaces to work together on projects or to meet for fun or business. Applications help people get connected and stay connected. That's the world of social media, and this chapter will guide you into that world.

You will learn . . .

- E-Mailing
- Chatting and Texting
- Microblogging
- Using Social Sites
- Visiting Virtual Worlds
- Blogging
- Using Message Boards and Newsgroups
- Using Wikis
- Using VOIP (Voice Over Internet Protocol)

E-Mailing

E-mail has been around since the earliest days of the Net. It is still around because it is so useful. To get the most out of e-mail, it helps to understand the following three things:

- **Text Versus HTML:** Some e-mail programs display only basic text, without special formatting. Other programs read the same HTML (**h**yper**t**ext **m**arkup **l**anguage) that formats Web pages. Text e-mail is less prone to viruses than HTML. It also loads faster, which is better for portable devices like cell phones.

Send Attach Fonts Colors Save

To: Merlene Monesti
From: Arnetta Monesti
Subject: Birthday Gift!
Attachments: 001-jpg; 002.jpg

Dear Grandma,

Thank you for the pullover sweater. I love it! Attached are photos of me wearing it at my birthday party.

Love you!

Arnetta

- **Attachments:** Most e-mail programs can send files attached to a message, but not everyone wants to receive them. For one reason, attachments are usually bigger than normal e-mail and take a long time to load. For another, e-mail programs have more trouble recognizing a virus in an attachment than inside an e-mail message. It's always best to ask before sending an attachment. Upload the file to online storage if possible, and provide a link to it inside your e-mail instead.
- **Spam:** Bulk advertisements by ground mail require postage, but Internet spam costs virtually nothing. Unscrupulous people use automated software to spam every e-mail address they can find. One way to fight this is to use a free e-mail service, which should have a good spam blocker. Another way to fight spam is to avoid posting your e-mail address online where spammers can find it.

Your Turn

How do you use e-mail? Do you use it for messages to friends, for tracking responses on social media, or for keeping track of online purchases? How do older people in your family use e-mail? Does the use of e-mail seem to be changing?

Chatting and Texting

Two of the most common ways to communicate digitally are chatting and texting.

Chatting

Internet chat, or instant messaging, is like a telephone conversation, but using your fingers instead of your voice. Some instant message programs can be open on your computer while you do other work. Many social Web sites and game sites have their own built-in chat services.

Chat tends to be casual, using abbreviations like LOL (laughing out loud). You can figure out these abbreviations from their context or look them up online. Remember to be polite when chatting. If you're busy, turn off the program or set your status to "away."

 DOVEY: Hey, Darren! What questions do we do for geometry?
December 23 at 4:15 pm • Like • Comment • See Friendship

 SK8TBOI: Questions 3-8. Watch those alternate interior angles!
December 23 at 5:00 pm • Like • Comment • See Friendship

Texting

Like chat, texting involves sending short messages by text. The difference is that these messages can wait for the recipient to read them and respond. Some texting is done online on special sites like Twitter. Text messages can also be sent from a cell phone to another mobile device.

Texting can be a convenient way to send a quick message like "I'm done with soccer practice" to your mother, or "Would you like to go to a movie tomorrow?" to a friend. Just remember that texting can cost money, especially on cell phones.

Your Turn

Use a chat service to talk with a friend or relative in another state or country. Then write an essay comparing chat with phone conversations.

Microblogging

Microblogging is a lot like text messaging. The difference is that your message is posted online instead of going directly to a friend's computer or phone. Twitter is one example of a microblogging site. Facebook "status" messages are another example of microblogging.

> **Fun Fact:** Microblogging gets its name from blogging, which in turn is short for "Web log." A Web log, or blog, is a personal online journal. (See "Blogging" on page 150.) Microblogging is like writing short blog posts.

Reading a Microblog Conversation

Read the following set of microblog posts from the bottom of the page upward, since microblog programs place newer posts above older ones.

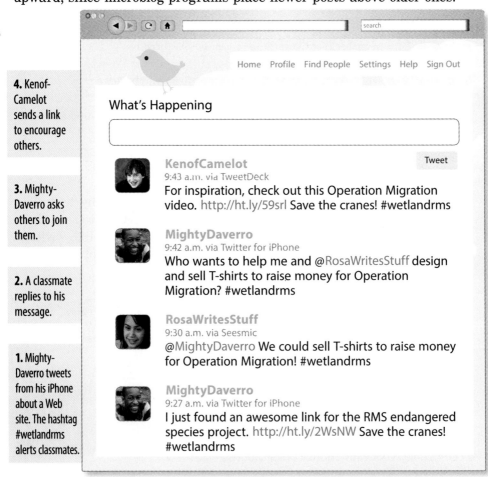

4. KenofCamelot sends a link to encourage others.

3. MightyDaverro asks others to join them.

2. A classmate replies to his message.

1. MightyDaverro tweets from his iPhone about a Web site. The hashtag #wetlandrms alerts classmates.

Home Profile Find People Settings Help Sign Out

What's Happening

Tweet

KenofCamelot
9:43 a.m. via TweetDeck
For inspiration, check out this Operation Migration video. http://ht.ly/59srl Save the cranes! #wetlandrms

MightyDaverro
9:42 a.m. via Twitter for iPhone
Who wants to help me and @RosaWritesStuff design and sell T-shirts to raise money for Operation Migration? #wetlandrms

RosaWritesStuff
9:30 a.m. via Seesmic
@MightyDaverro We could sell T-shirts to raise money for Operation Migration! #wetlandrms

MightyDaverro
9:27 a.m. via Twitter for iPhone
I just found an awesome link for the RMS endangered species project. http://ht.ly/2WsNW Save the cranes! #wetlandrms

Understanding Types of Posts

Microblogging is a form of broadcasting. Decide how far you want each message to travel. Most microblogging services support the following message types, although they may use different terms.

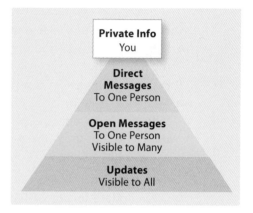

- **Private information** should not be microblogged.
- **Direct messages** go to a specific person, and no one else can see them. (Be aware that the other person might share the message.) A direct message is like whispering to someone.
- **Replies** are open messages that go to a specific person but can be seen by others following both people. A reply is like talking to a friend while other people listen in.
- **Updates** go to anyone following you or to anyone searching for a term or hashtag in the message. Writing an update is like giving an announcement in front of a room filled with people.

Your Turn

Imagine that it's your birthday today. What would you keep private? What would you write in a direct message, a reply, or an update?

Using Microblog Services

Various services can add features to your microblogging program.

- **Photo sharing** is made easy through add-on programs.
- **Social networking** connections can be made to your accounts on Facebook, a video site, and other social networking programs. (See pages 144–147.)
- **Aggregators** gather and sort microblog posts, making streams of comments easy to manage.
- **URL shorteners** help you to reduce long Web addresses to a manageable size to post.

Your Turn

Check out the features of your microblogging application. (Go to thoughtfullearning.com/p143 for suggested services.)

Creating a Microblog Post

Writing a microblog post takes very little time, but you should still use a short version of the inquiry process (see 235–314) to create the best post.

1. **Question, plan, and research** the microblog post.
   - **Subject:** What are you writing about? What links should you include? What keywords would help people find the post?
   - **Purpose:** Why are you writing? What effect do you want?
   - **Audience:** How broadly do you want to broadcast—to all followers, to a specific person and any others who are interested, to only one follower? Who are your followers? Who might follow or unfollow due to this tweet?

2. **Create** your microblog post, using one of these methods:
   - **Open update** for any followers to read.
   - **Open message (reply)** sent to one or two followers but open for others to read.
   - **Direct message** meant for one follower and not seen by others.

3. **Improve** your post before sending it.
   - **Evaluate** whether it fits your subject, purpose, and audience.
   - **Revise** your post:
     Remove words or characters that aren't needed.
     Rearrange words to grab the reader's attention.
     Rework the language to improve the flow.
     Add links to make the post more useful, or hashtags to make it easier to find.
   - **Perfect** your post by proofreading it.

4. **Present** the post by clicking "send." (Some third-party programs also allow you to schedule the post to send later.)

Twitter Tips

Twitter is one of the most popular microblogging services. Here are tips for using it.

Always ask a parent before creating any sort of online account.

Creating Your Profile

- **Username:** Use your own name (if your parent approves) or any sort of nickname.
- **Password:** Your password should be easy to remember but hard for strangers to guess. (**Tip:** Replace one or more letters with numbers. Example: *808Carter* is better than *BOBCarter*.)
- **Profile:** Your profile is a quick description of who you are and what you are interested in, so that other people can decide whether to follow you. Profiles are public, so don't list private information.

MightyDaverro
@MightyDaverro
Student, hockey player, bubble gum connoisseur. And I love space science!

- **Profile Picture:** You can upload a snapshot of yourself (with a parent's permission) or another image that represents you.
- **Twitter Terminology**

  Tweet: A microblog post on Twitter is called a "Tweet."

  Retweet: Repeating someone else's message is "retweeting."

  Followers: People who set their accounts to display your posts are called your "followers."

  Following: You are "following" the people whose posts show in your own account.

  Listed: You can make special lists (like "Basketball Stars" or "Classmates") to organize people you follow.

  Unfollow: You can always choose to stop following someone.

  Blocking: You can block an account from following you.

  Hashtag: By adding a keyword with a # in front (like #haiku or #geology), you can make your Tweets on that subject easy to find. Or you can easily search other people's Tweets with that hashtag.

  Trending: Topics that are popular today are called "trending" topics. You can scan the list to see what's happening.

Using Social Sites

Online social sites like Facebook allow people to share things like messages, photos, music playlists, and so on, with family, friends, and coworkers. People can also interact through built-in chat, mail-style messages, and even games.

Remember: Never post status updates or photos that you don't want the public to view. A future employer might see it.

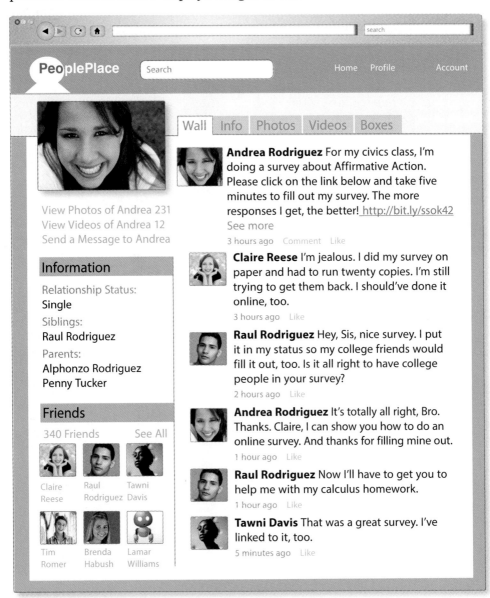

Understanding Social Networking Sites

Once you have built a profile on a social networking site, you can connect to friends and also explore the other options available to you.

- **Updates**, which are written by you and can be seen by your friends, tell what you are doing or what you are thinking about. Updates can include photos, videos, and links to other places on the Web.
- **Comments** are written by you in response to other people. By clicking in the "Write a comment . . ." box, you can respond to others. Your comments can be seen by your friends and by the other person's friends.
- **Messages** go only to the person you have selected. Messages are private, and you should not share the information you receive in a message in a general update or comment.
- **Like** is a feature you can click when you aren't sure what to say about an update or comment, but you like what the person shared.
- **Feeds** are different ways of sorting the comments of your friends. The "Top News" feed features the most popular comments. The "Most Recent" feed features the comments from newest to oldest.
- **Invites** allow you to alert others of events you want them to attend or causes you want them to support. Those who receive an invite can reply to let you know whether they are attending.
- **Groups** are gatherings of people with a common interest or background. By joining a group, you can receive news, take part in discussions, and learn about upcoming events.
- **Games** of all sorts—brain teasers, word and number games, role-playing games, and resource management games—are available on social networking sites.

Your Turn

Have you used a social networking site to spread the word about a project or ask for a recommendation? List different ways you've used such a site. Discuss with a classmate.

Creating a Social Site Profile

Your profile page is where people learn about you. Make sure it is carefully thought out.

1. **Question** the goal and situation for the social networking page.
   - **Subject:** What do you want to share? What should you keep private?
   - **Purpose:** Why are you creating this page? What do you want to get out of it? What do you want other people to get out of it?
   - **Audience:** Who will be your close contacts? Whom else will you connect to? What do these people know about you?
2. **Plan** your page on Facebook or another service.
3. **Research** and provide information for your page.
   - **About You:** Provide the name you want to use online. It can be your real name or a made-up one. Share some details about yourself, but do not provide private information.
   - **Education and Work:** List schools and workplaces to help others from the same school or workplace find you.
   - **Likes and Interests:** List favorite interests to help others find you. (Be aware that this also helps advertisers target you.)
   - **Contact Information:** Get your parent's approval before you post contact information of any kind.
4. **Create** your social networking page.
   - **Privacy:** Set the privacy options your parent approves.
   - **Profile Picture:** Upload a picture of yourself (with your parent's approval) or another image that represents you.
   - **Friend:** Search for others from the same school or community, or search by name. Request to "friend" those you know and trust.
   - **Status:** Tell what you are doing, or share an interesting thought. Link to photos or videos, or upload your own.
   - **Comment:** Respond to the status of your friends.
5. **Improve** your page.
   - **Evaluate** parts.
     Does this page fulfill your purpose? Does it represent you well?
   - **Revise** your page.
     Remove information or images that you don't want to share.
     Rearrange parts so that they make better sense to you.
     Replace your profile photo or rewrite parts you don't like.
     Add updates, photos, and links regularly.
6. **Present** your revised page and adjust as necessary.

Visiting Virtual Worlds

Virtual worlds are social media that simulate an environment—real or imaginary—for you to explore.

Exploring MUDs

The simplest virtual worlds are just text, sometimes with pictures, like a storybook you explore from link to link instead of page to page. Visitors to a MUD (Multi-User Dimension) can talk by text or voice chat, interact with the environment, change the contents of rooms or spaces, or even create new spaces for other people to explore. Some high schools and universities use MUDs for virtual campuses.

Visiting Virtual Reality Sites

Sites like the Second Life® world take the MUD idea a step further, using computer animation to create realistic-looking worlds. Visitors make characters, called "avatars," to represent themselves in these worlds. Virtual reality sites are used for business, education, and entertainment.

- **Business:** Some real businesses hold virtual meetings in these worlds. That way, members don't have to travel. Businesses may also hold career days to meet interviewees online, or they may run special events to promote their products.
- **Education:** Classes can meet in these worlds to do a virtual tour of a famous site like the Eiffel Tower, to interview an important person, to see concepts demonstrated, or simply to chat about what they're learning. Global Kids Island is one virtual location for classrooms in the Second Life world. Another is Kids Connect.
- **Entertainment:** Many people meet in worlds like Second Life just for the fun of it. Second Life characters can even fly!

Staying Safe

- **Protect your computer:** Nearly all virtual worlds require special software. Always ask an adult before downloading or installing anything from the Internet.
- **Protect yourself:** Not all virtual worlds are safe for kids, and not all visitors are kid friendly. Always follow a parent's or teacher's guidance about using a virtual world.

Blogging

A blog (short for Web log) is an online journal—sort of an electronic diary. Businesses use blogs to communicate with customers. Individuals use them to talk about topics important to them.

Using Common Features

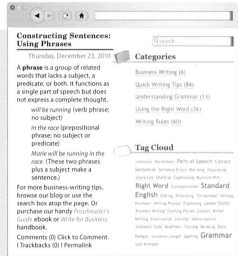

- **Entries Area:** Most blog pages have a main area where entries are posted. The newest entries are on top, with older ones below. This area may show whole entries or just excerpts. Clicking on an entry title takes you to a page with the full entry.
- **Search:** Most blogs have a search box so that you can easily find entries by keywords.
- **Categories:** Blogs often arrange their entries by category ("News," "Reviews," "Stamp Collecting," and so on). That way, you can quickly find all entries in a particular category.
- **Tag Cloud:** Many blogs also have a "tag cloud" in a sidebar. This is a collection of topics commonly discussed on the site. Clicking a tag brings up a list of entries involving that term.

Understanding Comments

On many blogs, visitors can leave comments or questions about posts, and the author can reply. (See pages 392–393.) When you leave a comment, remember the following:

- **Be polite.** The blog author is doing you a favor by providing the site and its information. So phrase any comments or questions politely, and be patient waiting for a reply. (If you would like a quick response, consider e-mailing the author to explain your need.)
- **Be clear.** Draft your comment in a word processor to make sure your comment or question is as clear and short as possible. The clearer and more concise it is, the more likely it is to be read and answered.
- **Be safe.** Never post your personal information on a blog. Your words can be seen by everyone on the Internet.

Using Message Boards and Newsgroups

Many people use message boards and newsgroups to discuss topics and share information.

Understanding Message Boards

A message board is something like a blog, except that anyone can make posts.

Before posting on a message board, you must create an account, and many boards have restricted membership. Most message boards have "moderators," people who keep discussions on track and polite. Here are some tips:

- **Understand categories.** Like blogs, message boards usually divide postings into categories. Unlike blogs, message boards do not have a main page that includes all posts.
- **Search smart.** Often a search engine will list results from message boards. Most message boards also have a search box on their pages to help you find what you need. Before doing a search, you should go to the most likely category for your topic.
- **Follow the rules.** To save visitors time and to avoid legal issues, message boards often have clearly stated rules for their use. Always read the FAQ (frequently asked questions) list and any "Introduction" section before using the board. This is especially important before posting a question or comment.

Understanding Newsgroups

Like message boards, newsgroups are group discussions of topics. The main difference is that while a message board is posted to a Web site, a newsgroup discussion takes place by e-mail. Archives of these discussions may be available online for you to search.

Your Turn

Think of a topic that interests you and search online for a message board or newsgroup that deals with the topic. With your parent's permission, read others' posts and respond to them.

Using Wikis

A wiki is a Web site that people can build and edit together using just a Web browser. This makes creating wikis quick and easy. ("Wiki" is a Hawaiian word for "fast.")

You've probably heard of the Wikipedia® site, an online encyclopedia written and edited by people all over the world every day. The Web also has a lot of specialized wikis, from medical wikis to dictionaries composed by students. You might use a wiki to . . .

- **Brainstorm ideas:** A wiki can be a great place to gather ideas, with links to images or information supporting each person's suggestions.
- **Assemble a group report:** In the example photos on this page and the next, a group of students has begun preparing a report about amphibians.
- **Publish a Web site:** Once your wiki project is completed, you might choose to publish it to the Web.
- **Build a dictionary:** New word entries can be added as they occur, and different people can write definitions for each one.
- **Write a manual:** Teachers often use wikis to collaborate on lesson materials. Students can work together the same way to write instructions on topics from origami (making art by paper folding) to instructions for using shop equipment.

Sample Class Project Wiki

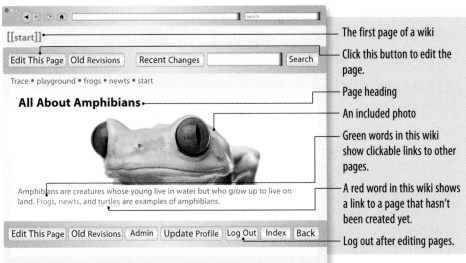

[[start]] — The first page of a wiki

Edit This Page | Old Revisions | Recent Changes | | Search — Click this button to edit the page.

Trace • playground • frogs • newts • start

All About Amphibians — Page heading

— An included photo

— Green words in this wiki show clickable links to other pages.

Amphibians are creatures whose young live in water but who grow up to live on land. Frogs, newts, and turtles are examples of amphibians.

— A red word in this wiki shows a link to a page that hasn't been created yet.

Edit This Page | Old Revisions | Admin | Update Profile | Log Out | Index | Back — Log out after editing pages.

Sample Class Project Wiki (cont.)

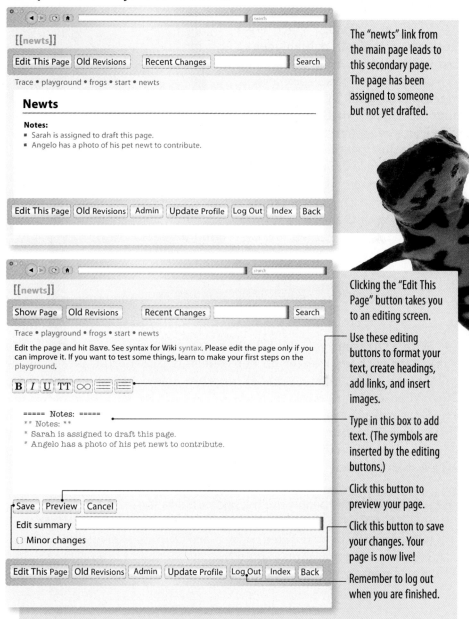

[[newts]]

Edit This Page   Old Revisions   Recent Changes   Search

Trace • playground • frogs • start • newts

Newts

Notes:
- Sarah is assigned to draft this page.
- Angelo has a photo of his pet newt to contribute.

Edit This Page   Old Revisions   Admin   Update Profile   Log Out   Index   Back

The "newts" link from the main page leads to this secondary page. The page has been assigned to someone but not yet drafted.

[[newts]]

Show Page   Old Revisions   Recent Changes   Search

Trace • playground • frogs • start • newts

Edit the page and hit Save. See syntax for Wiki syntax. Please edit the page only if you can improve it. If you want to test some things, learn to make your first steps on the playground.

B I U TT ∞ ≡ ≡

===== Notes: =====
** Notes: **
* Sarah is assigned to draft this page.
* Angelo has a photo of his pet newt to contribute.

Save   Preview   Cancel

Edit summary
☐ Minor changes

Edit This Page   Old Revisions   Admin   Update Profile   Log Out   Index   Back

Clicking the "Edit This Page" button takes you to an editing screen.

Use these editing buttons to format your text, create headings, add links, and insert images.

Type in this box to add text. (The symbols are inserted by the editing buttons.)

Click this button to preview your page.

Click this button to save your changes. Your page is now live!

Remember to log out when you are finished.

Your Turn

Brainstorm with classmates about ways you could use a wiki for a project. Visit thoughtfullearning.com/p153 for links to popular wiki applications

Using VOIP

VOIP stands for "Voice Over Internet Protocol," which means using the Internet for voice chat. If your computer has speakers, a microphone, and VOIP software like the Skype™ or Google Talk™ services, you can use it to talk for free to other people using that software. If your computer has a Webcam (short for "Web camera") attached, you can even have a video chat with them.

With VOIP chat you can talk to people anywhere in the world. You could talk with your sister on her college trip to Berlin, Germany, or your class could video-chat with another class at a school in Perth, Australia.

Some cell phones also allow VOIP calls if you are in a location with a wireless Internet connection. That way, the phone doesn't use up minutes from its wireless plan. Some phones even allow video chat by wireless connection.

Tip: Although many people use cell phones nowadays, a "landline" home phone can still be useful. ("Landline" means a cord runs from the phone to a telephone pole or other wired connection.) Landline phones allow police, firefighters, and ambulances to quickly locate the source of a call to 911 (the emergency service phone number).

Your Turn

Discuss with other students the ways your class could use a VOIP call for learning. Make a list of suggestions to present to your teacher.

Social-Media Activities

Use the following activities to improve your social-media skills.

Interview an Expert

The Internet can be a great way to get answers from an expert.

Your Turn

Follow these instructions to prepare an interview:
1. **Brainstorm** a list of experts who might be willing to be interviewed about a particular topic.
2. **Prepare** a list of questions you would like to have answered.
3. **Consider** social media you might use for the interview: e-mail, a VOIP call, a virtual-world visit, microblog posts, or an exchange of messages on a message board.
4. **Request** the interview and offer options for it.
5. **Conduct** the interview.
6. **Thank** the interviewee for participating.
7. **Write** an article about what you have learned.
8. **Publish** the article through a social-media service. (For more on interviews, see pages 275 and 446–449.)

Do a Microblog Search

Microblog posts are becoming recognized as an important historical record. (The Library of Congress has even created a Twitter archive for future historians!) These posts can also give insights into topics you are currently studying.

Your Turn

Follow these instructions to conduct a microblog search:
1. **Choose** a topic you'd like to learn more about, and search a microblog service like Twitter to discover what people are saying about it.
2. **Analyze** what you discover to gauge the attitude of the public.
3. **Research** the topic in your library to learn what the public may have missed about the topic.
4. **Report** to your class what you've learned about the topic and the public's perception of it.

E-Mail Your Elected Officials

Mayors, state senators and representatives, U.S. senators and representatives, judges, and even your local sheriff are all elected to represent public interests in government. It's not too early to begin preparing yourself to vote responsibly.

Your Turn

Do the following to e-mail a public official:
1. **Choose** an important topic for your city, state, or nation.
2. **Find out** who your government representatives are at that level.
3. **Choose** one representative and research news items to learn how he or she has voted on the topic.
4. **Decide** whether you approve or disapprove of your representative's vote.
5. **Send** an e-mail to your public representative, either thanking that person for his or her vote or expressing your disagreement.
6. **Report** to the class the response you received.

(For more on writing an e-mail, see pages 324–325.)

Build a Wiki

You can use a wiki to plan, organize, and prepare a group project. If your class has access to a wiki application, prepare a group report in that format.

Your Turn

Follow these steps to build a wiki:
1. **Brainstorm** a list of possible topics on a wiki page.
2. **Choose** the topic you like best, and make it the page title.
3. **Research** the topic, posting on the wiki page the information you find and links to the sources.
4. **Create** a rough outline for your project, assigning pages to individuals in the group.
5. **Draft** your page using the information you found earlier. Search for additional information as needed.
6. **Review** other people's pages, making helpful comments.
7. **Evaluate** and **discuss** the results.
8. **Revise** and **edit** to make improvements.
9. **Invite** other people to visit your wiki and discover what you learned.

(For more on writing in wikis, see pages 152–153.)

Chapter 10
Reading to Learn

Novelist Gary Paulsen once said, "Read like a wolf eats." In other words, read everything and anything—books, blogs, box tops, and billboards. Reading can definitely be enjoyable and exciting.

How do you feel about reading? The fact is that this is the information age. To be a good student and a lifelong learner, you need to develop strong reading skills. This chapter offers strategies for reading nonfiction materials and for enjoying fiction and poetry.

You will learn . . .

- Reading Nonfiction
- Reading Web Sites
- Using Reading Strategies
- Reading Fiction
- Reading Poetry

Reading Nonfiction

Nonfiction books and resources offer you all types of factual information. You can learn about the past and the present, how to put things together, what other people are thinking, and what is happening around the globe. To gain the most from reading, have a plan.

Before . . .

Understand why you are reading. *(What is your purpose?)*

Skim the selection, paying attention to headings, bold words, and the beginning and ending parts. *(What does it cover?)*

Decide on a reading plan. *(Will you complete it in one sitting or in several sittings?)*

During . . .

Use a study-reading strategy such as KWL. (See page 162.)

Take notes. (See page 163.)

Annotate or highlight the text (if you own it or are reading a photocopy). (See page 164.)

Reread parts that seem especially important or challenging.

After . . .

Summarize the reading to help you focus on its key points. (See pages 322–323.)

Write freely about the reading experience. *(What did you like about it? How will you use the information?)*

List questions that you still have about the material.

Your Turn

A writer named William Safire once said that reading can "tickle your thinking." What does he mean? When was the last time you read something that "tickled" your own thinking? What are your favorite types of nonfiction reading?

Nonfiction Page

This page shows some of the typical features of nonfiction reading selections. Become familiar with them. (See also pages 122–126.)

Title

Subtitle

Introduction

Heading

Bold words

Graphic

Caption

Heading

A Style Guide to the Inca Empire
How the People of the Inca Empire Dressed
By Mark Redding

You can tell a lot about a culture by what the people wear. For the Inca civilization of the sixteenth century, clothing reflected a person's social status.

Common Garb

Both Incan men and women's attire was made out of rectangular pieces of fabric. Noblemen's fabric was made of richly dyed **alpaca** wool, while common people wore coarser wool or cotton. Incan men wore sleeveless tunics called **onkas** and, depending on the weather, a thick cloak over their shoulders. The color pattern of the tunic reflected the man's position in society. Meanwhile, women wore a one-piece dress, made by pinning a blouse and skirt together at the waist along a sash. The pins could be used as knives for everyday use.

Emperor Atahualpa

The Emperor's Garment

The Inca Emperor wore a new outfit each day. His used clothing was then ceremoniously burned. He also wore an assortment of gold jewelry, including earrings and shoulder pads. The most distinguishing feature of his outfit was a gold head wrap with special bird feathers.

Wartime Attire

During wartime, Inca soldiers wore sleeveless tunics, which included a woven insignia of the soldier's unit. Higher-ranking soldiers sometimes received padded vests for protection. For head defense, the soldiers wore helmets made of wood or cane. Generals and warriors also adorned . . .

Reading Web Sites

Reading on the Web, as you know, is more of a multimedia experience than reading a book or a magazine. A Web site may contain links to interviews, film clips, and other articles, and it may also give you the chance to add your own comments.

Another important difference between the Web and printed material is the reliability of the information. Most books, newspapers, and magazines are reliable sources because trained writers and editors check them for accuracy. Some Web sites, however, are not carefully checked, and the information may not be reliable. When reading Web sites, keep the following points in mind. (See also page 137.)

What to ask . . .

Who authored the site? What do you know about his or her education and experience?

What group sponsored the site? An organization may be promoting a product or a certain way of thinking.

When was the site last updated? This is especially important if you need current information.

How accurate is the material? Compare it to other sources.

What to watch for . . .

The site offers no author or organization affiliation. Without this information, you cannot rely on the accuracy of a site's content.

The writing is poorly presented and contains errors.

The information seems one-sided (does not tell the whole story).

The site makes big claims. ("This site will tell you everything you need to know!")

The opinions are not backed by facts. (See pages 111–116.)

The language seems unfair, disrespectful, or even harmful.

 Focus

Government and education sites are usually reliable, as are the sites of most nonprofit organizations and professional sites. These types of sites usually end with *edu, org,* and *gov.*

Web Page

This page shows the typical features of informational Web sites.

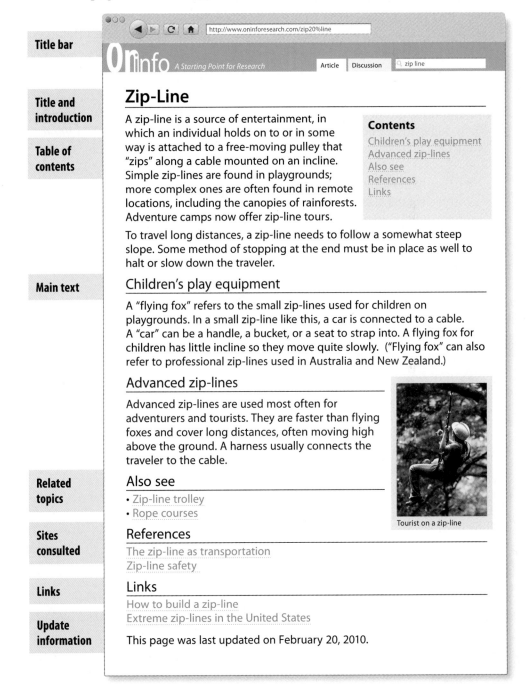

Title bar

Title and introduction

Table of contents

Main text

Related topics

Sites consulted

Links

Update information

http://www.oninforesearch.com/zip20%line

OnInfo *A Starting Point for Research*

Article | Discussion | zip line

Zip-Line

A zip-line is a source of entertainment, in which an individual holds on to or in some way is attached to a free-moving pulley that "zips" along a cable mounted on an incline. Simple zip-lines are found in playgrounds; more complex ones are often found in remote locations, including the canopies of rainforests. Adventure camps now offer zip-line tours.

Contents
Children's play equipment
Advanced zip-lines
Also see
References
Links

To travel long distances, a zip-line needs to follow a somewhat steep slope. Some method of stopping at the end must be in place as well to halt or slow down the traveler.

Children's play equipment

A "flying fox" refers to the small zip-lines used for children on playgrounds. In a small zip-line like this, a car is connected to a cable. A "car" can be a handle, a bucket, or a seat to strap into. A flying fox for children has little incline so they move quite slowly. ("Flying fox" can also refer to professional zip-lines used in Australia and New Zealand.)

Advanced zip-lines

Advanced zip-lines are used most often for adventurers and tourists. They are faster than flying foxes and cover long distances, often moving high above the ground. A harness usually connects the traveler to the cable.

Also see
• Zip-line trolley
• Rope courses

Tourist on a zip-line

References
The zip-line as transportation
Zip-line safety

Links
How to build a zip-line
Extreme zip-lines in the United States

This page was last updated on February 20, 2010.

Using Reading Strategies

You read nonfiction to learn new information. If the text is complex, you should use a reading strategy to help you understand the information more fully. The next three pages explain three effective reading strategies. (See also pages 268-272.)

Using KWL

KWL is an effective reading strategy, especially when you already know something about the topic. The letters KWL stand for what I *know*, what I *want* to know, and what I *learned*. Here's how the strategy works:

- Identify the topic of the reading at the top of your paper. Then create three columns, labeled K, W, and L.
- In the first column, jot down what you know.
- In the second column, list questions you would like to explore as you read.
- In the third column, identify what you have learned and still hope to learn.

Topic: **Electromagnetic Waves**

Know	**W**ant to know	**L**earned
EM waves have something to do with TVs, computers, and other technology. The waves may make connections.	Where do EM waves come from?	EM waves come from the sun and from technology.
	How do they move?	EM waves can spread in all directions and do not lose energy.
"Electro" means "electricity," a source of energy.	How are they used?	They move at a constant speed.
"Magnetic" suggests power or force.		Microwave ovens use EM waves. The waves add thermal energy to water.

Taking Reading Notes

Taking notes can be especially useful when the reading contains many facts and details. Notes keep track of information so you can use it later in projects, in reports, and on tests. Use these tips as a guide for taking reading notes.

- Use your own words as much as possible.
- Write down key phrases rather than complete sentences.
- Organize your notes, perhaps labeling important points with a plus (+) and supporting points with a dash (–).
- Devise shortcuts, using # instead of *number*, $ instead of *money*, and so on.

Sample Notes

React to the information by using a two-column note system: two-thirds of the page is for your main notes, and one-third is for your comments.

The Great Depression	*April 3*
+most serious economic downturn in industrial world	Investors and banks are hurt in today's recession, too!
–from 1929 at least thru 1939	
–started with the stock-market crash (10/29/29)?	I've seen a documentary showing long food lines.
+lack of confidence in econ. (banks) worsened things	
–25% of workforce (12-15 mil.) unemployed	
–agri., mining, and logging suffered	
+U.S. slump hurt Europe WWI recovery	I need to learn more about the WWI recovery.
–Ger., G.B., etc., dependent on U.S. $'s	
–tariffs imposed to protect domestic production (failed)	

Your Turn

Try using two-column notes to see if this method helps you to better understand and remember new information.

Annotating a Text

Highlighting, underlining, and making comments on the page of a text are all ways of *annotating*. You can do this if you own the book, or if you are reading a photocopy. Some common annotations are listed to the right.

- Write questions in the margin.
- Underline important ideas.
- Put an idea into your own words.
- Circle new words and define them.
- Draw arrows to connect ideas.

Sample Page

The Great Depression

What is meant by the "Western World"?

The Great Depression was the most serious economic downturn in the history of the industrialized Western World. It began in the United States in 1929 and continued at least through 1939. Some experts identify the stock-market crash on October 29, 1929 (Black Tuesday), as the starting point of this depression. The crash wiped out thousands of individual

How does a bank fail?

investors and destroyed many banks. By 1933, 11,000 U.S. banks had failed.

A lack of confidence in the economy and the banks led to less spending, less demand, and less production, which just made things worse. As the Great Depression worsened, unemployment continued to increase. At the height of the

Ms. Jones said these three were primary industries.

situation, more than 25 percent of the U.S. workforce, or between 12 and 15 million workers, was unemployed. People working in agriculture, mining, and logging suffered the most because there simply was no demand for materials used in industrial production. A severe drought in the U.S. only made things worse in the agricultural sector.

After World War I (1914-1919), the U.S. financed war-torn European countries trying to recover from the war. The economic slump in the U.S. greatly affected the recovery efforts

duties or fees placed on goods related to a certain country

in Germany, Great Britain, and many other countries, because these countries were dependent on U.S. dollars to rebuild. During this time, tariffs were imposed in the U.S. and in Europe to protect domestic production. Unfortunately, the tariffs greatly reduced international trade, which meant that they reduced the markets for new products. . . .

Reading Fiction

Fiction (novels and short stories) is literature or writing that is made up. While this type of writing flows from the writer's imagination, it may also relate to real life. As one writer says, "Fiction may not be real, but it shares the truth about life." (See pages 328–330.) When the fiction you are reading is challenging, you should make a plan for reading it.

Before . . .

Research the author. Where is the person from? What else has she or he written?

Skim the book. Think about the title. Review the chapter titles. Read the opening page or two.

Explore your first thoughts in a notebook or journal.

During . . .

Think about the story as it unfolds. What just happened? And what will happen next?

Consider the characters. Why do they act as they do?

Think about the setting (the time and place of the action). How does it affect the story? How does it connect with the author's life?

Consider the style. What stands out about the words and phrases that the author uses? Are there any descriptions that you really like?

After . . .

Consider how the main character changes by the end of the story. Is this change believable and logical?

Find the main message or theme in the story. Did the author effectively get this point across?

Explore your final thoughts in a notebook.

Your Turn

Use the plan above for reading your next novel or short story. Decide if it helps you to better understand and enjoy the writing.

Reading Poetry

A famous poet named Carl Sandburg once said, "Poetry is an echo, asking a shadow to dance." It's hard to tell what he means, isn't it? But that's Sandburg's point: Poetry cannot be simply explained in a factual way. It is a special form of writing that requires a special explanation. The following plan will help you "dance" with all sorts of poems.

In Focus

Writing about poems helps you enjoy them more fully, so be sure to have your class notebook ready to go whenever you read poetry. Explore your thoughts and feelings before, during, and after your reading. (See pages 332–333.)

Before . . .

Learn something about the poet. Where is the person from? Who or what does the poet usually write about?

Skim the poem. What are your first thoughts? Jot them down.

During . . .

Read the poem first for meaning. What is it saying?

Read it next for the flow and rhythm of the words. Does it flow smoothly or stop and start?

Read it another time for the special sound devices (like rhyme) and for figures of speech (like similes and personification).

Reread parts that challenge you or that you especially like.

After . . .

Think about the poem. Did you enjoy it right away? Or did it "improve" with additional readings?

Talk about the poem with friends or classmates.

Your Turn

Use the plan above for reading your next poem, exploring your thoughts and feelings in a notebook. Did the plan help you "dance" with the poem?

Reading Activities

Use these activities to help you practice and feel more comfortable with reading to learn.

Skimming a Printed Text

It's important to review or skim the main features of nonfiction texts before you do the actual reading. Once you can recognize and understand these features, they will guide your reading.

> **Our best advice:** Skimming informational texts for their main features is a reading strategy that you should practice regularly. It will help you read textbook chapters, newspaper or magazine articles, and other types of informational material for your classes.

Your Turn

Skim an important newspaper article for its main features. Either label the features on a printed copy of the article or identify them in a notebook. (See page 159 for an example.) Then explain in a few sentences what these features tell you about the article. Afterward, share your findings with your classmates.

Skimming a Web Site

Web sites also contain typical features that can serve as a guide for your Web reading.

> **Our best advice:** When you research Web sites for projects and reports, skimming a site is an important first step. You can identify the source of the site, how current it is, and what links it contains.

Your Turn

Skim a meaningful Web site for its main features. Label the features on a printed copy of the site. (See page 161 for an example.) Then explain in a few sentences what these features tell you about the Web site. Afterward, share your findings with your classmates.

Using a Reading Strategy

Using a study-reading strategy like KWL will help you to better understand and remember the informational material you are assigned. (See page 162.)

Our best advice: The KWL strategy helps you in three main ways. First, by writing down what you know already, you activate your prior knowledge about the subject. Then by writing what you wonder about, you start to make predictions about what you will read. These two activities awaken your thinking so that you are ready to learn from the text. Lastly, when you write what you have learned, you reflect on the reading and lock that learning into your mind. Use this strategy to retain and understand new information that you read.

Your Turn

Referring to the research report on pages 363–367, make and fill in a KWL chart in your notebook. Afterward, compare charts with a partner.

Sharing a Novel

When you and your friends read the same books or stories, have some fun comparing your thoughts about the plot lines and the characters. Many people belong to book clubs because they enjoy reading books, talking about them, and sharing them.

Our best advice: Make it a habit to read books and stories for enjoyment. Ask your classmates, friends, teachers, and librarian for their recommendations. Then get together with others to read and discuss good books.

Your Turn

Answer the following questions about one of your favorite books:
- Who is the main character? Do you like or dislike this person? Why?
- Where and when does the story take place?
- What is the most exciting event in the story? Why?
- How does the main character change by the end of the story?

Then share your thoughts about this book with a classmate who has also read it.

Chapter 11
Improving Vocabulary

In order to understand and interact effectively with your world, you need a strong vocabulary. Today, for example, it helps to know words like *hybrid, digital, geothermal, app,* and so on, if you want to engage in "the conversation."

As you advance in school, your vocabulary will naturally increase, but that may not be enough to keep up with all of the words you need to know. To really improve your word power, you must become a regular reader. No other activity will help you more. Then, for an even better vocabulary, refer to the word-building strategies in this chapter.

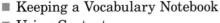

You will learn . . .

- Keeping a Vocabulary Notebook
- Using Context
- Using a Dictionary
- Using a Thesaurus
- Understanding Word Parts
- Common Prefixes, Roots, and Suffixes

Keeping a Vocabulary Notebook

Proactive is a word meaning "acting in advance" or "acting before." Keeping a vocabulary notebook is proactive because it is a way of taking control of your vocabulary building. Here is the type of information that you can include for each word you add to your notebook.

Example Words

Science

metamorphosis (mĕt-ə-mor′-fə-sĭs) ———— Pronunciation
-meta (change) + morph (form) + osis (process) ·———— Word parts
-a transformation, a clear change in appearance ·———— Definition
or character
-During its life cycle, an insect may undergo a ·———— In a sentence
metamorphosis or dramatic physical change.
-synonyms: alteration, change, changeover ·———— Synonyms

Art

illuminate (ĭ-loo′-mə-nāt′)
-il (into) + lumin (light) + ate (cause or make)
-to brighten with light
-Look how the moonlight illuminates the lake.
-synonyms: brighten, highlight, ignite

Technology

hypertext (hī′-pər-tĕkst′)
-hyper (over or above) + text (printed words)
-Web links among pages on the Internet
-How can I turn words on my Web site into hypertext?
-synonym: linkage

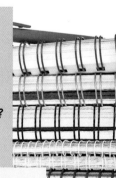

Your Turn

Reserve part of your class notebooks for vocabulary. Then list important new words that you learn during your course work. Your teacher may suggest certain words to include. Include as much information as necessary to help you understand each word.

Using Context

You constantly come across new words in your reading. Avoid the temptation to simply pass them over. Instead, try to figure out what unfamiliar words mean by studying them in context—looking for clues in the text surrounding the word. Here are some examples that you can use as a guide for learning new words in context.

Look for . . .

■ **Cause and effect connections**

Recommending the use of seat belts didn't work, so the state officials made seat-belt use *mandatory.*

■ **Definitions built into the text**

Dr. Williams is an *anthropologist,* a person who scientifically studies the physical, social, and cultural development of humans.

■ **Comparisons and contrasts**

Lynn Dery lives in New York, so she is used to a fast-paced life; Mandy Williams lives in the country, so she is used to a more *serene* lifestyle.

■ **Words in a series**

Spaghetti, lasagna, and *ziti* all have their own special shape.

■ **Synonyms (words with the same meaning)**

Hector's essay contains too many *banal,* overused phrases.

■ **Antonyms (words with the opposite meaning)**

Mrs. Wolfe still seemed strong and energetic after the storm, but Mr. Wolfe looked *haggard.*

■ **The tone and feeling created in the text**

The street was filled with *bellicose* protesters who pushed and shoved their way through the crowd. The scene was no longer peaceful and calm, as the marchers promised it would be.

Your Turn

Team up with a partner and define each of the italicized words above using the clues presented in the sentences. Afterward, check your definitions in a dictionary.

Using a Dictionary

The dictionary is the main resource to turn to whenever you have questions about new words. You'll find print versions in your classrooms and library. Did you know that dictionaries provide much more than simple definitions of words? Here is what you can find in most print-version dictionaries. (Also see page 173.)

Guide words at the top of the page list the first and last entry on a page. They help you find the page your word is on.

Each **entry** in a dictionary is in bold type and listed alphabetically.

The **syllable divisions** show you how to divide a word by syllables.

Parts of speech abbreviations tell how a word can be used. Many words can be used as more than one part of speech.

Pronunciations are included to help you pronounce the word.

Spellings and **capital letters** are given to help you use words correctly in your writing.

Illustrations offer visual information about words.

Accent marks aid in pronunciation of difficult words.

Synonyms and **antonyms** are provided for some words. (In this way, a dictionary serves as a thesaurus.)

Etymology gives the history of a word. This information will be set off by [brackets].

A **pronunciation key** serves as a guide to pronouncing words on the page.

English Usage

(In) Focus

Online and print dictionaries essentially provide the same information. However, online dictionaries may offer an audio option, helpful for pronouncing words, and other helpful links to related information.

THESAURUS

Dictionary

Dictionary Page

Guide Words — **deep dish**
defame

Entry Word — **deep dish** (dĕp′dĭsh′) *adj.* Made or used in a deep baking dish.

Syllable Division — **deep·en** (dē′pən) *tr. & intr.v.* **deep·ened, deep·en·ing, deep·ens** To make or become deep or deeper: *More digging slowly deepened the hole. Floodwaters deepened as the rain continued.*

deep-fry (dēp′frī′) *tr.v.* **deep-fried, deep-fry·ing, deep-fried** To fry by immersing in a deep container filled with oil or fat: *deep-fried the chicken wings.*

deep-root·ed (dēp′rōō′tĭd *or* dēp′rŏŏt′ĭd) *adj.* **1.** Firmly implanted below the surface: *a deep-rooted oak.* **2.** Firmly fixed; deep-seated: *deep-rooted beliefs.*

Part of Speech — **deep-sea** (dēp′sē′) *adv.* Of or relating to deep parts of the sea: *a deep-sea diver.*

deep-seat·ed (dēp′sē′tĭd) *adj.* **1.** Deeply implanted below the surface: *a deep-seated infection.* **2.** Firmly fixed; deeply rooted; strongly entrenched: *a deep-seated problem of long standing.*

Spelling and Capitalization — **Deep South** A region of the southeast United States, usually made up of the states of Alabama, Georgia, Louisiana, Mississippi, and South Carolina.

deep space *n.* **1.** The regions of space that are beyond the gravitational influence of Earth. **2.** The regions of space that are beyond our solar system.

deer (dîr) *n., pl.* **deer** Any of various hoofed mammals, such as the elk and the white-tailed deer, that chew their cud and usually have antlers in the males.

Etymology — [First written down before 899 in Old English and spelled *dēor* (meaning beast).]

■ *These sound alike:* **deer, dear** (loved one).

deer mouse *n.* A North American mouse having tan or brown fur, white feet, large ears, and a long tail.

Illustration —

deer mouse

deer·skin (dîr′skĭn′) *n.* **1.** The skin of a deer. **2.** Leather made from this skin. **3.** A garment made from such leather.

de·es·ca·late (dē-ĕs′kə-lāt′) *tr.v.* To reduce the scale, size, or intensity of: *Calm words de-escalated the crisis.* —**de·es′ca·la′tion** *n.*

Spelling of Verb Forms — **de·face** (dĭ-fās′) *tr.v.* **de·faced, de·fac·ing, de·fac·es** To mar or spoil the surface or appearance of; disfigure: *deface a poster with a crayon.* —**de·face′ment** *n.*

de fac·to (dĭ făk′tō *or* dā făk′tō) *adj.* **1.** Existing in fact but not by official recognition: *housing practices that resulted in de facto segregation.* **2.** Exercising power though not legally established: *a de facto government.*

Pronunciation — **def·a·ma·tion** (dĕf′ə-mā′shən) *n.* The act of making a statement that will damage a person's reputation; slander or libel: *defamation of a person's character.* —**de·fam′a·to·ry** (dĭ-făm′ə-tôr′ē) *adj.*

Accent Marks — **de·fame** (dĭ-fām′) *tr.v.* **de·famed, de·fam·ing, de·fames** To attack or damage the reputation of by slander or libel: *He defamed her good name by spreading false rumors.*

Using a Thesaurus

A thesaurus is a dictionary of synonyms and antonyms, and it can help you build your vocabulary. A thesaurus will prove most useful when you are looking for more specific words to substitute for those that you use over and over. Let's say you need a new word for "run." A thesaurus would offer interesting synonyms such as *bolt, dash, dart, sprint,* and *scamper.*

Print Version

You'll find a print thesaurus in your classroom or library. Some thesauruses organize words alphabetically as a dictionary does; the more traditional thesaurus refers you to the index for the word that you are interested in.

Word Entry

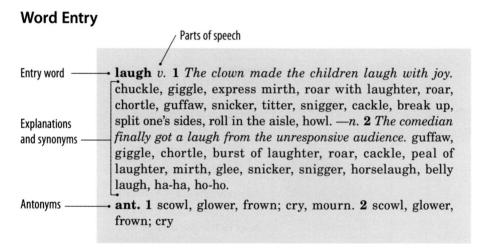

Parts of speech

Entry word —— **laugh** *v.* **1** *The clown made the children laugh with joy.* chuckle, giggle, express mirth, roar with laughter, roar, chortle, guffaw, snicker, titter, snigger, cackle, break up, split one's sides, roll in the aisle, howl. —*n.* **2** *The comedian finally got a laugh from the unresponsive audience.* guffaw, giggle, chortle, burst of laughter, roar, cackle, peal of laughter, mirth, glee, snicker, snigger, horselaugh, belly laugh, ha-ha, ho-ho.

Explanations and synonyms ——

Antonyms —— **ant. 1** scowl, glower, frown; cry, mourn. **2** scowl, glower, frown; cry

Online Version

You can also use an online version of a thesaurus, and you have many to choose from. For most of them, simply enter your word in the blank space, click the search box, and synonyms will appear. You'll find synonyms for your word as well as synonyms for different versions of your word. For example, you'll find synonyms for "run" as well as for "running," "run-on," "run-in," "run-around," and so on.

Your Turn

Think of two or three words that you may overuse. Then use a thesaurus to identify a few specific alternatives.

Understanding Word Parts

Many words in our language are made up·of different word parts—prefixes, suffixes, and roots. Often these word parts come from ancient languages, including Latin, Greek, Old French, and Old English. Learning how words are put together will help you better understand the language. (See pages 176–180 for common word parts.)

Example Words

These two examples show you how combinations of word parts create words in the language.

Respiration combines
- the prefix *re* meaning "again"
- the root *spir* meaning "breathe"
- and the suffix *tion* meaning "the act of or state of"

So *respiration* means "the act or process of breathing again and again."

Philosophy combines
- the root *phil* meaning "love"
- the root *soph* meaning "wise"
- and the suffix *y* meaning "inclined to" or "tending to"

So *philosophy* means "the love of wisdom."

In Focus

Many words in our language are root words themselves. For example, a word such as *nose* is not made up of other word parts. These words can be combined with other base words to form a word such as *nosebleed,* or they can be combined with other word parts, like the suffix *y,* to form a word such as *nosy.*

Your Turn

With the help of a partner, explain the combination of word parts that are used to form an important word in mathematics, science, and/or social studies. Use the glossary on pages 176–180 plus a dictionary to help you complete your work. Afterward, share your findings with your classmates.

Common Prefixes, Roots, and Suffixes

The next five pages list common prefixes, roots, and suffixes. When you are not sure of a new word, try to figure out its meaning by studying its parts.

Prefixes

Prefixes come before roots, or base words, to form new words. A list of common prefixes follows.

ambi, amphi *(both)* amphibious *(on both land and sea)*

ante *(earlier)* antedate *(to be of an earlier date)*

anti *(against)* antibiotic *(a substance fighting against disease)*

astro *(star)* astronomer *(studier of the stars and planets)*

auto *(self)* autocrat *(ruler with unlimited self-rule)*

bi *(two)* bisect *(to cut into two equal parts)*

circum *(around)* circumvent *(to avoid or get around something)*

dia *(through, across)* diameter *(a straight line passing through the center of a circle)*

epi *(upon, above, outer)* epicenter *(the point of the earth directly above the focus of an earthquake)*

ex *(out)* excavate *(to dig or hollow out)*

extra *(outside, beyond)* extrasensory *(outside the normal range of the senses)*

fore *(before, earlier)* foresee *(to see or know before)*

hemi *(half)* hemisphere *(half of a sphere or half of the human brain)*

hyper *(over)* hypercritical *(overly critical)*

in, im *(not)* improbable *(not probable)*

inter *(between)* interstate *(connecting or between two states)*

intra *(within)* intranet *(a network within the private control of a person)*

macro *(large)* macroclimate *(the climate of a large area)*

mal *(bad, poorly, or wrongly)* malformed *(poorly formed)*

micro *(small)* microcircuit *(a very small circuit)*

mono *(one)* monopoly *(control by one group)*

non *(not)* nonflammable *(not easily set on fire)*

over *(above, more, or too much)* overcharge *(to charge too much for something)*

poly *(many)* polygraph *(an instrument measuring many body actions)*

post *(after)* postwar *(a period of time after a war)*

pre *(before)* predict *(to make known before or in advance)*

re *(again, back)* readjust *(to adjust again)*

semi *(half or occurring twice)* semiautomatic *(partly automatic)*, semimonthly *(occurring twice a month)*

sub *(under)* subway *(an underground railroad)*

trans *(across, beyond)* transatlantic *(crossing the Atlantic Ocean)*

tri *(three)* triad *(a group of three)*

un *(not)* unreal *(not real)*

under *(below)* undercurrent *(a current beneath a surface)*

uni *(one)* unicellular *(having one cell)*

Roots

Roots serve as the starting point for most words. A list of common base words follows.

alter *(other)* <u>alter</u>native *(a different choice)*

anni, annu, enni *(year)* <u>anni</u>versary *(yearly event)*, <u>annu</u>al *(once a year)*, bi<u>enni</u>al *(lasting two years)*

anthrop *(human being)* <u>anthrop</u>ologist *(someone who studies the development of humans)*

aster *(star)* <u>aster</u>oids *(irregularly shaped bodies orbiting the sun)*

aud *(hear, listen)* <u>aud</u>iology *(the study of hearing)*

bibl *(book)* <u>bibl</u>iography *(list of books)*

bio *(life)* <u>bio</u>sphere *(the part of earth in which living things exist)*

chrom *(color)* <u>chrom</u>atic *(of or relating to colors)*

chron *(time)* <u>chron</u>ology *(the science dealing with the order of events)*

cise *(cut)* in<u>cise</u> *(to cut into or mark)*

claim *(cry out)* pro<u>claim</u> *(to announce or declare)*

cor, card *(heart)* <u>card</u>iac *(relating to the heart)*

corp *(body)* <u>corp</u>oration *(relating to a business group or body)*

cosm *(universe, world)* micro<u>cosm</u> *(a miniature world)*

cred *(believe)* in<u>cred</u>ible *(unbelievable)*

cycl, cyclo *(wheel, circular)* <u>cycl</u>ical *(occurring in cycles)*, <u>cycl</u>one *(strong circular wind)*

dem *(people)* epi<u>dem</u>ic *(an outbreak of a disease spreading among the people)*

dent *(tooth)* <u>dent</u>ist *(a person trained to work on teeth)*

derm *(skin)* epi<u>derm</u>is *(outer layer of skin)*

dic, dict *(say, speak)* <u>dict</u>ate *(to say or read aloud to be recorded or written by another)*, contra<u>dict</u> *(to speak against)*

dynam *(power)* <u>dynam</u>ic *(marked by intensity and power)*

equi *(equal)* <u>equi</u>lateral *(having all sides equal)*

fact *(do, make)* manu<u>fact</u>ure *(to make things)*

fin *(end, ended, finished)* <u>fin</u>al *(occurring at the end)*

flex *(bend)* re<u>flex</u> *(bending back)*

flu *(flowing)* <u>flu</u>id *(a substance that flows easily)*

fort, forc *(strong)* <u>fort</u>ify *(make strong)*, <u>forc</u>eful *(strong, full of force)*

fract, frag *(break)* <u>frag</u>ile *(easy to break)*, <u>fract</u>ure *(a break)*

gen *(birth, produce)* <u>gen</u>etics *(study of birth traits)*

geo *(earth)* <u>geo</u>logy *(study of the structure of the earth)*

grad *(step, go)* <u>grad</u>ual *(step by step)*

graph *(write, written)* auto<u>graph</u> *(a person's own signature)*

greg *(group, herd)* con<u>greg</u>ate *(to come together in a group)*

hab, habit *(live)* <u>habit</u>at *(the area in which animals or plants normally live)*

hetero *(different)* <u>hetero</u>geneous *(consisting of parts that are not alike)*

homo *(same)* <u>homo</u>geneous *(of the same or similar kind)*

hum *(earth)* <u>hum</u>us *(earth or dirt)*

hydr, hydro, hydra *(water)* <u>hydro</u>electric *(generating electricity using water)*, <u>hydr</u>ant *(an upright pipe fitted with a valve to draw water)*

ject *(throw)* e<u>ject</u> *(to throw out or force out)*

leg *(law)* <u>leg</u>islator *(a member of a government body that makes laws)*

liber *(free)* <u>liber</u>ation *(the process of setting free)*

log (word, study, speech) <u>log</u>ic (the study of thinking and reasoning)

lum (light) il<u>lum</u>inate (to provide with lights)

magn (great) <u>magn</u>ify (to make something appear larger)

man (hand) <u>man</u>acle (handcuffs)

mania (insanity) pyro<u>mania</u> (crazy urge to start fires)

medi (middle, between) <u>medi</u>an (located in the middle)

mega (great) <u>mega</u>bit (one million bits)

mem (remember) <u>mem</u>orial (something that serves as a remembrance)

meter (measure) thermo<u>meter</u> (an instrument that measures temperatures)

migra (wander) <u>migra</u>nt (a person who travels for work)

mit, miss (send) trans<u>mit</u> (send across), <u>miss</u>ile (suited for launching or sending off)

mob, mot (move) <u>mob</u>ilize (to move or gather together), pro<u>mot</u>ion (moved ahead or advanced)

mort (mortal, death) <u>mort</u>al (subject to death)

nat (to be born) <u>nat</u>ive (belonging to by birth or origin)

neur (nerve) <u>neur</u>ology (study of the nervous system)

nov (new) <u>nov</u>ice (a person new to an activity)

numer (number) <u>numer</u>al (a symbol or mark representing a number)

omni (all, completely) <u>omni</u>potent (all-powerful), <u>omni</u>vore (an organism that eats both plants and animals)

onym (name) syn<u>onym</u> (a word having the same meaning as another word)

pac (peace) <u>pac</u>ifist (a person who believes in peace)

pater, patr (father) <u>patr</u>iarch (father and head of family or clan), <u>pater</u>nal (characteristic of a father)

ped (foot) <u>ped</u>estrian (foot traveler)

pend (hang, weigh) <u>pend</u>ant (a hanging ornament, often linked to a necklace)

phil (love) <u>phil</u>osophy (love of wisdom)

phobia (fear) arachno<u>phobia</u> (fear of spiders)

phon (sound) tele<u>phon</u>e (an instrument that sends sounds)

photo (light) <u>photo</u>electric (electrical effects caused by light)

pop (people) <u>pop</u>ulate (to supply with people)

port (carry) <u>port</u>able (easy to carry)

proto (first) <u>proto</u>type (an original or first example of something)

psych (mind, soul) <u>psych</u>ology (the study of mental processes)

rupt (break) inter<u>rupt</u> (to break into a conversation)

sci (know) <u>sci</u>entist (someone who is an expert in a scientific field)

scope (see, watch) micro<u>scope</u> (an instrument that magnifies objects)

scrib, script (write) <u>scrib</u>ble (to write in a rush), in<u>script</u>ion (the act of writing, printing, or carving on a surface)

sen (old) <u>sen</u>ior (older person)

sequ, secu (follow) <u>sequ</u>ence (following of one thing after another), con<u>secu</u>tive (following in order)

soph (wise) <u>soph</u>isticated (having acquired more knowledge or refinement)

spect (look) in<u>spect</u> (to examine carefully)

sphere (ball) hemi<u>sphere</u> (half of the earth)

spir (breath) re<u>spir</u>ation (the act or process of breathing)

strict (tighten) con<u>strict</u> (draw tightly together)

tag (touch) con<u>tag</u>ious (transmitted by contact)

tele (far) <u>tele</u>phone (an instrument that sends sounds far away)

tempo (time) <u>tempo</u>rary (bound by time)

tend, tens *(stretch, strain)* ex<u>tend</u> (*to make longer*), <u>tens</u>ile (*relating to or capable of being stretched*)

terra *(earth)* <u>terra</u>in (*an area of land*)

therm *(heat)* <u>therm</u>al (*of or relating to producing heat*)

tom *(cut)* ana<u>tom</u>y (*the dissection or cutting of a plant or an animal for study*)

tox *(poison)* anti<u>tox</u>in (*acting against a poison*)

tract *(draw, pull)* at<u>tract</u> (*to cause to draw near*)

typ *(print)* <u>typ</u>ography (*the arrangement and appearance of printed material*)

vac *(empty)* e<u>vac</u>uate (*to remove or make empty*)

vert, vers *(turn)* re<u>vers</u>e (*turn back*), intro<u>vert</u> (*turn inward*)

vid, vis *(see)* <u>vid</u>eo (*visual parts of television*), <u>vis</u>ible (*possible to see*)

viv *(alive, life)* sur<u>viv</u>e (*to stay alive*)

voc *(call)* in<u>voc</u>ation (*the act of appealing or calling for help*)

vor *(eat greedily)* herbi<u>vor</u>ous (*plant-eating*)

zo *(animal)* <u>zo</u>ology (*study of animal life*)

Suffixes

Suffixes come after base words to form new words. A list of common suffixes follows.

able *(capable of or able)* mov<u>able</u> (*capable of being moved*)

age *(collection, act or result of)* mile<u>age</u> (*the collection or number of miles*), slipp<u>age</u> (*the result of slipping*)

al *(of, relating to)* season<u>al</u> (*relating to the seasons*)

an, ian *(born into, of or relating to)* Afric<u>an</u> (*born into Africa*), Hercule<u>an</u> (*of or relating to Hercules*)

ant *(a person or thing performing an action)* deodor<u>ant</u> (*something that performs or acts against odor*)

ary, ery, ory *(act of or relating to, connect with)* diction<u>ary</u> (*relating to a dictionary*), brib<u>ery</u> (*the act of bribing*)

ate *(characterized by or to act upon)* isol<u>ate</u> (*the act of setting apart*)

cide *(killer of)* insecti<u>cide</u> (*a chemical killer of insects*)

cy *(state, condition, quality)* bankrupt<u>cy</u> (*the state or condition of being bankrupt*)

dom *(condition, state)* serf<u>dom</u> (*the state of being a serf*)

ee *(a person who receives or benefits from)* train<u>ee</u> (*someone who benefits from training*)

en *(to cause to be or resembling)* streng<u>then</u> (*to cause to be stronger*), wood<u>en</u> (*resembling wood*)

ence *(state of or quality)* occurr<u>ence</u> (*the state of having occurred*)

er, or *(a person or thing that does something)* teach<u>er</u> (*someone who teaches*), act<u>or</u> (*someone who acts*)

escent *(beginning to or becoming)* lumin<u>escent</u> (*becoming light*)

ese *(relating to a certain place)* Chin<u>ese</u> (*relating to China*)

ess *(female)* princ<u>ess</u> (*female royalty*)

fy, ify *(to make or cause to become)* simpl<u>ify</u> (*to make simpler*)

ful *(full of)* wonder<u>ful</u> (*full of wonder*)

hood *(condition or quality)* false<u>hood</u> (*the condition or quality of being untrue*)

ic *(relating to, having)* atom<u>ic</u> (*relating to the atom*)

ion, sion, tion (act of, result of) format<u>ion</u> (*the act of forming*), preci<u>sion</u> (*the result of being precise or exact*)

ish (of or relating to) Swed<u>ish</u> (*of or being from Sweden*)

ism (state of, characteristic, quality) critic<u>ism</u> (*state of being critical*)

ist (one who) lobby<u>ist</u> (*someone who lobbies the government*)

ity (quality or condition) clar<u>ity</u> (*the quality of being clear*)

ive (tending toward or becoming a certain act) disrupt<u>ive</u> (*tending toward causing trouble*)

less (without, lacking) name<u>less</u> (*without a name or an identity*)

ling (a person connected with, something or someone that is small) earth<u>ling</u> (*someone connected with the earth*), duck<u>ling</u> (*a small or young duck*)

ly (having characteristics of, recurring, or in a specified manner) brother<u>ly</u> (*having the characteristics of a brother*), hour<u>ly</u> (*recurring on the hour*)

ment (act of, state of) govern<u>ment</u> (*act of governing*), amaze<u>ment</u> (*state of being amazed*)

ness (state, condition, quality) bright<u>ness</u> (*state of being bright*)

ology (study of) hydr<u>ology</u> (*the scientific study of water*)

osis (condition, process) tubercul<u>osis</u> (*the condition of being tubercular*)

ship (condition, quality of) companion<u>ship</u> (*the condition of being a companion or friend*)

some (apt, like, leading to) two<u>some</u>, lone<u>some</u>, grue<u>some</u>

ward (in a direction, toward) down<u>ward</u> (*toward a lower place*)

y (inclined, tending to) mess<u>y</u> (*inclined to messiness*)

🔍 In Focus

Knowing that words can belong to a family of words can also help you build your vocabulary. For example, you may know that one definition of *heart* is "the ability to feel love, kindness, or sympathy" as in this sentence: *Everyone loves my grandmother because she has a big heart.* Then, when you come across words such as *heartache, heartless, heartfelt,* or *heartwarming,* you will have a good chance of figuring out their meanings because they are part of the same word family.

Vocabulary Activities

The activities on the next two pages will help you work on your vocabulary-building skills.

Words in Context

Figuring out the meaning of new words in context is much quicker than looking them up in a dictionary. It also helps you focus on your reading because you don't have to do a lot of stopping. (See page 171.)

[**Our best advice:** Rather than passing over unfamiliar words, get into the habit of using context clues to find the words' meanings.]

Your Turn

List the italicized words below on a piece of paper. Then write down what each one means to you based on its use in the sentence. Finally, check your definitions against those provided in a dictionary.

1. In 1728, Boston officials enclosed the Commons to save the grass. Soon many people strolled within the *green*.
2. A serious outbreak of *influenza* occurred in New York City in 1733. It sickened three-fourths of the population.
3. In that same year, John Peter Zenger was relieved to earn an *acquittal* after being arrested for publishing false information.
4. *Conscription*, or the required enrollment in military service, went into effect in Prussia at this time.

Presenting a Challenging Word

A dictionary tells you just about everything you need to know about words—from their pronunciation to their history.

[**Our best advice:** Always have a dictionary handy whenever you are researching, reading, writing, or working on a project. And more importantly, use it whenever you have questions about words.]

Your Turn

Looking through a dictionary, choose a new word that attracts you. Then study all of the information given for that word. Present your findings to a small group of classmates or to the entire class.

Working with Synonyms

One word may have many synonyms, words that mean almost the same thing. Synonyms often provide different shades of meaning. For examples, synonyms for "cry," such as *sniffle* or *bawl*, certainly describe different types of crying.

Our best advice: Be sure to refer to a thesaurus when you need a specific alternative for a general word (such as *sniffle* for *cry*). Remember that there are electronic and print versions of this resource. (See page 174.)

Your Turn

For each of the following sentences, replace the italicized word with one or two more-specific synonyms. (Use a thesaurus as needed.) Afterward, compare your replacement words with a partner's.

1. The blizzard *left* a foot of snow on the city.
2. Because of the *strong* winds, it was difficult to walk.
3. People were *told* to stay indoors except for emergencies.
4. The *low* temperatures caused many pipes to burst.
5. Utility employees *worked* throughout the night to fix downed power lines.

Words in the Family

As you learned on page 180, many words belong to a family of related words. For example, the word *short* is used in *shorten, shortly, shortage,* and *shortcut.* Understanding this feature of the language can help you build your vocabulary.

Our best advice: Whenever you come across a new vocabulary word, see if it contains a shorter word (or base word) that you know. If it does, you have a good chance of identifying the meaning of the new word.

Your Turn

With the help of a partner, list as many words as you can that are related to *long* (as in *longing*), to *hang* (as in *hanger*), or to another base word of your own choosing. Then check for additional words in a dictionary. (Put a star next to each word that you found on your own.) Afterward, share your work with your classmates.

Chapter 12
Following Basic Conventions

It's true: The English language can trip you up once in a while. It's not always an easy skip along "the yellow brick road." After all, there are many rules to follow, and many exceptions to the rules.

This chapter explains the common conventions for using punctuation, mechanics, usage, and sentence structures.

You will learn . . .

- Using Basic Punctuation
- Following Proper Mechanics
- Understanding Commonly Confused Words
- Using Complete Sentences

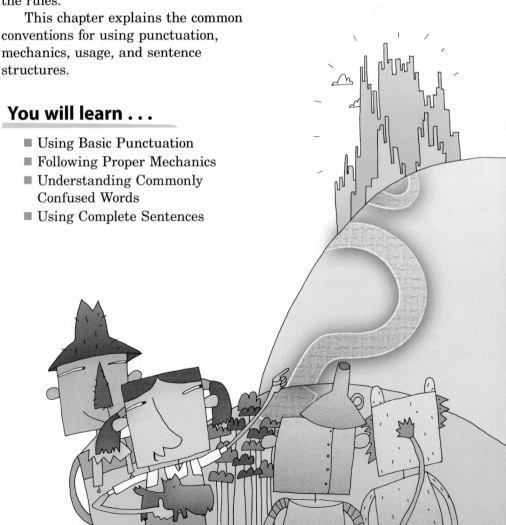

Using Basic Punctuation

Punctuation marks help you manage the ideas in your written communication. The next two pages list the top 10 basic punctuation rules to follow.

Rule 1: Place a period after a statement that makes a complete thought.
A period is used to end a sentence that makes a statement, request, or mild command.

> I went to see a movie last night.

Rule 2: Place a question mark after a sentence that asks a question.
A question mark is used after an interrogative sentence.

> Have you considered auditioning for the role in the play?

Rule 3: Place a single exclamation point after a word, a phrase, or a sentence to show emotion.
Multiple exclamation points are incorrect and unnecessary.

> **Unnecessary:** That's great!!!
> **Correct:** That's great!

Rule 4: Use a comma and a connecting word to join the parts of a compound sentence.
A compound sentence is made up of two or more simple sentences. Common connecting words include *and, but, or, nor, for,* and *so.*

> Carlos knocked twice on his friend's front door, **but** no one seemed to be home.

Rule 5: Place commas between items in a series.
Commas should be used to separate three or more words, phrases, or clauses in a series.

> We stuffed twigs, dry leaves, and newspaper scraps in between the firewood before igniting it.

Rule 6: Use commas in large numbers (1,000 and up), but not in years. Commas should be used to distinguish hundreds, thousands, millions, and so on. Commas are not used in years.

> In **2009**, Miley Cyrus's music video for "The Climb" surpassed **64,104,120** views on YouTube.

Rule 7: Use a semicolon to join two or more closely related simple sentences. A semicolon can be used to make a compound sentence without using a connecting word.

> You were absolutely right; that is the cutest cat I've ever seen.

Rule 8: Use apostrophes to show possession. To form the possessive of a singular noun, add an apostrophe and an *s*. To form a possessive of a plural noun ending in *s*, simply add an apostrophe. For plural nouns not ending in *s*, add an apostrophe and an *s*.

> **Singular noun:** Hannah**'s** knowledge of horses is impressive.
> **Plural noun ending in *s*:** The go-carts**'** wheels nearly touched.
> **Plural noun not ending in *s*:** The geese**'s** winter migration started sooner this year.

Rule 9: Use quotation marks to identify words that are spoken and for titles of songs, poems, short stories, and articles. But underline or italicize titles of books, magazines, and newspapers. Periods and commas at the end of the quoted material are placed inside quotation marks.

> "Here goes nothing," said Jaheim.
> Jaheim said, "Here goes nothing."
> "To Build a Fire" is a great short story.
> My sister just finished <u>The Giver</u>.

Rule 10: Use a colon to introduce a list. The colon often comes after summary words such as *the following*.

> My favorite instruments include the following: guitar, piano, and trumpet.

Following Proper Mechanics

The mechanics of writing deal with capitalization, plurals, abbreviations, and spelling. Here are the top 10 rules regarding mechanics.

Rule 1: Capitalize all proper nouns and words used as names.
A proper noun is the name of a particular person, place, thing, or idea.

> **Mark Zuckerberg** is one of the founders of the **Facebook** social media site.

Rule 2: Capitalize titles.
For titles, capitalize all first words, last words, and words in between except articles (*a, an, the*), short prepositions (*of, with, at*), and connecting words (*and, but, or, for, so, yet*). This rule counts for titles of books, newspapers, magazines, poems, plays, songs, articles, movies, artwork, historical documents, and so on.

> An advertisement for *The Phantom of the Opera* appeared in today's *Los Angeles Times*.

Rule 3: Capitalize the names of races, languages, nationalities, and religions, whether these words are used as nouns or adjectives.

> I was surprised to find some great **Egyptian** artwork in **Spain**. Many of the gallery owners spoke **Arabic**.

Rule 4: Capitalize geographic place-names.
Capitalize the names of planets, continents, countries, states, counties, cities, bodies of water, landforms, and public areas.

> The **Appalachian Mountains** run through many states, including **West Virginia** and **New Jersey**.

Rule 5: Form plurals.
Form plurals of most nouns by adding an *s* to the singular form. If the noun ends in *ch, s, sh, x,* or *z,* form plurals by adding *es.* For words ending with a *y* following a consonant, change the *y* to *i* and add *es.*

> Can we cannonball off the diving **boards** to make big **splashes**?
> Some **communities** have **waterslides** in their **pools**.

Rule 6: Use words for numbers under 10.
Numbers one through nine are usually spelled out, while numbers higher than nine are usually written as numerals.

> Christina should make **three** trays of granola bars for our class.
> She has **26** students to feed.

Rule 7: Use a combination of numerals and words for very large numbers.
You may use a combination of words and numerals for numbers in the millions and billions.

> Did you know that the United States makes **$40 billion** a year from exporting food?

Rule 8: Use abbreviations sparingly.
In formal writing, spell out words, except for titles and abbreviations such as these: Mr., Mrs., Ms., Dr., Jr., a.m., p.m.

> I can't wait for my dance lesson with **Ms.** Claiborne at 9:00 **a.m.**

Rule 9: Use *i* before *e*.
When spelling words with an *ie* combination, use *i* before *e* except after *c,* or when sounded like ā as in *eighty* or *freight.*

> To say that you feel **relieved** is to say that a great **weight** has been taken off your shoulders.

Rule 10: Understand the silent *e* rule.
If a word ends with a silent *e,* drop the *e* before adding a suffix that begins with a vowel: blame—blaming; date—dating.

> I have fun **using** virtual reality **gaming** systems.

Understanding Commonly Confused Words

This page and the next will examine 10 sets of commonly confused words. Learning the difference between these words will help you become a careful communicator.

Set 1: bring, take
Bring refers to movement toward the writer or speaker; *take* refers to movement away from the speaker or writer.

> Can you **bring** me a new trash bag? I want to **take** this one out to the dumpster.

Set 2: their, there, they're
Their is a possessive pronoun. *There* is an adverb that tells where. *They're* is the contraction of "they are."

> **They're** ready to deposit **their** donations in the collection box over **there**.

Set 3: to, too, two
To (preposition) indicates direction; it is also used to form an infinitive (*to go, to read*). *Too* (adverb) means "also," "very," or "excessively." *Two* is the number 2.

> I'm not **too** excited **to** go **to** the dentist, because I have **two** cavities.

Set 4: than, then
Than is used in a comparison; *then* refers to time.

> The movie starts later **than** the book sale, so let's go to the bookstore first. **Then** we can go to the movie.

Set 5: it's, its
It's is the contraction of "it is" or "it has." *Its* is the possessive form of "it."

> **It's** going to take a while for my broken arm to regain **its** strength.

Set 6: fewer, less

Fewer refers to countable units; *less* refers to value, degree, or bulk quantity.

> **Fewer** players on the team gives us **less** flexibility during a game.

Set 7: affect, effect

Affect is a verb that means "to influence." As a noun, *effect* means "the result"; as a verb, it means "to bring about."

> The bad special **effects** really negatively **affected** the movie's quality.

Set 8: capital, capitol

Capital can be a noun, referring to a city or money, or it can be an adjective, meaning "major" or "important." *Capitol* always refers to a building.

> Have you visited the **capitol** building in Indianapolis, the **capital** city of Indiana?

Set 9: good, well

Good is always an adjective. *Well* is almost always an adverb; however, when used to indicate a state of health, *well* is an adjective.

> Since you are feeling **well** again, we should celebrate with some yogurt. It's important to take **good** care of yourself.

Set 10: past, passed

Passed is the past tense of the verb "pass." It means "went by" or "gone by." *Past* can be used as a noun ("time gone by"), an adjective ("preceding"), or a preposition ("after" or "beyond").

> The rule was **passed** without any consideration for the lessons of the **past**.

Using Complete Sentences

The next three pages will help you use complete and correct sentences in your communication.

Sentence Basics

A **sentence** is one or more words expressing a complete thought.

> **This book will make you a better learner.**

A sentence must have a **subject** and a **predicate**.

■ The **subject** is the part of the sentence that is doing something or about which something is being said.

> **Learning** is a lifelong journey.

■ The **predicate** is the part of the sentence that says something about the subject.

> Learning **is a lifelong journey.**

The **subject** and **predicate** (the verb) must agree in number.

■ If you use a **singular subject**, you should use a **singular verb**.

> **Pedro learns** a lot from his father.

■ If you use a **plural subject**, you should use a **plural verb**.

> Many **students find** it easy to learn in groups.

■ If the **subject** is a word such as *everything, somebody,* or *anyone,* use a **singular verb**.

> **Everyone finds** it easy to learn from friends.

■ With *all, any, half, most, some,* or *one,* check the noun in the prepositional phrase that comes between the subject and verb. If the noun is plural, use a plural verb. If it is singular, use a singular verb.

> **Some** of my friends **enter** math contests.
>
> **Some** of the math **challenges** even the best students.

Common Sentence Errors

Fragments

A **sentence fragment** is a group of words that is missing a subject, a verb, or both. A fragment does not express a complete thought.

> **Incorrect:** Plays great music. *(missing subject)*
>
> **Correct:** The **disc jockey** plays great music.
>
> **Incorrect:** Once in a while, Keith and Bryan in the park. *(missing verb)*
>
> **Correct:** Once in a while, Keith and Bryan **run** in the park.

Comma Splices

A **comma splice** occurs when two simple sentences are connected with only a comma instead of a comma and a connecting word.

> **Incorrect:** Lisa changed into her uniform, then she entered the gym. *(comma splice)*

A comma splice can be corrected by forming two sentences, by using a semicolon, or by adding a coordinating conjunction.

> **Correct:** Lisa changed into her uniform. Then she entered the gym.
>
> **Correct:** Lisa changed into her uniform; then she entered the gym.
>
> **Correct:** Lisa changed into her uniform, **and** then she entered the gym.

Run-Ons

A **run-on** sentence occurs when two or more simple sentences are connected without punctuation or a connecting word.

> **Incorrect:** It's almost June I can't wait for some free time.
>
> **Correct:** It's almost June. I can't wait for some free time.
>
> **Correct:** It's almost June, and I can't wait for some free time.

Rambling Sentences

A **rambling sentence** occurs when loosely related ideas are included in one long, unfocused sentence. A rambling sentence should be rewritten or rearranged into shorter sentences using appropriate connecting words.

Rambling: Right before we left for our camping trip my mom took our dog to Doggy Day Care and I was in my room frantically searching for my sleeping bag and just then my brother decided to spill his milk all over the kitchen floor and it was complete chaos.

Improved: It was complete chaos right before we left for our camping trip. My mom was dropping our dog off at Doggy Day Care, and I was frantically searching in my room for my sleeping bag. Just then, my brother decided to spill his milk all over the kitchen floor.

Double Subjects

A **double subject** occurs when a pronoun is used immediately after the subject. It is corrected by deleting either the pronoun or subject, but not both.

Incorrect: **Shazam he** always is up to something. *(double subject)*

Correct: **Shazam** is always up to something.

Double Negatives

A **double negative** occurs when two negative words are unintentionally used in the same phrase.

Incorrect: **Don't** let **no** bully bother you. (*Don't* and *no* are both negative.)

Correct: Don't let any bully bother you. (*No* is replaced with the word *any*.)

Conventions Activities

Use these activities to help you review the basic conventions or rules of the language. (See also page 80.)

Making a Connection

Rule 4 on page 184 about compound sentences comes into play in almost everything you write, from a paragraph to a report.

[**Our best advice:** Using compound sentences can make your writing flow smoothly, so be sure to include them often.]

Your Turn

On your own paper, create a compound sentence with each of the following pairs of sentences. Use a comma and the most appropriate connecting word (*and, but, or, for, nor, so, yet*) to form each new sentence. Afterward, compare your work with a partner's.

- Our school has a new computer lab. I get to serve as a lab assistant.
- I usually eat a huge lunch. My stomach starts growling by four o'clock.
- It's always dark when I get up. I still try to run at least five miles.
- Gerald and Frank are sick. I don't have anyone to sit with on the bus.
- My aunt could take me to the museum today. She could take me sometime next week.

A Capital Place

Knowing when to capitalize the names of places may be challenging. There are many kinds of places, from bodies of water (*Colorado River*) to public areas (*Vietnam Memorial*), that can pop up in your writing.

[**Our best advice:** When you're not sure if a place-name should be capitalized, see page 186 and check the dictionary.]

Your Turn

With the help of a partner, write a brief paragraph or story about someone hiking through the Appalachian Mountains. This person must hike through, along, or near at least four or five specific places (states, cities, bodies of water, public areas). Be sure to capitalize the specific names of places. Afterward, share your writing with your classmates.

Partners Working with Pairs

There are many commonly confused words in the English language. Some of them are homonyms, or words that sound the same, such as *you're* and *your*. Others are words that are related in meaning but have their own special uses, such as *fewer* and *less*.

Our best advice: When you're not sure which word is correct, be sure to refer to pages 188–189. Also check the dictionary.

Your Turn

Review "Understanding Commonly Confused Words" on pages 188–189. Then write five or six sentences, using at least one of these words in each sentence. Take turns reading your sentences aloud to a partner. Have the listener (1) write down the correct spelling of any homonyms and (2) write *correct* or *incorrect* for the use of words such as *fewer* or *less*.

Rambling On

Writing that rambles has a breathless quality to it, going on and on without any breaks. Breaking up rambling ideas to form shorter, clear sentences will make the writing easier to follow.

Our best advice: When you revise or edit your writing, always check for rambling ideas.

Your Turn

Rewrite or rearrange the rambling idea that follows. (See page 192.) Afterward, share your writing with a partner.

I went to the doctor last week and when I got there, I had to wait forever to see him and when I finally met with him, he told me to get an x-ray so I had to go to another room and I had to wait there a long time and then I finally had my x-ray and then I went back to my doctor's examining room and he gave me a prescription for my bad cold.

Chapter 13
Improving Study Skills

You may have heard that some people have photographic memories. These people can apparently remember almost everything they read or learn. Wouldn't that be great! Well, according to most experts, having a photographic memory is probably more myth than reality. If some form of this ability does exist, very few people have it.

To be an effective learner, you can't rely on luck or your memory. Instead, you need to learn about and practice effective study and learning skills. These skills include taking effective notes, keeping a learning log, and studying for tests—all covered on the pages that follow.

You will learn . . .

- Taking Classroom Notes
- Using a Learning Log
- Preparing for Tests
- Using Test-Taking Skills
- Answering Objective Questions
- Responding to Prompts

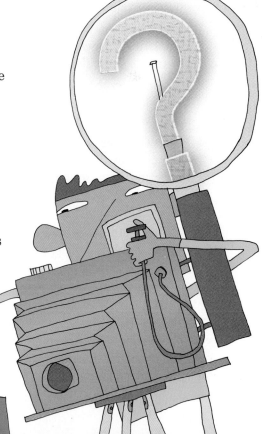

Taking Classroom Notes

Your teachers regularly introduce you to new concepts and subjects. To understand these ideas and put them to good use, you need to practice effective note taking. Use the information below as a guide.

- **Use an effective note-taking format.** A format is a plan or method of organization.

- **Label your notes** at the top of the page with the topic and date. Also number the pages to keep information in good order.

- **Record important information** that your teacher puts on the board.

- **Practice good listening skills** during discussions and lectures. Be alert for clues that important information is coming up— "There are four types of . . ." or "Please remember that . . ."

- **Number information** that is presented in steps.

- **Pay special attention to new vocabulary words.** Guess on the spelling, if you're not sure. Circle words as a reminder to check the spellings and definitions later.

- **Write down key words or phrases.** If you try to write complete sentences, you may not be able to keep up. Also try to use your own words as much as possible.

- **Use pictures, abbreviations, and your personal shorthand** to help you record important information. (Use + for "and," *u* for "you," and so on.)

- **Review your notes after class** and continue to review them from time to time. During your review, highlight or mark important facts and details.

In Focus

If you don't take complete notes, by the end of class, you may have forgotten as much as half of the information presented. After a few weeks, you may have forgotten 80 percent or even more!

Your Turn

On a scale of 1, meaning "ineffective," to 10, meaning "very effective," rate your note-taking skills. Are your notes organized? Are they clear? Do they help you to complete assignments and study the material? Explain your rating in a brief paragraph.

Sample Note Page

Keep your notes in a notebook or a binder. Use two-thirds of the page for your actual notes and the rest of the page for comments, questions, definitions, and extra information.

Algae	Nov. 3	p. 14

+ plant-like, single-celled organisms
  (protists)
+ includes a nucleus
+ don't belong to animal, plant,
  or fungi kingdom
+ often live in water
+ get energy from sunlight
    – contain chlorophyll to collect the
      sun's energy and release oxygen
      (photosynthesis)
    – organisms that use photosynthesis
      are important source of food

What is a nucleus?

flagella

cell wall

cell membrane

chloroplast
(traps
energy from
sunlight)

nucleus

Find out what each part does.

+ types of algae   single cell
– diatom (have chloroplasts)
– volvox (seaweed), multi-celled

Are there only two types?

Using a Learning Log

Taking good notes helps you *remember* important concepts covered in class, while keeping a learning log helps you *understand* the information better. A learning log is a special part of your class notebook reserved for writing about your course work.

- **Label and date your entries** to keep track of your writing.
- **Keep a regular writing schedule,** but write more often or for a longer time when you are studying something challenging.
- **Freely explore your thoughts and feelings.** Try writing nonstop for 3 to 5 minutes at a time.
  - Make connections in your writing: How do new ideas relate to what you already know?
  - Question what you are learning.
  - Argue for or against ideas or beliefs discussed in class.
  - Pay special attention to ideas that confuse you. Writing about them will help you understand them better.
- **Review your writing** to see how it has helped you better understand the material and concepts covered in class.

Specific Learning-Log Strategies

Here are four ways to write in your learning log.

- **Predicting** In your writing, predict what you think will happen next because of the new ideas or concepts you have learned about.
- **Summing Up** Summarize what was covered in a lesson or class. Consider its importance, value, and meaning.
- **Question of the Day** Try to answer a question such as "What if?" or "Why?" about a subject you are studying.
- **Dialoguing** Create a conversation between you and another person about a subject you are studying.

Your Turn

Write a learning-log entry about something that you have learned so far in this book. Be sure to review the guidelines above before you get started.

Learning-Log Entry

A student wrote the entry below after a class discussion on algae. In her writing, she explored her thoughts and feelings about the subject.

Algae   Nov. 4   p. 8

It's hard to think of something that is alive but not part of the animal, plant, or fungi kingdoms. How can that be? From the slides we saw, I'd call them plants, at least some of them. Seaweed is a type of algae, and it sure looks like a plant to me. Mr. Alvarez called them leftovers because they don't fit anywhere.

Algae may be way down on the food chain, but it is still important because it is a food source and provides energy. Plants do that, too. Hmm.

One slide showed that algae contains chlorophyll, and I know all about that. My mom makes me eat celery because it contains chlorophyll. She heard from my sister that chlorophyll is healthy, so we eat a lot of green food. Thanks, Sasha.

Algae, or at least some of it, is plankton because it floats in water and turns sunlight into energy (photosynthesis). Mr. Alvarez said that plankton makes most of the oxygen that animals breathe. So algae may be a tiny "leftover," but it is big in terms of its value.

Preparing for Tests

Everyone has different feelings about tests. Suzanne Farrell, a famous ballerina, says that she loved tests because they were another form of competition. Bruce Jenner, a gold-medal track star, still has nightmares about them. No matter how you feel about tests, they are a fact of school life. The next few pages will show you how to prepare for them.

Getting Started

Know what topics or information the test will cover.

Know what form the test will take *(multiple choice, short answer, true/false, essay)*.

Getting Organized

Make a list of everything that will be covered on the test.

Organize your notes and handouts accordingly.

Gather any notes that you may have missed.

Note the pages in your textbook that you need to review.

Getting to Work

Skim all of the material to get the big picture.

Write down questions that you may want to ask your teacher.

Continue to review the material.

Use study aids such as diagrams or flash cards.

Explain things out loud if that helps you remember.

Study the material with a classmate or family member.

 Focus

To remember a list of important terms, think of a special word or sentence based on the terms. For example, the word **homes** is spelled with the first letter of each of the Great Lakes—**Huron, Ontario, Michigan, Erie,** and **Superior.** (See pages 34–35.)

Using Test-Taking Skills

Make a plan for taking each of your tests. The suggestions below can help.

Before . . .

Come prepared with the right materials.

Listen carefully to your teacher's directions.

During . . .

Skim the test to see what you have to do.

Begin the test, following the directions for each section.

Watch for key words—*always, only, all, never*—in the questions.

Answer the questions you are sure of; then move on to the ones that you are not sure of.

Check with your teacher if you have any questions about the directions you have been given.

After . . .

Double-check your work before turning in your test.

Your Turn

Write down one or two problems that you have had with tests. Then write down two or three of the strategies mentioned above that you will try for your next test. Share your thoughts with your classmates.

Answering Objective Questions

Objective (factual) questions on tests ask for specific responses—true or false, matching, multiple choice, or fill in the blank. The information that follows will help you answer objective questions.

True or False

On this type of test, you must decide if a statement is either true or false.

- **Read each statement carefully.** If any part is untrue, then the entire statement is false.
- **Watch for key words** such as *all, every, always,* and *never.* Not many things are always true or never true.

> _False_ Every earthquake occurs along the borders of tectonic plates.
>
> *(Some earthquakes occur within tectonic plates.)*

- **Also watch for words that mean "not."** Be sure you understand how the word is used in the statement.

> _False_ You can't have a major earthquake if patches of rock move a few meters.
>
> *(A meter of shift can cause a major earthquake.)*

Matching

For matching questions, connect a word or phrase in one list to a word or phrase in a second list.

- **Read the directions carefully** so you know if answer choices can be used more than once, or if some may not be used at all.
- **Scan both lists before answering.**

> **1.** _b_ normal faults   **a.** the patch of rock moves up
> **2.** _a_ reverse faults   **b.** the patch of rock moves down
> **3.** _c_ strike-slip faults   **c.** the patch of rock moves sideways

Multiple Choice

For multiple-choice questions, decide which of several answers is correct.

- ■ **Watch for special answers** that may tell you all or none of the responses are correct.

> Which of the following is true about energy from earthquakes?
> **a.** It travels in one direction.
> **b.** It travels up.
> **c.** It travels down.
> **d.** none of the above

- ■ **Watch for words such as *except*,** which can completely change the question.

> These are recognized movements along fault lines except for . . .
> **a.** The rocks may slide along constantly.
> **b.** The rocks may snag.
> **c.** The rocks may melt from intense heat.
> **d.** The rocks may bend from stress.

Fill in the Blank

For fill-in-the-blank questions, write the missing words in sentences or paragraphs.

- ■ **Watch for the number of blanks.** Each one stands for one word or answer.

> The energy produced by an earthquake travels as ___seismic___ ___waves___.
> The best known fault is the ___San___ ___Andreas___ Fault in California.

- ■ **Watch for an article preceding the blank.** The article *an* tells you the word that follows should begin with a vowel sound. The article *a* tells you the word should begin with a consonant sound.

> Stress along a ___plate___ can cause rocks to break apart.

Responding to Prompts

Some tests ask you to respond to a prompt (or answer an essay question) by writing a paragraph or short essay in a limited amount of time.

A prompt includes three parts that will guide your writing. It will (1) give background information about a topic, (2) tell you what form of writing to use, and (3) name the purpose of your writing. Here's a sample prompt.

Sample Prompt

> We've studied earthquakes in chapter 4 and watched a documentary about them. In an expository paragraph, describe the occurrence of an earthquake. Consider *why, how,* and *where* they usually occur.

Your Turn

Name the three parts of this writing prompt.

Purpose Words

To know what to do in your response, you need to identify the purpose word in the prompt. In the prompt above, you are asked to *describe* something. Here is a list of common purpose words.

Compare: Show how two things are alike and different.

Contrast: Show how things are different.

Define: Tell what a word or subject means, what category it belongs to, or what it is used for.

Describe: Identify what something or someone looks like, sounds like, feels like, and so on.

Evaluate: Give your viewpoint about the value of something.

Explain: Show how something works or how something happened.

Persuade: Convince the reader to agree with your viewpoint or opinion.

Prove: Show that something is true or false, strong or weak, and so on.

Summarize: Present the main points in a clear, concise form.

Planning and Writing a Response

Even in a test situation, when time is short, responding to a prompt requires planning:

- **Follow all of the directions supplied by your teacher.** (Notice how much time you have to write your answer.)

- **Consider the parts of the prompt.** You need to know the topic, the form, and the purpose of your writing. (See the previous page.)

- **Write a topic sentence** or a thesis statement for your response, depending on whether you are writing a paragraph or a brief essay. Here is an example topic sentence for a response to the prompt on the previous page.

> An earthquake is the sudden shaking of the ground along a fault.

- **Make a quick list of supporting ideas.**

> – faults along tectonic plates
> – pieces of rocks in plates stick or snag
> – the stress builds and creates sudden movement
> – size depends on stress and distance of movement
> – Pacific Rim susceptible

- **Write your response,** starting with your topic sentence. Then include the ideas from your quick list. Add details as needed. End with a closing sentence.

- **Reserve time to review your response** to make sure that your ideas are clear and accurate.

In Focus

If you have 40 minutes to complete a response, consider this time schedule: 5 minutes for planning, 25–30 minutes for writing, and 5–10 minutes for reviewing.

Sample Response

The following response satisfies the prompt's three-part requirement by addressing the topic (how earthquakes occur), using the right form (an expository paragraph), and fulfilling the purpose (describing).

Prompt

We studied earthquakes in chapter 4 and watched a documentary about them. In an expository paragraph, describe the occurrence of an earthquake. Consider *why*, *how*, and *where* they usually occur.

Response

Topic sentence

Body (supporting) sentences

Closing sentence

An earthquake is the sudden shaking of the ground along a fault. Faults are usually found along the boundaries of tectonic plates, so that is where most earthquakes happen. Sometimes, though, earthquakes will also occur within tectonic plates. The earth's crust is made up of many tectonic plates, which are large and small patches of rock that fit together like a puzzle. When the pieces of rock within these plates stick or snag along a fault, they create stress. As this stress increases, the rocks can move because they are brittle. If this movement is sudden, an earthquake can occur. The size of an earthquake depends on the amount of stress that occurs and the distance that the pieces of rock move along the fault. People living along the plates that outline the Pacific Rim experience most of the world's earthquakes. Unfortunately, parts of the Pacific Rim, including California, are densely populated.

Your Turn

Plan and write a response to a prompt supplied by your teacher.

Study-Skills Activities

Use these activities to practice different study skills and become comfortable using them.

Comparing Notes

In the introduction to this chapter, you were reminded that you can't always rely on your memory to keep the information you are given in class. You need to take effective notes to keep track of the new material that you are introduced to.

> **Our best advice:** Become a regular note taker, using an effective method such as the one shown on page 197. Keep your notes in a class notebook rather than on individual sheets of paper, and record your notes neatly so that you can review them later on.

Your Turn

Team up with a partner for this activity. Select one page from a textbook that each of you will read and take notes on. Afterward, compare notes to see what each of you included.

Following a Lecture or Presentation

Taking notes during a lecture or presentation requires careful listening. And remember that your teacher won't necessarily write every important fact and detail on the board during the lecture.

> **Our best advice:** Practice good listening skills during lectures, presentations, and discussions. Also become skilled at knowing which facts and details to write down in the simplest way. (See page 196.)

Your Turn

Your teacher will lecture for two or three minutes about a topic, perhaps writing a few things on the board. Take notes as he or she goes along. Then your teacher will stop, erase the board, and choose you or one of your classmates to come to the front of the class and repeat the lecture you've just heard. If you are chosen, use your notes as a guide.

Logging On

The more you use new information, the better. Taking notes is a good first step, and writing about the new information in a learning log is an effective next step. In a learning log, you explore your thoughts and feelings about the new information.

Our best advice: Set aside part of your classroom notebook for learning-log entries. Then write in it about your course work for 5 to 10 minutes, every day or every other day. React to the notes you took or to ideas that were discussed in class.

Your Turn

Write learning-log entries about one of your classes for a week. Explore your thoughts about new information, class discussions, class work, and assignments. Consider what you learned, what questions you have, and what interests you the most. (See pages 198–199.)

Working with Prompts

Responding to a prompt may be the most challenging part of any test you take. Instead of answering a true/false or multiple-choice question, you must share your thoughts in a piece of writing. This requires an understanding of (1) the subject, (2) the form of the response, and (3) the purpose.

Our best advice: Practice responding to prompts until you are comfortable with this type of writing. To do this, write your own prompts, or questions, about a subject you are studying. Then respond to them within a limited amount of time. (See page 205.)

Your Turn

Select three purpose words from the list on page 204. For each word, write a prompt, or question, about something you are studying in one of your classes. Remember to include the three main parts in each prompt. Exchange prompts with a classmate and practice writing responses.

Chapter 14
Succeeding in School

Succeeding in school is important. Each accomplishment now is a stepping-stone to success in the future—at home and in your community and workplace.

To succeed, you'll need a positive attitude, good planning skills, and the desire to do well. We believe you can do this. Being serious about learning and working at it gives you a very good chance of succeeding in school. And the pages that follow will help you achieve this important goal.

You will learn . . .

- Getting Ready to Learn
- Creating a Positive Attitude
- Managing Stress
- Setting Goals
- Planning Your Time
- Completing Assignments

Getting Ready to Learn

To succeed in school, you have to be ready to learn. These guidelines will show you how.

- **Be alert.** Studies show that teenagers need eight or nine hours of sleep each night. With the proper sleep, you'll be alert. Without it, you won't be able to concentrate.
- **Be healthy.** Eating a healthy diet also keeps you alert and ready to learn. Say yes to healthy foods and no to high-fat munchies and sweets.
- **Be active.** Your brain needs oxygen to perform well. After 15 to 20 minutes of sitting, get up and move around to increase the blood flow to your brain.
- **Be positive.** Your best learning happens when you stop complaining and take an interest in your subjects. You don't accomplish much if you're in a bad mood or upset about something. (See page 212.)
- **Be social.** It's natural to interact with other people. So form groups to review for tests or develop projects. Learning is more fun when you do it with other people.
- **Be relaxed.** You'll learn the most when you are relaxed and stress free, yet still focused on the task in front of you. (See page 213.)

In Focus

There are many ways to learn. Reading, reviewing notes, and practicing math problems are common learning strategies. You can also try something new, like sketching your thoughts about a topic or exploring your feelings in a learning log. (See page 199.) Try teaming up with your classmates to debate the pros and cons of a topic, act out a concept, and so on.

Your Turn

Answer the following questions about your learning style: When and where do you do your best learning? What learning strategies work best for you? What new strategies would you like to try? Afterward, share your answers with your classmates.

Reasons for Learning

Why does learning take place in the first place? Here are four basic reasons.

1. **Learning drives you.** You just naturally seek out new information. New sights, sounds, smells, and ideas—they all interest you because you have a built-in need to know.

2. **Learning defines you.** New experiences, thoughts, and feelings add to your personal knowledge bank. The more deposits that you make in this bank, the more interesting and informed you become.

3. **Learning helps you.** Effective learning helps you solve problems, make decisions, build arguments, and enjoy life both in and out of school.

4. **Learning satisfies you.** Learning makes school, sports, hobbies, and friendships more rewarding and fun.

A Well-Prepared Learner

Carlos loves to discuss new ideas and solve problems. He plans interesting projects and seems to know a lot. How does he do it? Carlos is a well-prepared learner. He is . . .

Patient: Carlos knows that problems can be complicated. If he can't solve a problem right away, he doesn't give up.

Curious: Carlos often asks "Why?" or "What if?" And he enjoys surprises and making discoveries.

Logical: Carlos is able to think critically and logically about a subject. (See pages 13–30.)

Creative: Carlos can use his imagination to think in new ways. (See pages 31–48.)

Thorough: Carlos always looks for answers to questions he has about new subjects.

Careful: Carlos looks for true, accurate information. He may wonder who came up with a certain idea or question the accuracy of a particular Web site.

Focused: When Carlos needs to concentrate, he finds a quiet, well-lighted space to do his work.

Creating a Positive Attitude

The following tips will help you approach school in a positive way.

- **Be aware of your attitude.** Most people are not automatically positive; they have to work at it.
- **Decide what you want to achieve.** Having a clear goal will help you become and remain positive. (See page 214.)
- **Work hard, have fun, and be energized.** It is hard to be positive if you don't enjoy what you are doing.
- **Stay away from bad influences,** even if those "influences" are sometimes your friends.
- **Keep on course.** And try to find ways to overcome roadblocks. (See the story below.)
- **Expect to have things change.** Then be sure to adjust your goal or plan as needed.

A Positive Story

Huang NaiHui is the owner of three floral shops, an inspirational speaker, and a very charitable person. By all accounts, he is a success story, but once you learn about his background, you realize how special he really is.

Huang NaiHui was born in Taipe, Taiwan, in 1964, and he has been partially paralyzed since an early age. As a young child, he was abandoned by his immediate family and lived with his grandmother in the family's ancestral home. He didn't start school until he was 13 and found it very difficult to learn. Still, he continued to go to school.

When Huang NaiHui turned 24, tragedy stuck yet again because his grandmother died. Then his father told him to leave the ancestral home.

But that didn't stop Huang NaiHui. He built up his flower business and eventually became a spokesperson for those with handicaps. Today, he speaks all over the world about his life. Huang NaiHui succeeded because of hard work and a positive attitude.

Your Turn

Think of someone you know who has a positive attitude about life. How has this attitude helped the person? How does she or he serve as a model for other people? Share your thoughts with your classmates.

Managing Stress

Josie will be moving to a new city in three weeks. She's going to leave her school, lose her close friends, and never again play volleyball for the Comets. With all of this in mind, she's having a hard time concentrating in class.

DeWayne tried out for the school musical and really surprised himself by earning one of the lead roles. While that is good news, it also means that he'll be singing onstage for a large audience. The butterflies in his stomach are in full flutter.

Gerald promised his grandmother he would raise his math grade. He knows that she will be really disappointed if he doesn't keep his promise, but so far he hasn't tried to improve his grade. Every time he thinks about the situation, his confidence takes a hit.

What do these three students have in common? Clearly, they are all under stress. Stress produces different symptoms. Some people feel nervous, others get headaches, and still others may eat too much or too little.

Possible Approaches

Once you identify the cause of your stress, plan on a way to reduce it. Here are three possibilities:

Ask for help. Talk about the situation with someone you trust.

Step away from the problem. Going to a movie, reading a good book, exercising, or connecting with friends can relieve stress and help you address the problem more effectively.

Solve the problem. Addressing the source of the problem is the best way to deal with stress. For example, moving may be difficult for Josie, but hoping for the best in her new school and focusing on the school work in front of her, something she can still control, will greatly reduce her stress.

Your Turn

Team up with a partner and discuss what advice you would give to DeWayne and Gerald to relieve their stress.

Setting Goals

How can you complete excellent projects or improve an athletic skill? Start by setting goals. (See also pages 256–257.)

Working on Long-Term Goals

- **Know your limits.** Are you able to compose a complete rock opera, or wipe out world hunger? Probably not, but you can write some of your own music. And you can help organize a food drive in your community.
- **Prepare well.** Schedule specific times to work on your project or goal and stick to it. Reflect on your progress by writing about your experiences and work.
- **Keep on task.** Take the small steps as well as the big steps along the way. Every purposeful action can contribute to achieving your goal.
- **Adjust your goals as needed.** If you experience problems, be flexible. You may find that writing music is harder than you first thought, or that organizing a food drive is too challenging. When it is necessary, adjust your goals.
- **Learn from each project.** Planning and working on a project can be just as rewarding as reaching your goal. So dedicate yourself to enjoying the whole process—even the setbacks.

Getting Started

Kirk wants to improve his high jump. Here is part of his plan for reaching that goal.

Main Goal: Jump 5' 4" this track season
- set up a training schedule
- get Coach Smith's help to improve my strength and flexibility
- watch videos of my jumping technique
- read about great jumpers
- keep track of my progress

Your Turn

Identify a goal for yourself. Then make a brief plan, listing things you will do to meet the goal.

Planning Your Time

To meet important goals, you need to use your time wisely. This skill is called "time management," and planning and scheduling are important parts of it. (See also page 258.)

A weekly planner can help you make the best use of your time. Here is part of Kirk's preseason training plan for improving his high jump.

Weekly Planner

Day/Date	Training	Progress	Diet
Monday 2/6 a.m. p.m.	run 2 miles before school weight training: leg lifts (25 lbs) squats (50 lbs)	time: number:	Breakfast: peanut butter and banana Lunch: lean meat sandwiches and fruit Dinner: balanced meal Snacks: nuts and smoothies
Tuesday 2/7 a.m. p.m.	stretching exercises (from Coach Smith) flexibility training (from Coach Smith)		Add carbs to dinner for next day's run.

In Focus

Think carefully about each activity before you put it into your schedule. Everything that you do should point toward your goal. (Kirk would need to stay in touch with his coach to make sure that his plan is working.)

Completing Assignments

Completing assignments on time and in good order is an important part of being a successful student. Organizing your assignments and resisting the temptation to procrastinate, or put things off, will help you succeed.

Being Prepared

- **Understand the work.** What is the purpose of the assignment? What must you do? When is it due?
- **Determine how much time you will need** to complete the assignment.
- **Select the best spot to do your work**—the library, study hall, or home.
- **Collect the necessary materials**—pen, paper, laptop, and dictionary.

 Focus

You've heard that schoolwork should be a priority, but what's a priority? Notice the root word *prior,* which means "before." Making schoolwork a priority means putting it before other things—first on your list.

Working Smart

- **Review all of the directions** to make sure you understand everything.
- **Take breaks** as you need to when working on an assignment, but keep them short. If you're working at home, ask your family to help you create a private space so that you can concentrate.
- **Keep a list of any questions or concerns you have.** Then ask your teacher about them and get back to work.
- **Use good reading, note-taking, and studying strategies.** (See pages 157–168 and 195–208.)
- **Turn in your assignments on time.** And be sure that your work is neat and accurate.
- **Welcome any suggestions or advice** from your teacher for future assignments.

Your Turn

In a brief paragraph, describe your work habits: Share how, when, and where you usually do your homework.

School-Success Activities

The next two pages provide activities that will prepare you to succeed in school and beyond. Once you try them, think of other activities for additional practice.

Stress-Free Learning

Some learning situations are naturally more stressful than others. Working on a science project, for example, may produce more tense moments than working with a group of friends to assemble playground equipment for a community club.

Our best advice: You will do your best learning when stress is not a factor, or when it is managed effectively. (See page 213.)

Your Turn

Think of what stresses you. Make a chart listing stressors in the left column and solutions in the right column. Employ some of your solutions.

Stressors	Solutions
Noise	MP3 player
Tests	Study ahead
Hunger	Eat breakfast

Planning for Today

You have a full day of classes, from science to social studies. Setting goals for each class may help you do your best work.

Our best advice: Don't be a passive learner (someone not actively involved) in your classes. Instead, plan what you want to accomplish in each class.

Your Turn

Create a two-column chart in your notebook. In the first column, list the classes you are now taking. In the second column, list one goal for each class. For example, in math, your goal could be to ask for help whenever you don't understand a new concept or formula. Then use this chart as a learning guide for the semester.

Planning Way Ahead

There are many exciting career choices ahead for you in a variety of different fields—including science, math, engineering, and education. And, as technology advances, there will be even more career choices in the years to come.

Our best advice: It's never too early to think about careers that interest you, and what you can do now to prepare for them. In fact, career planning (or dreaming) can make learning more exciting and meaningful for you right now!

Your Turn

Create a two-column chart in your notebook. In the first column, list three or four careers that interest you. In the second column, list one thing that you could do right now to prepare for each one. For example, if you're interested in writing plays or acting, you could get involved in your school's drama program. Afterward, share your chart with your classmates.

Introducing . . .

Learning how other people have succeeded may encourage you to set goals for yourself. As you have learned in this chapter, planning and hard work are necessary for success. What do you think successful people have done to become so successful?

Our best advice: Learn as much as you can about successful people, especially people you admire in fields that interest you, such as science, medicine, technology, government, music, or sports.

Your Turn

Choose a successful person (famous or not so famous) to research. Consider the following questions to learn how this person achieved his or her goals: What triggered this person's interest and why? What challenges did he or she face? Who helped this person? What surprises or impresses you about his or her story? Afterward, present your findings to your classmates.

Chapter 15
Succeeding in the Workplace

You probably have already mowed lawns, vacuumed carpets, babysat, and perhaps helped out in a family-owned business or on your family's farm. Once you turn 14, however, you can apply for other kinds of jobs.

This chapter covers the basics of entering the workplace. You'll be using critical and creative thinking and be called on to collaborate and communicate. Follow the tips in this chapter to smooth your launch into the world of work.

You will learn . . .

- Child-Labor Laws
- Finding Job Opportunities
- Completing a Job Application
- Preparing for a Job Interview
- Developing Positive Work Habits
- Understanding Banking
- Creating a Business Idea

Understanding Child-Labor Laws

Before you begin looking for a job, you need to understand the laws meant to protect you from unfair and unsafe working conditions. Here is a summary of the federal child-labor laws.

Summary of Federal Child-Labor Laws*

The following regulations apply to nonfarm jobs and jobs for businesses that are not family owned.

1. **No hazardous work:** No one under the age of 18 can work in jobs deemed hazardous by the U.S. Secretary of Labor. Hazardous jobs include mining, working with heavy machinery, and so on.

2. **No workers under 14 years of age:** Those under the age of 14 are not allowed to hold jobs.

3. **Workers 14-15 years of age:**

   During School Year
   - Can work up to 3 hours on a school day
   - Can work up to 18 hours per week
   - Cannot work after 7:00 p.m.

   During Summer
   - Can work up to 8 hours per day
   - Can work up to 40 hours per week
   - Cannot work later than 9:00 p.m.

   > **Note:** Some states also require workers under 18 years old to have employment/age certificates. Check with your state's department of labor.

4. **Workers 16-17 years of age:** Can work unlimited hours per week.

5. **Workers 18 years of age and older:** Those over 17 years of age are not covered by child-labor laws.

* **Note: This information does not constitute legal counsel. Also note that your state may have stricter rules.**

Your Turn

For the exact language of these laws, go to the Web site for the United States Department of Labor and the Web site for your state's department of labor.

Finding Job Opportunities

Some people approach job searching with dread. Instead, try to think of a job search as a chance to explore opportunities. It's fun to imagine yourself working in different environments with different people.

Finding Opportunities

When you look for a job, check some or all of the following sources.

1. **Recommendations:** Ask family members and friends for ideas about good places to work. Also ask favorite teachers and neighbors if they know of anyone who is hiring.
2. **Favorite Places:** Think of places you like to be—movie theaters, ice-cream parlors, restaurants, camps, parks, stores, swimming pools—and list them as places you might work.
3. **Chamber of Commerce:** Many communities have chambers of commerce—associations of local businesses. Check with your local chamber of commerce about job openings for younger workers.
4. **Want Ads:** Check out local newspapers to see which companies are advertising for help. You can also search online, but make sure to check with your parent or guardian before pursuing any such opportunities.
5. **Help-Wanted Signs:** Look in shop windows for help-wanted signs.
6. **Community Bulletin Boards:** Grocery stores often have bulletin boards where people advertise events, offer products and services, and sometimes announce job openings.

Your Turn

Search one or more of the sources listed above and create a list of jobs that interest you. Then choose two or three jobs that you would like to consider more carefully.

Comparing Opportunities

As any adult will tell you, not all jobs are created equally. Once you have listed a few jobs that interest you, do a little research about each one. A gathering grid can help you compare different jobs.

Sample Gathering Grid

Jobs	Pay	Hours/ Week	Getting There	Training	Fun/ Friends
newspaper delivery	minimum	4-8	walk/ wagon	none needed	not fun/ alone
grocery bagger	minimum	up to 18	walk	little	fun if I like other people
busing/ dishwashing	minimum	up to 29	bike	some	not fun unless I like the people
lifeguard	minimum + $1	up to 40	ride in car	need lifesaving class	fun
movie theater usher	minimum	up to 18	ride in car	little	fun
babysitting	varies	varies	varies	little	depends

Your Turn

Make a gathering grid like the one above to compare the different jobs you are interested in. Research each position and fill in the grid with complete information. Then choose one or more jobs that you would like to apply for.

Completing a Job Application

Once you have found the job you'd like to have, you'll need to get an application form from the employer.

Tips for Completing Applications

1. Ask your parent or guardian for permission and help.

2. Photocopy the application so that you can do a rough copy first.

3. Gather the information.

4. Carefully read the directions and ask for help if you don't understand.

5. Complete the whole application.

6. Write NA if a part does not apply.

7. Check your work.

8. Create a clean, legible final draft to hand in.

APPLICATION FOR EMPLOYMENT

PERSONAL INFORMATION

NAME _Jeremy Williamson_   SOCIAL SECURITY NUMBER _368-21-XXXX_

ADDRESS _361 West Robinson Road, Elkhorn, WI 53200_

PHONE _(262) 555-3821_   ARE YOU 18 YEARS OR OLDER? Yes ☐ No ☑

EMPLOYMENT DESIRED

POSITION _Theater Usher_   DATE YOU CAN START _01/22/11_   SALARY DESIRED _$8.50_

CURRENT EMPLOYER _Elkhorn Media, Paper Deliverer_   MAY WE CONTACT YOUR EMPLOYER? Yes ☑ No ☐

EDUCATION	NAME AND LOCATION	YEARS	GRADUATE?
GRADE SCHOOL	Cooper School, Elkhorn	2003-2009	Yes
MIDDLE SCHOOL	Randall School, Elkhorn	2009-2011	Soon
HIGH SCHOOL	NA		
COLLEGE	NA		

FORMER EMPLOYERS (START WITH THE LAST ONE)

MONTH/YEAR FROM _____ TO _____	NAME AND ADDRESS/SALARY	POSITION	WHY LEFT?
	NA		
MONTH/YEAR FROM _____ TO _____	NA		

REFERENCES NAME THREE NONRELATIVES YOU HAVE KNOWN AT LEAST 1 YEAR.

NAME	ADDRESS	BUSINESS	YEARS
1. Jennie Hals	238 Pine, Elkhorn	Piano Instr.	5
2. David Johnson	1415 Maple Dr., Elkhorn	Pastor	3
3. Terry Lemon	3185 Oak, Elkhorn	Soccer Coach	2

SIGNATURE OF APPLICANT _Jeremy Williamson_   DATE _01/20/11_

Your Turn

Ask for a job application from the place where you would like to work. Follow the tips above as you complete the application form.

Preparing for a Job Interview

After you apply for a job, you may be called in for an interview. Here are some key interview tips.

Before . . .

- **Do your homework.** Research the company or organization. What do they do or sell? What is their goal or mission?
- **Prepare answers** for three key questions: Why are you interested in the job? What makes you qualified for the job? How can you help the company or organization?
- **Practice answering** interview questions with a friend or relative.
- **Dress appropriately.** Your attire should be conservative, even if everyone at the company dresses casually. Wear clean and ironed clothes—no jeans or T-shirts.
- **Show up on time.** Arriving late will make a bad first impression. Show up 5–10 minutes before the time of your interview.

During . . .

- **Greet the interviewer** with enthusiasm and shake her or his hand.
- **Be polite and courteous** throughout the interview.
- **Be yourself.** Show off the strengths of your personality.
- **Answer questions confidently.** Sit up straight and look the interviewer in the eyes. If you don't understand a question, politely ask the interviewer to state it in a different way.
- **Don't be afraid to ask questions** about the company and job.
- **Thank the interviewer** when the interview is over.

After . . .

- **Follow up** on the day after by sending a friendly e-mail or handwritten note to the interviewer. Thank him or her for the opportunity to meet and restate your interest in the job.
- **Call back** after a week if you haven't heard a final decision.

Your Turn

Practice interviewing by role-playing, asking a partner to act as the owner of the business. Afterward, review this page together and discuss the experience. What went well? How could you improve your interview skills?

Developing Positive Work Habits

Once you get a job, it's important to do the job well and get along with others. It all comes down to respect. Follow these tips.

Positive Work Habits

Respect your . . .

- **organization,** understanding the company's goals and working to achieve them.
- **boss,** knowing who the person is and following her or his directions.
- **coworkers,** treating them well and working together with them.
- **customers,** providing them the best products and services you can.
- **self,** dressing appropriately and conducting yourself professionally.
- **job,** following the schedule, arriving on time, and working hard.
- **career,** proving your value and taking on new challenges.

Resolving Conflicts

If you develop the work habits above, you will probably have very few problems at work. Sometimes, though, conflicts may arise between you and someone else. Here are four options for handling these conflicts:

- **Defer,** letting the other person have his or her way
- **Negotiate,** working out an arrangement in which you both give up something
- **Cooperate,** working out a way that you can help each other
- **Mediate,** having another trusted person help resolve the conflict

Every conflict is unique. Choose carefully when deciding how to resolve the issue, always keeping the company's and the other person's best interests in mind.

Your Turn

Which of the positive work habits do you have? Which do you need?

Understanding Banking

Once you are earning money on a regular basis, you'll probably want to open a bank account. Here are the basics of banking.

Types of Bank Accounts

There are two basic types of bank accounts: checking accounts and savings accounts.

- **Checking accounts** allow you to write checks or use a debit card to withdraw your money. Some checking accounts charge for their services and may also require a minimum balance.
- **Savings accounts** store money in a way that is less easy to access. You must visit the bank, access the account online, or do transactions over the phone. Savings accounts may also require a minimum balance. However, savings accounts are usually free and offer interest.

Banking Terms

When you open a bank account, you'll hear some terminology that you might not recognize. Here are quick definitions of the basic terms.

- A **deposit** is an amount of money put into your account.
- A **withdrawal** is an amount of money taken out of your account.
- The **balance** is the amount of money that is in your account.
- **Interest** is a percentage that your account balance earns.
- **Minimum balance** is the smallest amount of money an account can have to remain open and to avoid penalties.
- A **penalty** is a payment charged if you go below your minimum balance, make too many withdrawals from a savings account, or otherwise don't follow established rules.
- An **overdraft** occurs when you write a check but don't have the money in the account to cover it.
- A **statement** is a list of deposits, withdrawals, balances, and penalties for a certain period (usually a month). The statement may come in the mail or online.

Your Turn

If you would like to open a bank account, speak to your parent or guardian about the possibility. Show her or him this material and discuss options.

Opening a Bank Account

To set up a bank account, follow these steps.

1. **Get permission.** Ask your parent or guardian if you can open a bank account. You probably will need to use the same bank that your parent or guardian uses.
2. **Research options.** Research the types of accounts available. A gathering grid can help you compare different accounts. Choose the best type for you.

Account	Location	Monthly Fees	Minimum Balance	Interest	Overdraft Fee	Debit Card
Free Checking	L&M Bank	$0	$100	None	$30	Yes
High-Yield Checking	L&M Bank	$8.95	$500	0.5%	$30	Yes
Savings	L&M Bank	$0	$300	0.1%	None	No

3. **Sign up and deposit.** Go to the bank with your parent or guardian, fill out the application for an account, and make your first deposit in the account.
4. **Maintain the account.** Check your account online or in monthly statements mailed to you. Make sure deposits and withdrawals are accurate, and check the balance frequently so that you know how much money you have.

Understanding Checks and Debit Cards

A check is a slip of paper that provides your account information, tells how much you want to pay someone, and includes your signature for the amount. Once very common, checks are now being replaced by debit cards and online billing. A debit card is a plastic card that you can use like a credit card to access your checking account.

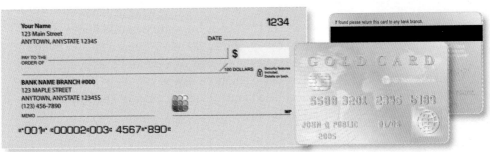

Creating a Business Idea

Many billionaires like Bill Gates and Mark Zuckerberg were young when they started their own businesses. You may not be ready to create the next Microsoft or Facebook, but you can create your own business opportunities. These pages can get you started.

Identifying a Need

Most businesses have the goal of making money, and the best way to make money is to provide a product or service that people need. The pyramid to the right, developed by Abraham Maslow, shows all of the different needs that people have. The creator of Facebook developed a service that helps people with friendship, family, and acceptance.

morality, creativity, problem solving

self-esteem, respect, achievement, confidence

friendship, family, acceptance

health, property, security, employment

air, water, food, clothing, shelter, sleep

Matching Needs with Skills

After identifying a need, consider your skills. What can you make or do that will meet this specific need? (Things you make are products. Things you do are services.) Brainstorm a list of ways that you could meet the need. The list below addresses the need "property."

Things I Could Make	Things I Could Do
birdhouses	lawn care
flower boxes	weeding gardens
compost bins	dog/cat sitting
corn mazes	walking dogs

Your Turn

Choose one of the needs from the pyramid above. Then brainstorm things you could make (products) and things you could do (services) that would meet that need.
Think of as many solutions as you can, even if some are impractical. Then choose one or more of the solutions to consider as business ideas.

Planning a Product or Service

Once you have an idea for a product or service that would meet a need, you can take your idea to the next level by developing a planning sheet. (See pages 255–262 and 455–470 for more information.)

Planning Sheet

Goal: I will create a service for pet sitting and dog walking.

Objectives:

Who? I will do the work, but Mom might need to drive.

What? I'll care for pets and walk dogs.

Where? I'll care for them at the owner's house or my house.

When? When people go on vacation, they hire me.

Why? Pets need care, and they don't like kennels.

How? I'll spread the word through the vets and the dog park.

Tasks:	**Time:**
Start	Now
1. List the services and figure out pricing.	April 7
2. Come up with a budget.	April 8
3. Make a name and a slogan for the service.	April 15
4. Come up with fliers.	April 16
5. Post fliers at vets and the dog park.	April 20
6. Ask friends with pets if I can pet sit during vacation.	April 22
7. Buy leashes, brushes, food bowls, and food.	May 1
8. Pet sit and walk dogs as hired.	Summer
Finish	Fall

Team:

I will do most of the work, and I can ride my bike to anyplace that's in town. Mom will have to drive me to places farther out. I need her permission for those.

Tools:

I'll need leashes, brushes, food bowls, a scoop, bags. I wonder if I'll need anything for fleas. I should make sure the pets are flea-free before bringing them home.

Your Turn

Fill out a planning sheet for your idea. (Go to thoughtfullearning.com/p229 to download a blank sheet.)

Pricing

The student with the pet-sitting service had to decide how much to charge for taking care of pets and walking dogs. He had a number of issues to consider:

- **Value:** What is a day of pet sitting worth? For a dog? For a cat? What is a half-hour dog-walk worth?
- **Competition:** How much does a kennel charge? What services do they give?
- **Market:** How much will people pay for these services?
- **Return on Investment:** What prices will make it worth the work?

Your Turn

Consider the price that you would set for your product or service. What value are you offering? What does the competition charge? What will the market bear? Will you get a good return on your investment?

Budgeting

Part of having a business is managing money. The first step in managing money is to set up a budget, which is a list of the expected income and expenses of a business. Here is a sample budget:

June Budget	Budget Amount	Actual Amount	Difference
INCOME			
Dog Sitting ($15 per day)	$105	$180	$75
Cat Sitting ($8 per day)	$40	$24	−$16
Dog Walking ($3 per half hour)	$18	$24	$6
Total June Income:	$163	$228	$65
EXPENSES			
Equipment (leashes, brushes, bowls)	$30	$24	−$6
Food and litter	$30	$55	$25
Total June Expenses:	$60	$79	$19

Your Turn

Create a budget like the one above for your business idea. (See also page 460.) Write down how much money you expect to take in to your business. Then write down the amounts of money you expect to pay out. As your business moves ahead, keep track of the money that is spent and keep updating your budget.

Workplace Activities

Use these activities to practice your workplace skills.

Dream Jobs

Your first job will probably not be your dream job, but a step toward bigger and better things. Take a moment to brainstorm dream jobs that you would like to have and the paths that will lead you there.

Dream Jobs	First I Could	Next I Could	Finally I Could
Veterinarian	Volunteer at the animal shelter	Work at a veterinary office	Go to veterinary school
Actor	Try out for school plays	Try out for community plays	Try out for professional plays
Marine Biologist	Study biology	Volunteer at the aquarium	Go to college for marine biology

Your Turn

Think about dream jobs by creating a chart like the one above. Then consider acting on your ideas.

Applying Yourself

Even if you aren't ready to apply for a job, you can practice the skill of filling out an application. Most businesses keep employment applications ready for anyone who asks.

[**Our best advice:** If you become comfortable with filling out an application, you'll be well prepared for the real experience. So be sure to practice this skill.]

Your Turn

Go to a local business and ask for an application. Take it home and sit down with your parent or guardian to fill it out. (Use the tips on page 223.) If you would like to work for the business, hand your application in.

R-E-S-P-E-C-T—Find Out What It Means to You

The key to succeeding in the workplace is to show respect. Think about ways that you can show respect in the workplace by completing the following activity.

Your Turn

Complete each sentence starter in this list:
Showing respect for my
    business means . . .
    boss means . . .
    coworkers means . . .
    customers means . . .
    self means . . .
    job means . . .
    career means . . .

Resolving Conflicts

Conflict resolution is important in the workplace, but it's best to practice it before you are in an actual conflict. Role-playing can help you practice conflict-resolution strategies. (See page 225.)

Your Turn

Imagine that you and a coworker are disagreeing about when to sweep your workplace entryway. You think it should be swept after closing, and your partner thinks it should be swept before opening. Role-play an argument. Then try one of the strategies below to end the conflict.

1. **Defer**—giving in and doing it the way the other person wants
2. **Compromise**—agreeing on a way in which both of you give up something
3. **Cooperate**—suggesting how you both could work together to accomplish the goal
4. **Compete**—both doing it your own way to see which is best
5. **Assert**—demanding that the partner does it your way

Discuss what happened in your role-playing. Then switch roles, asking your partner to try a different strategy for resolving the conflict. Finally, discuss which technique worked best.

Part II: Using the Inquiry Process

Part II: Using the Inquiry Process

This section leads you through the steps in the inquiry process, from questioning to creating to presenting. As you learn about this process, you will apply many of the skills that you learned in Part I. You will also use the inquiry process to complete the great projects in Part III.

Chapters in This Section

Chapter 16
Learning About the Inquiry Process

To inquire means "to ask questions." And we all know that a question ends with a question mark. So where did the question mark come from? No one is quite sure, but it is powerful. This mark signals a question, which may begin a search, and eventually land an answer . . . or bring to mind another question or two.

That's what the process of inquiry is all about—being hooked by a question and needing to find the answer. This process can help you learn whatever you need to know, and this chapter will show you how it works.

You will learn . . .

- Questioning
- Planning
- Researching
- Creating
- Improving
- Presenting

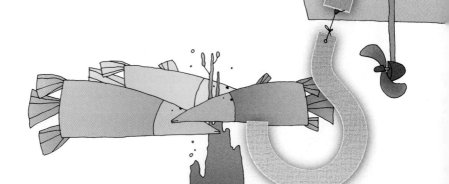

Understanding Inquiry

Inquiry is a process. You can't do everything all at once. At the beginning, you need to ask questions and explore. Then you plan what you want to do and research it, gathering the materials you need. Afterward, you create something, following your plan. When you've completed your creation, you check it against your goals to see how you can improve on what you have accomplished. In the end, you present your work to the wide world.

Here's a visual to help you understand the inquiry process:

1 Questioning

■ **Questioning:** You're just starting out, so now is the time to ask questions. Anything is possible. Ask creative questions and deep questions. Imagine, wonder, dream, brainstorm, hope.

2 Planning

■ **Planning:** Next, choose one possibility and plan how you will make it happen. Decide what you want to do, what your goals are, how much time you have, and what resources you have. Plot your course.

3 Researching

■ **Researching:** Then do research, gathering information and resources. Research involves working with media, technology, information, and people until you have what you need.

4 Creating

■ **Creating:** As you create, use your research and plan to make something new and amazing. Write. Draw. Build. Design. Sculpt. Arrange. This part of the process might be messy. Let it be.

5 Improving

■ **Improving:** After creating something, you need to take a close look at your creation. Does it meet your goals? Does it do what you want it to do? What works well? What could work better? How could you improve what you created?

6 Presenting

■ **Presenting:** Once your work is ready, present it to your audience. Is the work everything you wanted it to be? More? Less? What did you learn as you worked?

Your Turn

Which part of this process interests you most? Which part sounds most challenging?

1. Questioning

Inquiry begins by asking about the situation. The situation might be a school assignment, or your own backyard project. The basic questions you ask yourself are the same. (See also page 245.)

5 W's and H

Who is involved?	My science classmates and I
What is my goal?	To help an endangered species
Where is the situation?	In science class, in the school, and in my community
When is the situation?	Over the next three weeks
Why am I doing this?	It's an assignment with our endangered species unit.
How should I do it?	We could maybe have a fund-raiser for a charity.

Brainstorm

Once you have analyzed the situation, it's time to dream big. Let your brain—and the brains of your classmates and friends—storm up ideas. One way to do so is to use a cluster. Write a topic in the middle of a piece of paper or the middle of a board and then write ideas all around it, connecting them. Let your mind run wild. (See also page 247.)

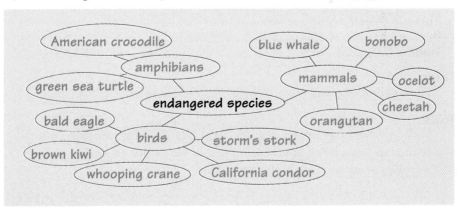

Your Turn
Analyze the situation you are in by answering the 5 W's and H about it. Then create a cluster like the one above.

2. Planning

After you've dreamed big—thinking about all the possibilities—it's time to plan exactly what you will do. Planning means outlining your goals and objectives and listing the tasks you'll need to accomplish. You should think about time, teams, and tools. A planning sheet can help.

Planning Sheet

Goal: I want to hold a fund-raiser to help save whooping cranes.

Objectives:

Who? I will run it, and I hope others will help out.

What? Will raise money to save whooping cranes.

Where In class, in the school, and in the community.

When? In the next three weeks.

Why? Whooping cranes are endangered.

How? We could sell something or have an event?

Tasks: **Time:**

Start

1. Find other people to help and get an advisor.   Oct. 1
2. Research charities and fund-raising ideas.   Oct. 1
3. Decide on an idea and divide up the work.   Oct. 4
4. Gather all the materials we need and get support. Oct. 5
5. Hold the fund-raiser.   Oct. 6-21
6. Send in the money.   by Oct. 22
7.
8.
Finish   by Oct. 29

Team:

I'll get Lupe, Jo, and Mike to help. They seem excited by the idea.

Tools:

We'll use the Internet to look for good charities for whooping cranes. We'll also search for fund-raising ideas. We'll have to decide on supplies when we have a clearer plan.

Your Turn

Go to thoughtfullearning.com/p238 to download your own planning sheet and complete it. (See also page 261.)

3. Researching

Each project you work on will require you to do some research (see pages 263–292). And any research you do must involve a good system for note taking. In the following example, Dave kept a two-column notebook. On the left, he wrote ideas for fund-raisers, and on the right, he wrote comments.

Your Turn

Make a list of possibilities for a project of your own.

Fund-Raising Ideas

_____ Just ask people to donate	My sister designed a T-shirt for her jazz choir. We could design and sell T-shirts to help save whooping cranes.
_____ Walk-a-thon	
_____ Bake sale	
_____ Sell flowers	
___✕___ Sell T-shirts	There's a company that rents lawn flamingoes for a fund-raiser. People pay to have their friends "flamingoed"—filling the front lawn with pink flamingoes. That's kind of like sending the cranes.
___✕___ Flamingoes in yards	
_____ Raking yards	
_____ Benefit concert	
___✕___ Benefit dance	
_____ Chicken dinner	Lupe's brother is a DJ. He would donate his time for free!

4. Creating

After you do your research and gather all the materials and knowledge you need, it's time to develop your project. This stage is the most fun, but also the most challenging. At this point, many of your ideas will become realities, but other ideas won't work, and you'll have to try something else. Don't get discouraged. That's part of the process! Enjoy the messiness of it, and enjoy the victories. (See pages 293–300.)

Here's the cool T-shirt design we came up with.

Save the **Cranes!**

Support Operation Migration

Whoop it up to save the cranes!

Come to the 2011 Whooping Crane
Benefit Dance
All profits go to Operation Migration

DJ!

Saturday, January 3, 7:00 p.m.
Brayford Gymnasium
Students $5

We made this poster to promote the dance. Lupe's brother wasn't free to DJ until January.

The flamingo idea was too expensive, but we've got two other fund-raisers that work together.

5. Improving

When you've finished your project, it's time to evaluate it. Start by going back to your goals to see if you met all of them.

Rubric Sheet

Goal:	Evaluation	Rating			Score
		Beat	Met	Didn't	
I want to hold a fundraiser to save whooping cranes.	We actually have 2 fundraisers going!	(60)	40	20	60
Objectives:					
1 I will run it with others from the class.	Mrs. Smith is our advisor.	Beat 10	Met (6)	Didn't 2	6
2 Will raise money to save whooping cranes.	$135 so far	Beat 10	Met (6)	Didn't 2	6
3 In class, in the school, and in the community.	We need more community support.	Beat 10	Met 6	Didn't (2)	2
4 In the next three weeks.	The dance will be in January.	Beat 10	Met 6	Didn't (2)	2
5 Whooping cranes are endangered.	We've really raised awareness!	Beat (10)	Met 6	Didn't 2	10
6 We could sell something or have an event?	We're having both.	Beat (10)	Met 6	Didn't 2	10
				Total:	96

Your Turn

Go to thoughtfullearning.com/p244 and download a rubric sheet. Use it to evaluate a project you have worked on. (See also page 303.) Then make improvements.

6. Presenting

When you are finally satisfied with your work, it's time to present it to the world. If you've been working on a writing project, you might post it to a class blog, present it to your class, or just read it out loud to family or friends. Dave, Lupe, Jo, and Mike continued selling "Save the Cranes" T-shirts right up through the holidays ("Makes a great present!") and at the benefit dance in January. They raised not just funds, but also awareness.

Inquiry Process in Review

If someone asked you what Dave and his friends did, you'd say they ran fund-raisers. But they were also using the inquiry process and building 21st century skills. This process and these skills work for big projects like running a fund-raiser, and also for everyday tasks like making a grocery list.

The Process of Inquiry	21st Century Skills
■ question	■ creative thinking
■ plan	■ critical thinking
■ research	■ communicating
■ create	■ collaborating
■ improve	■ reading/studying
■ present	■ using technology

Your Turn

Think of a time when you used the inquiry process, whether in or out of school. What did you do? What part was most challenging? What part was most fun? Were you happy with the results?

Chapter 17
Questioning

Sometimes you may say that you're bored. But in reality, you never have to be bored. Your brain is smarter than a supercomputer and more powerful than an X-Box® video-game system. Unleash it, and boredom will vanish. How? Float a few questions out there in your world—interesting or creative questions like *Why does red look angry and blue look calm?* or *What would happen if we brought back the mammoths?* But these are just examples. What do *you* need to know?

You will learn . . .

- Asking Creative and Deep Questions
- Asking Sensory and Thought Questions
- Asking About Your Past and Future
- Asking About Your World
- Asking About Things Around You
- Asking Socratic Questions

Asking Creative Questions

You've probably heard that there's no such thing as a stupid question. That's true. Here, for example is a question that might sound stupid:

> "How do you spell *h*?"

The answer seems obvious: "You spell *h* with an *h*." But there's another possible answer: "You spell *h* this way—A-I-T-C-H." And why doesn't the word *h* prominently feature the letter *h*, the same way that the word *dee* features the letter *d*? In fact, some people in England and Australia pronounce the letter *h* as *haitch*.

Do you see how creative questions lead you in interesting directions? Here are some more creative questions.

Why were the dinosaurs so big?
Why does money have value?
Can mosquitoes feel fear?
Why do people get old?
Is every electron the same?
Why did the Founding Fathers wear wigs?
Why do we call it Germany instead of Deutschland?
How does a water strider get a drink of water?
Do single-celled organisms need sleep?
Where is the Internet? Who runs it?
What happened to the mammoths?
How many personalities are there?
What makes funny jokes funny?
Why don't oil and water mix?
Could time move backward or sideways?
How do sunflowers know where the sun is?
Why was history so violent? Are we less violent now?
What is the purpose of music?
What is empty space made of?

Your Turn

Spend 5 minutes writing creative questions of your own.

Asking Deep Questions

Questions aren't all created equal. A researcher named Benjamin Bloom created a scale to show different kinds of questions. Here is the revised version of his scale. The farther down you go, the deeper the questions become. (See also pages 15 and 33.)

Levels of Thinking	One Student's Questions
To remember, ask about facts. **What** happened? **Who** was involved? **Where** did it take place? **When** did it happen?	The Cold War What happened in the Cold War? Who was involved in the Cold War? Where was the Iron Curtain? When did the war start and finish?
To understand, ask about meaning. **Why** did it happen? **What** does it mean? **How** does it connect to other things?	The Berlin Wall Why did the Soviets build the wall? What did the wall mean for Berlin? How did the wall affect other countries?
To apply, ask how to use ideas. **What** can I do with this idea? **How** could I use it?	Espionage What code-breaking skill can I use? What modern codes could I break?
To analyze, ask about the parts. **What** are the parts? **How** do they fit? **Why** do they work? **What** is their purpose?	Intelligence Agencies What were the CIA and KGB? How did they fight each other? Why was the KGB discontinued? What was their goal?
To evaluate, ask about quality. **What** is the value of this? **Does** it fulfill its purpose? **How** could it be better?	The Cold War What good was the Cold War? Did either country reach its goal? What could they have done better?
To create, ask about making something. **What** new thing can I make? **How** can I combine two things? **How** can I use something in a new way?	Propaganda What poster could I make? What words/images could I use? How could I use a real poster in a new way?

Your Turn

Think of a topic in social studies or science and ask a question about it from each of the six levels above. Note how your thinking deepens.

Asking Sensory Questions

You receive information through your senses, your memories, and your feelings.

What am I sensing?

As you explore a place, hold an object, or connect with a person, you should ask yourself what is pouring in through your senses. Filling out a sensory chart like the one below can help you heighten each of your senses. Make sure to choose especially descriptive words! Here is a sensory chart about a special place.

Sensory Chart

What do I . . .

see?	old railroad trestle, scraggy trees, chocolate-colored river, turtle island, bent metal ladder, boulders, graffiti, robin egg, fishing line
hear?	water chattering, wind in the leaves, goose honking, squirrel fight, trees creaking, grass crunching, plopping frog, rustling jacket
smell?	river water, warm grass, tar in rail ties, apple blossoms, sweat
taste?	clover bloom, wild mint
touch?	splintery ties, smooth boulder, dry grass, soft petal, rough stick, slick mud, cool air, flat stones

Your Turn

Make a sensory chart about a favorite location. (Download a template of a sensory chart at thoughtfullearning.com/p246.) Try to write down information from all five senses.

Asking Thought Questions

To discover what you think about any topic, you can create a mind map or cluster. A mind map traces your thoughts and helps you connect them.

Mind Map

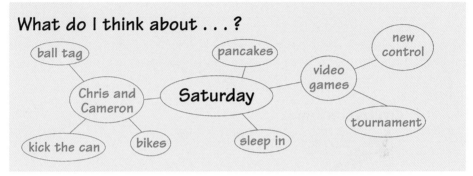

What do I think about . . . ?
- ball tag
- pancakes
- new control
- video games
- Chris and Cameron
- Saturday
- tournament
- kick the can
- bikes
- sleep in

> **Your Turn**
>
> Create your own mind map. In the center of a piece of paper, write a word or an idea and circle it. Then, around it, write other ideas and connect them to the first circle or to each other. Keep going until you have written all your thoughts on that topic.

Freewriting

You can also explore your thoughts by freewriting. Freewriting means writing for five or ten minutes without stopping, letting your thoughts flow freely.

> Saturday is the best day of the week. It's the one day that belongs to you. Instead of having to climb out of bed at the crack of dawn, you get to sleep. They also have marathons on Saturday. I mean TV marathons of the same show. Actually, I don't know why I even mentioned that. I don't like marathons. I can't sit still. Better to play video games. Mom always wants me to get outside. She practically pays my friends Chris and Cameron to come over. I guess it's cheaper than paying for an exercise program. . . .

> **Your Turn**
>
> Write for 5 minutes on any topic without stopping.

Asking About Your Past

Everything that has happened has led up to this moment. You are standing at the pinnacle of history, and of so many histories! In fact, where you are standing right now—*the now*—is the cross-point that decides the future. Ask what events led up to you right now.

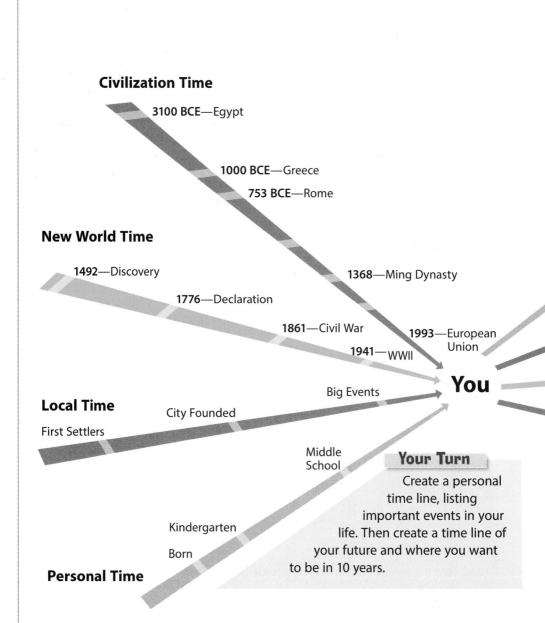

Civilization Time

3100 BCE—Egypt

1000 BCE—Greece

753 BCE—Rome

1368—Ming Dynasty

New World Time

1492—Discovery

1776—Declaration

1861—Civil War

1941—WWII

1993—European Union

Big Events

You

Local Time

City Founded

First Settlers

Middle School

Kindergarten

Born

Personal Time

Your Turn

Create a personal time line, listing important events in your life. Then create a time line of your future and where you want to be in 10 years.

Asking About Your Future

The same time lines that converge on you from the past shoot out from you into the future. What you decide today shapes your personal future and that of your city, your country, and your world. Imagine how your actions can shape those futures.

Personal Future

Who do you want to be and what do you want to do in
- 10 years?
- 20 years?
- 30 years?
- 40 years?
- 50 years?

Local Future

What do you want your home and city to be like when you are young, middle aged, and old?

Country Future

What will happen to your country in the next years and decades? What do you want to happen?

World Future

What will the world look like as you get older? What new wonders will there be? What challenges might we face?

Your Turn

Read the time line above.
Then write answers to the questions under one of the futures.

Asking About Your World

Our earth is an amazing, one-of-a-kind planet in the universe. It's the home world of millions of species of plants and animals. It has mountains that are six miles high and oceans that are six miles deep, deserts at 120° F and ice caps at −80° F, shifting plates and a molten core. Gaze for a while at the map of our world on the next page, and then ask yourself questions about our world.

Name: Alisha Simpson

1. Where do you live? Minneapolis, Minnesota, U.S.A.

2. Where do you wish you lived? The United Kingdom
   Why? I love British books and shows and British accents.

3. Where would you like to go for vacation? Canada
   Why? I want to see glaciers and moose.

4. Where would you not like to go for a vacation? Burma
   Why? I would be afraid to fly over the Pacific.

5. What country name do you like the best? Paupua New Guinea
   Why? It is fun to say.

6. What place intrigues you most? Brazil
   Why? Because of the Amazon River and the rain forest

7. What place scares you most? The Sahara Desert
   Why? It's as big as the United States.

8. What country would you like to lead? Australia
   Why? It's big, but it doesn't have a lot of problems.

Your Turn

Answer the questions above about your world. (Download a template from thoughtfullearning.com/p250.) Poll someone else in your class or online, asking these same questions. What answer surprises you most? How is your view of the world different from the other person's view?

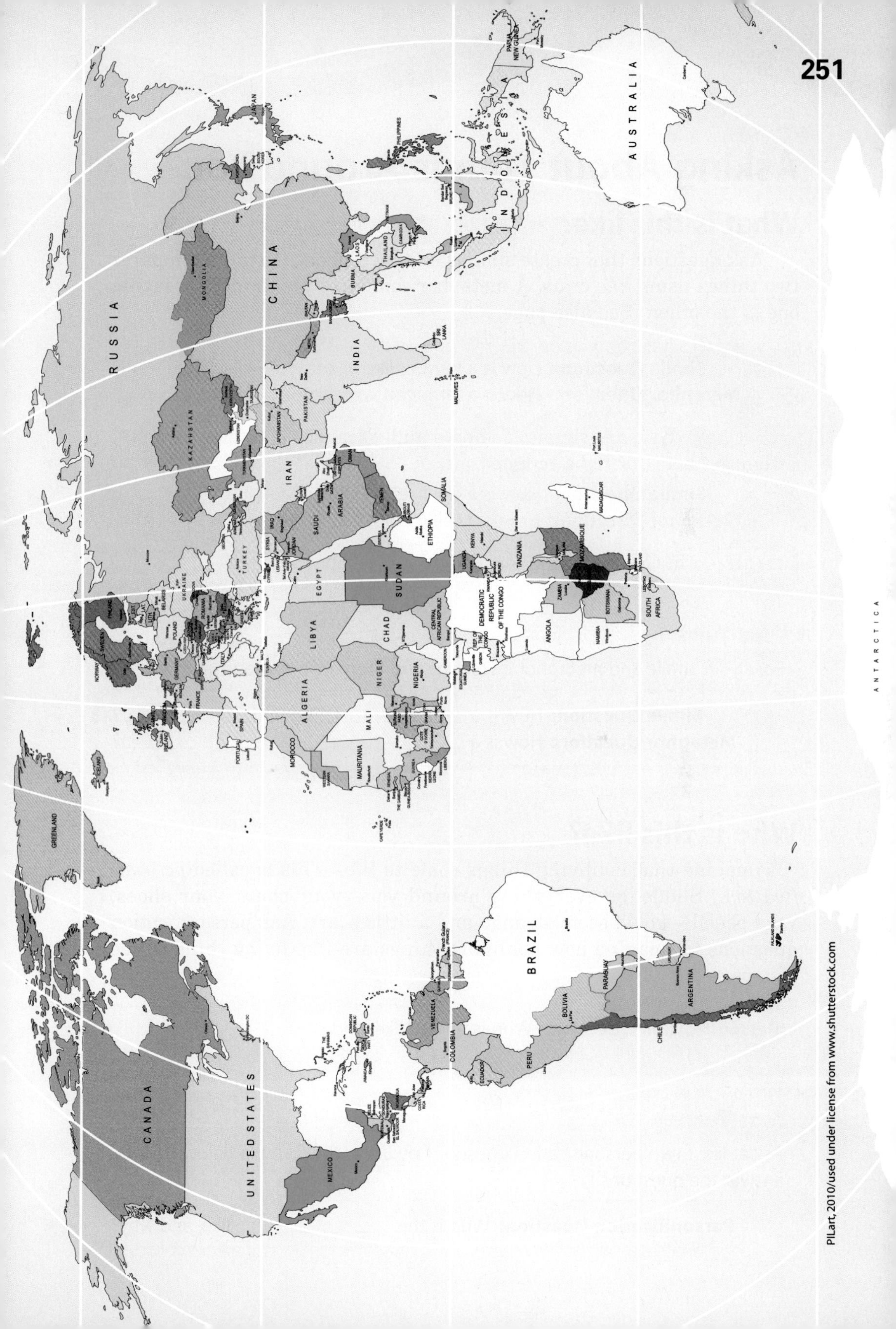
CANADA
UNITED STATES
MEXICO
GREENLAND
ICELAND
BRAZIL
ARGENTINA
CHILE
PERU
BOLIVIA
PARAGUAY
COLOMBIA
VENEZUELA
ECUADOR
FALKLAND ISLANDS
RUSSIA
CHINA
MONGOLIA
KAZAKHSTAN
INDIA
PAKISTAN
AFGHANISTAN
IRAN
SAUDI ARABIA
YEMEN
OMAN
TURKEY
UKRAINE
POLAND
GERMANY
FRANCE
SPAIN
PORTUGAL
ITALY
NORWAY
SWEDEN
FINLAND
BELARUS
ROMANIA
IRELAND
ALGERIA
LIBYA
EGYPT
MALI
NIGER
CHAD
SUDAN
NIGERIA
ETHIOPIA
SOMALIA
KENYA
TANZANIA
MOZAMBIQUE
MADAGASCAR
ZAMBIA
ANGOLA
NAMIBIA
BOTSWANA
SOUTH AFRICA
DEMOCRATIC REPUBLIC OF THE CONGO
CENTRAL AFRICAN REPUBLIC
MAURITANIA
MOROCCO
CAMEROON
BURMA
THAILAND
LAOS
VIETNAM
CAMBODIA
PHILIPPINES
JAPAN
INDONESIA
SRI LANKA
PAPUA NEW GUINEA
AUSTRALIA
ANTARCTICA

Asking About Things Around You

What is this like?

Ask questions that create similes and metaphors. A simile compares two things using *like* or *as*. A metaphor compares two things by saying one *is* the other. (See also page 36.)

> **Simile Question:** How is a temper like a volcano?
> **Metaphor Question:** How is a temper a volcano?
>
> Okay, those are simple. Tempers and volcanoes both erupt when they get hot. But try a tougher one.
> **Simile Question:** How is a cell like the solar system?
> **Metaphor Question:** How is a cell the solar system?
>
> In both, the center makes all of the other parts move.

Your Turn

Pose your simile and metaphor questions and then answer them.

> **Simile Question:** How is a _____ like a _____?
> **Metaphor Question:** How is a _____ a _____?

Who is this like?

Imagine that nonliving things come to life. (This is called *personification*.) Suddenly, everything around you—your chair, your shoes, your pencil—would seem strange and a little scary. Ask personification questions to imagine how nonliving things are like living things. (See also page 37.)

> **Personification Question:** Who is this TV like, and why?
> This TV is like my little brother because it is entertaining but loud.

Your Turn

Ask at least two personification questions by using the formula below. Then answer the questions.

> **Personification Question:** Who is this _____ like, and why?

How can I use SCAMPER?

A researcher named Bob Eberle came up with a set of great questions you can ask to deepen your thinking about any topic. He called these **SCAMPER**, taking the first letter from each type of question:

Question Type	Questions to Ask
Substitute	What else can I use instead? Who else can be involved instead? What other ingredients, materials, or power sources can I use? Where else could I do this?
Combine	How could I put two or more things together? How could I get two or more results from this? How can I appeal to more people about this?
Adapt	What changes would improve this? How could this better fit in the situation? What from the past could I copy?
Magnify	How can I make this bigger and more powerful? How can I increase performance or appeal? How can I slow this down or speed it up?
Put to Other Uses	What else could I do with this? Who else would be interested in this? Where else could I apply this?
Eliminate	How can I make this smaller and more precise? How can I decrease cost? How can I streamline this?
Rearrange	What other layout or order could I use? How can I look at this from a completely different perspective? How can I solve a different part of the problem? How can I reverse cause and effect?

Your Turn

Think of a project you are working on at school or at home. Answer one question for each letter in SCAMPER. What new possibilities come to mind? (Download a SCAMPER sheet from thoughtfullearning.com/p253.)

Asking Socratic Questions

The ancient Greek philosopher Socrates (SAW-cru-tees) did not lecture. Instead, he taught his pupils by asking them questions that made them sharpen and deepen their thinking. You can use the same questions in conversation to deepen thinking.

Socratic Questions

Clarifying questions ask the person to say exactly what is meant.
- Could you rephrase that, please?
- Could you provide an example?

Assumption questions ask the person to explore underlying ideas.
- Are you assuming that _____?
- Could you explain why/how _____?

Reasoning questions ask the person to trace the logic of an idea.
- What is the main cause of _____?
- What evidence shows that _____?

Perspective questions ask the person to consider other points of view.
- How would another person see the issue?
- How is _____ like and different from _____?

Consequence questions ask the person to consider what might happen.
- What could result from that idea?
- What is the value of _____ and why?

Recursive questions ask the person to think about the original question.
- Why are you asking this question?
- Why do you think I am asking this?

Your Turn

Pair with a partner and discuss a topic you are currently studying. One of you should play Socrates, asking questions from the list above while the other answers. Then switch roles. How do these questions deepen your thinking?

Chapter 18
Planning

Dreams are wonderful. But dreams, like clouds, can drift away. How can you grab those dreams, bring them down to earth, and make them real? The answer is planning.

Planning begins with these questions: What is my goal? How will I reach it? What resources will I use? What steps should I take?

This chapter gives you the tools you need to plan well, for anything from a class project to traveling to building an incredible gadget.

You will learn . . .

- Setting Goals, Objectives, and Tasks
- Scheduling Time
- Building Your Team
- Gathering Your Tools
- Creating a Planning Sheet
- Planning Throughout the Process

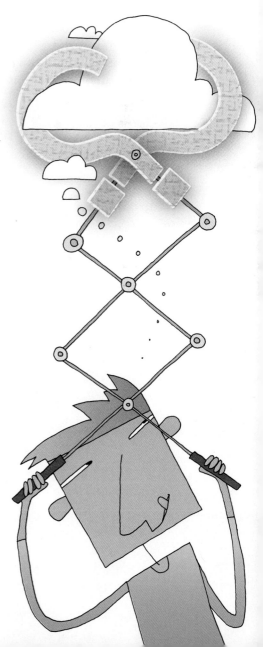

Setting Goals, Objectives, and Tasks

Whatever project you are taking on, you can plan it using the following strategy. First, you'll define your goal and objectives. Then you'll focus on a series of tasks. Finally, you'll need to manage your time, create a team, and gather the right tools and equipment.

Setting Your Goal

When you set a goal, use the asking strategies listed in the previous chapter to think about all the opportunities open to you. As you ask questions, cluster, and freewrite, you'll begin to realize which of these possibilities truly interest you. Using the following formula, write your goal:

Idea	+	Opportunity	=	Goal
Something you want or need to do		A time, place, or purpose for your idea to happen		An idea in focus
Create a short video.		Ms. Smith wants us to show what the westward expansion meant to settlers and Native Americans.		I will create a short video about the westward expansion to show what it meant to settlers and Native Americans.

Defining Objectives

After setting your goal, you need to make sure that you fully understand it. Defining objectives will make your goal clear to you and guide your work. You can create objectives for yourself by asking the 5 W and H questions.

Objectives

Who? | I'll write the script, direct the video, and act in it. I'll get friends to act in the video with me.

What? | We'll create a video about the westward expansion.

Where? | I'll write and plan in class, but we'll shoot the video in the park.

When? | We need to be done in two weeks.

Why? | Our video will show what the expansion was like for Native Americans and settlers.

How? | We'll use Mom's camera and make our own costumes and props.

Listing Tasks

The process of inquiry is different for each project. Take a moment to think about the tasks you will need to accomplish at each stage.

What do I need to do?	What do I need to learn?
1. Write a script.	I know a lot about the westward expansion, but I need to learn more about Tecumseh's War. I think maybe my video should be about the confrontation at Grouseland.
2. Find actors.	
3. Rehearse with them.	
4. Get a cameraperson.	
5. Set up a shooting schedule.	
6. Make costumes.	
7. Make props.	
8. Film scenes and edit the video.	

Your Turn

List your goal, objectives, and tasks for a current project or a potential one. (Download templates at thoughtfullearning.com/p257.)

Scheduling Time

Your schedule starts with the present moment and ends with your due date. Write these dates on a calendar and then divide the time between them by writing down some of the tasks you've listed. Here is a sample schedule for a student video:

Sunday	Monday	Tuesday	Wednesday	Thursday	Friday	Saturday
3	4 Assignment: Make a video of westward expansion.	5 Line up actors. Write script.	6 Finish script. Start on costumes and props.	7 Rehearse.	8 Finish costumes and props.	9 Film the narration and scene 1.
10	11 Film scene 2.	12 Film scene 3.	13 Edit the video.	14 Add titles/ music/ effects?	15 Project Due: In-class presentation	16

Making Adjustments: As you work on your project, keep checking your schedule. Speed up or slow down as needed.

- If you are going slower than you expected, figure out how to speed up or how to devote more time.
- If you still can't catch up, find out if the due date can be moved. If so, make a new schedule.
- If you are going faster than you expected, check your work to make sure it is as good as you want it to be. You can slow down to make improvements, or you can continue on, knowing you will have extra time at the end.

Your Turn

Get a calendar, either on paper or online. (Go to thoughtfullearning.com/p258.) Note your start date and your end date. Then schedule some of the tasks you have listed.

Building Your Team

In team sports, different people have different roles. As you build a team, think about your own role and the roles you need others to take on. Here is a list of roles, and one student's response:

actor	debater	leader	reporter
announcer	designer	manager	salesperson
artist	director	marketer	scientist
athlete	disc jockey	mechanic	screenwriter
boss	editor	musician	sculptor
builder	engineer	novelist	tailor
businessperson	entrepreneur	performer	teacher
caregiver	explorer	playwright	visionary
chef	friend	poet	welder
comedian	game designer	politician	zoologist
composer	host	programmer	
counselor	interviewer	promoter	

My Role: I will be the writer and director of the short video. I also want to be one of the actors in it, so I'll have to get someone else to run the camera. Once the video is done, I will be the editor, too.

Other Roles: I need actors and a cameraperson. I also may need help with sewing costumes and making props—unless I could borrow costumes and props from the local community theater. Maybe someone from the theater could join my team.

Possible Team:
Actors: Janice Johnstone, Maylee Turin, Zach Schotz, Tyrone Gree
Cameraperson: Ryan Willis, Mom
Costumes/Props: Mom, Barn Players

Note: Most of the roles above are jobs. The work you do on projects can sometimes turn into a career for you when you are older.

Your Turn

Write down the role/roles that you will play in your project. List the roles that others might play. Then list a possible team.

Gathering Your Tools

Every project needs specific tools, materials, information, and resources. Here is a list of tools created for a westward-expansion video:

Tools/ Equipment:
digital video camera
computer
video-editing program
USB cable
sewing machine?

Notes: Mom said I could use her video camera. I'll use the home computer. Don't need to sew.

Materials:
settler costumes
Native American costumes
settler's cabin
tomahawk
axe
musket

Notes: The Barn Players said I could borrow some costumes. Must get the actors' sizes. We'll use the settler's cabin in the library park for scene 3.

Information:
What tribes were in the Midwest? How did they dress? What conflicts were there between settlers and Native Americans?

Notes: The Shawnee, with Tecumseh as their commander. Tecumseh's War of 1811-1813; confronted William Henry Harrison at Grouseland.

Resources:
Internet
history book
library books
other actors
Mom

Notes: I'm basing Tecumseh's costume on a painting I found online.

Your Turn

Create a list of tools, materials, information, and resources. (Go to thoughtfullearning.com/p260 for a template.)

Creating a Planning Sheet

Here is a planning sheet for the westward-expansion video:

Planning Sheet

Goal: I will create a short video about the westward expansion to show what it meant to Native Americans and settlers.

Objectives: *Who?* I'll write, direct, and act. Friends will film and act.
What? We'll use a camera to make a short video.
Where? We'll write in class but shoot on location in the park.
When? We need to be done in two weeks.
Why? We want to show what the expansion was like for Native Americans and settlers.
How? We'll use Mom's camera to make a short video.

Tasks: **Time:**
Start ....   Oct. 4
1. Write a script.   Oct. 5-6
2. Find actors.   Oct. 5
3. Rehearse with them.   Oct. 7-8
4. Get a cameraperson.   Oct. 7
5. Set up a shooting schedule.   Oct. 7
6. Make costumes.   Oct. 6-8
7. Make props.   Oct. 6-8
8. Film scenes and edit the video.   Oct. 9, 11-14
Finish ....   Oct. 15

Team:
Actors: Janice Johnstone, Maylee Turin, Zach Schotz, Tyrone Green
Cameraperson: Ryan Willis, Mom
Costumes/Props: Mom, Barn Players

Tools:
Equipment: camera, computer, editing program, sewing machine
Materials: paper, costumes, cabin, axe, musket, tomahawk
Information: Midwest tribes, dress, wars fought
Resources: Internet, books, Ms. Smith, Mom, Barn Players

Your Turn

Create a planning sheet for a project. (Go to thoughtfullearning.com/p261.)

Planning Throughout the Process

A planning sheet can guide any project that you undertake, from choreographing a dance to building a wind turbine. The sheet is useful not just for the planning stage, but throughout the inquiry process. Here are the ways that a planning sheet will be used at various stages of a project.

Organizing

The planning sheet helps you get organized during the planning stage of your project.

Gathering

The planning sheet guides you as you carry out research, complete the tasks on time, and work with your team and the tools available to you.

Developing

The planning sheet helps you develop your project, targeting the goal and objectives to stay on course.

Evaluating

The planning sheet shows whether the project meets your goal and objectives, calling attention to specific areas that need improvement. It also lists the time, team, and tools you have for making improvements.

Chapter 19
Conducting Basic Research

The main character trait of all researchers is curiosity. William Least Heat-Moon was a man who was curious. He was so curious about the different people and traditions in the United States that he took a road trip to learn about them. He wrote about his discoveries in a book called *Blue Highways*.

What are you curious about? What questions do you have? Where will they lead you? This chapter will help you begin the journey.

You will learn . . .

- Asking Questions
- Finding Information
- Using the Library
- Taking Notes
- Organizing Your Information
- Using an Outline

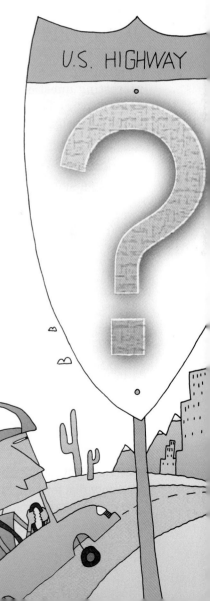

Asking Questions

As was stated in the introduction, the best research starts from your own curiosity and questions. You might be interested in the Slow Food movement, more specifically with food growers in urban areas: Who are some of the food growers in your own city? What do they grow? Where? And how?

Or maybe you have questions about all of the dogs you see: Why do so many people own dogs? How many dogs are too many? Why do some dogs bark so much? What is a dog park and how does it work?

Using Triggering Questions

Pages 243–254 tell you all about the importance of questioning. In that chapter, you may have generated a lot of interesting questions. If so, one of them may serve as an effective starting point for research. Otherwise, the sample questions listed below may trigger some of your own research questions.

People
- Which of my ancestors interests me the most?
- Who interests me in my community?
- Who is someone I admire?

Places
- What makes a certain restaurant so popular?
- What is the perfect living space for city dwellers?
- Why are deltas so important to the environment?

Things
- How fresh is our fresh air?
- What musical instrument is the most challenging to play and why?
- What exactly are peregrine falcons?

Ideas
- What is artificial intelligence?
- What does empathy mean and why is it important?
- Why is social networking so popular?

Your Turn

Review the questions above. Then write at least two questions under each category that interest you. Or identify a question or two that you wrote in the questioning chapter that you would be interested in researching. Share your ideas with your classmates.

Listing Pointed Questions

Once you identify main questions to explore, you can create another level of questions—called *pointed questions*—to help you plan and organize your research. Let's say that peregrine falcons have been seen in your city, and you want to learn more about them. Here are some pointed questions that could guide your research.

Main Question: <u>What exactly are peregrine falcons?</u>

Pointed Questions: <u>What does the peregrine falcon look like?</u>
<u>Where does it usually live?</u>
<u>What does it eat, and how does it get its food?</u>
<u>Who or what are its enemies?</u>
<u>How does it cope with "civilization"?</u>
<u>How many peregrine falcons are there?</u>
<u>What makes this bird interesting or different?</u>

Note: Think of your first list of pointed questions as a starting point. You may think of other questions once you start your research.

Using SCAMPER

You can use the SCAMPER strategy (page 253) to help you ask deeper questions about your topic. For example, you could *magnify* your research by asking a question like this:

How many birds of prey are coming into the city?

Or you could *combine* your research with something else by asking a question like this:

What is the relationship between the falcons and the existing bird populations in the downtown area?

Your Turn

Write down or circle one question that you asked on page 264 that could serve as the focus of a research project. Then list at least six or seven pointed questions that could help you explore the topic of your main question.

Finding Information

You have many options for investigating your questions—from searching the Internet to searching in-print materials, from talking with experts to making direct observations. Here's a basic review of your options.

- **The Internet** serves as a good starting point. Simply type in a keyword or keywords related to your main question and see what comes up: *peregrine falcons, peregrine falcons in the city, falcons and their prey.*
- **Reference books,** such as encyclopedias, atlases, and almanacs, can also serve as a good starting point for research.
- **Magazines** and **newspapers** provide up-to-date information on just about any topic, and most come in print and electronic versions. The *Readers' Guide to Periodical Literature* provides information, or any Internet databases that your library may subscribe to can help you find information in these resources.
- **Other people** can serve as excellent sources of information, plus they can direct you to additional sources. Consider your teachers, parents, members of your community.
- **Direct observations** or **experiences** allow you to see for yourself how something works or how something happens. This type of gathering makes research come alive for you.

Readers' Guide Entries

PEREGRINE falcon

Sky divers. J. Neinhaus. Sci Today 60: 77-81 Ag '10
Urban birds of prey. D. Michaels. Modern Life 21: 34-35 July '10

Your Turn

Do some early searching about your topic to see what types of information are available about one of your main questions. Consult the Internet, books and magazines, and other people for possible sources of information. Identify four resources.

Using the Library

Your school and city library contain many valuable resources to help you conduct research. The best way to start your library search is to consult your library's computer catalog. This service helps you identify specific books and materials related to your question or topic.

Using a Computer Catalog

Information is listed on this catalog according to titles, authors, and subjects.

1. **Title** If you know the title of a book, key it in to determine if your library has the book and, if so, where it is located.
2. **Author** If you know the name of the author you are interested in, enter his or her name. This will help you identify any titles by that author that are shelved in the library.
3. **Subject** Key in the subject, or a word or phrase related to your subject, to see what materials your library has to offer.

Computer Card Entry

Author:	Williams, Jordan
Title:	Birds of Prey in North America: A 21st Century Guide
Published:	National Science, 2007 150 pp.
Subjects:	Eagles, falcons, hawks, and owls
STATUS: Not checked out	**CALL NUMBER:** 500.32167
LOCATION: General collection	

Your Turn

Answer these two questions in your notebook: What are the three ways to use the computer catalog to find information in the library? What information on the sample entry would help you find Jordan Williams's book in your school's library?

Taking Notes

As you research a topic, you will need to take notes on what you learn. You may find it helpful to take notes on note cards, with a specific question at the top of each card. Then beneath the question, you can record important facts and details that answer the question. Number your note cards, and identify the source of the information to help you keep track of everything.

Note Cards

What does a peregrine falcon eat, and how does it get its food?

Where do peregrine falcons live and mate?

What does the peregrine falcon look like?
- usually between 15 and 20 inches in length
- long, pointed wings
- wingspan—43 inches
- hooked beak and razor-sharp talons for hunting

"Peregrine Falcon," Wikipedia

Note: While note cards work well, you can also take notes in your class notebook. Using a notebook, in fact, gives you more room to write. Simply write one of your questions at the top of the page, and record your notes beneath it. If you use the two-column system for note taking (see page 163), you will also have room to add your own comments.

What Information to Include

Use your own words as much as possible in your notes. And for the most part, write down key words and phrases rather than complete sentences. Write down word-for-word statements only when you feel they are really important. Put quotation marks around this information, and identify who wrote or stated these ideas. If you use the ideas of others in your research, you must give credit. (See pages 287–291.)

Using Electronic Notes

You may find taking notes on a laptop works well for you, especially if you can keyboard or type faster and more neatly than you can write. Your school might have special note-taking software for you to use. Ask your teacher or your school's technical advisor about this. Otherwise, you will have to use your basic word processing program. Here are the pros and cons for electronic note taking:

Pros

Your electronic notes are . . .

- always neat and readable.
- in a safe place, if you remember to save your work.
- easy to work with. You can quickly move information, delete ideas, and so on.
- portable since you can access them on a laptop or other electronic device.
- time-saving, in that you can save pictures and graphics right along with your notes.

Cons

Your electronic notes are . . .

- dependent on having a laptop or other electronic devices.
- essentially limited to words and ideas, unless you have special software that allows you to sketch or draw graphic organizers.

Electronic Note Page

Peregrine Falcon Notes

Fonts

What does the peregrine falcon look like?
- usually between 15 and 20 inches in length
- long, pointed wings
- wingspan—43 inches
- hooked beak and razor-sharp talons for hunting

Images of peregrine falcons
Peregrine Falcon Photos—Smithsonian Migratory Bird Center

Your Turn

Take notes on a note card, in a notebook, or on a laptop for one of the pointed questions you listed. Be sure to follow the advice or guidelines presented on these two pages.

Organizing Your Information

Once you have gathered information about your topic, the next step is to begin arranging or organizing the information you have found. If you are writing a report or working on a project, you may want to choose one main idea to serve as the focus of your work. For example, if you researched the peregrine falcon, your focus may be that it is one of the few animals taken off the endangered species list.

Then you should arrange the rest of your note cards in a logical order, keeping your focus in mind. You may also want to use a graphic organizer or an outline to help you organize your ideas. Common graphic organizers are shown on these two pages, and a guide to outlining appears on page 272.

Graphic Organizers

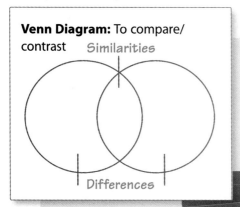

Venn Diagram: To compare/contrast

Similarities

Differences

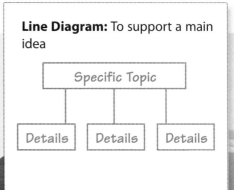

Line Diagram: To support a main idea

Specific Topic

Details   Details   Details

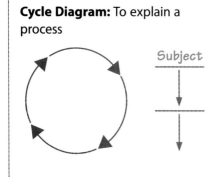

Cycle Diagram: To explain a process

Subject

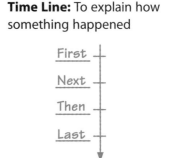

Time Line: To explain how something happened

First
Next
Then
Last

Cause/Effect: To analyze the causes and effects of something

Subject: _____

Causes (Because of . . .)	Effects (. . . these conditions resulted)
•	•
•	•
•	•
•	•

5 W's and H Chart: To identify the key details in a situation

Who?	
What?	
Where?	
When?	
Why?	
How?	

Before/After: To explain conditions before and after an event

Subject _____

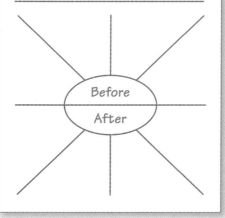

Before

After

Problem/Solution: To analyze a problem and solutions

Problem:

Causes of the Problem
•
•
•
•

Possible Solutions
•
•
•
•

Your Turn

Discuss the following questions with a partner: Which of these organizers have you used in the past? Why did you use them, and were they helpful? Also, which of these organizers would be helpful if you were writing a report on the question or topic that you have explored in this chapter? Why?

Using an Outline

An outline is an organized listing of main points and details that you would like to include in a report or project. Here are the basic guidelines to follow when creating a sentence outline.

- Begin your outline by turning the questions at the top of your note cards into statements.

> **Question:** How does a peregrine falcon cope with "civilization"?
>
> **Statement:** The movement of humans into the peregrine falcon's natural habitat also contributed to its endangered classification.

- List these statements in the order that you want to include them in your report or project. These are the main ideas in your outline that follow Roman numerals (I., II., III.).

- Leave enough space beneath each of these statements to include main supporting points. These points follow capital letters (A., B., C.).

- To include another level of detail under the capital letters, you would use regular numbers (1., 2., 3.).

- When outlining, if you have a I., you must at least have a II.; if you have an A., you must have a B., and so on.

Outline *(first part)*

I. The use of pesticides is the main reason the peregrine falcon became endangered.
  A. The falcons were infected when they ate other birds already infected with pesticides.
  B. Pesticides affected the falcon's ability to reproduce.
  C. They caused falcon eggs to have very thin, weak shells.
  D. The pesticides killed adult falcons.

II. The movement of humans into the peregrine falcon's natural habitat also contributed to its endangered classification.
  A. The use of wilderness land for farming, game preserves, and parks has damaged the falcon's natural habitat.
  B. Sonic booms from modern aircraft may also hurt the falcon population.

Chapter 20
Conducting Advanced Research

Research is the process of seeking answers to questions about anything and everything—from matters here on earth to secrets of the universe. During the process, you'll learn about yourself and what truly interests you.

As you search for answers to your questions, explore a variety of resources. And always share your discoveries honestly, giving credit for the ideas of others that appear in your work.

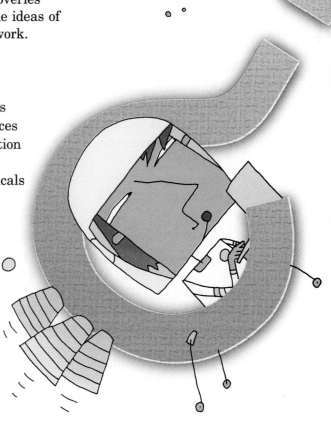

You will learn . . .

- Using Primary Sources
- Using Secondary Sources
- Understanding Nonfiction Books
- Understanding Periodicals
- Using the Internet
- Avoiding Plagiarism
- Using MLA Citation
- Evaluating Sources

Using Primary Sources

Whenever you begin a research project, your teacher may require that you consult primary sources of information along with secondary sources such as books and magazines. You are using a primary source of information when you collect information firsthand. Let's say you want to learn about the best way to train a dog. Observing dog training in action or actually participating in the training is a primary source of information.

Or let's say you are curious about the use of wind power in your area. Interviewing someone who sets up wind generators is a primary source of information, so is visiting a site with wind generators in action. Here are some of the primary sources available to you.

Types of Primary Sources

- Observing someone or something in action
- Experiencing something yourself
- Reading original letters, diaries, or documents
- Visiting a place
- Making something
- Attending an exhibit
- Completing an experiment
- Interviewing someone
  (See page 275.)
- Conducting a survey
  (See pages 276–277.)

For millions of primary sources, check out the Library of Congress (loc.gov) and the World Digital Library (wdl.org).

The Value of Primary Sources

Using primary sources gets you actively involved in research and makes the process more meaningful to you. If all of your information comes from books or the Internet, you miss a main point about conducting research—discovering things for yourself. How could you truly learn about training a dog without somehow getting involved in the activity?

Your Turn

Identify two or three primary sources of information that you could use to investigate the main question or topic that you worked with in the previous chapter. Share your choices with a classmate.

Conducting Interviews

Interviewing is an important primary source of information. During an interview, you either (1) talk in person with someone who knows about your topic, (2) communicate with someone by phone, or (3) e-mail the person the questions you would like her or him to answer.

Before . . .

Identify a person to interview. This could be someone you meet in person or someone you contact by phone or on the Net. (Get your parent's permission.)

Schedule for the interview. Be sure to set up a specific time and place for the conversation.

List important questions that you would like to ask. Arrange them in a sensible way.

During . . .

Be polite throughout the interview.

Give some background information about yourself and your research.

Get the person's permission before you use any recording devices or take any pictures.

Listen carefully.

Be prepared to reword a question if the person doesn't understand something. Also be prepared to ask follow-up questions.

Before you end the interview, review your notes to make sure that you have the information that you need.

Ask the person about other sources of information about the topic.

Thank the person for his or her help.

After . . .

Send a thank-you note to the person you interviewed.

Review your notes.

Contact the person, if necessary, to clear up any confusing points.

Consider sending the person a copy of your finished work.

Using Surveys

A survey is a detailed study used to gather data (statistics, feelings, or experiences) related to a topic you are exploring. You can use the data to help you form your research. The information that follows will help you create and use surveys. (Go to thoughtfullearning.com/p276 to find out about software for online surveys.)

1. **Identify the purpose and audience for your survey:** What do you want to learn, and whom do you want to contact?

2. **Form the survey according to your purpose.**
   - Write questions that are clear, and ask for the right type of information.
   - Word questions so they are easy to answer.
   - When possible, offer options to circle or underline.

3. **Consider two types of questions.**
   - Focused questions usually provide options and are easy to answer. (Yes-no, multiple choice, true-false, and fill-in-the-blank questions are examples.)
   - Open questions ask survey takers to write out short answers.

4. **Arrange the information in a logical way.**
   - Start with a brief explanation explaining who you are or who you represent, the purpose of the survey, how to complete it, and when and where to return it.
   - Number and label all of the information that follows so the survey is easy to understand.
   - Provide enough space for readers to make their responses.

5. **Give it a test run.**
   - Have a few classmates or friends complete the survey.
   - Revise it as needed.

6. **Carry out the survey.**
   - Distribute it to the intended group.
   - Collect and evaluate the responses.

Sample Survey

Dog Training Survey

My name is Theresa Brown, and I'm conducting research to learn about dog training. This survey will help me learn about any dog training experiences students at McKinley School may have had. Please answer the questions that follow, and return the survey to me or place it in the box next to room 205 by Friday. Thank you!

1. What is your gender?   male   female

2. What grade are you in?   5   6   7   8   9

3. Do you or your family own a dog?   yes   no
   Note: If you circled "no," skip to question 8.

4. If yes, has your dog had any dog training?   yes   no

5. What types of things has your dog learned?
   _____
   _____
   _____

6. How would you rate the effectiveness of the training?
   no effect   **very effective**
     1   2   3   4   5

7. What was your role in the training?
   _____
   _____
   _____

8. Have you ever volunteered to work with dogs in the neighborhood, at a kennel, or at a shelter?   yes   no
   Note: If you circled "no," turn your survey in.

9. If yes, did this work involve any dog training? yes   no

10. Explain this experience.
   _____
   _____
   _____

Using Secondary Sources

Secondary sources are the books and articles that you read for information, or documentaries and video presentations that you watch. Secondary sources provide secondhand information, or the thoughts and feelings of others.

If you were to read a how-to book about basic dog training, you would be using a secondary source. Or if you were to read about benefits of wind power in a science article posted on the Web, you would be referring to a secondary source. Here are some examples of secondary sources available to you:

Types of Secondary Sources

- Nonfiction books
- General reference books (See page 279.)
- Textbooks
- Informational brochures and pamphlets
- Magazine and journal articles (in print or online)
- Television specials and news shows
- Web podcasts and other video presentations
- Speeches by experts

The Value of Secondary Sources

Secondary sources provide expert explanations and analyses of topics that interest you. These sources should help you better understand topics and decide if your own thinking on the topic is realistic or on target.

What you don't want to do is rely too heavily on secondary sources. The main goal of any research project is to develop your own thoughts and feelings about a topic, not simply to repeat what others have said about it. You must also be careful that the secondary sources you use are up to date and reliable. (See page 292.)

Your Turn

Identify two or three types of secondary sources that would be of most value to you if you were researching a famous explorer. Share your choices with your classmates.

Selecting Reference Books

Your school or city library offers many reference books that may help you conduct your research. Some of the more common ones are listed here. But be sure to ask your librarian to learn about all of the reference books available in your library.

General Reference Books

- **Encyclopedias** are sets of informational books on just about any topic. They come in print or online versions. Also know that each set contains an index to help you find additional information on a topic. (See pages 280–281.)
- **Atlases** provide maps and other information about different areas. *National Geographic Atlas of the World* is an example.
- **Almanacs** offer charts, graphs, and lists of information about many topics. *The World Almanac and Book of Facts* is an example.

Specific Reference Books

- *Bartlett's Familiar Quotations* contains thousands of quotations organized from ancient history to the present time.
- *Current Biography* is published monthly and annually. Articles in this resource focus on the stories of interesting individuals.
- *Facts About the Presidents* is a reference book, but there are Web sites that offer similar types of information.
- *Famous First Facts,* available in print or electronically, offers "firsts" in all areas of life.
- The **Junior Authors & Illustrators** series, available in print or electronically, presents biographical information on children's and young adult authors.
- *Who's Who in America* gives biographical information on important people in the United States, past and present.

Your Turn

Identify two or three reference books that would help you learn about the topic or main question that you worked with in the previous chapter.

Understanding Nonfiction Books

To use nonfiction books effectively, you should understand how they are put together. For example, they usually contain a table of contents in the front and an index in the back to help you find information about specific topics. Here are the basic parts of a typical informational book.

- A **title page** gives the full title of the book, the author's name, the publisher's name, and the city of publication.
- A **copyright page** comes right after the title page. It tells you the year when the copyright was issued. (If the copyright is too old, the information might be outdated.)
- A **preface,** a **foreword,** or an **introduction** usually follows. It explains the purpose of the book.
- There may also be an **acknowledgment page,** listing people who helped with the book. (This information can also be combined with another page, as is shown in the example on the next page.)
- The **table of contents** identifies the page numbers of major divisions of the book (units, chapters, and topics).
- The **body** or main part of the book contains the core information in the text.
- An **appendix** sometimes follows the main text, and it contains extra information such as graphics, maps, lists, and other special information.
- A **glossary,** if it is included, provides an alphabetical listing of special words and terms. Refer to this part if you are unsure of the meaning of a certain word.
- A **bibliography** lists sources that the author used and other sources on the topic.
- The **index** lists in alphabetical order the page location of specific topics covered in the book. It appears at the end of the book.

Your Turn

Find the different parts in a nonfiction book of your choice. Pay careful attention to the type of information contained in each part, but remember that the book may not contain every part described above.

Parts of a Book

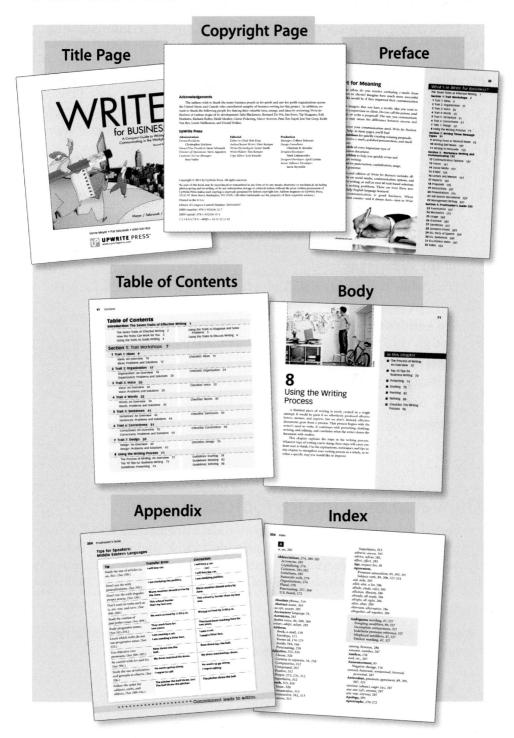

Title Page

Copyright Page

Preface

Table of Contents

Body

8
Using the Writing Process

Appendix

Index

Understanding Periodicals

Periodicals are magazines and journals that are published on a regular basis. Magazines are popular periodicals that focus on news, fashion, home improvement, and other areas of interest. Journals are periodicals that focus on a specific area of study (architecture, history) and contain articles written by scholars and experts.

To use periodicals properly, you need to understand their working parts. (Online versions will be arranged and accessed in different ways.)

- The **cover** will identify the title of the periodical. It may also identify the date of the issue and the volume and number of the issue.
- A **masthead** identifies publishing information related to the periodical, including the names of the editors and the location of the editorial offices.
- The **table of contents** lists the location of sections, features, and specific articles in the periodical.
- An **editor's note** or **from-the-editor section** often comes next, and in this part, the editor highlights the articles in the issue.
- **Letters** to the periodical may come next. These letters are submitted by readers in response to articles in earlier issues.
- The **body** or main part of the text contains the articles.
- **Indexes** may be included in some journals. These indexes might identify authors and titles in previous issues of the journal.

The Value of Using Periodicals

Periodicals provide you with up-to-date information. This is their true value. Most magazines even provide online updates in between issues. However, before you use articles in magazines or journals, be sure that they are reliable sources of information. (See pages 292.)

Your Turn

Working with a partner, identify the main parts of two periodicals contained in your school library. Share your discoveries with your classmates.

Parts of a Periodical

Cover

Table of Contents

Masthead

CREATIVETHINKING
MAGAZINE

Welcome
To the
Communication
Revolution

CREATIVETHINKING
MAGAZINE

Editorial and Executive Offices
770 East St. Tacoma, WA 98401
Telephone: 253. 444.4455

Publisher Nina Hinds
Advertising Director Michele Haggerty
Editor-in-Chief Mark Phillips
Associate Editor Grace Lawrence
Art Director Steven E. Mathews
Marketing Director Lee Olsen

Editor's Note

Article

From the Editor's Desk

Wooden on Success

By Mark Phillips,
Editor-in Chief

What are the keys to success? Teachers
and employers have tackled this question
for years. However, the answer is already
out there, and it comes from legendary
basketball coach John Wooden.

Wooden, a winner of 11 national
championships with UCLA Bruins,
defined success early in his career as "the
peace of mind from the self-satisfaction
in knowing you gave maximum effort in
your endeavor."

The Communication Revolution

By Shannon Miller

Leaders are taking advantage of a
communication revolution. Blogs,
Wikis, instant messengers, and social
media are connecting businesses
with customers, students with employers, and
politicians with constituents. So what are the
implications of this Communication Revolution?
Let's start on a global level.

Global Communicators

More people than ever are writing and
communicating with each other on a

Using the Internet

The Internet is a truly remarkable information resource. But having almost immediate access to so much information can be overwhelming. The next few pages provide helpful hints for navigating the Net. (See also pages 132–137.)

Navigating Tips

Keep these points in mind as you begin your searching.

- **Expect a long trip:** Finding the best information may take time.
- **Work smart:** Know the basics of Internet searching, including how to use keywords. (See below.)
- **Be creative:** If one route or keyword doesn't lead you in the right direction, choose a different one.
- **Check all choices:** For most searches, you will have many options to review.
- **Stay on task:** Avoid the temptation to take side trips while you research your topic.
- **Take notes:** Write down or print out key information.

A Basic Keyword Guide

The success of your Internet search depends on the quality of the keywords you use. Making simple changes to a keyword can provide you with completely different results.

1. To start, simply type in the topic of your research: *salmon, robots, falcons*.
2. Add a word, and you will call up pages that contain any of the words: *wild salmon, home robots, peregrine falcons*.
3. Enclose the phrase in quotation marks, and you will receive just the pages containing that phrase: *"wild salmon."*
4. Use words such as *and* (+) or *not* (-) to narrow or focus your search: *salmon and harvesting, salmon not farm-raised,* and so on.

Your Turn

Conduct a keyword search based on a topic of your choice, perhaps the one you worked with in the previous chapter. Try different combinations to see what you can discover. Afterward, evaluate your search.

Special Searching Options

Provided below are special options that you can use to conduct your online searches. Check with your teacher, technology resource person, or librarian about these options.

- The **Library of Congress** offers a great variety of online texts and resources.
- **National** and **state governments** provide research sites to help you learn about a variety of topics.
- A service such as **EBSCO** provides a database of newspapers, magazines, and journal articles.
- The **Internet Public Library** serves as a great online resource. As with all libraries, this one offers a lot of great information.
- **Network** with other people via e-mail, a chat room, text-messaging, and so on. Simply ask your questions, and see what others have to offer. (Get your parent's permission first.)
- Try a **metasearch site** to see what you can discover from multiple search engines. To use this feature, type "metasearch" into your basic search engine.
- Use a **directory** to learn about a topic, by starting with a general heading and working your way through more focused headings.

Your Turn

Experiment with two of these options to see how they work. Then compare the effectiveness of each one. Be sure to ask for help if you're not sure how to get started.

Parts of a Web Page

When you click on a specific source in your keyword search, a Web page will appear. Web pages may contain the following basic parts.

- A **title bar** usually appears at the top of the page and contains the name of the site or window.
- **Navigation buttons** help you navigate or "get around" the Net.
- An **address bar** is the space in which the Web site address appears.
- **Graphics** add visual interest to a Web page.
- **Text links** identify additional pages on the Web that can be accessed.
- **Radio buttons, pop-up selections, and check boxes** offer users choices.
- A **text box** is an on-screen frame in which you type text.
- A **status bar** appears at the bottom of the window and shows the progress of the loading of the Web pages.

Sample Web Page

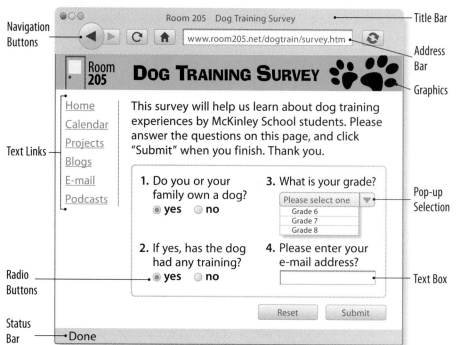

Avoiding Plagiarism

Neil Armstrong, the first man to step foot on the moon, has been involved in science, engineering, and exploration all his adult life. He sees research as the process of "creating new knowledge." By "new knowledge," he means making discoveries and learning things for yourself. You should approach research in the same way. That is why using primary sources of information is so important.

When your research uses primary sources, there's a good chance that you will avoid plagiarism in your work. Plagiarism is the use of the words and ideas of others as if they were your own. It is, in effect, a form of intellectual theft, and should be avoided.

Use the ideas of others only as support to help explain your own research. And always identify the source of each of these ideas. The graphic that follows identifies how to conduct responsible research and avoid plagiarizing.

Ways to Avoid Plagiarism

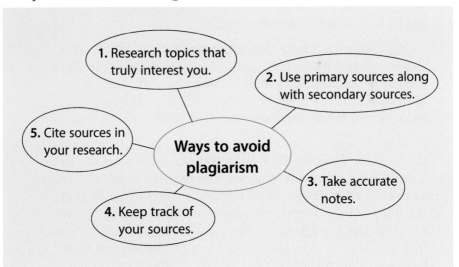

1. Research topics that truly interest you.

2. Use primary sources along with secondary sources.

5. Cite sources in your research.

Ways to avoid plagiarism

3. Take accurate notes.

4. Keep track of your sources.

Your Turn

With the help of a partner, find one or two important facts about plagiarism (other than a definition) on the Internet. Share what you have learned with your classmates.

What Plagiarism Looks Like

On these two pages, you will find an article about the homeless and different ways the article could be plagiarized. Use this information as a guide to check your own work for plagiarism.

People in Need
Anna Morales

On a chilly February afternoon, an old man stands on a city sidewalk and leans against a fence. In his hands a sign reads: "Will work for food. Please help!" Imagine, for a moment, the life this man leads. **He probably spends his days alone on the street begging for handouts, and his nights searching for shelter from the cold. He has no job, no friends, and nowhere to turn.**

Most Americans would like to believe that cases like this are rare. However, the National Coalition for the Homeless estimates that as many as 3 million people in this country share this man's condition. Who are these people we call "the homeless," and what factors have contributed to their plight?

According to Pastor Joel Warren, the director of the Greater Mission Shelter in San Angela, most of the homeless are unemployed males, and from 40 to 60 percent have alcohol or drug-related problems. Warren notes that the image of the typical homeless person is changing. He says that the average age of the homeless has dropped from fifty-five to thirty in the last ten years. National studies have also shown that this population is changing.

A recent study by the United States Conference of Mayors found that one-third of the homeless population consists of families with small children, and 22 percent of the homeless have full- or part-time jobs. Statistics seem to show that more and more of the homeless are entire families who have simply become the victims of a bad economy.

Common Types of Plagiarism

What follows are three common types of plagiarism (highlighted in the examples below.) Another type of plagiarism is using a photograph or graphic from another source without giving the proper credit.

Copying Text

With this type of plagiarism, a writer includes word-for-word sentences from the original source without giving credit.

> It's not hard to imagine what life is like for a homeless person. **He probably spends his days alone on the street begging for handouts, and his nights searching for shelter from the cold. He has no job, no friends, and nowhere to turn.** Such a life is becoming all too familiar to many because of the poor economy.

Forgetting Quotation Marks

With this type of plagiarism, a writer includes the exact words from a source without putting quotation marks before and after this information.

> Many people have no connection with a homeless man like the one just described, and it's not a problem that really enters their thinking. In "People in Need," Anna Morales states that **most Americans would like to believe that cases like this are rare. However, the National Coalition for the Homeless estimates that as many as 3 million people share this man's condition.** This lack of connection stems from the location of most homeless men.

Restating Ideas Without Citing Them

With this type of plagiarism, a writer restates a specific passage from an original article or book without identifying the source.

> **The economy has changed the profile of the homeless population. Studies indicate that families with children now make up more than 30 percent of this population. In addition, more and more homeless have part-time or full-time jobs.**

Giving Credit

You should always give credit for the ideas or words of others that you use in your research papers, reports, and presentations. By doing so, you avoid plagiarizing or using the words of others without crediting them in your work. (See pages 287–289.) Be sure to check with your teacher for instructions for giving credit, or follow the guidelines below.

Using MLA In-Text Citations

The Modern Language Association (MLA) has established an easy system for giving credit in your work. The examples come from the research paper on pages 363–367. (Go to thoughtfullearning.com/p290.)

- After the words from the source, identify the source of the quotation or information in parentheses. In most cases, that means including the author's last name and the page number where the information originated. Place this information at the end of the quoted or borrowed material, usually at the end of the sentence.

  > This obstacle is the driving force behind a state recommendation that the U.S. Fish and Wildfire Service delist the gray wolf as an endangered species in the Midwest (Nie 174). The recommendation . . .

- If you mention the author's name in your text, then you only need to include the page number in parentheses.

  > According to Nie, this obstacle is the driving force behind a state recommendation that the U.S. Fish and Wildfire Service delist the gray wolf as an endangered species in the Midwest (174). The recommendation . . .

- If no author is provided for a source, use a shortened form of the title and the page number, if it is given. (The following example is for a television show, so no page number is included.)

  > Farmers who can prove their livestock losses are caused by wolf attacks receive compensation from the state for their losses, but many farmers are frustrated by time delays for receiving the compensation ("Wolves").

- List on the works-cited page all of the sources of information that you credit in your work. This page comes at the end of your paper.

Creating an MLA Works-Cited Page

According to MLA style, you should create a works-cited page that lists the sources you noted in your paper or presentation. (It should not include sources that you may have read but did not use in your paper or presentation.) Here are the basics for creating this page:

- Include the works-cited page at the end of your paper.
- List the sources alphabetically, starting with authors' last names.
- If no author is given, start with the first word of the title, but not with a short word such as *A, An,* or *The.*
- Double-space all of the information on this page.
- If an entry is more than one line, indent each of the additional lines five spaces.

Citing Basic Sources

What follows is the basic type of information you should include for books, magazines, and online sources. The examples come from the research paper on pages 363–367. (Go to thoughtfullearning.com/p291 for more help.)

For a book include . . .

Author (last name first.) *Title.* City of publication: Publisher, copyright date. Print.

> Nie, Martin A. *Beyond Wolves: The Politics of Wolf Recovery and Management.* Minneapolis: University of Minnesota Press, 2003. Print.

For magazines include . . .

Author (last name first). "Title of the article." *Title of the magazine* Day month year: page numbers. Print.

> Lehmkuhler, Jess. "Effects of Wolves and Other Predators on Farms in Wisconsin." *Wisconsin Outdoor Journal* 1 May 2007: 15-20. Print.

For Web sources include . . .

Author (last name first). "Post title." Site title. Publisher (Host site), Post date or last update. Web. Date used.

> Ness, Erik. "To Kill a Wolf." *Grow Magazine.* University of Wisconsin-Madison, Spring 2009. Web. 10 Dec. 2010.

Evaluating Sources

When you conduct research, you need to make sure that your sources are reliable. Think about the special considerations below.

Experts and Other Primary Sources

Before deciding to interview an "expert," learn about the person. Does the person have the credentials (education and experience) to be an expert? Check with your teacher or a parent if you are not sure. And during an interview, try to gauge the quality of the person's responses. (See page 275 for more.)

Books and Other Print Materials

When selecting print material, learn about the author. Does she or he have the proper background? Check the material's publisher and date of publication to make sure that the information comes from a reputable source and isn't outdated. Then as you read, decide if the information seems fair and balanced. Does it raise any questions? (See page 126 for more.)

Telecasts and Broadcasts

When referring to TV or radio programs, be aware of the purpose of the program. Documentaries and news reports will be more reliable than TV movies or talk-radio conversations. Also, think about the show's intended audience and who sponsors the show. Check into the director and producer of the program, and check the information against other sources. (See pages 127–128 for more.)

Internet Sites

For Internet sites, be sure that the author (if identified) is reliable and respected in the field. Also check the type of site. Government (.gov), education (.edu), and nonprofit (.org) sites often are more reliable than commercial (.com) sites. In addition, determine if the site presents current information and if the information seems reliable and balanced. (See page 137 for more.)

Your Turn

Team up with a classmate to discuss the following: Why is it important to evaluate sources? What are the two most helpful tips on this page?

Chapter 21
Creating

Powerful Web pages, convincing oral presentations, and effective posters—finished products such as these are the result of a lot of planning, researching, and creating. You already know about the importance of planning and researching in the inquiry process. This chapter covers the creating step.

When you create something, you take your initial thoughts and grow them into something wonderful. An idea that once existed in your head becomes something other people can see and touch, respond to and use. This chapter will help you give shape to your project ideas.

You will learn . . .

- A Guide to Creating
- Creating Basic Structure
- Using Informational Structures
- Creating Narrative Structure
- Creating Visual Structure
- 10 Tips for Getting Unstuck

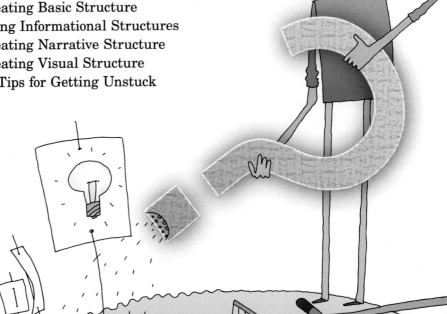

A Guide to Creating

At this point in the inquiry process, you are ready to create something, and the next section in *Inquire* covers all of the exciting possibilities open to you. The form your creation takes will depend on the topic, what you have learned, and how you feel about it.

Checking Your Readiness

You're ready to begin creating after you have . . .
- asked the right questions about your topic,
- completed your planning, including filling out a planning sheet (see page 261), and
- carried out the necessary research.

Getting Started

Here are a few tips that will help you make the best use of your team's talents and time.

- **Follow your schedule.** Check with your planning sheet to know what tasks you need to complete, when they need to be completed, and who will do what.
- **Be prepared.** Have all of the equipment and materials ready to go for each task.
- **Find a good spot to work.** That may be in the back of your classroom, in the art room, in the library, or perhaps in the basement of your home.
- **Reserve plenty of time to complete each task.** You need extended blocks of time, and the undivided attention of everyone involved, to work effectively.
- **Make adjustments as needed.** Expect a few things not to go as planned. Adjust your schedule if certain tasks take longer than expected.
- **Form a meaningful whole.** Your goal is to develop a complete first draft or design so that you have something to work with and improve upon.

In Focus

Having strong feelings about your project will help you do your best work. If, for some reason, you lose interest, rethink your approach.

Creating Basic Structure

Anything that follows a sequence needs a three-part structure: a beginning, a middle, and an ending. For example, oral presentations, essays, stories, plays, and videos should have this structure. Each part is described below. (Also see page 27.)

Beginning

The beginning gets the attention of your audience and provides the background information they need. The beginning should also identify the goal or main point of the product or project.

Appetizer: Think of the beginning part as the appetizer—something tasty that gets everybody ready for the main course.

Middle

The middle is the main part of your creation. It presents the important information, provides the key ideas or images, or develops the story line. It is important that you organize this part so it is easy to follow and has the impact you want. (See pages 26–28.)

Main Course: Think of the middle as the main meal—something hearty and satisfying.

Ending

The ending ties everything together and brings the creation to a logical or fitting close. It should remind the audience about the importance of the topic or provide a final key idea.

Dessert: Think of the ending as the dessert—something that leaves a sweet taste in your mouth and completes the experience in a gratifying way.

Using Informational Structures

When a project deals with a lot of information, organization becomes especially important. The material must be structured to deliver a clear message to your audience. The four organization strategies that follow will work for a variety of projects, including debates, essays, videos, speeches, and oral presentations.

Importance

Use order of importance to rank details or reasons from least important to most, or from most to least.

Most-to-Least Important	Least-to-Most Important
Detail 1	Detail 3
Detail 2	Detail 2
Detail 3	Detail 1

Participating in the community is the first work experience for many Parkview students. They learn about the importance of being on time and completing the work. They also learn about working together and communicating with adults. Anna Hernandez said, "I had to be at the senior center right at 3:00 p.m. because that's when board games started." Practicing these job skills helps students learn about the world of work.

The students' community service also helps them appreciate the problems and challenges facing Bington. Scott Thompson said, "I never realized how thoughtless people can be until I started cleaning up after them. Some people really trash the parks." Mansi Dass learned that some young children really need help with reading and learning. She said, "Some of these kids have hardly ever been read to, so they don't know how fun books can be." Community service helps connect students to their city.

Most importantly, students learn about giving back. For many students, their community service will be the first time they have helped strangers who need help. Ms. Sandra Williams, the community service advisor, said, "Working in the community shows students that a lot of other people need their help." Learning this lesson should help Parkview students become more involved in the community.

Problem-Solution

Use problem-solution order either to explain a problem or to outline a solution and argue for it.

Problem-Focused	Solution-Focused
Introduce the problem.	Introduce the problem.
Explain the severity of the problem.	Offer a solution.
Offer a solution.	Support the solution.

714 N. Harvey Street
East Lake, TN 37400
April 14, 2011

Editor
Jackson News
Jackson Middle School
31991 Lake Street
East Lake, TN 37400

Dear Editor:

Jackson Middle School does not currently offer boys' volleyball, but I think we should add a team. Here are the four main reasons:

1. Jackson High School already has a boys' volleyball program.
2. Other middle schools in the area, including West Lake and Monroe, have teams.
3. East Lake and surrounding cities have summer club teams. At least 12 Jackson boys that I know play club volleyball.
4. Volleyball would offer a good alternative for boys who are not interested in football, soccer, or cross-country.

Cause-Effect

Use cause-effect organization to focus on one cause and its many effects, many causes and their one effect, or many causes and many effects. The main point is to show the connections between events or conditions.

Cause-Centered
Cause
Cause
Cause
Effect

Effect-Centered
Cause
Effect
Effect
Effect

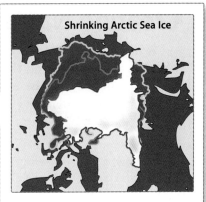

Shrinking Arctic Sea Ice

— 2000 minimum
— 2005 minimum
— 2007 minimum

Comparison-Contrast

Use comparison-contrast organization to show the similarities and differences between two things. Describe one thing and then the other, cover the similarities and then the differences, or describe both subjects point by point. (See also the Venn diagram on page 23.)

Subject by Subject
Subject 1
Subject 2

Similarities-Differences
Similarities
Differences

Point-by-Point

Point 1	
Subject 1	Subject 2

Point 2	
Subject 1	Subject 2

What do Abraham Lincoln and John F. Kennedy have in common?

• Former presidents
• Assassinated while in office
• Controversial

5

How were Abraham Lincoln and John F. Kennedy different?

Lincoln	Kennedy
Republican	Democrat
President for 5 years	President for 3 years
Fought the Civil War	Fought for Civil Rights

6

Creating Narrative Structure

A narrative has a very specific structure. Its plot can be graphed, with the x-axis following the story's beginning, middle, and ending, and the y-axis displaying the audience's level of interest.

Sample Plot Chart

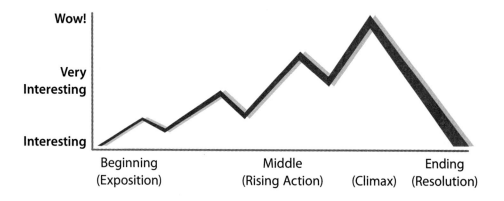

- **Exposition:** The characters are introduced and the setting (time and place) is established. An initial conflict sets up the problem for the main character.
- **Rising action:** The character faces more challenges as he or she tries to reach the goal. Each time, the stakes get higher.
- **Climax:** The character faces down the main challenge and either overcomes it or learns something. This is the most exciting point.
- **Resolution:** After the climax, the narrative wraps up in a satisfying way.

Note: You can use this structure to share personal experiences.

Your Turn

Using the model chart above, plot out a terrific experience—perhaps a great concert or show, a terrific party, an amazing camping trip, or a fun-filled day at a fair or an amusement park. Indicate how you felt at the beginning, middle, and ending by drawing the "plot line" for the experience. Then plot out a bad experience. How are the charts different? Why do you think writers create books whose plots are shaped like good experiences?

Creating Visual Structure

Some creations do not follow a sequence but are instead experienced all at once. Sculptures, paintings, and even posters like the one below have common visual elements. (See also pages 414–429.)

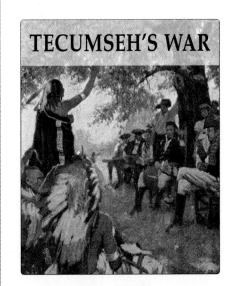

An American Tale of Courage and Honor
Presented by Ms. Smith's History Class

■ **Focus:** This is the main subject of the work.

■ **Figures:** People, animals, plants, or objects are often part of the scene.

■ **Arrangement:** Elements are placed to lead the eye or tell a story.

■ **Light:** Shadows and highlights increase visual interest.

■ **Color:** Blue, green, and purple have a calming effect, while red, orange, and yellow excite. Contrasts add energy.

■ **Background:** Figures usually appear in a specific time and place. A high horizon will focus attention on the ground, and a low horizon reveals the sky.

■ **Perspective:** The point of view and angle affect the audience's understanding.

■ **Other Elements:** Consider typography, framing, and the space in which your work will be displayed.

Your Turn

Analyze a favorite artwork, writing about each of its visual elements. Tell how each part affects the overall impact.

10 Tips for Getting Unstuck

In order to create something, you must keep going. Here are some tips to use in case you get stuck.

1. **Step back.** If you get stuck, you may be too close to your work. Take a step back and you will see more clearly.

2. **Review your planning.** Are you meeting your goal? If not, how can you get back on track?

3. **Define the hang-up.** Out loud or on paper, complete the following sentence: **"I'm having trouble moving forward because ..."** The part you add is the problem. Focus on it, define it, and decide how big it is.

4. **List ways around it.** Out loud or on paper, complete the following sentence: **"I can move forward again if ..."** The part you add is a solution. Complete the sentence several times to think of many solutions. Choose one and use it.

5. **Think upside-down.** If you're still struggling, flip your thinking. Ignore the problem and look at the rest of your project. How could changing something else get you moving again? What could you add, cut, rearrange, or rework?

6. **Ask for an opinion.** Ask someone else to look at your work. Explain the problem you are having and ask for suggestions.

7. **Take small steps.** You may not be able to solve the whole problem at once, but you *can* solve one part at a time.

8. **Work on other parts.** Often, solutions will present themselves as you go along. Keep going.

9. **Get away.** If all else fails, take a short break. Go do something completely different. When you are busy with other tasks, your subconscious mind may find the solution.

10. **Come back.** Return to the project and work through the issue.

Your Turn

Which of these tips will you try next time you get stuck?

Chapter 22
Improving

To create anything is a tremendous accomplishment, and you should feel happy and proud when you complete something. When it works hard, the creative mind deserves to be celebrated.

But after the celebration, when the creative mind is taking a break, you need to wake up your critical mind and take a hard look at what you have made. Did you achieve your goal? Did you exceed it? What parts aren't as good as you'd hoped? How could you make them better?

This chapter shows you how to improve what you create. Who knows— your idea might be the next big thing!

You will learn . . .

- Evaluating
- Using a Rubric Sheet
- Getting a Second Opinion
- Making Improvements
- Using an Improvement Plan
- Perfecting Your Work

Evaluating

The first step in improving your work is to evaluate it. When you evaluate, you decide what's good and what could be better about it. The best way to evaluate your work is to check it against your goal and objectives. That's right, you'll need to pull out your planning sheet and use it to create an evaluation sheet for your project, like the one on the facing page. Follow these guidelines:

1. **Copy your goal and objectives.** Fill in the goal and objectives for the project. Remember that your goal answers *what* and *why*, and that your objectives answer all of the 5 W's and H.

2. **Evaluate your project.** Write a sentence that describes how well you met your goal. Then write a sentence for each objective.

3. **Rate your project.** Decide how well you met or exceeded your goal and objectives. For each one, circle the correct answer:
   - **Beat:** You did better than you had planned.
   - **Met:** You did what you had planned.
   - **Didn't:** You fell short of what you had planned.

4. **Total your score.** Add up your goal (60 points possible) and your objectives (10 points possible for each of six objectives). Here is the scale of scores you can use, matching up to percentages.

120	100	90	80	70	60	40
Amazing!	Great	Strong	Good	Okay	Poor	Incomplete

Your Turn

Pull out your planning sheet and download a rubric sheet from thoughtfullearning.com/p302. Fill in the goal and objectives to create a rubric sheet that you, your teacher, or a peer could use to rate a project.

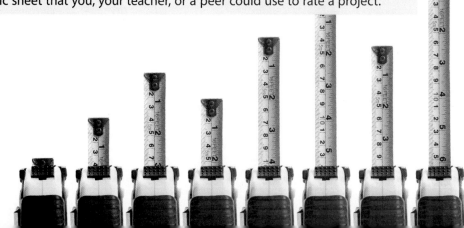

Rubric Sheet

The sheet below shows the evaluation that one student did for his westward-expansion video.

Rubric Sheet

Name: Kranti Modi   **Project:** Tecumseh's War

Goal:	Evaluation	Rating			Score
Make a video about the westward expansion	The footage looks good!	Beat 60	Met (40)	Didn't 20	40
Objectives: 1 I'll write, direct, and act.		Beat 10	Met (6)	Didn't 2	6
2 We'll make a short video.	It should be shorter. Part of it is boring.	Beat 10	Met (6)	Didn't 2	6
3 We'll write in class and shoot in the park.		Beat 10	Met (6)	Didn't 2	6
4 We need to be done in 2 weeks.	We have 2 days to go!	Beat (10)	Met 6	Didn't 2	10
5 We'll show what the expansion was like for Native Americans.	We need another scene showing Tecumseh's side.	Beat 10	Met 6	Didn't (2)	2
6 We'll use Mom's camera and make props/costumes.		Beat 10	Met (6)	Didn't 2	6

TOTAL: 76

Your Turn

Evaluate your project. Read your goal and objectives, and evaluate how well you have achieved them. Then rate your project, comparing your score to the scores on the facing page. (Go to thoughtfullearning.com/p303 for a rubric sheet.)

Getting a Second Opinion

Your evaluation of the project is critical, but you also need the evaluation of others. A classmate or your teacher can offer a second opinion that can help you. It's never easy to hear someone say what isn't working quite right with your project, but that information is very important if you want to improve it.

Your Role

Remember that you are in charge. You've put much more thought and effort into this project than anyone. The reviewer is only helping you make a good thing even better. Use the following tips to get the most out of a second opinion.

- **Introduce the project:** Explain briefly what you have made.
- **Outline your goal and objectives:** Provide the reviewer a rubric sheet and discuss the goal and objectives you have listed.
- **Focus the feedback:** Tell the reviewer the kind of feedback you need.
- **Present your project:** Let the reviewer interact with your project, whether by reading it, watching it, or using it.
- **Give the reviewer space:** Let the person fill out the rubric sheet in private. When the person is finished, ask to discuss the rubric sheet.

Your Turn

Present your project to a reviewer, giving the person a rubric sheet that shows your goal and objectives. Follow the tips above and ask the reviewer for help with improving the project.

The Responder's Role

An outside perspective allows the responder to point out things that the project leader can't see. A good responder helps the person make big improvements. A bad responder provides no help or, worse, makes the person give up. To be a good responder, follow these tips:

- **Connect with the project leader:** Start with respect. Make sure the project leader knows you believe in her or him. By creating this common ground, you shift the focus from personalities to the project.
- **Connect with the goal and objectives:** Read the goal and objectives and restate them to the project leader. Understanding the goal and objectives shows that you and the leader are on the same side and that you want to help the person succeed.
- **Focus first on the positive:** Show the project leader that you appreciate what is working with the project.
- **State the negative in positive terms:** When you mention a problem, show how it is not as good as another part of the project. Emphasize how you want this problem not to detract from the good things that are working.
- **Provide options:** Follow up a statement of a problem with one or more solutions to solve the problem. When a project leader hears of a problem, the natural result is panic, but when you offer one or more solutions, you give the person lifelines to escape the problem.
- **Step back:** Once you have given your opinion and your suggestions, let the project leader go back to fixing the problems. Give the leader room to work through changes.

Your Turn

Help another person with his or her project. Learn about it, review the goal and objectives, and then carefully consider the work. Use the tips above.

Making Improvements

After evaluating your work and receiving a second opinion, you should be ready to improve it. Some of your improvements may be critical in nature; others will be more creative.

Critical Improvements

Cutting

Ask yourself the questions below. Then plan which parts you will cut.

■ What part or parts do not help me reach my goal or objectives?
■ How can I make my work simpler, smaller, cleaner, or clearer?

Rearranging

Ask yourself the following questions to plan which parts to rearrange.

■ What part or parts are in the wrong place?
■ How can I rearrange my work to make it more effective, efficient, and smooth?

Creative Improvements

Reworking

Ask yourself the following questions to plan which parts to rework.

■ What part or parts need to work better?
■ How can I rework these parts so that they help me achieve my goal?

Adding

Ask yourself the following questions to plan which parts to add.

■ What is missing from my creation?
■ How can I add just what is needed?

Your Turn

Answer these questions about your own project, completing an improvement plan like the one on the following page.

Using an Improvement Plan

Here is an improvement plan created by the student who was making a video about the westward expansion. (Go to thoughtfullearning.com/p307 to download an improvement plan of your own.)

Name: Kranti Modi   **Project:** Tecumseh's War (Video)

Critical Improvements

Cutting: What part or parts do not help me reach my goal or objectives? How can I make my work simpler, smaller, cleaner, or clearer?

I don't need the part when Jacob and Martha are reading by candlelight. It's boring and doesn't add important information.

Plan: I'll cut the reading scene and just have Jacob and Martha reading when Tecumseh knocks on the door.

Rearranging: What part or parts are in the wrong place? How can I rearrange my creation to make it more effective, efficient, and smooth?

I should have them meet Tecumseh before the war begins. That way they'll understand his side of the story better.

Plan: I'll move the scene about meeting Tecumseh.

Creative Improvements

Reworking: What part or parts need to work better? How can I rework these parts so that they help me achieve my goal?

The scene with the battle looks fake because nobody actually makes contact.

Plan: I'll shoot that scene over again, but with tight shots so it is harder to tell what is happening.

Adding: What is missing from my creation? How can I add just what is needed?

I need to add a final scene for Tecumseh.

Plan: I'll write a new scene, and we'll film it on Friday at the park.

Perfecting Your Work

Once you have made major changes to your work, you'll want to give everything a final polish. The amount of polishing that you do depends on the situation. The more formal the situation, the more time you should spend polishing.

Your work should always be clean, clear, and correct. For more important situations, it should also be effective, efficient, and enjoyable. For the most important or formal situations, it should also be precise, powerful, and poetic. How much time you spend perfecting your work depends on how important the final product is to you. Why stop short?

	Casual	Semiformal	Formal
Clean	X	X	X
Clear	X	X	X
Correct	X	X	X
Effective		X	X
Efficient		X	X
Enjoyable		X	X
Precise			X
Powerful			X
Poetic			X

Your Turn

Think about a recent project you completed. Was it casual, semiformal, or formal? Did you follow through to the right level of perfecting? What might you do differently next time?

Chapter 23
Presenting

The final stage in the inquiry process is presentation—setting your work before other people. Yes, this can be scary. What if they don't like it? What if they are bored by it? Then again, what if they love it?

So loosen your grip on the thing and let your audience hold it awhile. Let them read it, study it, watch it, listen to it, use it. To finish well, you need to march your work out into the world and share it.

You will learn . . .

- Understanding the Situation
- Presenting in Person
- Presenting on the Web
- Promoting Your Project

Understanding the Situation

Before "going public," ask yourself the 5 W and H questions about the situation. Here is a set of questions and answers from a student who made a video.

Situation Analysis

Name: Kranti Modi   **Project:** Tecumseh's War

1. **Who** will interact with your work?
   Anybody on Youtube can see my video. I want to make sure my friends and classmates watch it.

2. **What** do you want the audience's experience to be like?
   I want people to think about the clash of cultures between settlers and Native Americans.

3. **Where** do you want to present your work?
   I'll host the video at Youtube, but I'll also use Facebook and Twitter to link to it, and I'll put a link on my blog, as well.

4. **When** do you want your work to be presented?
   I want to make a big splash with the video, so I'll put it up on my birthday so I can promote it at school and on my Facebook page.

5. **Why** do you want to present your work to them?
   We worked really hard on this video, and it turned out great. I want to show it off but also help teach people.

6. **How** will your work be presented?
   It will be a low-resolution video, so I think I should maybe host it also on my site so people can see the quality of it better.

Your Turn

Answer the questions above about your own presentation situation. (Download your own version from thoughtfullearning.com/p310.)

Presenting in Person

Often, you'll need to make an oral presentation of a project. Here are three ways you can prepare an oral presentation.

Note Cards

One common way to prepare a presentation is to use note cards. Write out your introduction and conclusion word for word. Then write out the main points on other cards. Order them and number them. (See page 75.)

Introduction	1
Imagine that you lived in the 1700s in the Ohio Territory. That's where Tecumseh lived. When he was growing up, his village was attacked five times by settlers. As a grown man, Tecumseh fought bravely, as this video will show.	

Outlines

Another common presentation format is an outline. It contains the key points of your presentation, written as sentences or phrases to remind you what to say. (See also pages 442–443.)

Sample Outline

1. Give background about Tecumseh
2. Tell about making the video
   A. Planning the westward expansion project
   B. Script writing
   C. Costumes, props, sets, filming
   D. Editing the video
3. Invite audience to relax and enjoy "Tecumseh's War"

Manuscripts

A manuscript is the full presentation written out word for word. If you use a manuscript, practice with it so that you can look up from the page and make eye contact. (See also pages 440–441.)

Your Turn

Create note cards, an outline, or a manuscript for your presentation.

Presenting on the Web

When you present a project on the Web, think about the following:

Purpose

Understand what effect you want the posting to have. Are you just wanting to show off your great work, or do you have other reasons for posting? Here are some common reasons to post.

- **To entertain:** You can post videos and stories online to entertain people who have similar interests.
- **To inform:** Blog posts, book or movie reviews, and how-to articles are often posted to provide information to others.
- **To persuade:** Editorials, letters to the editor, and protest songs are often posted to convince others of something.
- **To invite:** Photos, drawings, videos, fiction, and many other types of projects are posted online in sharing sites in order to attract like-minded individuals, forming a community.

Place

You can post your work on a private site and have complete control over it, on a classroom wiki and share it with those you know, or on a public site and get the widest possible audience. Here are the pros and cons of each type of site:

Location	Pro	Con
Your Own Site	■ You keep control. ■ You keep ownership. ■ You can make changes to your work at any time.	■ You may have little traffic. ■ The site might not handle special media well.
A Classroom Wiki	■ The site is safe. ■ Friends and family will see your work. ■ Your work is in context.	■ The material might be taken down after a while. ■ Class sites have only so much room.
A Public Site	■ You get the most traffic. ■ You get the most effective presentation.	■ You may have to give up rights. ■ Posting may require membership and a fee.

Timing

Obviously, you should post your work when it will have the best effect—depending on what you are trying to accomplish.

- **To just get finished . . .** post as soon as you are done. Afterward, draw people's attention to it using social media and telling everyone that the special occasion is simply that you have completed the project.
- **To complete a broadcast . . .** post when the project best fits the schedule. For example, if you always post a podcast on Tuesdays, post your podcast then so your audience can find it.
- **To draw in an audience . . .** post in connection with an event or a holiday. Mention the special occasion, and link back to your work from places that feature that event or holiday.

Procedure

Every site will have different rules about file sizes, file types, content, and so on. Make sure that you understand the site specifications. Also, most sites will require you to digitally sign an agreement. Be sure to read the agreement. If posting on the site means that you give up rights to your material, you might want to think twice before doing so.

Once you fully understand the specifications and property considerations, follow the instructions that the site provides for uploading material. (You may have to become a member before making a post.)

Your Turn

Answer these four questions yourself.
1. Why should I post?
2. Where should I post?
3. When should I post?
4. How should I post?

Then make your posting.

Promoting Your Project

Here are basic tools for promoting a project.

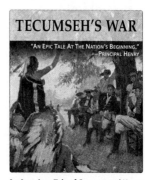

TECUMSEH'S WAR

"An Epic Tale At The Nation's Beginning."
—Principal Henry

An American Tale of Courage and Honor
Presented by Ms. Smith's History Class

Watch It Now Online!

Posters or Handouts

Of course, you can promote your work by creating posters to hang in the school hallways or small brochures or handouts to leave on the counter of a store. Make sure to include a graphic to grab people's attention and get them to remember your message. (See pages 418–419, 422–423.)

Your Turn

Create paper promotions for your project, including the elements listed above. Remember that these promotions can also be sent out using social media.

Social Media

Promote your project by sending an e-mail message (with attached poster) to your friends and family members. Include a link if your project is available online. You can also upload your poster to Facebook or Twitter and provide links there. (See pages 139–156 for more on social media.)

Your Turn

Log onto your social networks and promote your project. Invite others to see what you have done and ask for their comments and feedback.

Community Calendar

Don't forget about traditional promotional opportunities, such as submitting a promotion to the community calendar section of a newspaper, writing a feature story about your project for the local paper, or taking out an ad. You can also submit your slogan to local businesses that have electronic message boards, if they provide community announcements.

Your Turn

Submit promotional materials to local newspapers and businesses with message boards.

Part III:
Developing Projects

Part III: Developing Projects

This section is overflowing with project ideas using the inquiry process. There are writing projects, graphing projects, Web projects, design projects, and much more. Each specific project includes guidelines, visuals, and examples. Listed below are the types of projects covered in Part III. Remember that these are just starting points. Let inquiry lead you to make these projects your own.

Chapters in This Section

Chapter 24
Basic Writing Projects

Writing is a powerful vehicle for success. In school, writing helps you explore your thoughts and become a better learner. Outside of school, good writers and communicators are more likely to land jobs and achieve their career goals.

Being a good writer doesn't mean you have to be the next Shakespeare. Just writing an effective banner is an accomplishment. But you also need to be able to complete the other forms of writing covered in this chapter.

You will learn . . .

- Writing Paragraphs
- Writing Summaries
- Writing E-Mail
- Creating Instructions
- Writing Narratives
- Writing Poems
- Writing Plays
- Building Essays

Project Overview

Here is a quick overview of the writing projects in this chapter.

Paragraph

A paragraph introduces an idea or a topic and supports it with details and reasoning. Here you'll learn the parts of a complete paragraph and how to arrange them. (See pages 320–321.)

The Science of Speed

Unlike race cars or trains, roller coasters do not rely on powerful engines for speed. Instead, coasters let gravity and momentum do all the work. Gravity is the force that constantly pulls objects of mass toward the ground. When a roller-coaster track slopes down, the passenger cars accelerate forward because gravity pulls the front car downward. When the track tilts up, the cars decelerate because gravity pulls the back car downward. These changes in acceleration are what make roller coasters so thrilling. But gravity is not the only factor in maintaining speed. Another is momentum. On most roller coasters, the first drop is t... designed this way... cars forward thro... especially needed... gravity pulls the... of-war between gr... ride!

Half Plant, Half Animal

In "A Biological Fusion," Mercedes Matthews introduces a scientific study of the first known animal to produce chlorophyll. Chlorophyll is the green pigment that plants use to get energy from the sun during photosynthesis. The animal's biological name is *Elysia chlorotica*, but a non-scientist would more likely call it a sea slug. Biologist Sidney K. Pierce ran the study of the sea slugs, which live in the marshes and creeks along the Atlantic coast of the United States. His study concluded that the sea slugs picked up the power to produce chlorophyll by stealing genes from the algae they ingest. The manufacturing of chlorophyll allows the slugs to convert light to energy and survive for a long time without eating. An *Elysia chlorotica*, then, can actually be considered part animal, part plant.

Summary

Writing a summary means capturing the main point of a reading selection in your own words. (See pages 322–323.)

E-Mail

E-mail is a popular form of electronic communication. Here you'll find guidelines for writing effective e-mail. (See pages 324–325.)

Field Trip Idea

Send Attach Address

To: cbaker@redwoodms.edu

Subject: Field Trip Idea

Hi, Ms. Baker:

Since we have been studying the history of automobiles in social studies, I suggest we take a field trip to the Virginia Museum of Transportation. I looked at the Web site and saw the museum has a big collection of the old locomotives and automobiles we have been talking about in class.

I know we don't have a lot of money for field trips this year, but guess what? Students get in for free! They even do guided tours at no charge. It would be so cool to see the classic ca... person.

If you have time, you should check out the museum... Here is the link:

http://www.vmt.org/education/school...

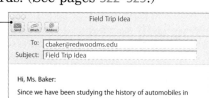

Instructions for Calculating the Windchill Factor

Windchill factor is the effect wind speed has on how cold temperatures feel. Wind causes a person's body to cool more rapidly, just as it would at a lower temperature. Here are the steps for calculating the windchill.

Materials Needed: thermometer, anemometer, paper, pencil, windchill chart

Steps:
1. **Set up equipment.** Place the thermometer outside in a shaded spot away from buildings or other heat sources. Set up the anemometer in an open area away from buildings. *Caution: Avoid prolonged exposure to low temperatures and high winds.*
2. **Take readings.** Every five minutes for half an hour, check the anemometer and write down wind speeds. After the first ten minutes, begin checking the thermometer and writing down Fahrenheit temperatures every five minutes.
3. **Average the readings.** Add the anemometer readings and divide by the number of readings to get an average wind speed. Add the thermometer readings and divide by the

Instructions

Instructions are useful for explaining how to do something or showing how something works. (See pages 326–327.)

Narrative

Narratives are stories about real or imagined events that mean something. Here a writer gives a fictionalized account in a diary form. (See pages 328–330.)

> 1
>
> August 28, 1943, Day 396: Hot. It is scorching hot out here. At home in Los Angeles, I enjoyed the warm weather. Even on those rare summer days when temperatures hit 90, I was able to cool off at the fountains near my house or the crowded public swimming pool on the outskirts of Little Tokyo.
>
> But this Arizona desert heat is different. It is dry and constant and unbearable. I am thirsty all the time, but we have to be careful about how much water we drink. There is no play fountain or swimming pool. The only running water is in the mess hall and hospital.
>
> August 29, 1943, Day 397: I spent the whole day in the barracks today, cooped up, trying to stay cool. Finally, that blazing ~~sun~~ dropped behi~~nd~~ cool breezes ~~~~
> Dad and ~~I~~ the sunset. ~~~~ the sky. It ma~~~~ think it'll be ~~~~ He just s~~~~

Mercury

This metal is liquid at eighty degrees
And measures your temperature after a sneeze.
It isn't an alloy and never would settle
For being mislabeled "transitional metal."

It's element eighty on charts on the wall
And powers the battery-pack of your doll.
It's gleaming and runny and glossy and odd
And registers heat when it's in a glass rod.

Oh mercury, why be so shiny and slick?
Oh quicksilver, why do you make people sick?
Your vapors are toxic; your contact so bad
That you made the sane hatter of Wonderland mad!

Poem

Poetry is a great outlet for expressing an idea in an interesting way. (See pages 332–333.)

When Washington Met Sally

GEORGE WASHINGTON, first U.S. president
SALLY RIDE, first woman in space

SCENE 1:
Setting: Coffee shop, Mount Vernon, VA, present day
(SALLY RIDE sits at a table and sips coffee from a mug. GEORGE WASHINGTON enters.)
WASHINGTON: How do you do, Ms. Ride? *(Removes hat)*
SALLY RIDE: Very well. And you, Mr. President?
WASHINGTON: Splendid. *(Sitting across from her)* That accent of yours . . . Are you a Pennsylvanian?
SALLY RIDE: No, Californian.
WASHINGTON: *(Confused)* You don't look Spanish!
SALLY RIDE: I'm not. I'm American.
WASHINGTON: *(Clearly dumbfounded)* Don't be preposterous! The Treaty of Paris sets clear borders for the United States. Anything west of the Mississippi belongs to the Spaniards.
SALLY RIDE: You clearly have a lot of catching up to do, Mr. President.
WASHINGTON: Do I? *(Tastes his coffee and shakes his head in disgust.)* Then explain to me how you can be both American *and* Californian.
SALLY RIDE: That requires a bit of a history lesson.

Play

Playwriting takes a creative mind. Find out how to put your story ideas into play format. (See pages 334–336.)

In Your Dreams

Dreams are one of life's greatest mysteries. For centuries, people have tried to figure out why we dream and what our dreams mean. Dream interpreters even accompanied military leaders during battles. Today scientists know more about dreams but are still unclear on what causes dreams and why they are so hard to remember.

What scientists do know is that every person dreams every night, even though most people do not remember what they dreamed. In fact, on most nights, people dream several times, with each dream lasting between 5 and 20 minutes. In a lifetime, the average person will spend an equivalent of six years dreaming. Even people who have been blind since birth dream. The only difference is that they dream in sounds, smells, and feelings instead of in images.

Scientists note that within 5 minutes of waking up, people forget half of what they dreamed. Within 10 minutes, they forget 90 percent. Why it is so difficult to recall dreams is debatable. One theory is that people dream information that they don't want to remember, because it

Essay

Essays provide writers with the space to explore a topic in great detail. Guidelines will help you construct complete essays. (See pages 337–340.)

Inquire   To Write a Paragraph

1. **Question** the situation for the paragraph.
   - **Subject:** What specific topic will you write about?
   - **Purpose:** Why are you writing—to explain, to describe, to narrate?
   - **Audience:** Who will read this paragraph?

2. **Plan** your paragraph.
   - **Identify your topic.** Make it specific enough to cover in one paragraph.

3. **Research** your topic.
   - **Searching:** Consult primary and secondary sources as needed to learn about your topic. (See pages 274–279.)
   - **Focusing:** Decide on a focus—the part of the topic that you want to emphasize in your paragraph.

     Topic: *Mrs. Brown*   **Focus:** *is a great math teacher*

     State the focus in a topic sentence.

     Topic sentence: *Mrs. Brown makes learning math fun.*

   - **Shaping:** List important details that support or explain your topic. Arrange the details in the most logical order.

4. **Create** the first draft of your paragraph.
   - **Start with your topic sentence.**
   - **Follow with your supporting details.**
   - **End with a sentence that ties everything together.**

5. **Improve** your first draft.
   - **Evaluate** your first draft.
     Purpose: Does the paragraph effectively fulfill your purpose?
     Audience: Will the paragraph hold the reader's interest?
   - **Revise** your writing.
     Rewrite sentences that are confusing or unclear.
     Add details to explain your topic more fully.
     Reorder sentences that are out of place.
   - **Edit** your revised writing.
     Replace general nouns and verbs with specific ones.
     Check your writing for accuracy.

6. **Present** the final copy of your paragraph to your classmates or to friends or family members.

Paragraph

Here is a sample paragraph created by a student for her science class. The writer has included a clear topic sentence, body sentences that share supporting details, and a closing sentence.

The **topic sentence** (underlined) tells the reader what the paragraph is about.

The **body sentences** provide support for the topic sentence.

The **closing sentence** refers again to the main idea and offers a final point.

The Science of Speed

Unlike race cars or trains, roller coasters do not rely on powerful engines for speed. Instead, coasters let gravity and momentum do all the work. Gravity is the force that constantly pulls objects of mass toward the ground. When a roller-coaster track slopes down, the passenger cars accelerate forward because gravity pulls the front car downward. When the track tilts up, the cars decelerate because gravity pulls the back car downward. These changes in acceleration are what make roller coasters so thrilling. But gravity is not the only factor in maintaining speed. Another is momentum. On most roller coasters, the first drop is the tallest and steepest. Coasters are designed this way to create enough momentum to carry the cars forward through the rest of the track. Momentum is especially needed to make it up hills and through loops, as gravity pulls the cars in the opposite direction. This tug-of-war between gravity and momentum makes for one fun ride!

Inquire   To Write a Summary

1. **Question** the situation for your summary.
   - **Subject**: What specific topic does the reading selection address?
   - **Purpose**: What is the goal of the selection—to inform, to persuade, to tell a story—and how can its contents be summed up?
   - **Audience**: Who reads this type of material?

2. **Plan** your summary.
   - **Identify** the main point of the writing.

3. **Research** your topic.
   - **Searching**: Reread the selection and write down the key points.
   - **Focusing**: Find the focus of your summary—the selection's main idea.
     > **Topic**: *"Strange Sneezing Situations"*
     >   *by Hannah Holmes*

     State the focus in a topic sentence.
     > **Topic sentence:** *In "Strange Sneezing Situations," Hannah Holmes describes how genetics influence a person's sneezing habits.*
   - **Shaping**: List the key points of the article in your own words.

4. **Create** the first draft.
   - **Start with your topic sentence.**
   - **Follow with supporting details.** Recount the selection's most important details in your own words.
   - **End with a sentence that restates the main point** of the topic sentence.

5. **Improve** your first draft.
   - **Evaluate** your first draft.
     Purpose: Does the paragraph effectively sum up the selection?
     Audience: Would a person reading the summary understand what the reading selection was about?
   - **Revise** your writing.
     Add details to summarize the selection more fully.
     Cut any unnecessary details.
   - **Edit** your revised writing.
     Check your writing for accuracy.

6. **Present** the final copy of your summary to your classmates or post it on your classroom blog or discussion site.

Article and Summary

A summary captures the main points of a reading selection. Here is a science article followed by a student's summary, which includes only the most important details from the article in the student's own words.

A Biological Fusion
By Mercedes Matthews

Plants are plants and animals are animals. An organism can't be a combination of the two, right? Think again. A new study by biologist Sidney K. Pierce suggests a sea slug living in the marshes and creeks along the U.S. Atlantic coast is part animal, part plant. Biologically known as *Elysia chlorotica,* the sea slug is the first known animal to manufacture chlorophyll, the green pigment in plants that captures energy from sunlight during photosynthesis.

Scientists believe the green, leaf-shaped slugs acquired the ability to make chlorophyll by stealing genes from their main source of food—algae. Instead of digesting algae whole, the slugs retain and save the algae's chloroplasts in their own cells. What makes the *E. chlorotica* even more remarkable is that Pierce proved the species has developed the ability to make chlorophyll without the assistance of the chloroplast reserves stolen from algae. This ability allows the slugs to convert energy from the sun and survive long stretches without any food.

So how did Pierce make this discovery? He used a radioactive tracer that tracked the chemical processes in the slug cells. The results showed that the slugs themselves were making the green chlorophyll pigment, not simply relying on the algae they ingested. For further proof he looked at slugs that hadn't eaten algae for five months and discovered chloroplasts still existed in their bodies. If the chloroplasts came from the algae, they would have been digested long ago. Thus, the slugs were producing their own chlorophyll. An animal with plant parts: What an extraordinary discovery!

Student Summary

The **topic sentence** introduces the title, author, and main point.	### Half Plant, Half Animal

In "A Biological Fusion," Mercedes Matthews introduces a scientific study of the first known animal to produce chlorophyll. Chlorophyll is the green pigment that plants use to get energy from the sun during photosynthesis. The animal's biological name is *Elysia chlorotica,* but a non-scientist would more likely call it a sea slug. Biologist Sidney K. Pierce ran the study of the sea slugs, which live in the marshes and creeks along the Atlantic coast of the United States. His study concluded that the sea slugs picked up the power to produce chlorophyll by stealing genes from the algae they ingest. The manufacturing of chlorophyll allows the slugs to convert light to energy and survive for a long time without eating. An *Elysia chlorotica,* then, can actually be considered part animal, part plant.

The **body sentences** give key details.

The **closing sentence** completes the summary.

Inquire   To Write an E-Mail

1. **Question** the situation for the e-mail.
- **Subject:** What is the specific topic of your e-mail message?
- **Purpose:** Why are you choosing to write an e-mail? What type of response do you hope to get?
- **Audience:** Who will read your e-mail—a teacher, a classmate, a friend?

2. **Plan** your e-mail.
- **Be clear** about the purpose of your message.

3. **Research** your topic.
- **Searching:** Find the correct e-mail address of the receiver.
- **Focusing:** Decide on your focus—the topic and reason for writing the e-mail.

    Topic: *art contest results*   **Reason:** *to say congratulations*
    Focus: *You won first prize in the art contest. Way to go!*

- **Shaping:** List any other important details you want to include.

4. **Create** the first draft of your e-mail.
- **Complete the e-mail header.** Create a clear subject line that tells the reader what the message is about.
- **Start the message** by greeting the reader and stating your focus.
- **Follow with any additional details** you wish to include.
- **Politely end the message.** If any follow-up information is needed, spell it out. Then provide a polite closing and your name.

5. **Improve** your first draft.
- **Evaluate** your first draft.
    Purpose: Does the e-mail fulfill your purpose for writing?
    Audience: Is the language clear and appropriate for the reader?
- **Revise** your e-mail.
    Cut any careless or unnecessary comments.
    Break up any lengthy passages into short, double-spaced paragraphs with lists and headings.
- **Edit** your revised e-mail.
    Check your message for spelling and punctuation errors.

6. **Present** the e-mail by sending it to the receiver.

E-Mail

Here is an e-mail from a student to his teacher. The student is careful to avoid sloppy errors because he wants to make a good impression. His message is clear and easy to read.

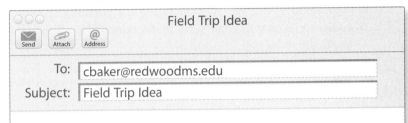

Field Trip Idea

Send   Attach   Address

To: cbaker@redwoodms.edu

Subject: Field Trip Idea

The beginning states the main point of the message.

Hi, Ms. Baker:

Since we have been studying the history of automobiles in social studies, I suggest we take a field trip to the Virginia Museum of Transportation. I looked at the Web site and saw the museum has a big collection of the old locomotives and automobiles we have been talking about in class.

The middle provides additional details.

I know we don't have a lot of money for field trips this year, but guess what? Students get in for free! They even do guided tours at no charge. It would be so cool to see the classic cars in person.

If you have time, you should check out the museum's Web site. Here is the link:

http://www.vmt.org/education/school.html

The ending politely completes the message.

Thanks for reading my idea about a field trip to the Museum of Transportation. Hopefully we can make it there someday soon.

Thanks again.

Tony Stanley

Inquire To Create Instructions

1. **Question** the situation for your instructions.
   - **Subject:** What specific topic will your instructions cover?
   - **Purpose:** Why are you writing these instructions?
   - **Audience:** Who will read your instructions? How much do they know about the subject?

2. **Plan** your instructions by creating a list of steps.

3. **Research** your topic.
   - **Searching:** Consult primary and secondary sources to learn all about your subject. (See pages 274–279.)
   - **Focusing:** Decide on a focus—your topic and main reason for writing the instructions.

     Topic: *greeting a dog*   **Importance:** *make the dog feel safe*
     Topic sentence: *Following a few simple steps when greeting a dog will make the dog feel safe and comfortable around you.*
   - **Shaping:** List the steps of the instructions in the correct order. Also list any materials or tools required to complete the task.

4. **Create** the first draft of your instructions.
   - **Start by introducing the process,** explaining its importance, and stating its goal. Then, if necessary, list any materials needed.
   - **Follow by writing numbered, step-by-step instructions.** If possible, add visual aids.
   - **End with a brief description of the final outcome.**

5. **Improve** the first draft.
   - **Evaluate** your first draft.
     Audience: Are your instructions clear and helpful?
   - **Revise** your writing.
     Rewrite steps that are confusing or unclear.
     Add steps or visual aids as necessary.
     Cut steps that don't belong.
     Reorder steps that are out of place.
   - **Edit** your revised writing.
     Replace passive verbs with command verbs (*place* instead of *should be placed*).
     Check your writing for accuracy.

6. **Present** your project by printing a copy and posting it where the instructions will be most helpful.

Instructions

Here a student explains how to calculate windchill in easy-to-follow steps.

The beginning introduces the activity, tells why it is important, and lists the materials.

Instructions for Calculating the Windchill Factor

Windchill factor is the effect wind speed has on how cold temperatures feel. Wind causes a person's body to cool more rapidly, just as it would at a lower temperature. Here are the steps for calculating the windchill.

Materials Needed: thermometer, anemometer, paper, pencil, windchill chart

Steps:

1. **Set up equipment.** Place the thermometer outside in a shaded spot away from buildings or other heat sources. Set up the anemometer in an open area away from buildings. *Caution: Avoid prolonged exposure to low temperatures and high winds.*

An important caution is mentioned.

2. **Take readings.** Every five minutes for half an hour, check the anemometer and write down wind speeds. After the first ten minutes, begin checking the thermometer and writing down Fahrenheit temperatures every five minutes.

The **middle** presents numbered steps.

3. **Average the readings.** Add the anemometer readings and divide by the number of readings to get an average wind speed. Add the thermometer readings and divide by the number of readings to get an average temperature.

4. **Check the windchill chart.** Find the average temperature in the top row and the average wind speed in the left column. Trace your finger down the temperature column and across the wind-speed row to find the windchill factor.

Windchill Chart

Temperature (°F)

Calm	30	25	20	15	10	5	0	-5	-10
5	25	19	13	7	1	-5	-11	-16	-22
10	21	15	9	3	-4	-10	-16	-22	-28
15	19	13	6	0	-7	-13	-19	-26	-32
20	17	11	4	-2	-9	-15	-22	-29	-35
25	16	9	3	-4	-11	-17	-24	-31	-37
30	15	8	1	-5	-12	-19	-26	-33	-39
35	14	7	0	-7	-14	-21	-27	-34	-41
40	13	6	-1	-8	-15	-22	-29	-36	-43
45	12	5	-2	-9	-16	-23	-30	-37	-44
50	12	4	-3	-10	-17	-24	-31	-38	-45

Wind (mph)

The **ending** provides an informative chart.

Source: http://www.weather.gov/om/windchill

■ Frostbite in 30 minutes ■ Frostbite in 10 minutes

Inquire To Write a Narrative

1. **Question** the situation for the narrative.
   - **Subject:** Who is the main character? What other characters will be in it?
   - **Purpose:** What conflict will the main character encounter? What is your reason for writing this narrative?
   - **Audience:** Who will read the narrative?

2. **Plan** your narrative. (Go to thoughtfullearning.com/p328 for more.)
   - What are the key plot points? How will the narrative begin, develop, and end? (See page 298.)

3. **Research** your narrative.
   - **Searching:** Consult primary and secondary sources as needed to learn about the location, plot, and characters in your narrative.
   - **Focusing:** Decide on what mood you wish to convey in your narrative—tension, doom, excitement, and so on.
   - **Shaping:** Decide on a climax for your narrative. The climax shows the outcome of the central conflict. The main character faces her or his greatest challenge and either succeeds or fails.

4. **Create** the first draft of the narrative.
   - **Start** by grabbing the reader's attention. Good narratives often begin somewhere in the middle of the action.
   - **Follow** with rising action, unfolding and building the conflict.
   - **Lead** up to the climax, the most exiting part.
   - **End** with the resolution, showing how the character is changed by the events in the narrative.

5. **Improve** your first draft
   - **Evaluate** your first draft.
     Subject: Is the main character memorable?
     Purpose: Is the conflict in the narrative interesting?
   - **Revise** your writing.
     Rewrite any dialogue or action that does not fit the personality or voice of the characters.
     Add any missing details or background information.
   - **Edit** your revised writing.
     Replace any general nouns or verbs with specific ones.
     Check your writing for accuracy.

6. **Present** the final copy online or read it out loud to your classmates or another group.

Narrative (Historical Diary Entries)

The following historical diary entries were created by a student for his social studies class. The writer speaks from the perspective of a young person who is forced to live in a Japanese internment camp during World War II.

1

In the **beginning**, the writer starts in the middle of the action and gives the reader a sense that not all is right.

August 28, 1943, Day 396: Hot. It is scorching hot out here. At home in Los Angeles, I enjoyed the warm weather. Even on those rare summer days when temperatures hit 90, I was able to cool off at the fountains near my house or the crowded public swimming pool on the outskirts of Little Tokyo.

But this Arizona desert heat is different. It is dry and constant and unbearable. I am thirsty all the time, but we have to be careful about how much water we drink. There is no play fountain or swimming pool. The only running water is in the mess hall and hospital.

The **middle** provides details and observations about the day.

August 29, 1943, Day 397: I spent the whole day in the barracks today, cooped up, trying to stay cool. Finally, that blazing sun slid down through the barbed wire and dropped behind the sandy hills. The sky was on fire, but cool breezes began to blow.

Dad and I went out and stood there and looked at the sunset. Red and yellow and purple battled across the sky. It made me think of the war. "When do you think it'll be done, Dad?" I asked. "The war, I mean."

He just shook his head.

August 30, 1943, Day 398: I couldn't stand it anymore. I couldn't stay inside for another minute. I ran outside at the hottest part of the day and just yelled at that blazing sun, "Go away! Leave us alone!"

(Over) →

2

August 30 (Continued)

Dad came to the doorway and called out, "Who are you shouting at?"

"The sun!" I shouted, pointing up. "The stupid sun!" It just kept pouring heat down on me. My bare feet were burning on the hot sand. I started hopping from one foot to the other as I shouted at the sun.

Dad laughed. "What are you doing? A rain dance?"

"Ow, ow, ow, ow!" I yelled as I ran back into the barracks.

August 31, 1943, Day 399: My rain dance worked.

Today, clouds rolled across the sky, blocking the sun. They bunched together until no blue remained. They boiled high into the sky and darkened to gray and then black. Then they burst open, pouring water down.

Back in Los Angeles, we would stay inside when it rained. But here, we went out and stood in it. The rain felt so good—cool and wet and pounding down. Gullies started to run through the camp, and then they were streams, and then rivers. The other camp kids and I ran through the water and made boats out of sticks and laughed. We watched our stick boats float through the fences and keep on going, out into the desert, traveling far away.

The cool rain gives me hope. I know we will someday leave this place and go back to our homes. I know we will be free.

The **ending** looks to the future.

Using Transitions

Transitions are useful in all types of writing. In paragraphs, transitions connect sentences and ideas. In longer writing, transitions can connect one paragraph to the next. Here are some effective transitions to use in your writing.

To Show Location

above	below	between	inside	next to
around	beside	by	near	over

To Show Time

after	during	first	meanwhile	second
before	finally	later	next	until

To Compare Things

also	in the same way
as	like
both	similarly

To Contrast Things

although	however
but	on the other hand
even though	yet

To Add Information

additionally	and	besides	for instance
along with	another	finally	in addition
also	as well	for example	next

To Conclude or Summarize

as a result	in conclusion
finally	lastly

To Clarify a Point

for example	in other words
for instance	that is

Inquire To Write a Poem

1. **Question** the situation and your goal for writing a poem.
   - **Subject:** What will be the poem's focus?
   - **Purpose:** Why are you writing the poem?
   - **Audience:** Who will read the poem?

2. **Plan** your poem, using a free-verse or traditional form.
   - Free-verse poetry doesn't have a strict rhythm and rhyme scheme.
   - Traditional poetry has a specific rhythm and rhyme scheme.

3. **Research** your topic.
   - **Gathering:** Brainstorm details about your topic. Consider making a word cluster around the topic word.
   - **Imaging:** Think in images, trying to capture the topic using the five senses—sights, smells, tastes, sounds, and touch.
   - **Researching:** Study poetic forms and techniques. (To learn much more, go to thoughtfullearning.com/p332.)

4. **Create** the first draft of your poem.
   - **Focus** first on ideas and imagery.
   - **Experiment** with the sounds in your poem.
   - **Create** similes (comparing two things using *like* or *as*), metaphors (saying one thing *is* another), and personification (giving objects or animals human characteristics).
   - **Shape** your ideas into the form you have planned to use—free-verse or a traditional form.

5. **Improve** the first draft.
   - **Evaluate** your first draft.
     Does the poem present your topic in a fresh way? Does it achieve your purpose and connect to your audience?
   - **Revise** your poem.
     Add sensory details to make your topic clearer.
     Cut parts of the poem that are not needed.
     Rearrange parts that are out of order.
     Rewrite material that isn't working well.
   - **Edit** your poem to make it read smoothly.

6. **Present** your poem during a classroom poetry reading or post it online for others to read.

Poem

Poetry is a creative way of capturing your thoughts and feelings about the subjects you are studying. This rhyming poem shares important information about one of the chemical elements, mercury.

The poem consists of three stanzas, with each one four lines in length.

Mercury

This metal is liquid at eighty degrees
And measures your temperature after a sneeze.
It isn't an alloy and never would settle
For being mislabeled "transitional metal."

Each quatrain (*four-line stanza*) follows a similar rhyme scheme (*aabb*).

It's element eighty on charts on the wall
And powers the battery-pack of your doll.
It's gleaming and runny and glossy and odd
And registers heat when it's in a glass rod.

Each line presents an important detail about the topic.

Oh mercury, why be so shiny and slick?
Oh quicksilver, why do you make people sick?
Your vapors are toxic; your contact so bad
That you made the sane hatter of Wonderland mad!

Inquire | To Write a Play

1. **Question** the situation for the play.
   - **Subject:** What will the play be about? Who will be featured?
   - **Purpose:** Why are you writing a play? What mood should you create?
   - **Audience:** Who will perform the play? Who will watch it?

2. **Plan** your play by thinking about characters and plot. (Go to thoughtfullearning.com/p334 for much more on writing plays.)

3. **Research** your play.
   - **Characters:** List traits about each character, including personality, attitude, and voice. If the characters are real or historical figures, learn as much as you can about them.
   - **Conflict:** Create conflicts based on the characters' goals or differences.
   - **Plot:** Sketch out a plot for your play.
   - **Setting:** Decide on a time and a place for your play's action.

4. **Create** your play.
   - **Beginning:** Set the scene, introduce the characters, and create the conflict.
   - **Rising Action:** Intensify the conflict to a crisis.
   - **Climax:** Have the characters either succeed or fail.
   - **Resolution:** Wrap up the play, showing how the characters changed.

5. **Improve** your play.
   - **Evaluate** the play.
     Are the characters interesting and likable? Is the conflict believable and exciting? Will people like the play?
   - **Revise** your story to create major improvements.
     Remove characters, scenes, or details that do not help the play.
     Rearrange parts so that they flow in the best way.
     Rewrite parts that are unclear or confusing.
     Add description, dialogue, and action as needed.
   - **Edit** your play, proofreading and checking it for accuracy.

6. **Present** your play, performing it for its intended audience.

Note: Ask your teacher where and when you should present your play. See pages 452–454 and thoughtfullearning.com/p334 for more on performing plays.

Play Sketch

The following sketch describes a meeting between a historical figure and a modern-day hero.

The **beginning** introduces the characters and sets the scene.

When Washington Met Sally

GEORGE WASHINGTON, first U.S. president
SALLY RIDE, first woman in space

SCENE 1:
Setting: Coffee shop, Mount Vernon, VA, present day
(SALLY RIDE sits at a table and sips coffee from a mug. GEORGE WASHINGTON enters.)
WASHINGTON: How do you do, Ms. Ride? *(Removes hat)*
SALLY RIDE: Very well. And you, Mr. President?
WASHINGTON: Splendid. *(Sitting across from her)* That accent of yours . . . Are you a Pennsylvanian?
SALLY RIDE: No, Californian.
WASHINGTON: *(Confused)* You don't look Spanish!
SALLY RIDE: I'm not. I'm American.
WASHINGTON: *(Clearly dumbfounded)* Don't be preposterous! The Treaty of Paris sets clear borders for the United States. Anything west of the Mississippi belongs to the Spaniards.
SALLY RIDE: You clearly have a lot of catching up to do, Mr. President.
WASHINGTON: Do I? *(Tastes his coffee and shakes his head in disgust.)* Then explain to me how you can be both American and Californian.
SALLY RIDE: That requires a bit of a history lesson.
WASHINGTON: I'm all ears.
SALLY RIDE: *(Takes deep breath)* Back in 1821, Mexico gained its independence from Spain and briefly took ownership of California. Then in 1846, the United States declared war against Mexico because Mexico failed to recognize the annexation of Texas. That war lasted for three years until American troops seized control of the Mexican capital in the Battle for Mexico City. Are you still with me?

In the **middle**, the dialogue develops the story line in the play.

Stage directions in parentheses describe the character's actions.

WASHINGTON: *(Still confused)* Uh, I think so.

SALLY RIDE: Good. Because the Mexican-American War officially ended with the signing of the Treaty of Guadalupe Hidalgo in 1848. As part of the treaty, Mexico conceded California to the United States. And that's how California became the thirty-first state in the Union.

WASHINGTON: *(Pauses to think and then bursts out laughing)* <u>Thirty-first</u> state? You're not serious!

SALLY RIDE: Yes, well, currently there are fifty states.

WASHINGTON: *(Still laughing)* What a wonderful fairy tale! *(Sarcastic)* Do tell me: Who was the president during this Mexican-American fable? Don't tell me it was Jefferson!

SALLY RIDE: No, this was long after Jefferson's time in office. It was . . . *(Pauses to think)* You know, I've completely forgotten. Give me a moment to look it up. *(Takes out a cell phone)*

WASHINGTON: What in the name of freedom is that shiny device?

SALLY RIDE: *(Amused)* It's called a cell phone, Mr. President. I'm just going to Google your question. This place has free wi-fi.

WASHINGTON: Why fly what?

SALLY RIDE: *(Looks at cell phone)* Ah, here we go. James Polk, our eleventh president, oversaw the Mexican-American War.

WASHINGTON: *(Chuckles)* I do say, Ms. Ride, you are quite the storyteller. Let me guess, the next thing you'll tell me is that you've been to outer space?

SALLY RIDE: *(Sighs)* How much time do you have?

(The curtain falls. End of SCENE 1.)

The **conflict** (problem) is heightened as the dialogue continues.

A **scene break** indicates a change in the time and place of the action.

Building Essays

Essays allow you to explore a topic in great detail. An essay has a clear beginning, middle, and ending. The following chart compares the working parts of paragraphs and essays. The chart below takes a closer look at the parts of an essay.

Paragraph	Essay
Topic sentence ——————▶	Beginning paragraph (with thesis statement)
Body ————————————▶	Middle paragraphs
Closing sentence ————▶	Ending paragraph

Basic Structure of Essays

Beginning

Build the reader's interest. Introduce your topic in an interesting way.

Find a direction. Briefly explain why the topic is important.

State your focus. Write a thesis statement.

Middle

Support your thesis. Supply background information and include important points.

Structure your paragraphs. Start each paragraph with a separate main point.

Add details. Clarify each main point with supporting details.

Ending

Restate the focus. Remind the reader of the essay's purpose and rephrase the thesis statement.

Speak to the reader. Sum up the essay with a final point that speaks directly to the reader.

Inquire | To Write an Essay

1. **Question** the situation for the essay.
   - **Subject:** What specific topic will you write about?
   - **Purpose:** Why are you writing—to explain, to persuade, to describe, to narrate?
   - **Audience:** Who will read this essay? How would you like them to react to your writing?

2. **Plan** your essay.
   - **Pick a topic** and narrow it down from a general to a specific subject.

3. **Research** your topic.
   - **Searching:** Consult primary and secondary sources as needed to learn about your topic. (See pages 274–279.)
   - **Focusing:** Form a thesis statement, expressing a specific thought about the topic of your essay.

     Topic: *dreaming*   **Thought:** *mysterious to science*

     Thesis statement: *Scientists are still unclear on what causes dreams and why they are so hard to remember.*
   - **Shaping:** Arrange important details that support or explain your topic in an outline or other graphic organizer.

4. **Create** the first draft of your essay.
   - **Start with an opening paragraph** that introduces your topic and includes a thesis statement.
   - **Follow with middle paragraphs** that support your thesis.
   - **End with a closing paragraph** that revisits your thesis.

5. **Improve** your first draft.
   - **Evaluate** your first draft.
     Purpose: Does the essay effectively fulfill your purpose?
     Audience: Will the essay hold the reader's interest?
   - **Revise** your writing.
     Rewrite any sentences that are confusing or unclear.
     Add connecting words or transitions.
     Cut any parts that don't fit or aren't necessary.
   - **Edit** your revised writing.
     Check your writing for accuracy.

6. **Present** the final copy of your essay on a personal blog or read it out loud to your classmates.

Essay

In the following expository essay, a student explores the strange but all-too-familiar world of dreams.

The **beginning** introduces the topic in an interesting way and includes a thesis statement (underlined).

Both **middle** paragraphs focus on a different part of the topic and support the thesis statement.

The **ending** paragraph revisits the thesis and offers some thought-provoking questions.

In Your Dreams

Dreams are one of life's greatest mysteries. For centuries, people have tried to figure out why we dream and what our dreams mean. Dream interpreters even accompanied military leaders during battles. Today scientists know more about dreams but are still unclear on what causes dreams and why they are so hard to remember.

What scientists do know is that every person dreams every night, even though most people do not remember what they dreamed. In fact, on most nights, people dream several times, with each dream lasting between 5 and 20 minutes. In a lifetime, the average person will spend an equivalent of six years dreaming. Even people who have been blind since birth dream. The only difference is that they dream in sounds, smells, and feelings instead of in images.

Scientists note that within 5 minutes of waking up, people forget half of what they dreamed. Within 10 minutes, they forget 90 percent. Why it is so difficult to recall dreams is debatable. One theory is that people dream information that they don't want to remember, because it is too painful or scary. Another theory is that dreams are so unique that they don't allow for memory enhancers like association and repetition. Research has yet to prove either theory.

Today people are still fascinated by dreams. Even with all the breakthroughs in brain science, dreams remain a puzzle to scientists. Why can't people remember dreams? What causes nightmares? Do dreams mean anything? These questions may never be answered, but that won't stop people from dreaming.

Different Types of Essays

There are three main categories of essays: narrative, expository, and persuasive. Each category includes specific types of essays with different purposes.

Narrative essays tell a story.

- In a **personal narrative,** a writer tells about something significant that happened in his or her life. Personal narratives often are published as short stories, blog entries, and journals.
- In a **descriptive essay,** a writer uses sensory details to depict a scene, portray a person, or describe an object.
- In an **autobiography,** a writer reflects on the story of her or his life. Autobiographies are sometimes turned into books and movies.

Expository essays explain something.

- In a basic **expository essay,** a writer explains something or demonstrates how something works. Most of the articles you read in newspapers and magazines are examples of expository essays.
- In a **cause-effect essay,** a writer examines the causes and effects of an event or occurrence to see how they are connected.
- In a **comparison-contrast essay,** a writer looks at the similarities and differences of two subjects.

Persuasive essays give an opinion.

- In a basic **persuasive essay,** a writer provides an opinion and supports it with strong reasoning. The articles in the "Opinion" section of a newspaper are examples of persuasive essays.
- In a **position paper,** a writer takes a stand on an issue and encourages the reader to agree with the position.
- In a **problem-solution essay,** a writer presents a problem and offers solutions for solving it.

Chapter 25
Advanced Writing Projects

Certain forms of writing, such as lab reports and research papers, require advanced levels of thinking. For example, with these forms, you will need to *evaluate* information. Careful thinking will also help you write strong business letters and argument essays.

This chapter provides guidelines for and examples of several advanced writing projects.

You will learn . . .

- Writing News Reports
- Writing Observation Reports
- Writing Lab Reports
- Writing Proposals
- Writing Business Letters
- Writing Argument Essays
- Writing Research Papers

Project Overview

Here is a quick overview of the advanced writing projects in this chapter.

News Report

News reports tell about the information and current events that impact the world around us. (See pages 344–345.)

Students Adopt-A-Stream

Students from Redwood Middle School replaced their backpacks and pencils with hip waders and test tubes last Friday in an effort to protect the environment.

Thirty eighth graders tested the water quality and picked up trash and litter along the Wabash River in Clinton as part of the national Adopt-A-Stream program.

The students learned about the Adopt-A-Stream program while studying river ecosystems in their science class. The program hopes to build awareness for water pollution in America's rivers and streams by having middle school students care for a local waterway.

"We've learned that rivers are really important because they are home to lots of great plants and animals and are a huge source of fresh water," said eighth grader Maria Gonzalez. "So we
the environment

The students
along the river fo
color. The results
report and sent t
in charge of the
analysis.

Lab Report: Greener Lawns

Question: Will using the high setting on the lawn mower help create a healthier, thicker lawn?

Hypothesis: I believe that the high setting will create a healthier, thicker lawn than the middle setting that I have regularly used in the past.

Materials: Lawn mower with adjustable settings, lawn, sketch book, and pencils

Procedure:
1. Our family lawn was mowed once a week for a period of six weeks, from the middle of June through the first three weeks of July.
2. For the front yard, the high setting on the lawn mower was used. For the back yard, the middle setting was used. (The low setting was not tested because a neighbor uses it, and his lawn almost always appears dry and patchy.)
3. No fertilizer was used either in the front or the back.
4. The lawn was watered once, during the fifth week, due to dry conditions. The watering was timed and measured to ensure that both the front and back received the same amount of water (one inch of soaking).
5. Observations were made on the same day of the week on designated sections of the front and back lawns. Both sections were free of shade.
6. Sketches of each section were made during each observation, noting the location of weeds or dry patches.

Observation and Lab Reports

An observation report captures a moment in time with great detail. A lab report documents the entire process of an experiment. (See pages 346–351.)

Date: February 17, 2011
To: Mrs. Cindy Anderson
From: Lester Williams
Topic: Vertical Farming Project for the Learning Fair

Project: For my project for the district learning fair, I will construct a diorama showing two floors in a vertical farm along with a report explaining this new form of farming. (Vertical farming is carried out in abandoned city warehouses.)

Materials:
- Current articles on vertical farming
- Foam-core sheets for the basic structure of the diorama (rectangular box shape)
- See-through plastic sheet covering one end for viewing
- Other materials to consider for interior parts: colored paper, tape, balsa wood, Popsicle sticks, toothpicks, string, cotton swabs, and miniature plants (from hobby store)
- Markers for labeling and coloring

Description:
The interior of the diorama will show planting beds, plants, lighting, and watering on two floors. Labels will guide the viewer.

Steps and Due Dates:
1. Research vertical farming by February 24.
2. Plan my diorama on paper and gather supplies by March 3.
3. Build my diorama by March 17.

Proposal

A proposal presents a plan of action and requests permission to implement it. (See pages 352–353.)

Business Letters

Business letters are a common form of correspondence in the workplace. Requesting information and applying for a job are common reasons to write a business letter. (See pages 354–359.)

Benton Middle School
6830 Parkview Drive
Benton, MO 63330
October 14, 2011

Mr. Ron Kramer
Director of EMT Training
Edinburgh Technical College
314 Kinzie Avenue
Astor, MO 63331

Dear Mr. Kramer:

I'm an eighth-grade student at Benton Middle School, and I am interested in learning about the career of being an emergency medical technician (EMT).

I was excited to learn in last Sunday's *Standard* that Edinburgh Technical College has just started an EMT program and that you are the program's director. Since Benton is so close to Astor, it would be easy to attend your school once I graduate from high school.

714 N. Harvey Street
East Lake, TN 37400
April 14, 2011

Editor
Jackson News
Jackson Middle School
31991 Lake Street
East Lake, TN 37400

Dear Editor:

Jackson Middle School does not currently offer boys' volleyball, but I think we should add a team. Here are the four main reasons:

1. Jackson High School already has a boys' volleyball program.
2. Other middle schools in the area, including West Lake and Monroe, have teams.
3. East Lake and surrounding cities have summer club teams. At least 12 Jackson boys that I know play club volleyball.
4. Volleyball would offer a good alternative for boys who are not interested in football, soccer, or cross-country.

I know that adding another sport means finding coaches, scheduling practices and meets, and purchasing uniforms. But that shouldn't stop us from seriously exploring the possibility.

Letter to the Editor

A letter to the editor is written to a newspaper or magazine as a way to comment on a story, raise a question, or respond to another reader. (See page 358.)

Argument Essay

An argument essay is a form of persuasive writing in which a writer takes a stand on a relevant issue. (See pages 360–361.)

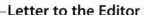
The Value of Serving

Anna Hernandez plays board games with residents at Bington's Senior Living Center. Scott Thompson helps pick up trash at Wilson Park during the city's spring cleanup campaign. Mansi Dass reads to preschoolers enrolled in the Head Start program. Parkview's community service requirement gives students life-changing experiences not available in the classroom.

Participating in the community is the first work experience for many Parkview students. They learn about the importance of being on time and completing the work. They also learn about working together and communicating with adults. Anna Hernandez said, "I had to be at the senior center right at 3:00 p.m. because that's when board games started." Practicing these job skills helps students learn about the world of work.

The students' community service also helps them appreciate the problems and challenges facing Bington. Scott Thompson said, "I never realized how thoughtless people can be until I started cleaning up after them. Some people really trash the parks." Mansi Dass learned that some young children really need help with reading and learning. She said, "Some of these kids have hardly ever been read to, so they don't know how fun books can be." Community service helps connect students to their city.

Romero 1

Carlos Romero
Mrs. Becker
Science 8
February 11, 2011

Wolves in Wisconsin

The gray wolf is one of the most controversial animal species in North America. In no state is this more evident than in Wisconsin. A great number of gray wolves roamed the northern woods of this state from the time of the retreating glaciers to the 1950s, when the wolf population all but disappeared. Today, however, gray wolves are back in Wisconsin. Their return is an ecological triumph, but it also brings up old concerns. Hunters and farmers worry about the impact of wolves on deer populations and livestock, and state environmental officials say the wolf population

Research Paper

A research paper uses a variety of sources to take an in-depth look at an interesting topic. Research papers are often written about controversial topics. (See pages 362–367.)

Inquire To Write a News Report

1. **Question** the situation for your news report.
   - ■ **Subject:** What specific topic will you write about?
   - ■ **Purpose:** Why are you writing—to explain, to inform, to entertain?
   - ■ **Audience:** Who will read the report? Where will it appear?

2. **Plan** the basics for your report.
   - ■ **Identify your topic.** Make it timely and important to readers.
   - ■ **Identify your deadline.** Know the due date for your report and plan accordingly.

3. **Research** your topic.
   - ■ **Searching:** Search for information and conduct interviews. (See page 275.)
   - ■ **Focusing:** Decide on a focus and state it in a single sentence.
   - ■ **Shaping:** List additional details and answer the 5 W's about your topic.
   - ■ **Arranging:** Put the details in the best order. Most news reports form an inverted pyramid, moving from the most to the least important details.

4. **Create** the first draft of your news report.
   - ■ **Start with a lead** that gets attention and identifies the focus.
   - ■ **Follow with other details** in descending order of importance.
   - ■ **End with the last detail,** or with a closing statement.

5. **Improve** your first draft.
   - ■ **Evaluate** your first draft.
     Purpose: Does the report achieve its purpose?
     Audience: Will the report hold the reader's interest?
   - ■ **Revise** your writing.
     Rewrite sentences that are confusing or unclear.
     Add details to explain your topic more fully.
     Cut parts that don't support the topic.
     Reorder sentences that could be more effectively arranged.
   - ■ **Edit** your revised writing.
     Replace general nouns and verbs with specific ones.
     Check your writing for accuracy using pages 183–192 as a guide.

6. **Present** the final copy to your newspaper.

News Report

News reports tell readers about important things happening in the world around them. This news report explains how a science class is caring for a local river.

The **beginning** (lead) presents the most important details in an interesting way.

The **middle** paragraphs present other details in descending order of importance.

The **ending** provides final details.

Students Adopt-A-Stream

Students from Redwood Middle School replaced their backpacks and pencils with hip waders and test tubes last Friday in an effort to protect the environment.

Thirty eighth graders tested the water quality and picked up trash and litter along the Wabash River in Clinton as part of the national Adopt-A-Stream program.

The students learned about the Adopt-A-Stream program while studying river ecosystems in their science class. The program hopes to build awareness for water pollution in America's rivers and streams by having middle school students care for a local waterway.

"We've learned that rivers are really important because they are home to lots of great plants and animals and are a huge source of fresh water," said eighth grader Maria Gonzalez. "So we felt this would be a great way to protect the environment and give back to our hometown."

The students tested water at three different points along the river for temperature, toxins, pH levels, and color. The results of the water tests were compiled in a report and sent to Delta Labs, the nonprofit organization in charge of the Adopt-A-Stream program, for further analysis.

Along with testing the water, students also picked up bagfuls of trash. They mostly found empty plastic bottles, broken glass, and crumpled food wrappers.

"It was crazy how much litter there was around," said Dylan Green, an eighth grader at Redwood Middle School. "I think it looks a lot nicer now."

Their efforts did not go unnoticed. Mayor Josie Siegel stopped by to commend the students for their work.

Inquire   To Write an Observation Report

1. **Question** the situation for your observation report.
   - **Subject**: What specific location will you write about?
   - **Purpose**: Why are you writing—to observe or to describe?
   - **Audience**: Who will read this report? What do they need to know?

2. **Plan** the basics for your report.
   - **Identify your topic.** Make sure you can describe it in a brief report.
   - **Prepare for your observing.** Prepare a sensory chart (see page 246).

3. **Research** your topic.
   - **Searching**: Write down sensory observations, record sounds, and take pictures.
   - **Focusing**: Consider a focus for your report.
   - **Shaping**: Decide how you want to arrange your observations.

4. **Create** the first draft of your report.
   - **Start with the first observation** or develop a more traditional introduction by identifying the focus.
   - **Organize the rest of your observations** in the best order.
   - **End with your last observation** or an idea that captures the location.

5. **Improve** your first draft.
   - **Evaluate** your first draft.
     Purpose: Does the report fulfill your goal?
     Audience: Will the report hold the reader's interest and provide enough details about the location?
   - **Revise** your writing.
     Rewrite parts that are confusing or unclear.
     Add details as needed to enhance the observation.
     Cut parts that don't support the topic.
     Reorder sentences that could be more effectively arranged.
   - **Edit** your revised writing.
     Replace general nouns (*flip-flops* instead of *shoes*) and verbs (*hums* instead of *makes noise*).
     Check your writing for accuracy using pages 183–192 as a guide.

6. **Present** the final copy of your report on a blog, share it out loud with your classmates, or turn it into a multimedia report with actual sights and sounds.

Observation Report

A student who attended the San Francisco Chinese New Year Festival and Parade wrote the following observation report.

The **beginning** introduces the topic.

The **middle** paragraphs focus on sights, sounds, and emotions.

The **ending** reflects on the moment.

Chinese in America

Dad and I wait in the huge crowds on Kearny Street in San Francisco. People who got here first sit in bleachers along the road. We bunch together, hip to hip. Little kids are sitting half on the curb and half on our toes. Taller people stand in rows behind us, with others farther back going into the decorated shops of Chinatown. Red lanterns hang from the pagoda roof overhead. Red is supposed to bring good luck and prosperity.

The parade begins, led by two boys with a street-wide banner welcoming us to the San Francisco Chinese New Year Festival and Parade. Behind them is a float with a red pagoda and the mayor and other politicians smiling and waving. People walking beside the float hurl candy. The kid sitting on my toes bounds up to grab the stuff. With the candy are little red envelopes with coupons inside. Girls are dancing past. They wear lime-green coats with sleeves that reach down to their knees. They swirl around, letting the sleeves whip through the air. They are smiling. Everyone is smiling. Behind them come more girls, these in red silken blouses and feathery headdresses. The girls play snare drums.

Not everybody in the parade is Chinese. High school bands march here, too. Their uniforms aren't red, their saxophones and trumpets aren't traditional Chinese instruments, but they are playing the theme from the American movie *The Last Emperor*. Dad says they don't have Chinese New Year Parades in China. This parade was started in the 1860s by immigrants who used it to teach others about their culture. I guess it's still working.

Now a dragon with a white-furred head and a gaping mouth appears. In the mouth stands a man clutching the dragon's teeth and making the head dance. He snakes back and forth along the way and approaches us. One little kid shouts, "I'm not scared of you!" His mother tells him the dragon isn't a monster. It brings good luck. Behind the dragon's head, a coiling, scaly body stretches out, carried along by people with poles. What a great idea, to make a monster into a defender!

I like this parade. It makes me think of Macy's Thanksgiving Day Parade. It's American like that, but also Chinese. It celebrates being Chinese in America.

Inquire To Write a Lab Report

1. **Question** the situation for your report.
   - **Subject:** What specific topic will you report on?
   - **Purpose:** Why are you writing—to explain or to describe?
   - **Audience:** Who will read the report? What will they need to know?

2. **Plan** the basics for your report.
   - **Identify your topic.** Your topic will be the scientific question that you have explored and tested.
   - **Become familiar with the appropriate form** for reporting on experiments, either a form provided by your teacher or the one on pages 349–351.

3. **Research** your report.
   - **Searching:** Conduct your experiment using the scientific method (see page 57). Take thorough notes.
   - **Focusing:** Draw conclusions from the results of your experiment.
   - **Shaping:** Arrange the supporting details for your report.

4. **Create** the first draft of your report.
   - **Start your report with your scientific questions and hypothesis.**
   - **Follow with the materials, step-by-step procedure, and observations.**
   - **End with the conclusions based on your findings.**

5. **Improve** your first draft.
   - **Evaluate** your first draft.
     Purpose: Does the report effectively fulfill the reason you are writing—to explain or to describe?
     Audience: Will readers be able to follow your report?
   - **Revise** your writing.
     Rewrite any parts that are confusing or unclear.
     Add details as needed.
     Cut parts that don't relate to the topic.
     Reorder sentences or parts that are out of order.
   - **Edit** your revised writing.
     Replace general nouns and verbs with specific ones.
     Check your writing for accuracy using pages 183–192 as a guide.

6. **Present** the final copy of your lab report on a blog or Web site or use it to lead classmates through the same procedure.

Lab Report

On a Web site, Li Cheng learned that using the high mower setting is one way to grow a thicker, healthier lawn and to fight weeds. He conducted an experiment to test this claim. The following lab report shares his findings.

The **beginning** identifies the question and hypothesis that prompted the experiment.

Lab Report: Greener Lawns

Question: Will using the high setting on the lawn mower help create a healthier, thicker lawn?

Hypothesis: I believe that the high setting will create a healthier, thicker lawn than the middle setting that I have regularly used in the past.

Materials: Lawn mower with adjustable settings, lawn, sketch book, and pencils

The **middle** spells out the procedure step by step.

Procedure:
1. Our family lawn was mowed once a week for a period of six weeks, from the middle of June through the first three weeks of July.
2. For the front yard, the high setting on the lawn mower was used. For the back yard, the middle setting was used. (The low setting was not tested because a neighbor uses it, and his lawn almost always appears dry and patchy.)
3. No fertilizer was used either in the front or the back.
4. The lawn was watered once, during the fifth week, due to dry conditions. The watering was timed and measured to ensure that both the front and back received the same amount of water (one inch of soaking).
5. Observations were made on the same day of the week on designated sections of the front and back lawns. Both sections were free of shade.
6. Sketches of each section were made during each observation, noting the location of weeds or dry patches.

Observations:

Week 1: No real difference between the thickness and health of the two sections was observed. Both sections contain a few patches of clover and a limited number of dandelions.

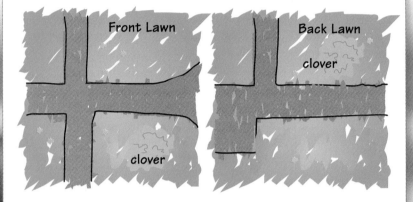

Week 2: Same as week 1.

Week 3: The front lawn appears thicker and greener than the back lawn. Weed coverage is greater in the back than in the front, but the change is not that significant.

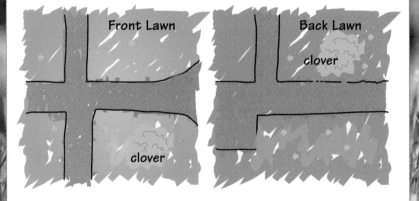

Week 4: Pretty much the same as week 3.

Week 5: The front lawn appears healthy even with the dry conditions; clover and dandelions are still limited. The back lawn clearly contains dry patches and seems more stressed; weed coverage increased somewhat.

Sketches bring observations to life.

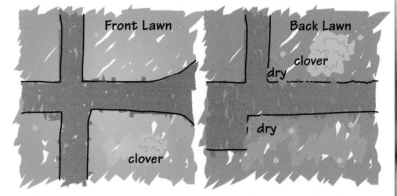

Week 6: The front lawn has maintained its health and weeds are hard to find. The back lawn has benefited from the watering, but does not appear as thick and green as the front lawn.

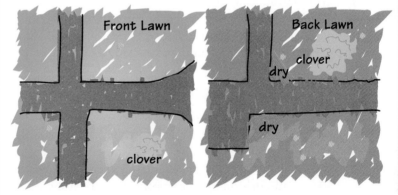

Conclusions: Using the high setting on the lawn mower produced a healthier lawn than using the middle setting. The differences were most obvious when conditions became drier. So for the test period, which means during a rather dry period, my hypothesis proved true. I will use the high setting for both parts of the lawn for the rest of the mowing season to see how it works.

The **ending** explains the findings.

Inquire | To Write a Proposal

1. **Question** the situation for your proposal.
   - **Subject:** What specific topic will you propose?
   - **Purpose:** Why are you writing—to explain, to suggest, to plan?
   - **Audience:** Who will read the proposal? What do they need to know?

2. **Plan** the basics for your proposal.
   - **Identify your topic.** Write down your specific topic and goal.
   - **Learn about the form.** Review the example proposal (page 353).

3. **Research** the topic.
   - **Searching:** Learn as much as you can about your topic. Consult primary and secondary sources. (See pages 274–286.)
   - **Focusing:** Identify the key features of your writing—materials, steps, and due dates.
   - **Shaping:** Arrange the key features as shown on page 353 or according to requirements provided by your instructor.

4. **Create** the first draft of your proposal.
   - **Start by introducing the topic.**
   - **Follow with the supporting details** (materials, steps, and timeline) that explain your proposal.
   - **End with an explanation of the expected results of your proposal.**

5. **Improve** your first draft.
   - **Evaluate** your first draft.
     Purpose: Is the proposal convincing?
     Audience: Is the proposal clear to readers? Does it call them to act?
   - **Revise** your writing.
     Rewrite parts that are confusing or unclear.
     Add details to explain your proposal more fully.
     Cut parts that don't support your topic.
     Reorder sentences that could be more effectively arranged.
   - **Edit** your revised writing.
     Replace any words that seem too general.
     Check your writing for accuracy using pages 183–192 as a guide.
     Follow an accepted format for your proposal.

6. **Present** the final copy of your proposal or submit it to a social or blogging site.

Proposal for a Project

Date: February 17, 2011
To: Mrs. Cindy Anderson
From: Lester Williams
Topic: Vertical Farming Project for the Learning Fair

The **beginning** introduces the project.

Project: For my project for the district learning fair, I will construct a diorama showing two floors in a vertical farm along with a report explaining this new form of farming. (Vertical farming is carried out in abandoned city warehouses.)

Materials:

The **middle** part identifies the materials, steps, and due dates.

- Current articles on vertical farming
- Foam-core sheets for the basic structure of the diorama (rectangular box shape)
- See-through plastic sheet covering one end for viewing
- Other materials to consider for interior parts: colored paper, tape, balsa wood, Popsicle sticks, toothpicks, string, cotton swabs, and miniature plants (from hobby store)
- Markers for labeling and coloring

Description:
The interior of the diorama will show planting beds, plants, lighting, and watering on two floors. Labels will guide the viewer.

Steps and Due Dates:

1. Research vertical farming by February 24.
2. Plan my diorama on paper and gather supplies by March 3.
3. Build my diorama by March 17.
4. Prepare my report and present my project on March 24.

The **ending** states the value of the project and asks for approval.

Outcome: My project will show how abandoned warehouses in big cities can be used to grow food for city dwellers, grocery stores, and restaurants.

Please let me know if this proposal is acceptable. I am willing to make changes as needed.

Inquire   To Write a Business Letter

1. **Question** the situation for your letter.
   - **Subject:** What topic will you address?
   - **Purpose:** Why are you writing?
   - **Audience:** Who will read this letter? What response do you want?

2. **Plan** the basics for your letter.
   - **Identify a topic** and narrow it from a general to a specific subject.
   - **Learn the receiver's** name, title, and address.

3. **Research** your letter.
   - **Searching:** Gather details that you need to include in your letter.
   - **Focusing:** What specifically do you want to accomplish or gain?
   - **Shaping:** Organize the body of your letter into three main parts.
     Beginning: Introduce your subject and reason for writing.
     Middle: Present important details in brief, clear paragraphs.
     Ending: Explain what action you would like the receiver to take.

4. **Create** the first draft of your letter.
   - **Start with the heading, inside address, and salutation.**
   - **Follow with the body**—the beginning, middle, and ending parts.
   - **End with a complimentary closing and signature.**

5. **Improve** your first draft.
   - **Evaluate** your letter.
     Purpose: Does it achieve your goal?
     Audience: Does it give the reader all necessary information?
   - **Revise** your writing.
     Rewrite sentences that are confusing or unclear.
     Add details to explain your topic more fully.
     Cut parts that are unnecessary.
     Reorder sentences that could be more effectively arranged.
   - **Edit** your revised writing.
     Replace general nouns and verbs with specific ones (*Jefferson West* instead of *school, donate* instead of *give*).
     Check your writing for accuracy using pages 183–192 as a guide.

6. **Present** the final copy of your letter by sending it out.

Letter Requesting Information

This letter follows the full-block letter format.

Benton Middle School
6830 Parkview Drive
Benton, MO 63330
October 14, 2011

Mr. Ron Kramer
Director of EMT Training
Edinburgh Technical College
314 Kinzie Avenue
Astor, MO 63331

Dear Mr. Kramer:

The **beginning** explains the reason for the letter.

I'm an eighth-grade student at Benton Middle School, and I am interested in learning about the career of being an emergency medical technician (EMT).

I was excited to learn in last Sunday's *Standard Press* that Edinburgh Technical College has just started an EMT program and that you are the program's director. Since Benton is so close to Astor, it would be easy for me to attend your school once I graduate from high school.

The **middle** presents the important details.

I would appreciate any details you could share with me about your program. I am especially interested in the following types of information:

1. Qualifications to enter the program
2. Program description
3. Career opportunities
4. Visits or tours of the school

The **ending** states the next step.

Any information that you can give me will be much appreciated. You can contact me by letter at the above address or via e-mail at lbunker@bentonms.edu.

Sincerely,

Larry Bunker

Larry Bunker

Parts of a Business Letter

A business letter includes the *heading, inside address, salutation, body, complimentary closing,* and *signature.* (It may also include the word *Enclosure* or the abbreviation *Encl.* at the bottom of the letter if any additional pages are included.)

The **heading** includes the writer's address and the date of the letter. It is placed about an inch from the top of the page.

The **inside address** includes the name and address of the person or group you are writing to. Identify the title of the person after his or her name. (If the title is brief, place it after the name, separated by a comma. If the title is long, place it on the next line.) Place the inside address usually four to seven spaces beneath the heading.

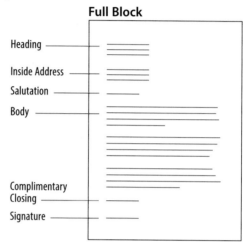

Full Block

Heading
Inside Address
Salutation
Body
Complimentary Closing
Signature

The **salutation** politely addresses the receiver of the letter. Use *Dear* followed by *Mr., Mrs., Ms,* or *Miss;* the person's last name; and a colon. If you don't know the person's name, use *Dear Sir or Madam, Dear EMT Director,* or *Dear Edinburgh Technical School,* followed by a colon. Place the salutation two spaces beneath the inside address.

The **body** is the main part of the letter and should consist of brief paragraphs that get right to the point. (Remember to create beginning, middle, and ending parts.) Single-space each individual paragraph, but double-space between the paragraphs.

The **complimentary closing** announces the end of the main part of the letter with *Sincerely, Very truly,* or *Yours truly* followed by a comma. Double-space after the last body paragraph for the closing.

The **signature** gives the letter writer's name (in type) four spaces after the closing. The writer adds her or his written signature above the typed name.

Note: The business letter on page 355 and the graphic here follow full-block style, which means all of the information is placed at the left-hand margin.

Sending a Letter

To send a letter, you must (1) correctly address the envelope and (2) neatly fold the letter and insert it into the envelope.

Folding a Business Letter

Use these steps for folding a letter for a basic business envelope.

1. Divide the letter into thirds. Begin by folding up the bottom third of the letter.
2. Then fold the top third of the letter down. Crease the edges firmly and neatly.
3. Place the letter into the envelope with the open end at the top.

```
LARRY BUNKER
6830 PARKVIEW DR
BENTON MO 63330




          MR RON KRAMER
          DIRECTOR OF EMT TRAINING
          EDINBURGH TECHNICAL COLLEGE
          314 KINZIE AVE
          ASTOR MO 63331
```

Addressing the Envelope

Follow these steps for addressing your business envelope.

1. Write or type the full name and address of the receiver slightly to the left of the middle of the envelope.
2. Write your return address in the upper left-hand corner.
3. Place the correct postage in the upper right-hand corner.

Regular Form	**Postal Form**
Mr. Ron Kramer	MR RON KRAMER
Director of EMT Training	DIRECTOR OF EMT TRAINING
Edinburgh Technical College	EDINBURGH TECHNICAL COLLEGE
314 Kinzie Ave.	314 KINZIE AVE
Astor, MO 63331	ASTOR MO 63331

Note: The U.S. Postal Service prefers all capitals and no punctuation.

Letter to the Editor (Promoting a Cause)

714 N. Harvey Street
East Lake, TN 37400
April 14, 2011

Editor
Jackson News
Jackson Middle School
31991 Lake Street
East Lake, TN 37400

Dear Editor:

Jackson Middle School does not currently offer boys' volleyball, but I think we should add a team. Here are the four main reasons:

1. Jackson High School already has a boys' volleyball program.
2. Other middle schools in the area, including West Lake and Monroe, have teams.
3. East Lake and surrounding cities have summer club teams. At least 12 Jackson boys that I know play club volleyball.
4. Volleyball would offer a good alternative for boys who are not interested in football, soccer, or cross-country.

I know that adding another sport means finding coaches, scheduling practices and meets, and purchasing uniforms. But that shouldn't stop us from seriously exploring the possibility. After all, the purpose of middle school is to offer students a wide range of educational and extracurricular opportunities.

Students who feel the same way about boys' volleyball should contact their student council representatives. They also should discuss the topic with Ms. Jones, the athletic director, and with their parents. Parents should raise the issue at the next PTA meeting.

By working together, we can make our athletic program even stronger with the addition of boys' volleyball.

Sincerely,

Greg Cheney

Greg Cheney

Letter Applying for Work

758 Katie Drive
High Point, AZ 85087
September 8, 2011

Josh Sorenson, Director
Camp Maclean
1561 Lake Drive
High Point, AZ 85087

Dear Mr. Sorenson:

The beginning names the position of interest.

I am applying for the position of day camp counselor, which was posted on the job board at our school.

I am 13, in the eighth grade, and the oldest of four children. In school, I have participated in volleyball, basketball, and softball. I'm also an honor student and have missed very few days of school during the past three years. Last summer, I earned my Junior Lifesaving Certificate as well.

The **middle** explains qualifications.

When I was an elementary student, I attended Camp Maclean for two summers. Because of this experience, I understand the responsibility and hard work required to be an effective counselor.

Please feel free to contact Ms. Shirley Avercamp, my volleyball coach, and Mrs. Christine Jones, a neighbor and babysitting client, for references. See the attached sheet for contact information.

The **ending** asks for an interview and provides contact information.

May I call you after 3:00 p.m. on Tuesday, September 13, to set up a time for an interview? If this is not convenient, please contact me any day after 2:30 p.m. at (520)555-0002 or lbutler2815@link.com.

Sincerely,

Lateesha Butler

Lateesha Butler

Inquire To Write an Argument Essay

1. **Question** the situation for your essay.
   - **Subject:** What specific topic will you write about?
   - **Purpose:** Why are you writing? What are you arguing for?
   - **Audience:** Who will read this essay? What do they need to know?

2. **Plan** the basics for your essay.
   - **Identify a topic.** Make sure it is timely and interesting.
   - **Learn about forming an argument.** (See pages 103–118.)

3. **Research** your topic.
   - **Searching:** Consult primary and secondary sources. (See pages 274–286.) Take notes during your research.
   - **Focusing:** Decide on a focus and state it in a thesis statement.
   - **Shaping:** List key points that support or explain your thesis. Also identify any important arguments against your thesis.

4. **Create** the first draft of your essay.
   - **Start by introducing your topic** and stating your thesis.
   - **Follow with your supporting points.** Also deal with any important opposing arguments.
   - **End with a paragraph that stresses the importance of your thesis.**

5. **Improve** your first draft.
   - **Evaluate** your first draft.
     Purpose: Does the essay achieve your goal?
     Audience: Will the reader be able to follow your argument?
   - **Revise** your writing.
     Rewrite parts that are confusing or unclear.
     Add details to explain your topic more fully.
     Cut parts that don't support the topic.
     Reorder parts that could be more effectively arranged.
   - **Edit** your writing.
     Make sure that you have cited sources correctly. (See pages 290–291.)
     Check your writing for accuracy using pages 183–192 as a guide.

6. **Present** the final copy of your essay in person to your classmates or submit it to an appropriate social or blogging site.

Argument Essay

The **beginning** paragraph introduces the topic and states the thesis (underlined).

The Value of Serving

    Anna Hernandez plays board games with residents at Bington's Senior Living Center. Scott Thompson helps pick up trash at Wilson Park during the city's spring cleanup campaign. Mansi Dass reads to preschoolers enrolled in the Head Start program. <u>Parkview's community service requirement gives students life-changing experiences not available in the classroom.</u>

    Participating in the community is the first work experience for many Parkview students. They learn about the importance of being on time and completing the work. They also learn about working together and communicating with adults. Anna Hernandez said, "I had to be at the senior center right at 3:00 p.m. because that's when board games started." Practicing these job skills helps students learn about the world of work.

The **middle** supporting paragraphs lead up to the most important point.

    The students' community service also helps them appreciate the problems and challenges facing Bington. Scott Thompson said, "I never realized how thoughtless people can be until I started cleaning up after them. Some people really trash the parks." Mansi Dass learned that some young children really need help with reading and learning. She said, "Some of these kids have hardly ever been read to, so they don't know how fun books can be." Community service helps connect students to their city.

    Most importantly, students learn about giving back. For many students, their community service will be the first time they have helped strangers who need help. Ms. Sandra Williams, the community service advisor, said, "Working in the community shows students that a lot of other people need their help." Learning this lesson should help Parkview students become more involved in the community.

A main opposing argument is discussed and countered.

    Some people think that the community service requirement may feel like a punishment to some students. They point out that people who get in trouble are often required to complete community service. But most students quickly discover that community service is a pleasure, not a punishment. They feel better because they've done good and made a difference.

The **ending** paragraph stresses the importance of the thesis.

    Bington students are in school for 180 days, 8 hours each day. Depending on their grades, they have to complete between 6 and 12 hours of community service. When you look at the program in this way, students aren't asked to do much. What students gain from their experience far outweighs anything they may have to give up. Their community service gives them a taste of real life at just the right time.

Inquire To Write a Research Paper

1. **Question** the situation for your research paper.
   - **Subject:** What specific topic will you research and write about?
   - **Purpose:** Why are you writing—to inform or to persuade?
   - **Audience:** Who will read this paper? What do they need to know?

2. **Plan** your paper.
   - **Identify your topic.** Be sure it interests you and you can find enough information about it.
   - **Establish a work schedule.** (See pages 255–262.)

3. **Research** your topic.
   - **Searching:** Consult primary and secondary sources to learn about your topic. (See pages 274–286.) Take careful notes and track sources.
   - **Focusing:** Decide on a focus and state it in a thesis statement.
   - **Shaping:** Determine the best order of supporting details for your thesis.

4. **Create** the first draft of your research paper.
   - **Start strong.** Get the reader's attention and state your thesis.
   - **Support your thesis.** Use your organizing plan as a guide.
   - **End strong.** Tie everything together and restate your thesis.

5. **Improve** your first draft.
   - **Evaluate** the first draft of your research paper.
     Purpose: Does the paper achieve your goal?
     Audience: Will the paper engage and enlighten the readers?
   - **Revise** your writing.
     Rewrite parts that are confusing or unclear.
     Add more details to explain your topic more fully.
     Cut parts that don't support your thesis.
     Reorder parts that could be more effectively arranged.
   - **Edit** your revised writing.
     Review your documentation. (See pages 290–291.)
     Check your writing for accuracy using pages 183–192 as a guide.

6. **Present** the final copy of your research paper by sharing it in person, by submitting it to an appropriate Web site, or perhaps by incorporating it into a multimedia project of some type.

Research Paper

Romero 1

Carlos Romero

Mrs. Becker

Science 8

February 11, 2011

Wolves in Wisconsin

The gray wolf is one of the most controversial animal species in North America. In no state is this more evident than in Wisconsin. A great number of gray wolves roamed the northern woods of this state from the time of the retreating glaciers to the 1950s, when the wolf population all but disappeared. Today, however, gray wolves are back in Wisconsin. Their return is an ecological triumph, but it also brings up old concerns. Hunters and farmers worry about the impact of wolves on deer populations and livestock, and state environmental officials say the wolf population is too large to manage. <u>Decisions concerning these key issues will determine the future of gray wolves in Wisconsin</u> ("Wolves").

Evidence of gray wolves (*Canis lupus*) in Wisconsin traces back 10,000 years. The wolves thrived in the thick forest habitat of northern Wisconsin, where retreating glaciers formed many lakes and streams. By the 1800s, there were believed to be between 3,000 and 5,000 wolves living in the state (Wydeven). Around this same time, many European settlers arrived in the area. These settlers, who were mostly hunters and farmers, feared that the wolves would diminish the deer

Fig. 1 Gray Wolf Yawning, photo from Public-Domain-Image.com, 29 Mar. 2010. Web. 14 Dec. 2010.

The beginning gets the reader's attention about the topic and states the thesis (underlined).

A visual is included along with a source note.

The first few **middle** paragraphs provide background information.

population and endanger their livestock. Consequently, Wisconsin passed bounty laws, which paid hunters up to $20 for every wolf killed ("Wolves"). The law was revoked in 1957, but the damage was already done. Hundreds of wolves were killed, and the survivors took refuge in Minnesota and Michigan. By 1960, there were no gray wolves in Wisconsin ("Wolves").

Gray wolves started to come back to Wisconsin in 1975. They trickled in from Minnesota and were protected by two new laws. First, 1974 federal legislation made gray wolves an endangered species at the national level. Second, Wisconsin placed the gray wolf on its state endangered species list. Both laws made it illegal to hunt, harm, or sell gray wolves in Wisconsin. For further protection, the Wisconsin Department of Natural Resources (DNR) administered a wolf recovery plan in the late 1980s, with a goal of maintaining a wolf population of 80 for three straight years. The goal was easily met. The wolf population reached 205 in 1999 and has surged since then. Today, between 690 and 733 gray wolves live in Wisconsin (Wydeven).

The supporting paragraphs contain many facts and supporting details.

The steep rise in wolf populations is a problem. Conservationists are thrilled with the growing population of wolves but must contend with key questions: How many wolves can Wisconsin support? And how many wolves are the citizens of Wisconsin willing to put up with? In its Wolf Management Plan, Wisconsin Wolf Science Advisory Committee (WWSAC) members recommend that a suitable wolf population is between 300 and 500 wolves (WWSAC 3). Of course, the current wolf population is much more.

Sources are cited using MLA style. (See pages 290–291.)

Wisconsin farmers and hunters have serious concerns about the large number of wolves in the state. Wolves are extremely

Romero 3

The key issues about the problem are explained.

shy and don't pose a threat to humans, but they do threaten livestock. With wolf populations on the rise since the mid-1990s, wolf attacks on livestock have been increasing. Numbers of Wisconsin farms with livestock kills increased from an average of 2.8 animals annually in the 1990s to 14 annually between 2000 and 2005 (Lehmkuhler 17-18). In addition, from 2002 to 2005, the state's wolf population increased 32 percent while farms with livestock attacks increased 178 percent (15). Farmers who can prove livestock are killed by wolf attacks receive compensation from the state for their losses, but many farmers are frustrated with the time delays for receiving their money ("Wolves").

Statistics add an important level of support.

Hunters are also concerned about the wolf population. In 2009, the National Rifle Association of America reported that deer hunters harvested their lowest numbers of deer in 27 years. Some hunters blame wolves for lowering deer populations. According to DNR reports, wolves killed approximately 13,000 deer in 2009, but that number accounts for a small percentage of deer mortalities. By comparison, bears and coyotes combined were responsible for 49,000 deer mortalities (Wisconsin DNR).

Conservationists, hunters, and farmers do, however, agree on two key points: (1) Wolf populations have grown too large in Wisconsin, and (2) a wolf management plan should be put into action to control the population. Carrying out such a plan is nearly impossible unless the gray wolf is taken off the federal endangered species list. This fact is the driving force behind a state recommendation that the U.S. Fish and Wildlife Service (USFWS) no longer considers the gray wolf an endangered species in the Midwest (Nie 174). The recommendation has gained

Romero 4

support in the ecological community, and the USFWS is expected to approve the change in 2011 (Smith).

If the gray wolf is no longer considered endangered, Wisconsin plans to enforce an already federally approved wolf management plan (Smith). The plan calls for capping the total population of wolves to 350 outside of Native American reservations. To achieve this goal, the DNR would allow landowners in wolf territory to hunt problem wolves that threaten their livestock. The DNR would also perform a broader hunt in isolated wolf territories to achieve the recommended wolf population (Wisconsin DNR). The question now is whether the state will ever get a chance to enforce the plan. And if it does, will wolves disappear from Wisconsin for a second time?

The attitude toward the gray wolf in Wisconsin is a story of extremes. When Europeans first settled in the state, wolf populations were thought to be too big and too dangerous. But when wolves vanished, there was an outcry to bring them back. Now that wolves are back, some favor an all-out removal, while others say wolves deserve to stay. The answer, according to David Mladenoff, an ecology professor at the University of Wisconsin, is somewhere in the middle. "Neither [extreme] is going to be an appropriate model for living with wolves," said Mladenoff. "Ultimately, to learn to live with wolves, we have to figure out how to make fair rules and live with each other" (Ness). Whether Wisconsin can create a policy that protects gray wolves and keeps the people near them satisfied is still unclear. Until then, the future of wolves in Wisconsin remains uncertain.

A last supporting paragraph is developed.

The **ending** paragraph ties everything together.

The final thought expands the scope of the paper.

Romero 5

Works Cited

Lehmkuhler, Jess. "Effects of Wolves and Other Predators on
    Farms in Wisconsin." *Wisconsin Outdoor Journal* 1 May
    2007: 15-20. Print.

Ness, Erik. "To Kill a Wolf." *Grow: Magazine.* University of
    Wisconsin-Madison, Spring 2009. Web. 10 Dec. 2010.

Nie, Martin A. *Beyond Wolves: The Politics of Wolf Recovery and
    Management.* Minneapolis: University of Minnesota Press,
    2003. Print.

Smith, Paul A. "DNR Reiterates Support of Wolf Delisting." *On
    the Trail,* JSOnline, Mon. 13 Dec. 2010. Web. 14 Dec. 2010.

Wisconsin Department of Natural Resources. *Wolves and Deer in
    Wisconsin.* Madison: WI DNR, Oct. 2009. PDF file.

Wisconsin Wolf Science Advisory Committee. *Wisconsin Wolf
    Management Plan Addendum 2006 and 2007.* Madison:
    Wisconsin Department of Natural Resources, 15 Aug. 2007.
    PDF file.

"Wolves in Wisconsin." *In Wisconsin.* PBS. MPTV, Milwaukee, 2
    Nov. 2010. Television.

Wydeven, Adrian. *The History of Wolves
    in Wisconsin.* Madison: Wisconsin
    Department of Natural Resources, 14
    June 2010. PDF file.

The works-cited page lists all the sources cited in the paper.

The works are listed alphabetically by author or other information.

Each entry provides enough information to locate the source. (See pages 290–291.)

The first line of each entry is flush left; second or third lines are indented.

Researching Tips

Refer to these tips for additional guidance whenever you are developing a research paper.

Selecting

A worthy topic should meet the following criteria: (1) It should truly interest you; (2) it should be within your abilities to research; (3) and it should be specific. (Researching all endangered birds would be too broad; researching one of them is specific enough.)

Organizing

If your purpose is to inform, arrange your supporting details by logical order, time (process), cause-effect, and so on. But if your purpose is to persuade, consider organizing your supporting details by order of importance—beginning or ending with your most convincing argument.

Formatting and Documenting

The research paper on pages 363–367 follows the Modern Language Association (MLA) style for formatting and documentation. Check with your teacher to see what style you should use. (You can learn more about MLA style on the Web.)

Point of View

Traditional research papers are written from an objective point of view, or without any personal thoughts or feelings. However, personal research projects are written from a subjective point of view, meaning that they will include your personal thoughts and feelings.

Chapter 26
Graphing Projects

Seeing is believing. That's why pictures are such a powerful form of communication. Instead of filling page after page with words and numbers that *tell* what you mean, create graphs that *show* what you mean. This chapter explains how to make several kinds of graphs, tables, and charts that can energize your projects.

You will learn . . .

- Creating Pie, Line, and Bar Graphs
- Creating Tables
- Creating Diagrams, Time Lines, and Flowcharts
- Creating Infographics

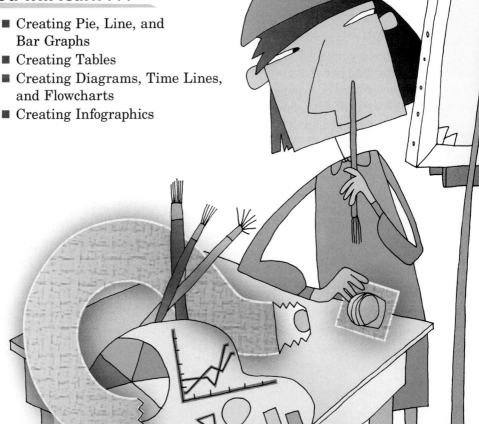

Project Overview

Here is a quick overview of several ways to present information graphically.

Pie Graph

A pie graph shows how a whole amount is split up into different segments. Each segment represents a part of the total. (See page 373.)

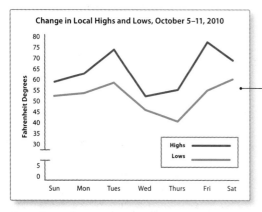

2010 Computer Lab Expenditures

$262 Hardware Repairs
$775 Paper Supplies
$415 Hardware Upgrades
$484 Software Upgrades

Total Expenditures: $1,936

Change in Local Highs and Lows, October 5–11, 2010

Line Graph

A line graph shows changes over time. The horizontal axis shows time and the vertical axis shows quantity. A line traces from one quantity to the next. (See page 374.)

Bar Graph

A bar graph compares amounts. The horizontal axis shows time or groups and the vertical axis shows quantity. Bars reaching to various quantities display the comparison. (See page 375.)

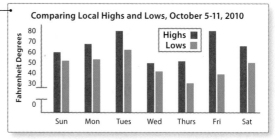

Comparing Local Highs and Lows, October 5-11, 2010

Table

A table arranges raw information in rows and columns. Often subjects are listed down the first column, and traits are listed across the top. (See page 377.)

Planet Facts

Planet	Distance from Sun (million mi.)	Diameter (mi.)	Type	Surface Temp. (F)	Length of Day	Length of Year
Mercury	36.0	3,032	Rock	-290 to 800°	176 days	87.9 days
Venus	67.24	7,521	Rock	864°	243 days	225 days
Earth	92.96	7,926	Rock	-126.9° to 136°	23.9 hours	365.25 days
Mars	141.6	4,222	Rock	-125° to -23°	24.6 hours	687 days
Jupiter	483.7	88,846	Gas	-234°	9.9 hours	11.86 years
Saturn	885.9	74,898	Gas	-288°	10.7 hours	29.45 years
Uranus	1,783.9	31,764	Gas	-357°	17.2 hours	84.0 years
Neptune	2,771.0	30,776	Gas	-353°	16.1 hours	164.8 years

Diagram

A diagram shows a picture and labels the parts of it. The diagram may be a photo, a painting, a drawing, or a cutaway, as shown here. (See page 379.)

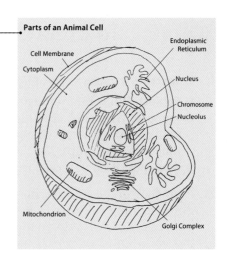

Parts of an Animal Cell

Major Civil War Battles of 1862

March	Monitor and Merrimac
April	Shiloh
	New Orleans
May	
June	Seven Pines (Fair Oaks)
July	The Seven Days Battles
August	Pope's Campaign
September	Harper's Ferry
	Antietam
October	
November	
December	Fredericksburg

Time Line

A time line shows events in the order they occurred. (See page 380.)

Flowchart

A flowchart outlines a process. Ovals indicate start and end points, diamonds show decision points, rectangles indicate steps, and arrows show the flow. (See page 381.)

Composing a Personal Essay

Start
Purpose
Describe — Narrate
Draft with order of location.
Draft with time order.
Evaluate — Changes
No Changes — Improve
Present
End

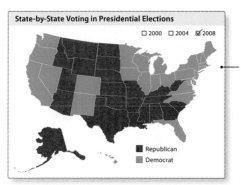

State-by-State Voting in Presidential Elections

☐ 2000 ☐ 2004 ☑ 2008

■ Republican
■ Democrat

Infographic

An infographic is an interactive online graphic that can combine elements from other graphics. (See page 383.)

Inquire To Create a Graph

1. **Question** the overall situation for the graph.
   - **Subject:** What information do I want to present?
   - **Purpose:** Why am I creating the graph? To show parts of a whole (pie graph)? To show changes over time (line graph)? To compare amounts (bar graph)?
   - **Audience:** Who will read the graph? What do they need to know?

2. **Plan** your graph by studying the type you will make. Explore graph-making software or gather supplies (graph paper, ruler, compass, protractor) to create the graph by hand. (Go to thoughtfullearning.com/p372 for suggestions.)

3. **Research** your topic.
   - **Gather** raw data from experiments, surveys, reports, or tables.
   - **Organize** the raw data for your graph.

4. **Create** your graph.
   - **Pie graphs** show the parts of a whole. See page 373 for tips on creating pie graphs.
   - **Line graphs** show changes over time. See page 374 for tips on creating line graphs.
   - **Bar graphs** compare amounts. See page 375 for tips on creating bar graphs.

5. **Improve** your graph.
   - **Evaluate** your graph.
     Does it clearly portray your topic? Is it accurate? Is it attractive?
     Does it include a title and clear labeling?
     Does the graphic achieve its purpose? Do readers understand it?
   - **Revise** your graph.
     Remove any distracting visuals or unneeded words.
     Rearrange parts that may be out of place.
     Redo parts that are unclear or confusing.
     Add any missing information and label the parts.
   - **Perfect** your graph, making it clean and correct.
     Ink the drawn lines.
     Color the parts or leave them black and white, as you wish.

6. **Present** your graph online, in a report, or in a presentation. (Go to thoughtfulllearning.com/p372 for more help creating graphs.)

Pie Graph

The following pie graph displays the amount of money that a school has spent in one year on its computer lab. The graph tells what part of the whole amount was spent for each type of expense.

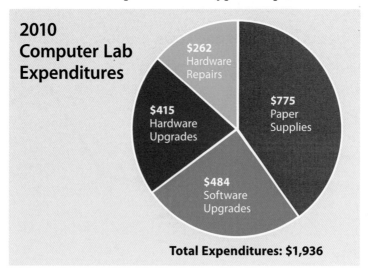

2010 Computer Lab Expenditures

$262 Hardware Repairs

$415 Hardware Upgrades

$775 Paper Supplies

$484 Software Upgrades

Total Expenditures: $1,936

Tips for Pie Graphs

Use a pie graph to divide a whole into parts.

- **Include no more than six slices.** Combine small slivers into a "miscellaneous" slice.
- **Start at the twelve o'clock position** with the largest slice and move clockwise.
- **Add the other slices** in descending order, from largest to smallest.
- **Label each slice horizontally** and provide amounts or percentages.
- **Use the equation below** to calculate the width (in degrees) for each slice.

a. Part quantity ÷ whole quantity x 100 = percentage
b. Percentage x 3.6 = number of degrees

Slices	$1,936	100%	360 degrees
Part 1	$775	40.03%	144.1 degrees
Part 2	$484	25.00%	90.0 degrees
Part 3	$415	21.44%	77.2 degrees
Part 4	$262	13.53%	48.7 degrees

Line Graph

In the following line graph, a student records the high and low temperatures in his hometown for a week. Notice how the graph shows changes in temperature over time.

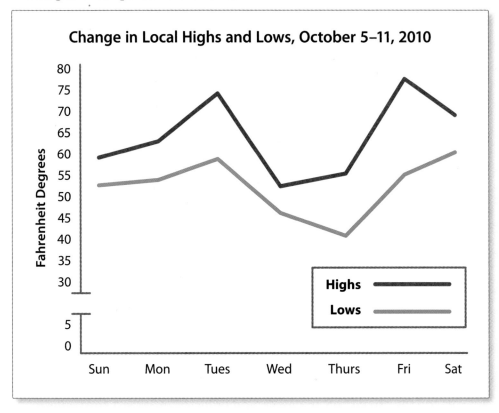

Tips for Line Graphs

Use a line graph to compare changes in quantity over time.

- **Plot time horizontally.** Mark units of time on the *x* axis (horizontal).
- **Plot quantity vertically.** Mark units of quantity on the *y* axis (vertical), starting at 0. If you need to skip a range to save space, show a break in the vertical axis.
- **Mark a dot** where the quantity and time intersect.
- **Draw lines** to connect the dots.
- **Create a legend** if you are using more than one line.
- **Title the line graph** clearly.

Bar Graph

The multiple bar graph below compares high and low temperatures, while the single bar graph compares highs on different days.

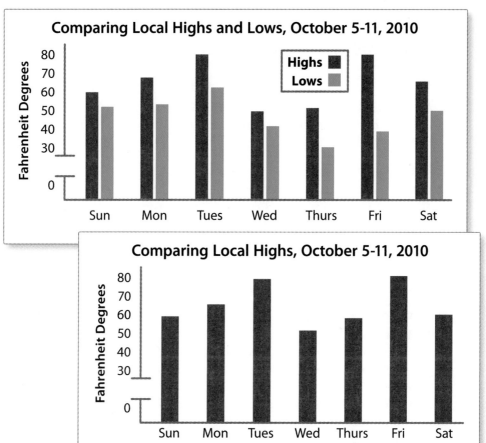

Tips for Bar Graphs

Use a bar graph to compare quantities.

- ▪ **Plot time horizontally.** Mark units of time or items to compare on the *x* axis.
- ▪ **Plot quantity vertically.** Mark units of quantity on the *y* axis, starting at 0. If you need to skip a range, show a break.
- ▪ **Present your data accurately.** Don't exaggerate or minimize differences.
- ▪ **Create consistent bars.** All should be the same width.
- ▪ **Use different colors** for different items, and provide a legend.
- ▪ **Give your graph an informative title.**

Inquire To Create a Table

1. **Question** the overall situation for the table.
   - **Subject:** What topics am I dealing with? What traits or amounts do I want to show?
   - **Purpose:** Why am I creating the table? How will it be used? What information is most important?
   - **Audience:** Who will use the table? What information do they need?

2. **Plan** your table, exploring table-making features of your word processor or spreadsheet program. (Go to thoughtfullearning.com/p376 for assistance.)

3. **Research** your topic.
   - **Gather** the data that you will present in your table.
   - **Decide** how to use rows and columns to effectively present the data.

4. **Create** your table. (See also "Tips for Tables" on page 377.)
   - **Choose** the number of columns and label them at the top.
   - **Create** the rows, labeling them at the left.
   - **Provide** a title that clearly identifies the table's content.

5. **Improve** your table.
   - **Evaluate** the table.
     Is each column and each row clearly labeled? Is the information in each cell accurate? Does the table include units of measure as needed?
     Does the table achieve its purpose? Do readers understand it?
   - **Revise** your table.
     Remove any columns or rows that do not provide essential information.
     Rearrange columns or rows for a better order.
     Redo any part of the table that is unclear or confusing.
     Add columns or rows as needed.
   - **Perfect** your table, making it clean and correct.

6. **Present** your table in the best context—perhaps online, in a report, or in a presentation. (Go to thoughtfullearning.com/p376 for more information.)

Table

The following sample table contains information about the eight planets of our solar system. The information is arranged in rows and columns.

Planet Facts

Planet	Distance from Sun (million mi.)	Diameter (mi.)	Type	Surface Temp. (F)	Length of Day	Length of Year
Mercury	36.0	3,032	Rock	-290 to 800°	176 days	87.9 days
Venus	67.24	7,521	Rock	864°	243 days	225 days
Earth	92.96	7,926	Rock	-126.9° to 136°	23.9 hours	365.25 days
Mars	141.6	4,222	Rock	-125° to -23°	24.6 hours	687 days
Jupiter	483.7	88,846	Gas	-234°	9.9 hours	11.86 years
Saturn	885.9	74,898	Gas	-288°	10.7 hours	29.45 years
Uranus	1,783.9	31,764	Gas	-357°	17.2 hours	84.0 years
Neptune	2,771.0	30,776	Gas	-353°	16.1 hours	164.8 years

Tips for Tables

Use a table to compare lists of data.

- **Make rows and columns.** Label the rows with item names down the left side, and label the columns with the traits at the top. (If the traits outnumber the items you will compare, you can reverse the position of these elements.)
- **Fill in boxes.** Where rows intersect columns, fill in the information that applies to that item and that trait.
- **Provide units of measure.** When numbers are given, provide the units for each or for a whole row or column.
- **Provide a title.** Clearly identify the topic of the table.

Inquire To Create a Diagram, Time Line, or Flowchart

1. **Question** the overall situation for the graphic.
   - **Subject:** What is the topic of the graphic?
   - **Purpose:** Why am I creating the graphic? To show the parts of something (diagram)? To show a sequence of events (time line)? To show the steps in a process (flowchart)?
   - **Audience:** Who will read the graphic? What information do they need?

2. **Plan** your graphic, deciding whether you'll use software or will create your diagram, time line, or flowchart by hand. (Go to thoughtfullearning.com/p378 for more help.)

3. **Research** your topic.
   - **Consult** resources to gather the information you need.
   - **List** the parts of the object, the steps of the process, or the events in the time line.

4. **Create** your graphic.
   - **Diagrams** show the parts of an object. Find or create a picture of the object and label the parts. Include a title. See page 379 for tips on creating diagrams.
   - **Time lines** show a sequence of events. See page 380 for tips on creating time lines.
   - **Flowcharts** show the steps in a process. Use ovals for start and end points, diamonds for decisions, rectangles for steps, and arrows to connect them. See page 381 for tips on creating flowcharts.

5. **Improve** your graphic.
   - **Evaluate** your graphic.
     Does it make the topic clear, achieving its purpose? Is it accurate and attractive? Does it include a title and clear labeling? Do readers understand it?
   - **Revise** your graphic.
     Remove any parts that do not communicate clearly.
     Rearrange parts that are out of order.
     Redo parts that are confusing.
   - **Perfect** your graphic, making it clean and correct.

6. **Present** your graphic in the best context—online, in a report, or in a presentation.

Diagram

The following diagram identifies the main parts of an animal cell.

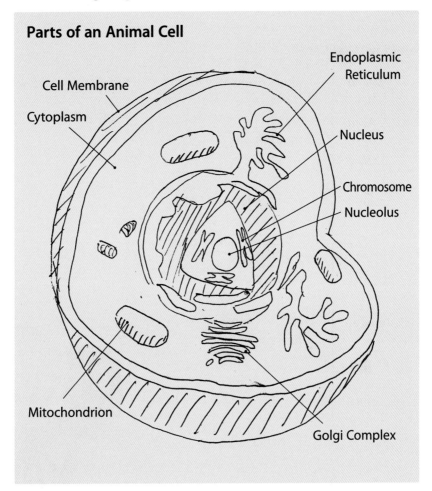

Parts of an Animal Cell

Endoplasmic Reticulum

Cell Membrane

Cytoplasm

Nucleus

Chromosome

Nucleolus

Mitochondrion

Golgi Complex

Tips for Diagrams

Use diagrams to show the parts of complex things.

■ **Select a topic** that you need to show in a diagram.

■ **Consider types of images,** such as a simple illustration, a cutaway (as shown above), or an "exploded view," in which the parts are pulled away from each other to show them individually.

■ **Draw, photograph, or find** the image that you want to present.

■ **Label the parts of the image** and draw lines to each.

■ **Provide a descriptive title** for the diagram.

Time Line

The following time line traces the major battles of the Civil War in 1862.

Major Civil War Battles of 1862

March	*Monitor* and *Merrimac*
April	Shiloh
	New Orleans
May	
June	Seven Pines (Fair Oaks)
July	The Seven Day's Battles
August	Pope's Campaign
September	Harper's Ferry
	Antietam
October	
November	
December	Fredericksburg

Tips for Time Lines

Use time lines to show a sequence of events.

- **Choose the right scale** for your topic—hour by hour, day by day, and so on. Size your project so that it fits easily on one page or screen.
- **Record your information.** Place each event in sequence.
- **Title the time line,** accurately naming its contents.

Flowchart

The following flowchart demonstrates the process of drafting, revising, and presenting a personal essay.

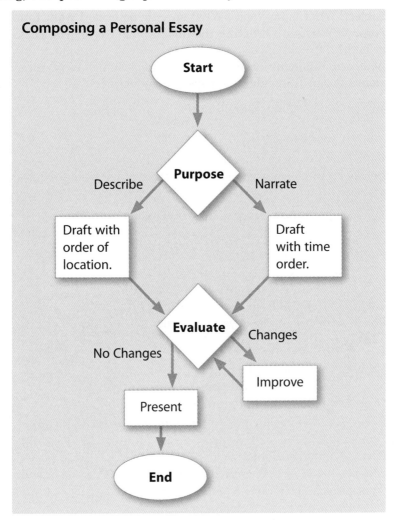

Composing a Personal Essay

Tips for Flowcharts

Use a flowchart to show a sequence with decision points and alternate routes.

- ▪ **Use ovals** to indicate the start and end points.
- ▪ **Use diamonds** to indicate decision points.
- ▪ **Use rectangles** to indicate steps in the process.
- ▪ **Use arrows** to connect the parts.

Inquire To Create an Infographic

1. **Question** the overall situation for the infographic.
   - **Subject:** What is my topic? What specific point do I want to make?
   - **Purpose:** Why am I creating the infographic? To inform, persuade, or both?
   - **Audience:** Who will interact with the infographic? What interactive elements can I provide to engage the audience?

2. **Plan** your infographic, searching the Web for options.

3. **Research** your topic.
   - **Gather** data from reliable print and online sources.
   - **Decide** on the format you will use—map, graph, table, diagram, or other.

4. **Create** your infographic. (See also "Tips for Infographics" on page 383.)
   - **Prepare** the graphic, using the examples earlier in this chapter as a guide.
   - **Add** animation to the graphic if appropriate.
   - **Title** the infographic so users can quickly understand its contents.
   - **Provide** any necessary keys or legends.

5. **Improve** your infographic.
   - **Evaluate** your infographic.
     Does the infographic present the important information? Is it accurate? Does the infographic use animation?
     Does the infographic achieve its purpose? Do readers understand it?
   - **Revise** your infographic.
     Remove any parts or animation features that do not provide essential information.
     Rearrange parts for a clearer presentation.
     Redo parts that aren't working.
     Add missing information, titles, legends, or animations.
   - **Perfect** your infographic, making it clean and correct.

6. **Present** your infographic online and use social media to attract readers. (Go to thoughtfullearning.com/p382 for more on infographics.)

Infographic

The following infographic shows how states voted (Republican or Democrat) in three recent presidential elections. In its online form, this infographic is interactive, allowing the user to click the election year to see the states changing color.

Tips for Infographics

Create infographics online to give users the chance to make selections and interact with the information. Any of the graph types shown on the previous pages could be made into infographics by adding animation and additional layers of information.

- **Choose the graph type** that will best describe your topic.
- **Create versions of the graph** to show changes over time, or connect the graph to others with similar information. For example, the line and bar graphs on pages 374–375 could be linked in an infographic to show the same information in three ways.
- **Link the graphs** so that users can click through the different versions.

Additional Infographics

Here are two additional example infographics.

Animated Maps

Another way to use an animated map is to show gradual changes over time. The three shots below come from an infographic that shows the progressive shrinking of the Arctic Sea ice from 2000 to 2007.

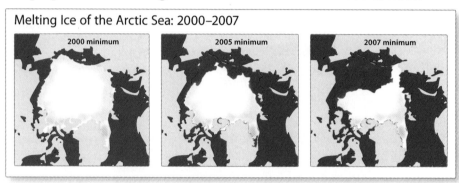

Melting Ice of the Arctic Sea: 2000–2007

Word Clouds

A word cloud is a cluster of words used frequently in a piece of writing. The more often a word is used, the larger it appears. You can scan the cloud to see the most important concepts in a reading. The word cloud below comes from all of the text in this chapter. (Go to wordle.net to create your own word cloud, or go to thoughtfullearning.com/p384 for more information.)

Word Cloud from Text in This Chapter

Chapter 27
Web Projects

You are probably older than Twitter, Facebook, or YouTube™. You're probably even older than Wikipedia and Google. These sites and services have come rushing onto the scene very recently, and they have transformed our world.

The World Wide Web, which itself is only about 20 years old, is continuing to transform the world. And the good news is that it's your world, your Web—a place for you to search and publish. This chapter will show you how.

You will learn . . .

- Designing Glogs
- Making Digital Stories
- Creating Blog or Wiki Posts
- Building Web Sites

Project Overview

On the pages that follow, you'll find directions for making your own glog, digital story, blog or wiki post, and Web site. You'll also find examples that other students have made.

Glog

Glog stands for "graphical blog." (See pages 150 and 392–393 for a discussion of blogs and an example blog project.) Think of a glog as a digital poster. Besides using pictures and text, a glog can also link viewers to further information. (See page 388–389.)

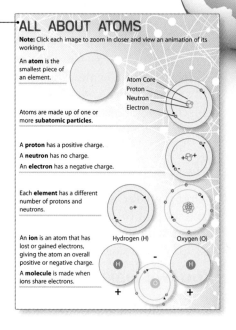

ALL ABOUT ATOMS

Note: Click each image to zoom in closer and view an animation of its workings.

An **atom** is the smallest piece of an element.

Atom Core
Proton
Neutron
Electron

Atoms are made up of one or more **subatomic particles**.

A **proton** has a positive charge.
A **neutron** has no charge.
An **electron** has a negative charge.

Each **element** has a different number of protons and neutrons.

An **ion** is an atom that has lost or gained electrons, giving the atom an overall positive or negative charge.

A **molecule** is made when ions share electrons.

Hydrogen (H)   Oxygen (O)

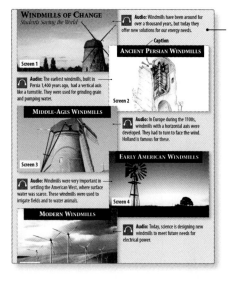

WINDMILLS OF CHANGE
Students Saving the World

Screen 1

Audio: Windmills have been around for over a thousand years, but today they offer new solutions for our energy needs.

Caption

ANCIENT PERSIAN WINDMILLS

Audio: The earliest windmills, built in Persia 1,400 years ago, had a vertical axis like a turnstile. They were used for grinding grain and pumping water.

Screen 2

MIDDLE-AGES WINDMILLS

Audio: In Europe during the 1100s, windmills with a horizontal axis were developed. They had to turn to face the wind. Holland is famous for these.

Screen 3

EARLY AMERICAN WINDMILLS

Audio: Windmills were very important in settling the American West, where surface water was scarce. These windmills were used to irrigate fields and to water animals.

Screen 4

MODERN WINDMILLS

Audio: Today, science is designing new windmills to meet future needs for electrical power.

Digital Story

Like a glog, a digital story relies on visuals to present its information. However, a digital story presents those images one at a time. Most digital stories also include audio to tell more about the pictures. (See pages 390–391.)

Blog or Wiki Post

Either a blog or a wiki can be a quick way to collaborate with other people on a Web project. The administrator can assign privileges for individuals to create pages, write content to fill them, and/or edit that content. (See pages 392–393.)

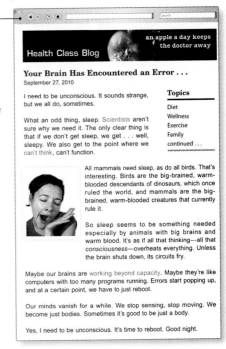

Health Class Blog

an apple a day keeps the doctor away

Your Brain Has Encountered an Error . . .
September 27, 2010

I need to be unconscious. It sounds strange, but we all do, sometimes.

What an odd thing, sleep. Scientists aren't sure why we need it. The only clear thing is that if we don't get sleep, we get . . . well, sleepy. We also get to the point where we can't think, can't function.

Topics

Diet
Wellness
Exercise
Family
continued . . .

All mammals need sleep, as do all birds. That's interesting. Birds are the big-brained, warm-blooded descendants of dinosaurs, which once ruled the world, and mammals are the big-brained, warm-blooded creatures that currently rule it.

So sleep seems to be something needed especially by animals with big brains and warm blood. It's as if all that thinking—all that *consciousness*—overheats everything. Unless the brain shuts down, its circuits fry.

Maybe our brains are working beyond capacity. Maybe they're like computers with too many programs running. Errors start popping up, and at a certain point, we have to just reboot.

Our minds vanish for a while. We stop sensing, stop moving. We become just bodies. Sometimes it's good to be just a body.

Yes, I need to be unconscious. It's time to reboot. Good night.

Web Site

If you have enough information to share that it should be divided into separate pages, you have enough to build a Web site. Ask an adult to help you post the pages once you have all your information prepared. (See pages 394–396.)

Home History Warfare Modern Sparta Gallery

HISTORICAL BOUNTY: SPARTA

HISTORY OF SPARTA

The Ancient City of Sparta was located slightly to the west of the Eurotas River. The city was south of Nemea and Argos, which were bitter rivals of Sparta since the beginning. The city had different districts, which welcomed different citizens depending on the individual's rank and whether or not he or she was born in the city. The Acropolis, however, was open to all.

Courtesy of Shutterstock

A BLOODY RIVALRY BEGINS

Sparta started out as a city with a limited amount of land and a serious problem with the growing population. To gain more territory, Spartan warriors marched across the Taygetos Mountains to annex Sparta's neighbor Messenia. Other neighbors were not pleased. Argos, for example, backed the Messenian Revolt, which nearly destroyed Sparta. In the end, the battle-hardened Spartans won their war against Argos.

These Spartan victories in turn angered the Athenians, who had been allies of Messenia and Argos. The Spartan-Athenian rivalry was born. The Peloponnesian War resulted, pitting Sparta and the Peloponnesian League against Athens. The two sides battled each other many times. The only time they fought on the same side was when Greece was attacked by Persia at Thermopylae and when Alexander the Great of Macedonia invaded the southern parts of Greece.

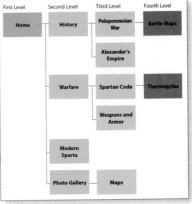

Inquire | To Design a Glog

1. **Question** the situation for your glog (graphical blog).
   - **Subject:** What information will your glog cover?
   - **Purpose:** Why are you making this glog? What do you hope to accomplish with it?
   - **Audience:** Who will see your glog? What do they need or want to gain from it?

2. **Plan** your glog by making a sketch on a large sheet of paper.

3. **Research** your topic.
   - **Gather** information that your glog will present. Look for images that help to show that information.
   - **Explore** other glogs for inspiration. (Go to thoughtfullearning.com/p388 for ideas.)
   - **Organize** your images in the best order.

4. **Create** your glog, considering the following components.
   - **Visuals:** Use photos and illustrations that both communicate well and look good together. The first impression your glog makes will determine whether people look at the details.
   - **Text:** Keep text to a minimum. Make clear captions or titles for each image. Add a sentence or two of explanation where needed.
   - **Links:** Because your glog is an online document, you can provide links to sources with more details if your viewers want them.

5. **Improve** your glog.
   - **Evaluate** the glog.
     Does it accurately portray your message? Does it look good as a whole? Could elements be better arranged? Do some images need to be replaced with better ones? Is the text clear and helpful?
   - **Revise** your glog.
     Remove visuals and text that distract or don't contribute.
     Rearrange parts so that the viewer's eye moves smoothly from one to another.
     Rework any elements that don't look or feel right.
     Add visuals, text, and links to make your glog stronger.
   - **Perfect** your glog, making each part the best it can be.

6. **Present** your glog to other people by sharing a link to it.

Glog

In her science class, Callie Leavitt created a glog to show what atoms and molecules are made of. She included short definitions of each and used drawings to reveal more information.

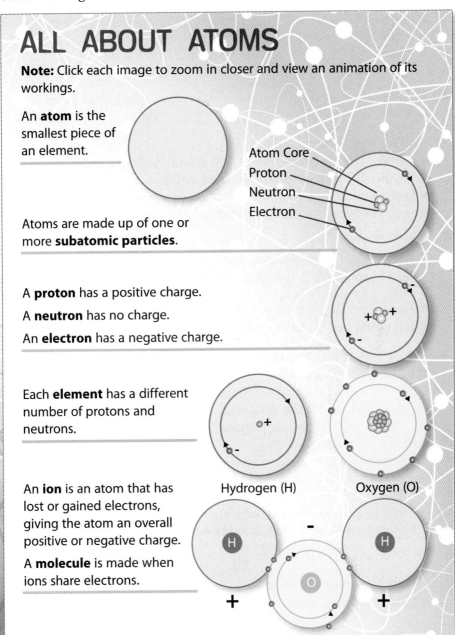

ALL ABOUT ATOMS

Note: Click each image to zoom in closer and view an animation of its workings.

An **atom** is the smallest piece of an element.

Atom Core
Proton
Neutron
Electron

Atoms are made up of one or more **subatomic particles**.

A **proton** has a positive charge.

A **neutron** has no charge.

An **electron** has a negative charge.

Each **element** has a different number of protons and neutrons.

Hydrogen (H)   Oxygen (O)

An **ion** is an atom that has lost or gained electrons, giving the atom an overall positive or negative charge.

A **molecule** is made when ions share electrons.

H   H

+   +

-

O

Inquire To Make a Digital Story

1. **Question** the situation for your digital story.
   - **Subject:** What information will your digital story provide?
   - **Purpose:** Why are you making this digital story? How will it communicate better than another medium would?
   - **Audience:** Who will see your digital story? What do they need or want from it?

2. **Plan** your digital story by using a storyboard to organize your pictures, text, and audio. (See page 409.)

3. **Research** your topic.
   - **Gather** information that your digital story will present, along with any needed photos, video clips, and audio.
   - **Explore** other digital stories to see what works best.
   - **Organize** your images in the best order.

4. **Create** your digital story, considering the following components.
   - **Visuals:** Use photos or video that will hold your audience's attention.
   - **Text:** Keep text to a minimum. It should be little more than a caption for the visuals.
   - **Audio:** Provide most information in audio with each visual.
   - **Links:** Add text links to other sources to provide more information.

5. **Improve** your digital story.
   - **Evaluate** the presentation.
     Is the digital story interesting from start to finish? Is the subject clear and are all the details helpful? Does the story do what you want it to? Will people respond well to it?
   - **Revise** your digital story.
     Remove visuals, audio, and text that don't contribute.
     Rearrange parts so that the story flows smoothly.
     Rework any elements that don't sound, look, or feel right.
     Add visuals, audio, text, and links to improve your digital story.
   - **Perfect** your digital story, making each part the best it can be.

6. **Present** your digital story online.

Note: Digital stories can be created in many media: as a video, a photo album with captions, or an online slide-show presentation.

Digital Story

The screens below show a simple digital story. Note how captions give the main idea, while audio accompaniment adds important details.

Caption (Title)

WINDMILLS OF CHANGE
Students Saving the World

Screen 1

Audio: Windmills have been around for over a thousand years, but today they offer new solutions for our energy needs.

Caption

ANCIENT PERSIAN WINDMILLS

Audio: The earliest windmills, built in Persia 1,400 years ago, had a vertical axis like a turnstile. They were used for grinding grain and pumping water.

Screen 2

MIDDLE-AGES WINDMILLS

Audio: In Europe during the 1100s, windmills with a horizontal axis were developed. They had to turn to face the wind. Holland is famous for these.

Screen 3

EARLY AMERICAN WINDMILLS

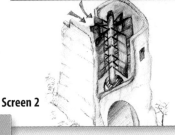

Audio: Windmills were very important in settling the American West, where surface water was scarce. These windmills were used to irrigate fields and to water animals.

Screen 4

MODERN WINDMILLS

Audio: Today, science is designing new windmills to meet future needs for electrical power.

Screen 5

Inquire   To Create a Blog or Wiki Post

1. **Question** the situation for your post.
   - **Subject:** What do you want to write about?
   - **Purpose:** Why are you making a post? Are you explaining, persuading, entertaining? How do you want readers to respond?
   - **Audience:** Who will read the post? What will readers gain?

2. **Plan** your blog or wiki post by brainstorming, clustering, or using other prewriting activities.

3. **Research** your topic.
   - **Gather** information about your topic, watching for links you can provide to other articles or videos.
   - **Focus** your ideas about the topic with a thesis statement.
   - **Organize** the details with a quick list.

4. **Create** your post, including the following parts.
   - **Beginning:** Get the reader's attention and introduce your topic. Provide your thesis up front, or build to it.
   - **Middle:** Support your thesis, placing details in the best order.
   - **Ending:** Wrap up your post, giving the reader a final thought.
   - **Title:** Create an interesting title that will work well on Twitter, Facebook, and other social media. (You can use these services to promote your post.)
   - **Visuals:** Include an attention-getting image.
   - **Links:** Include links to related articles, videos, or pages within the wiki.

5. **Improve** your post.
   - **Evaluate** the post.
     Does the post fulfill your purpose? Does it have an interesting topic and clear focus? Does it have the right impact? Will readers respond well to it?
   - **Revise** your post.
     Remove ideas and details that aren't needed.
     Rearrange ideas so that they are in the best order.
     Rework parts (beginning, middle, or ending) that don't work.
     Add new details that help you achieve your goal.
   - **Perfect** your post, checking it for errors.

6. **Present** your post and send the link via other social media.

Blog Post

In the following blog post written for a health-class Web site, a student reflects on the strangeness of sleep. Her post is meant to be entertaining but also thought provoking.

Health Class Blog

an apple a day keeps the doctor away

A title sparks interest.

Your Brain Has Encountered an Error . . .

September 27, 2010

I need to be unconscious. It sounds strange, but we all do, sometimes.

The beginning introduces the topic.

What an odd thing, sleep. Scientists aren't sure why we need it. The only clear thing is that if we don't get sleep, we get . . . well, sleepy. We also get to the point where we can't think, can't function.

Topics

Diet
Wellness
Exercise
Family
continued . . .

The middle gives details.

All mammals need sleep, as do all birds. That's interesting. Birds are the big-brained, warm-blooded descendants of dinosaurs, which once ruled the world, and mammals are the big-brained, warm-blooded creatures that currently rule it.

A photo draws the eye.

So sleep seems to be something needed especially by animals with big brains and warm blood. It's as if all that thinking—all that *consciousness*—overheats everything. Unless the brain shuts down, its circuits fry.

Links connect to related information.

Maybe our brains are working beyond capacity. Maybe they're like computers with too many programs running. Errors start popping up, and at a certain point, we have to just reboot.

Our minds vanish for a while. We stop sensing, stop moving. We become just bodies. Sometimes it's good to be just a body.

The ending provides a final thought.

Yes, I need to be unconscious. It's time to reboot. Good night.

Inquire To Build a Web Site

1. **Question** the situation for your Web site.
   - **Subject:** What should the site focus on?
   - **Purpose:** Why are you creating a Web site? What need does it fill?
   - **Audience:** Who will use the site? What do they want?

2. **Plan** your Web site by completing a planning sheet. (See page 261.)

3. **Research** your topic.
   - **Gather** the information and images that you will present on your site. Track sources so that you can credit them.
   - **Sort** the information into separate pages and features you will offer on your site.
   - **Organize** your site by drawing a map of the site's pages and the connections between them.
   - **Find** site-building software online, and buy a domain name and hosting, if needed. (Go to thoughtfullearning.com/p394 for suggestions.)

4. **Create** your Web site, considering the following components.
   - **Home Page:** Give visitors a starting point, summing up site content, explaining its purpose, helping people navigate, and making them care about the site.
   - **Content Pages:** Create different pages for different parts of the topic.
   - **About Us Page:** Create a page telling who you are.
   - **Contact Us Page:** Create a page telling readers how to e-mail you.
   - **Headings, Text, Visuals, Links:** Use these features for clarity.

5. **Improve** your Web site by evaluating each page.
   - **Evaluate** the Web site.
     Does the site fulfill your goal? Does each page focus on an important part of the topic? Will people find what they need? Will the site draw traffic?
   - **Revise** your Web site.
     Remove text, images, or whole pages that aren't needed.
     Rearrange pages or parts of pages for a better flow.
     Rewrite pages that don't work well.
     Add new pages and features to meet the audience's needs.
   - **Perfect** each page and the whole site, correcting any errors.

6. **Present** the Web site online and promote it with other media.

Web Site Map

In his history class, Aidan King created a map for his Web site about ancient Sparta. The map shows the arrangement of Web pages. Aidan planned four levels of pages in order to share details with those who were interested.

Site Map for *Historical Bounty: Sparta*

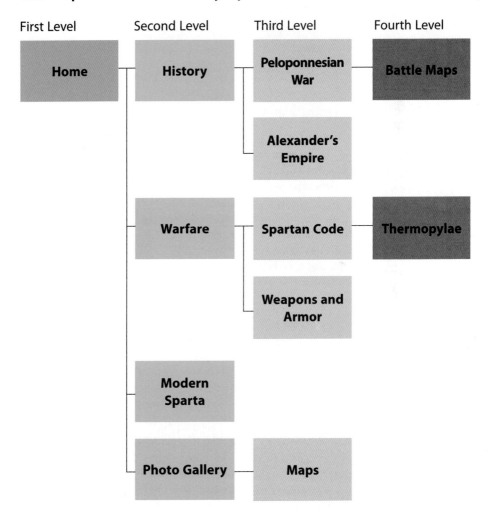

First Level   Second Level   Third Level   Fourth Level

Home

History   Peloponnesian War   Battle Maps

Alexander's Empire

Warfare   Spartan Code   Thermopylae

Weapons and Armor

Modern Sparta

Photo Gallery   Maps

Your Turn

Create a site map for your own Web site. Include different levels of details, and show how they are connected.

Web Site

Here is the beginning of the history page from Aidan's Web site about Sparta. Note the other pages listed in the title bar.

The title bar identifies the site and provides links on the site.

The text, photos, and **design** share the student's information.

Headings help readers navigate the text.

Links to sources of ideas are in blue.

Home   History   Warfare   Modern Sparta   Gallery

HISTORICAL BOUNTY: SPARTA

HISTORY OF SPARTA

The Ancient City of Sparta was located slightly to the west of the Eurotas River. The city was south of Nemea and Argos, which were bitter rivals of Sparta since the beginning. The city had different districts, which welcomed different citizens depending on the individual's rank and whether or not he or she was born in the city. The Acropolis, however, was open to all.

Courtesy of Shutterstock

A BLOODY RIVALRY BEGINS

Sparta started out as a city with a limited amount of land and a serious problem with the growing population. To gain more territory, Spartan warriors marched across the Taygetos Mountains to annex Sparta's neighbor Messenia. Other neighbors were not pleased. Argos, for example, backed the Messenian Revolt, which nearly destroyed Sparta. In the end, the battle-hardened Spartans won their war against Argos.

These Spartan victories in turn angered the Athenians, who had been allies of Messenia and Argos. The Spartan-Athenian rivalry was born. The Peloponnesian War resulted, pitting Sparta and the Peloponnesian League against Athens. The two sides battled each other many times. The only time they fought on the same side was when Greece was attacked by Persia at Thermopylae and when Alexander the Great of Macedonia invaded the southern parts of Greece.

Chapter 28
Audio-Visual Projects

You're lucky to live at a time when audio and video technology is relatively inexpensive and reliable. Once upon a time, only big movie studios could make and distribute films. But today, you can make a video in your backyard, post it that night, and have thousands of viewers by the next morning.

The technology is there for you to use, and this chapter offers guidelines for creating several different audio and video projects. But most important, it focuses on what you will personally bring to the process—ideas worth sharing.

You will learn . . .

- Creating Podcasts
- Creating Slide Shows
- Creating PSAs
- Making Videos
- Basic Types of Videos

Project Overview

You'll find the following audio-visual projects in this chapter. You'll find added help for creating a video at thoughtfullearning.com/p406.

Podcast

A podcast is an audio or audio-video feature made available on the Internet. Podcasts can follow an interview format, provide information, and even entertain. (See pages 400–401.)

Our **Supermassive Black Hole**

Jason: This is Jason Smith with *Real-World Role Models*. Today, I'm talking with the father of a friend of mine. This is Dr. Mike Lattimore, who is an astronomer at our local UW campus. Thanks for coming in, Dr. Lattimore.

Dr. Lattimore: You're welcome, Jason.

Jason: So, you've been telling me there's a monster at the center of our galaxy.

Dr. Lattimore: Well, yes. In the region called Sagittarius A, there's a supermassive black hole. It's about 4.3 million times as massive as our own sun.

Jason: Whoa! That's a lot of mass. But how does anybody know it's there? I mean, it's a black hole, right?

Dr. Lattimore: We can't see it directly, but we can track the movement of stars around it. One of those stars—we call it S2—goes around the center every 15.2 years. That's about 11 million miles an hour! By measuring S2's speed and orbit, we can determine the mass of the object it is orbiting. And the only way to crunch 4 million solar masses into that small a space is to have a supermassive black hole there.

Jason: Should we be afraid?

Dr. Lattimore: No. Not at all. We're 27 thousand light years away from it—very safe. In fact, we now believe that most if not all galaxies have supermassive black holes at their centers. Instead of jeopardizing these galaxies, the

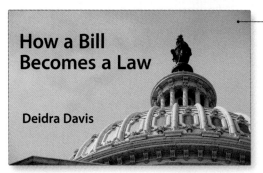

How a Bill Becomes a Law

Deidra Davis

Slide Show

A slide show (for example, a PowerPoint presentation) uses words and images to communicate to an audience. Some slide shows accompany a speech, but others have a sound track and can stand alone. (See pages 402–403.)

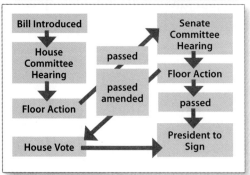

Bill Introduced → House Committee Hearing → Floor Action → House Vote

passed → Senate Committee Hearing → Floor Action → passed → President to Sign

passed amended

Public Service Announcement

A public service announcement (PSA) is a message meant to persuade people to do something that will help them or their communities. It is a type of commercial, but the purpose is to help people rather than to sell a product. (See pages 404–405.)

What Book?

EXT. MEADOW—AFTERNOON

A girl sits against a tree, reading *The Hobbit*.

  NARRATOR
  (voice-over)
  What book made you fall in love with reading?

  CUT TO:

INT. SCHOOL HALLWAY—MORNING

A boy sits on a window ledge and reads *The Hunger Games*.

  NARRATOR
  What book could help someone else love reading, too?

  CUT TO:

INT. LITERACY CENTER—EVENING

A literacy teacher hands a copy of *The Last Olympian* to an adult reader. It has a note attached that says, "Get ready for a great adventure! –Terrell Davis"

  TERRELL DAVIS
  (voice-over)
  Get ready for a great adventure!

The adult reader smiles, opens the book, and begins to read.

  NARRATOR

Video

A video is a movie of any length, from short features suitable for YouTube to full-length films that could be shown in a theater. Creating a video is a process that involves scriptwriting, directing, storyboarding, acting, filming, and editing—with many people involved. (See pages 406–410.)

Lincoln, Time Traveler

INT. CLASSROOM—MORNING

A TEACHER stands at the front of the classroom, writing the words "Prime Numbers" on the whiteboard, and the camera pans back from her down one of the rows of students sitting at their desks.

  TEACHER
  Prime numbers are numbers that cannot be divided by anything except themselves and one.

The camera pans back to the class to show one student wearing a black suit, stovepipe hat, and a black Abe Lincoln beard.

  TEACHER
  Which one of you can give me an example of a prime number?

The student with the beard raises his hand solemnly and stands. The TEACHER turns to acknowledge him.

  TEACHER
  Yes, Abe?

  LINCOLN
  Four score, and seven.

Inquire　To Create a Podcast (Audio)

1. **Question** the situation.
   - **Subject:** What main idea do you want to get across?
   - **Purpose:** Do you want to entertain, inform, persuade, or narrate?
   - **Audience:** Whom do you want to reach with your podcast?

2. **Plan** your podcast using a planning sheet. (See page 261.)

3. **Research** your topic and technical requirements.
   - **Tools:** Find audio recording and editing equipment and software. Find a site for posting your podcast. Learn to use the equipment and software, and experiment with posting on the Web site. (Go to thoughtfullearning.com/p400 for tips.)
   - **Team:** Work with your team of scriptwriters, audio engineers, and on-air personalities to arrange your recording session.
   - **Topic:** Research your subject until you have enough information.

4. **Create** your podcast using one of these approaches.
   - **Scripted:** Use a script with a beginning, a middle, and an ending and record a reading by on-air personalities. Rerecord parts as needed.
   - **Mixed:** Script some parts (opening, interview questions, main points, closing), but let on-air personalities improvise the rest. Do repeat takes and prepare for moderate editing.
   - **Improvised:** Have on-air personalities make up dialogue about the topic, but be ready for heavy editing and retakes.

5. **Improve** the rough cut.
   - **Evaluate** your podcast against your goal and situation.
     Goal: Did you meet it? How could you improve your work?
     Situation: Did you cover the subject? Did you achieve your purpose? Are you reaching your audience?
   - **Revise** your podcast as necessary.
     Cut material that does not help you achieve your goal.
     Reorder parts to create a better flow.
     Redo weak parts to be stronger.
     Add new material to fill gaps.
   - **Perfect** your podcast, polishing it to professional standards.

6. **Present** your podcast by posting it to a Web site.

Podcast

Here is the first page of a podcast transcript in which a student interviews an astronomy professor who happens to be the father of a friend.

Our Supermassive Black Hole

The **beginning** identifies the podcaster, the topic, and the interviewee.

Jason: This is Jason Smith with *Real-World Role Models*. Today, I'm talking with the father of a friend of mine. This is Dr. Mike Lattimore, who is an astronomer at our local UW campus. Thanks for coming in, Dr. Lattimore.

Dr. Lattimore: You're welcome, Jason.

Jason: So, you've been telling me there's a monster at the center of our galaxy.

Dr. Lattimore: Well, yes. In the region called Sagittarius A, there's a supermassive black hole. It's about 4.3 million times as massive as our own sun.

The **middle** part contains a series of questions and answers.

Jason: Whoa! That's a lot of mass. But how does anybody know it's there? I mean, it's a black hole, right?

Dr. Lattimore: We can't see it directly, but we can track the movement of stars around it. One of those stars—we call it S2—goes around the center every 15.2 years. That's about 11 million miles an hour! By measuring S2's speed and orbit, we can determine the mass of the object it is orbiting. And the only way to crunch 4 million solar masses into that small a space is to have a supermassive black hole there.

Follow-up questions prompt the interviewee to explain his ideas.

Jason: Should we be afraid?

Dr. Lattimore: No. Not at all. We're 27 thousand light years away from it—very safe. In fact, we now believe that most if not all galaxies have supermassive black holes at their centers. Instead of jeopardizing these galaxies, the black holes at their centers actually help hold the galaxies together.

Jason: Which came first, our supermassive black hole or our galaxy?

Dr. Lattimore: Now that's an excellent question. . . .

Inquire To Create a Slide Show

1. Question the situation.
- **Subject:** What is your topic? What is your specific focus?
- **Purpose:** Are you trying to inform, persuade, or narrate?
- **Audience:** Who will view the slide show? Will it stand on its own, or will you present it in person?

2. Plan your slide show using a planning sheet. (See page 261.)

3. Research your topic and technical requirements.
- **Write** research questions to guide your search.
- **Read** about your topic, taking notes and tracking sources.
- **Gather** images—photos, graphs, tables, diagrams—that support your ideas. (See also page 443.)
- **Organize** information in a reasonable way (cause-effect, compare-contrast, and so on).

4. Create your slide show, using software such as the PowerPoint program.
- **Beginning:** Provide an opening slide with the title of the presentation, your name, and a visual that engages the viewer. Then provide a few slides that introduce the idea and give your thesis, or focus.
- **Middle:** Create middle slides that support your thesis. Use text in lists paired with strong visuals.
- **Ending:** Sum up the main point of your slide show and leave the audience with a strong final thought. If you want to persuade, include a call to action. (See page 107.)

5. Improve your slide show.
- **Evaluate** your slide show against your goal and situation.
  Goal: Did you meet your goal? How could you improve?
  Situation: Did you cover the subject? Did you achieve your purpose? How does your audience respond?
- **Revise** your slide show as necessary.
  Cut slides that don't help you meet your goal.
  Reorder slides for better flow.
  Redo slides that are overcrowded or ineffective.
  Add new slides to improve support.
- **Perfect** your slide show, polishing and proofreading it.

6. Present your slide show in person or on the Web.

Slide Show

Here are some slides from a presentation about how a bill becomes a law. Note how the student uses photos, graphics, and lists to get the point across.

The **beginning** slide includes the title, the student's name, and an image.

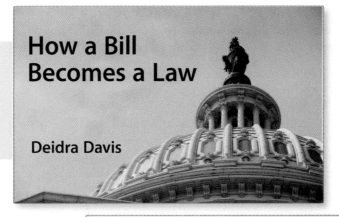

A **flowchart** provides an overview of the process.

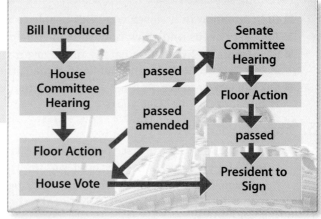

The **closing** slide uses a bulleted list to review key points.

Three Branches

- Legislative makes laws.
- Executive enforces laws.
- Judicial interprets laws.

Inquire To Create a PSA (Video)

1. **Question** the situation.
   - **Subject:** What idea are you presenting in your public-service announcement (PSA)? Why?
   - **Purpose:** What do you want viewers to do after seeing the PSA?
   - **Audience:** Whom are you trying to convince? What do they want?

2. **Plan** your PSA using a planning sheet. (See page 261.)

3. **Research** your topic and technical requirements.
   - **Tools:** Create props, costumes, and backdrops. If recording, borrow recording and editing equipment as needed.
   - **Team:** Rehearse your PSA with your actors and the recording crew.
   - **Topic:** Research your subject and write a short script.

4. **Create** your PSA, writing the script, acting it out, and perhaps recording it.
   - **Grab attention** in a clever way. Get people to watch and listen.
   - **Appeal to needs** and show how your idea helps. (See page 466.)
   - **Be memorable** by using a catchy name or an easy-to-remember slogan. Use repetition and music to cement the idea.
   - **Call the viewer to act.** Ask for a specific action using a command verb: "Join us!" or "Get yours today!"

5. **Improve** your PSA.
   - **Evaluate** your PSA against your goal and situation.
     Goal: Did you meet it? How could you improve your work?
     Situation: Did you focus on the audience's needs? Did you feature your subject? Are viewers likely to take the action that you suggest?
   - **Revise** your PSA as necessary.
     Cut parts that don't work, making the PSA short and sweet.
     Reorder parts to grab attention up front and call the audience to act at the end.
     Redo weak parts to be stronger.
     Add new material to meet your goals.
   - **Perfect** your PSA, polishing it to professional standards.

6. **Present** your PSA live or play the recording.
   - **Share** with classmates and family members or post online.

Public-Service Announcement

The following public-service announcement promotes a book drive for a literacy center—all in about 30 seconds. Note how the writer grabs attention, focuses on needs, and delivers the idea in a catchy way.

The script identifies the setting, gives directions, and provides dialogue.

The **beginning** lines get the audience's attention.

The **middle** part makes an emotional appeal.

The **ending** makes a call to action.

What Book?

EXT. MEADOW—AFTERNOON

A girl sits against a tree, reading *The Hobbit*.

NARRATOR
(voice-over)
What book made you fall in love with reading?

CUT TO:

INT. SCHOOL HALLWAY—MORNING

A boy sits on a window ledge and reads *The Hunger Games*.

NARRATOR
What book could help someone else love reading, too?

CUT TO:

INT. LITERACY CENTER—EVENING

A literacy teacher hands a copy of *The Last Olympian* to an adult reader. It has a note attached that says, "Get ready for a great adventure! –Terrell Davis"

TERRELL DAVIS
(voice-over)
Get ready for a great adventure!

The adult reader smiles, opens the book, and begins to read.

NARRATOR
Donate your favorite book to the Racine Literacy Center. Drop off the book in Mr. Brown's English class, Room 233, by October 21. Remember to include a note telling what you love about it. Help someone else fall in love with reading, too.

Inquire To Make a Video

1. **Question** the situation.
   - **Subject:** What main idea do you want to get across in your video?
   - **Purpose:** Why do you want to create a video? How do you want people to react? What type of video will you make?
   - **Audience:** Who will watch this video?

2. **Plan** your video using a planning sheet. (See page 261.)

3. **Research** your topic and technical requirements.
   - **Tools:** Gather the camera, computer, software, lighting, props, and costumes you need. (Go to thoughtfullearning.com/p406 for tips.)
   - **Team:** Ask people to be actors, artists, costumers, prop people, and camera operators. Set up a shooting schedule.
   - **Topic:** Research your topic.

4. **Create** your video, following these tips.
   - **Write your script.** Use your research to create real characters and believable dialogue. (See pages 407–408.)
   - **Choose the best order.** Shoot scenes in whatever order works best for the actors, the lighting, or the camera.
   - **Shoot scenes a number of times.** Try different takes and choose the best one when you edit.
   - **Guide team members.** Tell people exactly what to do, but be considerate.
   - **Edit.** Use video-editing software to create a rough cut of your video.

5. **Improve** your rough cut.
   - **Evaluate** your video against your goal and situation.
     Goal: Did you meet it? How could you improve your video?
     Situation: Do the characters and dialogue get the main idea across? Does the video have the effect you want?
   - **Revise** your video as necessary.
     Cut parts that aren't working. When in doubt, leave it out.
     Reorder scenes to create a better flow.
     Reshoot or digitally alter parts that have problems.
     Add new material as needed.
   - **Perfect** your video, polishing it to professional standards.

6. **Present** your video on a file-sharing site or on disk.

Video

This page and the next offer the introductory text for a sample video script. (Free screenwriting software is available on the Internet.)

Lincoln, Time Traveler

INT. CLASSROOM—MORNING

The script indicates the place and time of the action.

A TEACHER stands at the front of the classroom, writing the words "Prime Numbers" on the whiteboard, and the camera pans back from her down one of the rows of students sitting at their desks.

TEACHER
Prime numbers are numbers that cannot be divided by anything except themselves and one.

Camera directions explain the action.

The camera pans back to the class to show one student wearing a black suit, stovepipe hat, and a black Abe Lincoln beard.

TEACHER
Which one of you can give me an example of a prime number?

The student with the beard raises his hand solemnly and stands. The TEACHER turns to acknowledge him.

TEACHER
Yes, Abe?

LINCOLN
Four score, and seven.

TEACHER
(quickly calculating)
Um, yes. That's right. Eighty-seven is a prime number. Excellent once again. Students, you could all learn something from our exchange student.

Action and **dialogue** move the plot along.

LINCOLN
Pardon me, ma'am, but I'm not an exchange student. I'm Abe Lincoln. Somehow I have been brought forward in time.

The class laughs and the TEACHER joins them.

An interesting **story line** with a conflict is developed.

TEACHER
Oh, now, enough of the jokes.

LINCOLN
I'm not joking, ma'am. As the sixteenth president of these United States, I am much needed to save our nation from splitting in two. But I have been snatched out of time and placed here, perhaps to solve an even greater problem.

TEACHER
(humoring him)
Can't think of a greater problem than the American Civil War.

LINCOLN
What about the lack of decent clothing? Is there some sort of textile crisis? Where is the wool, the cotton? Where are the starched linen collars?

The class laughs again, but another student raises his hand and stands. He is HENRY BOTICCINI, a straight-A student, and he tilts his eyebrow.

HENRY
It's not a crisis here that has sent you forward, Abe. It's the Civil War. Someone wanted to take you away from it. Someone wanted to make sure that the United States split apart!

The class gasps, and the TEACHER suddenly becomes very serious, accepting LINCOLN's story.

TEACHER
Who would have done such a thing?

Rising action created by the dialogue builds interest in the story.

HENRY
There's any number of people, but I think we can start by taking a look at JOHN WILKES BOOTH!

Another gasp comes from the students.

LINCOLN
Very good idea. What's your plan?

Storyboarding

After writing a script, you can storyboard it. A storyboard is a series of pictures that shows a video shot by shot. It helps the director of the video communicate to others what he or she is thinking. Here is the beginning of a storyboard for the *Lincoln, Time Traveler* video. A storyboard can be created by hand (as this one is) or in a slide-show program.

Basic Types of Videos

The type of video you make is limited only by your imagination. Here are a few basic types to consider.

Fiction

A fiction video tells a made-up story.

- **Drama:** A drama is a serious story, often about important issues. A drama could be a detective story, spy thriller, romance, biopic, historical epic, science-fiction story, and so on.
- **Comedy:** A comedy is a funny story, often about crazy characters, misunderstandings and mistaken identities, or absurd situations. A comedy could be a farce, buddy film, sitcom, mockumentary, parody, romantic or musical comedy, and so on.

Nonfiction

A nonfiction video tells a true story. It may report an event or a situation, make a persuasive pitch about an issue, or document what is going on.

- **Report:** A report tells about an event and usually includes real footage of the incident, interviews with those involved, and the words of a reporter. A report should be objective.
- **Documentary:** A documentary is an in-depth report especially suitable for complex issues. It includes a lot of footage and provides a careful study of the subject.
- **Opinion:** An opinion piece is like a report, except that the narrator offers her or his opinion about the event or issue. An opinion piece is sometimes called an editorial or a perspective.
- **Music Video:** A music video is a film that features a specific song. It may show people performing the song, depict a scene from the song, or just provide interesting images that go with the music.

Your Turn

For more on making videos and films, go to thoughtfullearning.com/p410.

Chapter 29
Design Projects

Look around you. Most things you see were designed and built by human beings, from the room you are in to the shoes you are wearing to the computer in the corner. We design things to make life easier, safer, more beautiful, and more fun.

This chapter includes a range of design projects, from cartoons and posters to scale models and Rube Goldberg machines.

You will learn . . .

- Creating Cartoons
- Creating Posters
- Designing T-Shirts
- Designing Brochures
- Building Dioramas
- Drafting Blueprints
- Building Scale Models
- Building Rube
  Goldberg Machines

Project Overview

Here is a quick overview of the design projects in this chapter.

Cartoon

Cartoons use images and words to tell a story or express an idea. You'll find examples of comic strips, gag comics, political cartoons, vocabulary cartoons, and photo comics. (See pages 414–417.)

Poster

Posters use words and images to persuade audiences or to provide information. (See pages 418–419.)

T-Shirt

A T-shirt can be a walking poster, helping you get the word out. (See pages 420–421.)

Brochure

A brochure makes your case with just a few pages of images and words. (See pages 422–423.)

Diorama

A diorama is a three-dimensional scene that depicts a specific place and time. (See pages 424–425.)

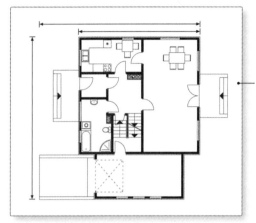

Blueprint

A blueprint is a plan for a building or an object, often showing multiple perspectives. (See pages 426–429.)

Scale Model

A scale model is a miniature version of a larger building or object. The model is built "to scale," meaning that its measurements are in proportion to those of the full-size object. (See pages 430–431.)

Rube Goldberg Machine

A Rube Goldberg machine is a complicated device that performs a simple task. (See pages 432–436.)

Inquire　To Create a Cartoon

1. **Question** yourself about the goal or objective of the cartoon.
   - **Subject:** What specific topic will be my focus?
   - **Purpose:** What should my cartoon do? Entertain? Persuade?
   - **Audience:** Who will see this cartoon? What do they already know and what do they need to know about the subject?

2. **Plan** your cartoon using a planning sheet. (See page 261.)

3. **Research** the following:
   - **Topic:** Study your subject and come up with an initial concept for a cartoon.
   - **Tools:** Gather paper, pencils, and pens, or use a computer program for digital sketching. (Go to thoughtfullearning.com/p414 for tips.)
   - **Team:** Create the whole piece yourself, or split the task with others—storyboarding, drawing, lettering, inking, and coloring.

4. **Create** your cartoon.
   - **Finalize** your idea for the cartoon.
   - **Storyboard** the cartoon frame by frame, sketching figures and adding narration, dialogue, and thought bubbles.
   - **Draw** each frame of your cartoon.
   - **Letter** each caption or thought bubble neatly.

5. **Improve** your cartoon.
   - **Evaluate** the cartoon.
     Does the cartoon fulfill your goals and objectives? Does it focus on a clear topic? Does it achieve its purpose? Does the audience respond appropriately?
   - **Revise** your cartoon.
     Remove extra words or unneeded frames.
     Rearrange frames for a more effective story.
     Redraw frames that do not work well.
     Add new frames as needed.
   - **Perfect** your cartoon, making it clean and correct.
     Ink the drawn lines.
     Color the cartoon, or leave it black and white, as you wish.

6. **Present** your cartoon online, on a bulletin board, or, if appropriate, send it to a school or community newspaper.

Comic Strip

A comic strip uses a series of pictures to tell an often humorous story that makes a point.

The **beginning** frame introduces the situation.

The **middle** frame develops the joke.

The **ending** frame provides the punch line.

Gag Cartoon

A gag cartoon is a single panel that tells a joke. The *New Yorker* has raised gag cartoons to an art form. This gag cartoon uses a play on words from math class.

Political Cartoon

A political cartoon satirizes politicians, often using symbolism. This form of cartooning is hundreds of years old. This example refers to the birth of Canada, flanked by Uncle Sam and Mother Britannia.

This image is in the public domain in both Canada (its country of origin) and the United States.

Vocabulary Cartoon

A vocabulary cartoon illustrates the meaning of a word or a group of words.

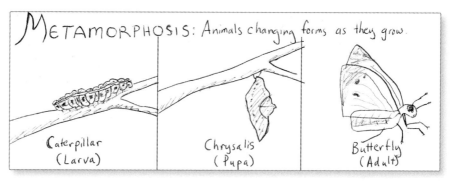

Photo Cartoon

A photo cartoon uses photos instead of drawings to tell the story. In this photo cartoon, students have found and identified fractions.

1 apple + 1/2 apple + 1/4 apple = 1 3/4 apple

9/10 closed

1/10 open

Inquire   To Create a Poster

1. **Question** the overall situation or goal for the poster.
   - **Subject:** What is the general subject of my poster? What is my specific topic or focus?
   - **Purpose:** What should the poster do? Persuade? Inspire? Amuse?
   - **Audience:** Who will see this poster? Where will it be displayed? How far away will it be from viewers?

2. **Plan** your poster using a planning sheet. (See page 261.)

3. **Research** the following:
   - **Topic:** Research your topic, gather all the information you need, and write an attention-getting slogan.
   - **Tools:** Gather paper, poster board, pencils, and markers or paint, or create your poster digitally and mount it on poster board.
   - **Team:** Create the poster yourself, or have others help with the initial concept, creating a slogan, finding images, and putting the poster together.

4. **Create** your poster.
   - **Sketch** your idea on regular-sized paper.
   - **Transfer** the concept in light pencil onto your poster board.
   - **Letter** the message neatly and use spacing that enhances readability.

5. **Improve** your poster.
   - **Evaluate** the poster.
     Does the poster meet or exceed your goals and objectives?
     Does the poster focus on a clear topic? Does it achieve its purpose?
     Does the audience respond appropriately?
   - **Revise** your poster.
     Remove unneeded words or visuals.
     Rearrange parts to make a more effective composition.
     Redo unclear lettering or drawings that do not work.
     Add missing information or a helpful graphic.
   - **Perfect** your poster, making it clean and correct.
     Check all information to make sure it is complete and correct.
     Ink or paint the lines so they can be read from a distance.

6. **Present** your poster by displaying it in an appropriate place.

Poster

The following event poster advertises a benefit dance for an organization that is helping to save whooping cranes. Note how the poster answers the 5 W's and H about the event, provides a strong visual, and persuades the reader to attend.

A **call to action** is made.

A **photograph** helps viewers understand the purpose of the dance.

The **5 W's** of the event are identified.

Inquire To Design a T-Shirt

1. **Question** the overall situation or goal for the T-shirt.
   - **Subject:** What do I want to feature on the T-shirt? Will I use text and images?
   - **Purpose:** Why am I designing a T-shirt? To promote a cause? Raise funds? Outfit a team? Commemorate an event?
   - **Audience:** Who will wear this shirt? Who will see it?

2. **Plan** your T-shirt using a planning sheet. (See page 261.)

3. **Research** the following:
   - **Topic:** Research your topic, gathering images and ideas that you would like to use on your shirt.
   - **Tools:** If you are doing your own silk-screening, gather a silk screen, emulsion, a light source, and the other tools you will need (go to thoughtfullearning.com/p420 for links).
   - **Team:** Do the whole project yourself or get help from artists, writers, and companies that print custom T-shirts.

4. **Create** your T-shirt pattern.
   - **Measure** the image space you have to work with or choose a shirt style on a T-shirt company Web site.
   - **Create** a design on paper or digitally. (T-shirt company Web sites have special programs to help.) For basic silk-screening, use one color.
   - **Compose** words and images to create the best effect.

5. **Improve** your T-shirt.
   - **Evaluate** the shirt's design.
     Does the T-shirt meet or exceed your goals and objectives?
     Does the T-shirt accomplish its purpose? Do people like it?
   - **Revise** your T-shirt.
     Remove unneeded words or visuals.
     Rearrange parts to make a more effective composition.
     Redo unclear lettering or images.
     Add missing information or helpful graphics.
   - **Perfect** your T-shirt, making it clean and correct.

6. **Present** your T-shirt.
   - **Silk-screen** the design onto the shirt.
   - **Submit** the design to the T-shirt company for printing.

T-Shirt

This T-shirt was designed and sold by a science class who wanted to raise money to support a program designed to save whooping cranes.

The **design** is balanced and attractive.

The **words** carry an important message and make a call to action.

The **visual** enhances or supports the message.

Note: To learn more about Operation Migration, go to www.operationmigration.org.

Inquire   To Design a Brochure

1. **Question** the overall situation for your brochure.
   - **Subject:** What is the general subject of my brochure? What is its specific topic?
   - **Purpose:** What should the brochure do? Explain? Promote? Persuade?
   - **Audience:** Who will read this brochure? Will it be read online, downloaded, distributed as a printed piece, or some combination of these?

2. **Plan** your brochure using a planning sheet. (See page 261.)

3. **Research** the following:
   - **Topic:** Research your topic and gather details.
   - **Tools:** Decide on a production method: online? color printer? photocopier? Take pictures or gather photos from another source. Access a computer with software for editing words and photos.
   - **Team:** Create the brochure on your own or work with others to decide on images, words, and layout. If your brochure represents a club or group, get their approval of the content.

4. **Create** your brochure.
   - **Write** text that gives your main point and achieves your purpose.
   - **Include** images that draw the eye but also explain the text. Use black-and-white art for a brochure that you plan to photocopy.
   - **Use** an easy-to-read type style that connects smoothly with the images around it. Consider a single fold (front, back, and two inside pages) or a double fold (three outside panels, three inside panels).

5. **Improve** your brochure.
   - **Evaluate** the brochure.
     Does it meet your goal? Does it focus on a clear topic? Does it achieve its purpose? Do readers respond well?
   - **Revise** your brochure.
     Remove unneeded words or visuals.
     Rearrange parts to make a more effective composition.
     Redo parts that are unclear or confusing.
     Add missing information or a helpful graphic.
   - **Perfect** your brochure, making it clean and correct.

6. **Present** your brochure online, print it, or copy it.

Brochure

The following brochure was created to promote an after-school club that designs and builds model cities of the future. The cities are then entered into a national engineering competition. This brochure was distributed as a printed piece to interest students at an open house.

Back Page   **Front Page**

Frequently Asked Questions

Q: Do I have to be good at math and science?
A: Future Builders welcomes all skill levels. You learn by doing!

Q: What do we build our scale models from?
A: You can choose. Some use common household items such as cardboard, toothpicks, egg cartons, and Popsicle® sticks. Others use LEGO® bricks. The materials are limited only by your imagination.

Q: If I build a city, do I have to enter the competition?
A: No one is required to compete, but if you are proud of your work, you'll want to enter to win!

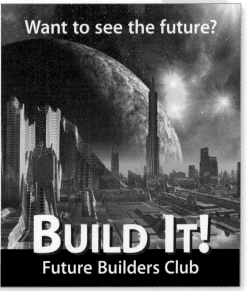

Want to see the future?

BUILD IT!
Future Builders Club

Inside Pages

What is the Future Builders Club?

The Future Builders Club is an after-school group that designs and builds scale models of future cities. We then enter our best cities in local and even national contests. Here are the specifics:

Who? Cooper School students

What? Design and build a future city

Where? Room 302

When? Tuesdays from 2:30 to 4:00 p.m.

Why? To solve city problems—and to win a national contest

How? Design first in the SimCity® game and then build actual scale models

Where do we compete?

When students complete their future cities, they can enter them in local competitions. Local winners go on to a national competition in Washington, D.C., and may get a chance to shake hands with the president!

Inquire To Build a Diorama

1. **Question** the situation for your diorama.
   - **Subject:** What scene do I want to show? Who or what is the focus of the scene? What background should I depict?
   - **Purpose:** Why am I building a diorama? What effect do I want to create?
   - **Audience:** Who will see the diorama? What impression do I want to give them?

2. **Plan** your diorama using a planning sheet. (See page 261.)

3. **Research** the project.
   - **Learn** all about your subject. Look for pictures, paintings, and blueprints.
   - **Gather** the materials you need: a box, felt, clay, pipe cleaners, Popsicle® sticks, glue, paint, brushes, markers, and so on. Print photos for the background if you wish.

4. **Create** your diorama.
   - **Create** the background, either painting it or pasting printed photos together in a panorama. Paint the floor or cover it with grass, stone, or wood.
   - **Construct** physical structures using toothpicks, Popsicle® sticks, cardboard, or premade materials like LEGO® bricks or LINCOLN LOGS™ sets.
   - **Add** people or animals, forming them out of clay or clothespins, or perhaps using premade figures such as plastic dinosaurs or army soldiers. Position the figures to tell a story.
   - **Insert** helpful labels and explanatory text, and title the diorama.

5. **Improve** your diorama.
   - **Evaluate** your diorama.
     Does the diorama clearly depict your subject? Do the figures, structures, and background tell a clear story? Does your audience respond well to it?
   - **Rework** your diorama.
     Remove parts that don't look right or tell your story.
     Rearrange figures and structures to make a better composition.
     Rebuild parts that are weak.
     Add missing parts that are needed to tell your subject or story.
   - **Perfect** your diorama, providing finishing touches.

6. **Present** your diorama to your class, school, or community.

Dioramas

The top photo shows a diorama of a forest at the time of the dinosaurs. The bottom two images show scenes from a professionally made diorama about World War II.

The **materials** used include sticks, clay, wire, paint, and even actual vegetables.

Each **scene** captures a specific action with props and the position of the characters.

Inquire To Draft a Blueprint

1. **Question** the situation for the blueprint.
   - **Subject:** What building or object do I want to plan?
   - **Purpose:** What do I want to achieve with this plan?
   - **Audience:** Who will see and work with the blueprint?

2. **Plan** the blueprint using a planning sheet. (See page 261.)

3. **Research** your project.
   - **Topic:** Sketch parts of your structure, experimenting.
   - **Tools:** Gather drafting tools (see page 428) or download free blueprint software. Find example blueprints, drawings, and photos of the type of object or building you want to plan with your own blueprint. (Go to thoughtfullearning.com/p426 for suggestions.)

4. **Create** one or more of the following parts.
   - **Floor Plan:** Create a top-down view, to scale, of each main level of the structure.
   - **Elevation:** Create a side-on view, to scale, of each side of the structure.
   - **3-D:** For an overall impression, make a 3-D view.

5. **Improve** your blueprint.
   - **Evaluate** the blueprint.
     Does the blueprint meet your goal? How could you do a better job of meeting it? Did you carefully represent the subject? Does the blueprint make sense to your audience?
   - **Revise** your blueprint.
     Cut parts of the drawing that clutter the overall plan.
     Reorder parts to create a clear plan.
     Redo parts that are not well drawn or thought out.
     Add missing parts that complete your vision.
   - **Perfect** your blueprint.
     Check the scale, appearance, and labeling of each part.

6. **Present** the blueprint to your instructor, your class, or your friends.
   - Discuss the building plan.
   - Launch a building project with others who want to help.

Blueprint

Here are sample blueprints showing the floor plan, front elevation, and architectural rendering of a fishing cottage. A student created them using the Google Sketchup™ computer-aided-design program.

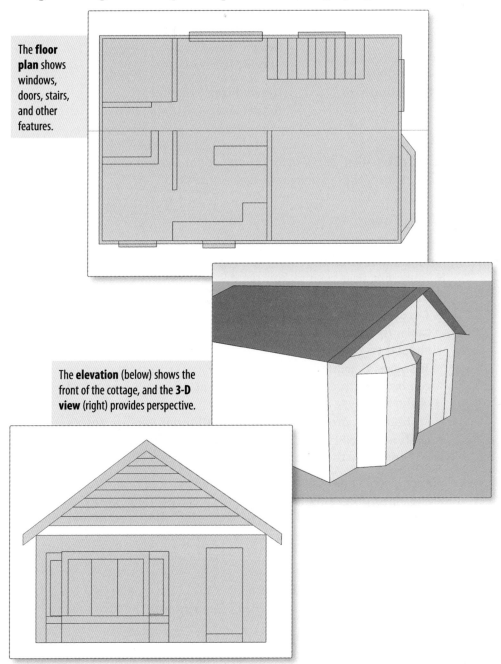

The **floor plan** shows windows, doors, stairs, and other features.

The **elevation** (below) shows the front of the cottage, and the **3-D view** (right) provides perspective.

Parts of a Blueprint

A blueprint is a drawing that shows the plan for a building, a vehicle, or an object. A blueprint needs to be correctly proportioned. That means each part of the subject is the right size when compared to the other parts. The key is to use a scale.

Scale

The scale is the ratio between the drawn size and the actual size.

Drawn Size: 1 inch
Actual Size: 12 inches
$= \frac{1}{12}$ scale

Drawn Size: 1 centimeter
Actual Size: 100 centimeters
$= \frac{1}{100}$ scale

Your Turn

Choose a scale that will work for your blueprint. Use measurements that will be easy to use for both drawn size and actual size.

Drafting Tools

You can create a blueprint by hand, using these tools:

- **Table:** For best results, use a table with ninety-degree edges.
- **Drafting paper:** Drafting paper can be unlined or graphed.
- **T-square:** A T-square is used to orient the drafting paper on the table, to draw horizontal lines, and to accommodate various-shaped triangles.
- **Triangles:** A triangle with points at 30, 60, and 90 degrees combines with another with points at 45 and 90 degrees to make angles.
- **Protractor:** A protractor calculates all other needed angles.
- **Drafting pencils:** Sharp pencils make clean lines.

Many people nowadays use drafting software. These CAD (computer-aided design) programs make it easy to create floor plans, elevations, and three-dimensional structures. They also allow you to add material types to plans—from wood to cement to shingles.

Your Turn

Gather drafting tools or download a free CAD program. (For CAD programs, go to thoughtfullearning.com/p428.) Experiment with the tools until you are comfortable using them.

Views

Because a blueprint uses a flat picture to show a three-dimensional structure, multiple views will offer the best overall vision. Here are different options:

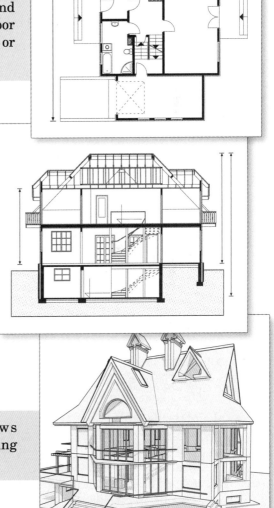

Floor Plan: This basic view shows an overhead image of the building or object, indicating length and width. Blueprints include a floor plan of each level of a building or an item.

Elevation: This view shows the side of the building or object, indicating height and length. Blueprints often include an elevation of each side of the item.

Note: Advanced building projects also have special views to show plans for plumbing, electricity, and other systems.

3-D View: This view shows length, width, and height, using perspective.

Your Turn

Decide which views you will draw for your blueprint project. Select the best tools for creating your plan.

Inquire To Build a Scale Model

1. **Question** the situation for your scale model.
   - **Subject:** What am I representing with this model? A building? A machine? A boat or an aircraft? What size should it be and what scale should I use?
   - **Purpose:** Why am I building a model? What effect do I want?
   - **Audience:** Who will see the model? Who will use it or judge it?

2. **Plan** your scale model using a planning sheet. (See page 261.)

3. **Research** your scale model.
   - **Learn** everything you can about the subject of your model. Look at photos, drawings, blueprints, maps, and other resources to help you.
   - **Decide** on a workable scale: for example, converting meters to centimeters or feet to inches. (See page 428.) Make sure your model won't be too big or too small.
   - **Gather** materials. For buildings, consider using cardboard or foam core. For vehicles, consider buying a model kit. For working prototypes, consider using building kits such as Erector sets.

4. **Create** one of these scale models.
   - **Building:** Follow the architectural plans for the building, perhaps even copying the blueprint onto your base and building on top of it.
   - **Vehicle:** Assemble the kit by following the instructions, or combine parts of different kits to create something altogether new.
   - **Machine prototype:** Create each piece according to the established scale and connect them. Test the movable pieces.

5. **Improve** your scale model.
   - **Evaluate** your model.
     Does it adequately depict your subject? Are all parts the right shape and proportion? Do moving parts move? What does your audience think?
   - **Rework** your scale model.
     Remove parts that don't look or work right.
     Reposition elements to make the model authentic.
     Rebuild parts that are not to scale or should look better.
     Add missing parts.
   - **Perfect** your model, providing finishing touches.

6. **Present** your model to its intended audience.

Scale Models

The top photo shows a scale model of a log house. The bottom two photos show prototypes of vehicles.

This model shows exact dimensions and precise architectural details.

These prototypes show how large-scale vehicles would be built.

Inquire To Build a Rube Goldberg Machine

1. **Question** the situation for your Rube Goldberg machine.
   - **Subject:** What theme should I use? How many steps should it take?
   - **Purpose:** What task must the machine do?
   - **Audience:** Who will see or judge the machine? What rules apply?

2. **Plan** your machine using a planning sheet. (See page 261.)

3. **Research** the construction of your machine.
   - **Materials:** Gather pieces that you find interesting and that will work with your theme. Experiment with ways to store and release energy in each piece. (See page 436.)
   - **Team:** Enlist others who are interested in the project and have the talent and time to contribute to it. Collaborate with them as you experiment.

4. **Create** your Rube Goldberg machine.
   - **Build** a frame that will hold or organize the other pieces of the machine. For contests, follow the size and mobility requirements.
   - **Set up/attach** the pieces that form your machine, working backward from the final reaction that completes the task. Test each piece to make sure it functions properly, and make the whole assembly easy to reset.

5. **Improve** your machine.
   - **Evaluate** the machine.
     Does the machine accomplish its final task? Does it include enough steps to make it interesting? Does it fit the theme? Does it abide by contest rules? How can the machine be more reliable, amusing, or convenient?
   - **Rework** your machine.
     Remove pieces that don't work or aren't reliable.
     Reposition pieces that are not aligned correctly.
     Rebuild pieces that are hard to set up, uninteresting, or unreliable.
     Add new pieces to make your machine more elaborate or effective.
   - **Perfect** your machine, testing every system and overall function.
     Fine-tune each part of the machine.
     Decorate it in keeping with your theme.
     Give the machine an amusing, memorable name.

6. **Present** your machine before an audience.

Rube Goldberg Machines

The following photos show Rube Goldberg machines entered into a Milwaukee-area competition. The photos were taken by Cory Militzer, a physics teacher and longtime adviser for a Rube Goldberg machine club. The drawing comes from Arnold Zucker's burglar alarm patent.

These Rube Goldberg machines were built by high school students from Wisconsin.

This elaborate burglar alarm showered the sleeper awake.

Designing a Rube Goldberg Machine

Rube Goldberg was an inventor and a cartoonist who created many fanciful machines to do ordinary tasks, such as striking a match or putting mustard on a hot dog. The more elaborate and crazy the machines, the better.

The Rube Goldberg machine is all about the final goal—to spread butter on toast, to turn a page in a book, to untie a shoelace. So the first thing you need to do is define the goal.

Goal

What final task must your machine perform? If you are entering a contest, this task may be defined for you. Otherwise, make your own list of possible tasks. Here's a starting point:

open a door	wake someone up	turn on a light
clean a window	extinguish a candle	clip a flower
turn an hourglass	open a drape	stir the soup
put on a slipper	blow a bubble	start an MP3 player
lick an envelope	zip a zipper	peel a banana

Once you have chosen a task, brainstorm a list of ways that the machine could accomplish it. Here are ways to extinguish a candle:

blow with a bellows	sponge the wick	lower a glass over it
blow with a balloon	dump water on it	use a snuffer
pop a balloon on it	drop it in a bucket	use a fire extinguisher
smother it	fan it out	spray water on it

Next, eliminate ways that are too dangerous, too costly, too messy, too unpredictable, or otherwise unworkable. Then choose an option.

Your Turn

Define the goal for your Rube Goldberg machine. What task is it supposed to perform? (If you are entering a competition, the goal may already be established for you.)

Theme

The theme of a Rube Goldberg machine connects the various pieces into a single story. One episode of the TV program *Mythbusters* featured a Rube Goldberg machine with a Christmas theme. Consider holidays or seasons, sports or games, movies or books, monsters or myths to come up with a theme that works for your project.

Your Turn

List possible themes for your Rube Goldberg machine. Let your imagination run wild. After creating a long list, select the theme you like best.

Pieces

With these things in mind—your goal, the way your machine will finally accomplish the task, and your theme—continue planning. Work backward, imagining a series of reactions that will trigger that final result. Experiment with these reactions, using everyday objects in new ways. The following lists of objects are sorted by theme.

Food	History	Sports	Music
eggbeater	powdered wig	golf ball	trombone
frying pan	bust of Socrates	bowling ball	accordion
toaster	model train	basketball	drum
whisk	plastic dinosaur	tennis ball	drumsticks
garlic press	toy sword	tennis racket	cymbal
egg timer	pirate hook	baseball bat	harmonica
fork	clay pot	hockey puck	ukulele
spoon	sandal	lacrosse stick	bugle
chopper	quill and ink	basketball hoop	baton
plastic bottle	toy cannon	skis	guitar
soda can	crown	inner tube	MP3 player

Your Turn

Gather objects that you could use to make the pieces of your Rube Goldberg machine. Consider the listed objects above, but think of other possibilities, perhaps making your own themed list of items. Experiment with the pieces you gather.

Energy

When you build your Rube Goldberg machine, you are setting up a series of potential-energy "batteries." The following actions, for example, store energy in an object:

- stretching a rubber band
- placing something up high
- compressing a spring
- filling a water jug
- suspending a mallet from a ribbon
- stacking dominoes so that they fall in lines and rows
- winding up a toy

Consider other ways to store potential energy in everyday objects. Then consider how to trigger the release of that energy.

Your Turn

Experiment with ways to store and release energy in your Rube Goldberg machine.

Frame

A Rube Goldberg machine entered in a competition will need to be portable, easily assembled, and properly sized for a defined space. A well-designed frame can help with all these requirements. The frame here had a baseball stadium theme.

Your Turn

Create a frame for your Rube Goldberg machine, making sure that it follows the specifications of the competition and that it also connects the many pieces of your machine in a stable way.

Chapter 30
Performing Projects

Performing means doing something in front of a real audience. Delivering a speech, acting in a play, participating in a debate, entering a talent show, or even conducting a formal interview are all performances.

Performing requires preparation. You must plan, build, practice, and then perform. This chapter provides guidelines and models that will help you prepare and present quality performances.

You will learn . . .

- Preparing Speeches
- Giving Demonstration Speeches
- Conducting Live Interviews
- Debating Issues
- Staging Plays

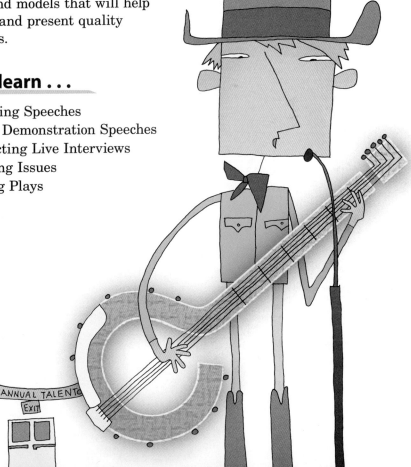

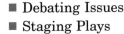

Project Overview

Here is an overview of the performing projects in this chapter.

Basic Speeches

Speeches are formal presentations in front of different audiences. A persuasive speech is an important type of formal presentation to use in school. (See pages 440–443.)

> **Speech for School Board Open Meeting**
> **September 23, 2010**
>
> School board members, faculty, parents, and fellow students. My name is Kevin Lee, and I am a seventh grader at Parkview. Thank you for the opportunity to speak today. These are tough times, and the board needs to make difficult cuts. The proposal to cut foreign-language classes, however, is cutting into our future.
>
> Studies show that it's easier to learn a new language when a person is young. So delaying foreign-language ...chool means taking away some of ...uctional time for learning Spanish, ...ther language.
>
> ...ay, "So what? Why does it matter ...nother language?" Well, it matters ...bal society, so the ability to ...han one language is more important ...earning other languages opens up

Student Survey: Class to Save?

40	
30	
20	
10	
0	Art Music Gym Language

How to Balance a Chemical Equation

In physical science class, we have learned that chemical equations show how the atoms are arranged in a chemical reaction. Since the number of atoms remain the same before and after the reaction, a chemical equation describing this process must be in balance. In this demonstration speech, I will show you how to balance chemical equations. Once you learn the steps, you will find it fun to do yourself.

Balanced Equation
$$C + O_2 \rightarrow CO_2$$

Parts of a Chemical Equation

First, I need to explain a few terms.

Reactants are substances in place before a chemical reaction.
Products are the results or changes produced by the chemical reaction. (The arrow indicates the direction of the reaction.)

Reactants   Product
$$H_2 + O \rightarrow H_2O$$
Subscripts

Subscripts are the numbers below a chemical formula identifying the number of atoms in a molecule.
Coefficients show how many molecules are involved in a reaction. If there is no coefficient, then only one molecule of that type is involved in the reaction.

No Coefficient
$$O_2 + O$$
With a Coefficient
$$2 O_2$$

Demonstration Speeches

Demonstration speeches are common assignments in many of your classes. What makes these speeches different is that they actually show how to do something or how something works. (See pages 444–445.)

Live Interviews

Interviewing is a carefully planned conversation that you conduct to learn about a topic. Interviews are often used in podcasts.
(See pages 446–449.)

Interview with Marcie Smith

Josh Williams: Today's blog features Marcie Smith, a local historian who will share information about the Crazy Horse Memorial. Ms. Smith, thank you for sharing your time with us today.

Marcie Smith: I'm delighted to be with you.

JW: First of all, could you tell us something about the Crazy Horse Memorial?

MS: Sure, the memorial is located in the Black Hills region of South Dakota, not far from Mt. Rushmore.

JW: Why is the memorial located in this region?

MS: Crazy Horse was a member of the Lakota Sioux, and this area has always been considered sacred by the Lakota.

JW: What exactly will a visitor see at the memorial?

MS: Well, a visitor won't see a completed carving. Only Crazy Horse's head, about 87 feet in height, is done.

JW: When will the carving be complete?

MS: No one really knows. It depends on a number of factors including continued funding of the project.

JW: What will the completed carving look like?

MS: Crazy Horse will be seen leaning over his horse's head, pointing his left hand toward his sacred lands.

Attention to Athletes: Good or Bad?

Moderator (*Teacher*): Today, we will hear a debate addressing the following position: *The special attention given to professional athletes is bad for our society.* The affirmative team on my right will argue that this attention does more harm than good. The opposition on my left will argue that this attention is earned and beneficial.

We will start with speaker number one for the affirmative followed by speaker number one for the opposition. Each speaker will have two minutes to present his or her argument. Please give each speaker your undivided attention. Tonya Jones, the podium is yours.

Tonya Jones (*first speaker for the affirmative*): Thank you, Ms. Wilson and my fellow classmates. We constantly see and hear about star professional athletes. We see them perform, interviewed, and talked about on television. And of course, we see many young adults wearing their jerseys. We on the affirmative team feel that all of this attention does more harm than good in our society.

Professional athletes are performers, paid to entertain us, and that is fine. But the attention given to them goes far beyond playing a game. Many people, especially young people, come to idolize athletes because these stars are seen and heard so often. According to Byron King, author of *The*

Debates

A debate is a formal discussion about an important topic. Debaters must research a topic thoroughly before a debate and be prepared to defend or oppose a point of view about the topic. (See pages 450–451.)

Plays

Staging a play can involve many activities, from choosing or writing a play to casting the different roles to building the set. (See pages 452–454.)

Inquire | To Prepare a Speech

1. **Question** the situation for your speech.
   - **Subject:** What should I talk about? What should my focus be?
   - **Purpose:** What should my speech do? Inform? Persuade? Memorialize?
   - **Audience:** Who will hear this speech? What does the audience know about the subject? What do they need to know?

2. **Plan** your speech by completing a planning sheet. (See page 261.)

3. **Research** your speech.
   - **Topic:** Gather information about your topic and prepare any necessary handouts for the audience. Also gather props or demonstration materials.

4. **Create** your speech.
   - **Beginning:** Get the listeners' attention and present your main idea.
   - **Middle:** Provide details that support or explain your main idea.
   - **Ending:** Return to your main point and leave the audience with a strong final thought.
   - **Visuals:** Present visuals through a slide show, during a demonstration, or with handouts.

5. **Improve** your speech.
   - **Evaluate** the speech after practicing it three or four times.
     Does the speech focus on my topic?
     Does it achieve its purpose?
     Does a test audience get the point? Are they interested?
   - **Revise** your speech.
     Remove extra words or unneeded parts.
     Rearrange details that appear out of order.
     Rework parts (beginning, middle, ending) that don't work well.
     Add stories, statistics, quotations, or other support as needed.
   - **Perfect** your speech, making sure it is clear and correct.

6. **Present** your speech in person or record it for later use. Follow these tips for a successful presentation.
   Take a deep breath before you begin.
   Greet your audience politely and get their attention.
   Speak slowly and loudly.
   Look up frequently and make eye contact with your audience.

Persuasive Speech

In the following speech, a student speaks to an open meeting of his school board, arguing to preserve foreign-language instruction.

Speech for School Board Open Meeting
September 23, 2010

The **beginning** greets the audience and gives the main point.

School board members, faculty, parents, and fellow students. My name is Kevin Lee, and I am a seventh grader at Parkview. Thank you for the opportunity to speak today. These are tough times, and the board needs to make difficult cuts. The proposal to cut foreign-language classes, however, is cutting into our future.

The **middle** supports the main point.

Studies show that it's easier to learn a new language when a person is young. So delaying foreign-language instruction until high school means taking away some of the most valuable instructional time for learning Spanish, French, German, or another language.

To persuade, the speaker answers an objection.

Some people may say, "So what? Why does it matter if students can speak another language?" Well, it matters because we live in a global society, so the ability to communicate in more than one language is more important now than ever before. Learning other languages opens up to us whole new cultures and countries and many exciting opportunities.

The **ending** includes a call to action.

I urge you to reconsider cutting foreign-language instruction. We need it more than ever. Without these classes, we are taking a troublesome step backward.

Thank you.

Other Speech Formats

The speech on the previous page is written out word for word in manuscript format. This format works well when every word has to be right. For other situations, try one of the following speech formats.

Outline

An outline provides an organized listing of the main points to be covered in a speech. Here is the speech from the previous page in a simplified outline format. (Also see page 272.)

School Board Speech

I. Beginning: Greet school board members, faculty, parents, fellow students

The proposal to cut foreign-language classes is cutting into our future.

II. Middle: Develop support; address objections
   A. Studies: Easier to learn language when younger
   B. Objection: Why need another language?
   C. Answer: We live in a global society.

III. Ending: Stress main point

Don't cut foreign-language instruction. Without these classes, we are taking a troublesome step backward.

List

If you are comfortable speaking with only a few notes, consider making a simple list. A list provides words or phrases to help you remember what to say.

School Board Speech
1. Greet group
2. Oppose cutting foreign-language classes
3. Studies show . . .
4. Why? Global society
5. Don't cut FL instruction

Your Turn

Create an outline, a list, or a manuscript for a speech of your own.

Adding Slides

Visuals are common in demonstration speeches (see pages 444–445), but also consider using them to enhance the story in your persuasive speeches. For the speech on page 441, for example, the student could develop a slide-show presentation with the following elements.

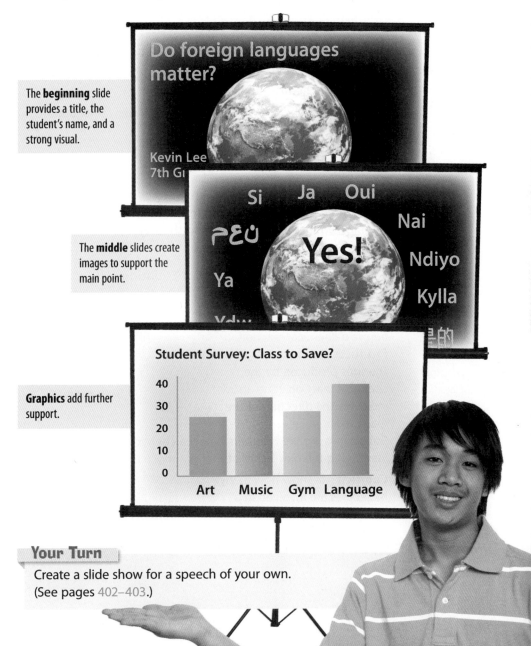

The **beginning** slide provides a title, the student's name, and a strong visual.

The **middle** slides create images to support the main point.

Graphics add further support.

Your Turn

Create a slide show for a speech of your own.
(See pages 402–403.)

Demonstration Speech

In a demonstration speech, you show how to do something or how something works. The following speech explains an important operation in physical science: How to balance chemical equations with coefficients. The speaker used PowerPoint slides in her demonstration.

How to Balance a Chemical Equation

The **beginning** sets the scene and names the topic (underlined).

In physical science class, we have learned that chemical equations show how the atoms are arranged in a chemical reaction. Since the number of atoms remain the same before and after the reaction, a chemical equation describing this process must be in balance. <u>In this demonstration speech, I will show you how to balance chemical equations</u>. Once you learn the steps, you will find it fun to do yourself.

Balanced Equation
$$C + O_2 \rightarrow CO_2$$

Parts of a Chemical Equation

First, I need to explain a few terms.

Reactants are substances in place before a chemical reaction.
Products are the results or changes produced by the chemical reaction. (The arrow indicates the direction of the reaction.)

The **middle** first identifies key terms.

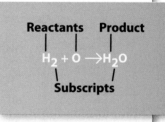

Reactants   Product
$$H_2 + O \rightarrow H_2O$$
Subscripts

Subscripts are the numbers below a chemical formula identifying the number of atoms in a molecule.

Coefficients show how many molecules are involved in a reaction. If there is no coefficient, then only one molecule of that type is involved in the reaction.

No Coefficient
$$O_2 + O$$
With a Coefficient
$$2\,O_2$$

Steps in the Process

Now that you know the basic parts, I will next show you how to balance a chemical equation for burning methane (CH_4).

Then the steps in the process are explained.

Step 1: Count the number of atoms in the equation. As you can see in the slide, H and O are not balanced. The reactants contain four atoms of H and two atoms of O. And the products contain three atoms of O and two atoms of H.

Step 1: Count the atoms.

$$CH_4 + O_2 \rightarrow CO_2 + H_2O$$

C-1	C-1
H-4	O-2
O-2	H-2
	O-1

Each step is demonstrated in a visual.

Step 2: Use a coefficient to add atoms to one side of the equation. Start by balancing an element that appears in only one reactant and product, such as H. A coefficient of 2 added to H in the product balances the number of H atoms. There are now four atoms of H on each side of the equation.

Step 2: Use a coefficient on one side.

$$CH_4 + O_2 \rightarrow CO_2 + 2H_2O$$

coefficient

Step 3: Now add another coefficient as needed to balance the equation. Because the coefficient in the product increases the number of O atoms, we need to add a coefficient to the O in the reactant to balance the number of O atoms.

Step 3: Add another coefficient as needed.

$$CH_4 + 2O_2 \rightarrow CO_2 + 2H_2O$$

coefficient

Step 4: If no other coefficients are needed, then check your work. You can do this in the same way that you counted the number of atoms in step 1. But this time, multiply the coefficient times the subscript, as shown in the slide. Now the equation is in balance.

Step 4: Check your work.

$$CH_4 + 2O_2 \rightarrow CO_2 + 2H_2O \; (1)$$

C-1	C-1
H-4	O-2
O-4	H-4
	O-2

The ending gives a review of the process.

Remember that the atoms in a chemical reaction must be in balance, and you can use coefficients to achieve this balance.

Inquire To Conduct a Live Interview

1. **Question** the situation for the interview.
   - **Subject:** Who will you interview? What will you discuss?
   - **Purpose:** Why are you interviewing the person?
   - **Audience:** Who will see, hear, or read this interview? What does the audience need to know about this person? About the subject?

2. **Plan** your interview by completing a planning sheet. (See page 261.)

3. **Research** the interview:
   - **Topic:** Gather information about the person and subject. Make a list of possible questions. Focus on questions that require thoughtful answers (not just a *yes* or a *no*).

4. **Create** your interview.
   - **Greet** the interviewee and thank the person for being interviewed.
   - **Explain** the subject and purpose of the interview.
   - **Ask** your prepared questions and follow-up questions based on the answers given.
   - **Record** responses if the interviewee agrees, or write them down.
   - **Thank** the person again.

5. **Improve** your interview for a later presentation, perhaps in a blog or a podcast.
   - **Evaluate** each part.
     Does each question and answer connect with the goal of the interview?
     Is each interesting? Does each one reveal something interesting about the person or subject?
   - **Revise** your interview.
     Remove any questions and answers that are off the topic.
     Rearrange parts to provide a natural flow.
     Rework awkward wording without changing direct quotations.
     Add an introduction and a conclusion if needed.
   - **Perfect** your interview, making sure it is accurate.
     Share the interview with the interviewee for final edits.

6. **Present** your interview online or on a bulletin board, or submit it to a school or community newspaper if appropriate.

Live Interview

In the following interview, a student speaks with a local historian about an important Native American memorial.

The **beginning** introduces the interviewee and the topic.

The **middle** part consists of a series of questions and answers.

Both planned and follow-up questions are asked.

The **ending** provides a final thought and a thank you.

Interview with Marcie Smith

Josh Williams: Today's blog features Marcie Smith, a local historian who will share information about the Crazy Horse Memorial. Ms. Smith, thank you for sharing your time with us today.

Marcie Smith: I'm delighted to be with you.

JW: First of all, could you tell us something about the Crazy Horse Memorial?

MS: Sure, the memorial is located in the Black Hills region of South Dakota, not far from Mt. Rushmore.

JW: Why is the memorial located in this region?

MS: Crazy Horse was a member of the Lakota Sioux, and this area has always been considered sacred by the Lakota.

JW: What exactly will a visitor see at the memorial?

MS: Well, a visitor won't see a completed carving. Only Crazy Horse's head, about 87 feet in height, is done.

JW: When will the carving be complete?

MS: No one really knows. It depends on a number of factors including continued funding of the project.

JW: What will the completed carving look like?

MS: Crazy Horse will be seen leaning over his horse's head, pointing his left hand toward his sacred lands.

JW: So why is Crazy Horse being memorialized?

MS: That is a great question. Crazy Horse has been described as a courageous fighter, a humble man, a giver and provider, and someone who remained true to the Lakota way of life.

JW: Is there anything else we should know about him?

MS: Believe it or not, there is no verifiable photograph of Crazy Horse. So what is captured in the carving is the spirit of this great man.

JW: Thank you for this information. You've certainly got me interested in Crazy Horse.

Live Interview

The following interview is a transcript of a school podcast. In the podcast, a student interviews Chris Cook, an architectural engineer who specializes in environmentally friendly buildings.

Interview with Chris Cook

The **beginning** introduces the interviewee and the topic.

Mackenzie Allen: Today's podcast features an interview with Chris Cook, a Cincinnati-based architectural engineer who specializes in designing environmentally friendly buildings. Thanks for talking with us today, Chris.

Chris Cook: I'm glad to be here.

MA: Can you tell us what you do for your job?

CC: Well, I'm in the business of green architecture, which means I help design sustainable buildings. A "sustainable" building is one that utilizes natural resources like sunlight and wind power in an effort to be energy efficient and have less of an environmental impact.

MA: I've often heard about "environmental impact" but don't know exactly what it means. Will you explain it?

CC: That's an excellent question. A building's environmental impact describes its negative effect on the environment. Too much environmental impact is wasteful in terms of energy and water use. It can also pollute the air around us.

MA: And one way to decrease the environmental impact is through solar power, correct?

The **middle** part consists of a series of questions and answers.

CC: Absolutely. To utilize solar power, we design windows, walls, and floors in a way that distributes solar energy as heat in the winter and deflects the sunlight in the summer. We also place solar paneling on roofs to capture energy.

MA: What about ways to make a building less wasteful with its water?

CC: There's actually many ways to reduce water use. We install low-flow showers and toilets in bathrooms. There are even big water aquifers, which you put in a basement, that collect extra water, purify it, and reuse it on site.

Both planned and follow-up questions are asked.

MA: If students wanted to reduce the environmental impact of our school building, what could we do? Is it even possible?

CC: Yes, it is very possible. You may need to modify a few lifestyle habits. For example, drink water out of the fountain rather than buying bottled water. Turn off the faucets in the bathrooms when you're done washing your hands. Finally, recycle as much as possible. Do you pack your own lunch?

MA: My mom does.

CC: Good. Well, request fresh, homemade meals rather than prepackaged meals. This will cut back on trash.

MA: Besides these lifestyle choices, is there anything we can do to the building to make it a greener school?

CC: One really cool way is to build a green roof. Basically, a green roof is a garden on the top of your school. It takes time to build, but the benefits are worth it.

MA: A garden on the roof? Wow! What are some of the benefits of building one?

CC: Green roofs reduce storm-water runoff by up to 40 percent as well as provide insulation to reduce heating and cooling needs. They also can be used to grow plants and fresh vegetables. Studying the plant growth is a great way to learn biology while growing fresh veggies.

MA: That's awesome. I'd love to suggest this idea to my principal.

The ending provides a final thought and a thank-you.

CC: Go for it! Let me know if I can be of any help.

MA: I definitely will. And thanks so much for answering my questions.

CC: You're welcome.

Inquire To Debate an Issue

1. **Question** the situation for the debate. (Often a debate centers around a proposition with one team arguing for it and one team arguing against it.)
   - **Subject:** What is the topic (issue) that will be debated?
   - **Purpose:** Why are you putting on the debate? What is the goal of the experience?
   - **Audience:** Who will witness the debate? Will the audience have an opportunity to ask questions? Will they choose the winning team?

2. **Plan** your debate by creating a proposition, forming two teams, and giving team members specific roles.

3. **Research** the issue.
   - **Topic:** Learn as much as you can about the topic so you know both sides of the issue. (Of course, pay special attention to the side you will argue for.)
   - **Support:** Fill out a pro-con chart, listing reasons for and against the position.

4. **Create** your side of the debate.
   - **Decide** as a team on your best arguments and supporting evidence. Also discuss how you will counter the opposition. (See pages 103–118.)
   - **Develop** each team member's presentation.
   - **Practice** first by rehearsing your side's presentations. Then practice with one member taking on the role of the opposition.

5. **Improve** your team's performance.
   - **Evaluate** the team's main arguments.
     Are your arguments strong enough?
     Have you prepared arguments for countering the opposition?
   - **Improve** your presentations as needed.
     Remove any weak points.
     Rearrange details that may not be in the best order.
     Rework any parts that are not clear enough.
     Add main points and supporting details as needed.

6. **Present** the debate to your class. Take questions from the class at the end of the debate and ask them to vote on the winning team.

Debate

The model below shows how a debate typically begins. Included are the moderator's opening remarks and parts of the first two speakers' speeches.

Attention to Athletes: Good or Bad?

In the **beginning**, a moderator sets the scene for the debate.

Moderator (*Teacher*): Today, we will hear a debate addressing the following position: *The special attention given to professional athletes is bad for our society.* The affirmative team on my right will argue that this attention does more harm than good. The opposition on my left will argue that this attention is earned and beneficial.

We will start with speaker number one for the affirmative followed by speaker number one for the opposition. Each speaker will have two minutes to present his or her argument. Please give each speaker your undivided attention. Tonya Jones, the podium is yours.

In the **middle**, the first speaker for the affirmative states her team's position.

Tonya Jones (*first speaker for the affirmative*): Thank you, Ms. Wilson and my fellow classmates. We constantly see and hear about star professional athletes. We see them perform on the field and get interviewed afterward on television. And of course, we see many young adults wearing their jerseys. We on the affirmative team feel that all of this attention does more harm than good in our society.

An authority is cited as evidence.

Professional athletes are performers, paid to entertain us, and that is fine. But the attention given to them goes far beyond playing a game. Many people, especially young people, come to idolize athletes because these stars are seen and heard so often. According to Byron King, author of *The New Royalty,* this generation of youth rate athletes as more important than people in almost all professions requiring advanced education. This is wrong. . . .

The first speaker for the opposition establishes his team's position.

Ben Rodgers (*first speaker for the opposition*): It is true that professional sports play an important role in our society, which is fine, because many people enjoy cheering for their favorite players. That these stars receive a lot of attention is understandable. They are the top performers in their sports, and they have worked hard. Why shouldn't they be recognized . . . ?

Inquire To Stage a Play

See pages 334–336 for tips on writing a play.

1. **Question** the situation for the play.
   - **Subject:** What is the subject of the play? Is it a comedy? A tragedy? A mystery? Is it a new play or a classic?
   - **Purpose:** Why are you putting on the play? What effect should it have? What mood do you want to create?
   - **Audience:** Who will see this play? How can you connect with the audience?

2. **Plan** your play by completing a planning sheet. (See page 261.)

3. **Research** the play.
   - **Actors:** Cast actors. (Conduct tryouts if necessary.) Get copies of the play for all of those with speaking parts and read through it.
   - **Technical crews:** Enlist others to help design and build sets, work backstage, run lights and sound, provide publicity, create a program, and handle ticket sales.

4. **Create** your production of the play.
   - **Read** through the script together.
   - **Block** scenes by deciding where actors enter, stand, move, and exit.
   - **Run scenes** to help actors learn lines and blocking.
   - **Practice music** first offstage. Then add music to the practice runs.

5. **Improve** your performance by evaluating and revising it.
   - **Evaluate** your play.
     Does the performance suit the goal of the project?
     Do the performers get the ideas across? Do they create the right emotional impact? Does the audience respond appropriately?
   - **Tighten** the performance.
     Remove awkward pauses and unnecessary actions.
     Rearrange blocking so that speakers can be seen and heard.
     Rework scenes that aren't functioning well.
     Add subtle reactions to lines and actions.
   - **Perfect** your performance.

6. **Present** your performance. Listen to the audience's response; then continue to refine your work to improve your next performance.

   (Go to thoughtfullearning.com/p452 for more on plays.)

Play Script

What follows is the first part of a play script. It includes all of the main parts of a standard script.

Title

The New Recruits
By Tyrone Davis

Cast of Characters

Cast

JOHN BOROUGHS, a farmer
DAVID BOROUGHS, his twelve-year-old son
SERGEANT MARSHALL, a drillmaster
SARAH GOODWIN, a boarding-house owner
SOLDIERS, the comrades in arms

Act

ACT I, SCENE 1

Scene

SETTING: Williamsburg, Virginia, 1776, at a training grounds for recruits into the Continental Army. SERGEANT MARSHALL marches SOLDIERS along the fence line as JOHN and DAVID BOROUGHS approach.

Dialogue

JOHN: Hail, good sir!

MARSHALL: (*Gesturing for the SOLDIERS to continue marching*) I am not a "sir"—in bondage to King George and his titles.

JOHN: Forgive me, Captain.

MARSHALL: I am Sergeant Marshall of the Continental Army of George Washington.

JOHN: (*Bowing*) And I am John Boroughs, farmer, though I wish to be a militiaman. I and my son both wish to join your army.

Stage direction

(*SERGEANT MARSHALL nods, walking around the two recruits and observing their clothing.*)

MARSHALL: How old is the boy?

JOHN: He's thirteen.

Songs

DAVID: (*Sings*) HARK, THE SOUND OF WAR IS HEARD,
AND WE MUST ALL ATTEND;
TAKE UP OUR ARMS AND GO WITH SPEED,
OUR COUNTRY TO DEFEND.

School Play

Here are photos from a school play, both in rehearsal and in performance.

Students practice a song for an upcoming production.

Students rehearse a scene and later perform it in costume.

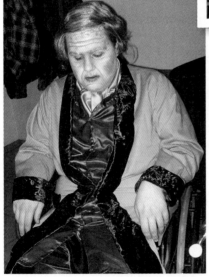

Makeup transforms this student into an elderly man.

Actors run lines.

Chapter 31
Community Projects

You've probably learned about bees and how they cooperate. The worker bees, drones, and queen all have their jobs to do. Bees feed each other, look for nectar, guard and clean the hive, and on and on. The hive, or community, thrives because the individuals help each other.

In a similar way, a city, a company, or a school thrives when its citizens, workers, or students do their jobs and cooperate. And when a problem or a need arises, these same individuals often come together to work on solutions. They plan community projects, and this chapter focuses on several—everything from organizing an event to creating a club.

You will learn . . .

- Organizing Events
- Running Contests
- Running Campaigns
- Creating Clubs

Project Overview

Here is a quick overview of the community projects in this chapter.

Events

Organizing a successful event like a fund-raising event requires careful planning. Planning sheets help get the job done. (See pages 458–461.)

Planning Sheet

Goal: Host a pancake-breakfast fund-raising event to support the jazz choir.

Objectives:
Who? Students in jazz choir and parent volunteers will organize the event.
What? We'll need food, beverages, tables, tickets, and kitchen equipment.
Where? We'll host the fund-raiser at the Community Terrace in McKinney Park.
When? The fund-raiser will take place Friday, October 7, 2011, from 8–11 a.m.
How? We'll divide the tasks among jazz choir members.

Tasks: | **Time:**
Start .... Aug. 20
1. Host a kickoff meeting. Aug. 20
2. Plan the budget. Aug. 24
3. Reserve the Community Terrace. Aug. 25
g. 25 – Sept. 2
pt. 5 – Sept. 26
pt. 5 – Oct. 7
pt. 10
t. 5
t. 7
t. 8
t. 9
nny Curtis,
g, Monique
don, Terri Turk,

Pancake-Breakfast Work Roster

Job	Arrive By	Volunteers
Food Set up griddles, warming pans; prepare pancakes, sausage	6:30 a.m.	**Students:** Lon Chan, Tricia King, Monique Morris
		Adults: Lee Chan, Terrence McDonald, Clara Morris, Linda Peters
Beverages Brew coffee, mix punch, keep milk and orange juice on ice	6:30 a.m.	**Students:** Eli Goldberg, Tawny Reynolds, Lisa Vera
		Adults: Donna Goldberg, Ron Vera
Tables Set out place settings; bus tables; clean floors	6:45 a.m.	**Students:** Bendon Davis, Patty Seldon, Terri Turk
		Adults: David Davis
Tickets Set up table, cash box; sell tickets	6:45 a.m.	**Students:** Ashley Archer, Juan Rodriguez
		Adults: Pepe Rodriguez

Harrison Student-Council Motto Contest

Promote your school and win a month's worth of free hot lunches in the school motto contest! The Harrison Student Council is seeking a new school motto that shows off our pride. We want to hear from you!

Contest Rules
1. **Who can enter?** Anyone can enter the school motto contest.
2. **What can I win?** The first-place winner will receive a month's worth of free hot lunches and recognition as the creator of the winning motto. Three runners-up will also be recognized for their mottoes.
3. **How do I enter?** First, come up with a short, punchy motto that shows school pride. Then go to the Harrison Student Council Web site, click on the "Motto Contest" button, and fill out the form. Or go to the office and fill out the same form on paper.
4. **How long does the contest run?** The contest runs from Monday, September 27, through Tuesday, October 12.
5. **When will winners be announced and where?** The winner and runners-up will be announced on Monday, October 18, in the morning announcements, on the Web

Contests

Running a contest is a fun way to kick-start creativity in and out of the classroom. However, it takes a lot of careful planning. (See pages 462–463.)

Campaigns

Running a campaign means promoting an idea or a cause on a large scale. Targeting a campaign, publicizing it, and writing a campaign speech are all important tasks. (See pages 464–467.)

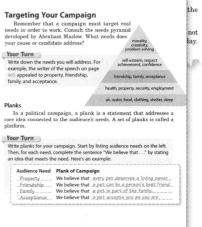

Help Take Care of Pets-to-Be

Do you have a pet at home? Did you once have a pet? Think of your pet's eyes as it looked up at you. Now imagine the hopeful eyes of dogs and cats waiting to become someone's pets. Until they do, the animals at the Dover Humane Society need you. There are many ways you can help them:

1. **Donate food and supplies:** Dog and cat food as well as rawhides, litter, and chew toys cost a little but help a lot.
2. **Donate time:** For just a few hours a week, you can help the trained veterinarians care for the animals at the shelter.
3. **Consider adopting a pet:** The animals in the shelter need good homes and loving owners.
4. **Avoid buying from pet stores:** Instead of increasing demand for dogs from "puppy mills," help a homeless

Targeting Your Campaign

Remember that a campaign must target real needs in order to work. Consult the needs pyramid developed by Abraham Maslow. What needs does your cause or candidate address?

Your Turn
Write down the needs you will address. For example, the writer of the speech on page 465 appealed to property, friendship, family, and acceptance.

morality, creativity, problem solving

self-esteem, respect achievement, confidence

friendship, family, acceptance

health, property, security, employment

air, water, food, clothing, shelter, sleep

Planks

In a political campaign, a plank is a statement that addresses a core idea connected to the audience's needs. A set of planks is called a platform.

Your Turn
Write planks for your campaign. Start by listing audience needs on the left. Then, for each need, complete the sentence "We believe that . . ." by stating an idea that meets the need. Here's an example:

Audience Need	Plank of Campaign
Property	We believe that *every pet deserves a loving owner.*
Friendship	We believe that *a pet can be a person's best friend.*
Family	We believe that *a pet is part of the family.*
Acceptance	We believe that *a pet accepts you as you are.*

Live Poets Society Charter

Mission Statement
The Live Poets Society is a student club for anyone interested in writing, reading, and talking about poetry. Our purpose is to
- **encourage** people to write and share poetry.
- **help** poets improve their work by providing helpful feedback.
- **create** a community for poets and poetry lovers.
- **promote** poetry reading and writing in our school and community.

Meetings
The Live Poets Society meets every Tuesday after school in Mrs. Schmaling's room, 201, from 3:00 to 4:00 p.m.

Membership
The Live Poets Society is open to any student a[t] School. To join, students only need to show up[.]

Leadership
The Live Poets Society has a student leader wh[o] each year at the first meeting of the club. The s[tudent] a faculty advisor (Mrs. Schmaling).

Clubs

Joining a club is a fun way to interact with people who share your interests. Effective clubs start with a thoughtful charter. (See pages 468–470.)

Inquire To Organize an Event

1. **Question** the situation for the event.
   - **Subject:** What sort of event is it? What is the focus? Is it a one-time event or one that happens often?
   - **Purpose:** Why are you putting on the event? What do you want to accomplish? Why will people attend?
   - **Audience:** Who will attend the event? What do they expect? What response do you want from them?

2. **Plan** the event by completing a planning sheet. (See page 261.)

3. **Research** the event.
   - **Gather** the information and ideas you need. Ask a team of people to help you plan and carry off the event. List whatever decorations, refreshments, tickets, and supplies you may need, and the places you can get these.
   - **Arrange** to use the location you need for the event. Assign the different preparation and event tasks to the team members.
   - **Publicize** the event using posters, fliers (both paper and digital), and other forms of publicity. (See pages 466–467.)

4. **Create** the event, considering the following roles.
   - **Decorators** to transform the space
   - **Sign makers** to draw people in and direct them
   - **Ticket takers** to collect tickets or money for paid events
   - **Refreshment** people to provide and sell refreshments
   - **Host** to guide the group through the event
   - **Cooks/servers/dishwashers** for meal events
   - **Entertainers/DJs** for dance events

5. **Improve** your event.
   - **Evaluate** the event.
     Did the event fulfill its goals and objectives?
     Did it focus on an appropriate idea or activity? Did it achieve its purpose? Did people attend? What did they think? How could it be improved next time?
   - **Improve** the event by adding value, removing inefficiency, rearranging the sequence, and reworking parts to make them more effective.

6. **Present** the event again if it happens more than once.

Event Planning Sheet: Fund-Raiser

A planning sheet lays out the basic details needed to put on an event. The following example describes the basic plan for a pancake-breakfast fund-raiser.

Planning Sheet

Goal: Host a pancake-breakfast fund-raising event to support the jazz choir.

Objectives: *Who?* Students in jazz choir and parent volunteers will organize the event.

What? We'll need food, beverages, tables, tickets, and kitchen equipment.

Where? We'll host the fund-raiser at the Community Terrace in McKinney Park.

When? The fund-raiser will take place Friday, October 7, 2011, from 8–11 a.m.

How? We'll divide the tasks among jazz choir members.

Tasks:	**Time:**
Start	Aug. 20
1. Host a kickoff meeting.	Aug. 20
2. Plan the budget.	Aug. 24
3. Reserve the Community Terrace.	Aug. 25
4. Design posters and fliers.	Aug. 25 – Sept. 2
5. Post posters and fliers.	Sept. 5 – Sept. 26
6. Build awareness using social media.	Sept. 5 – Oct. 7
7. Reserve 10 tables and 60 chairs.	Sept. 10
8. Purchase supplies for the event.	Oct. 5
9. Run the pancake breakfast.	Oct. 7
10. Clean up and return equipment and materials.	Oct. 8
Finish	Oct. 9

Team: Jazz choir members—Ashley Archer, Lon Chan, Donny Curtis, Brendon Davis, Eli Goldberg, Raul Jones, Tricia King, Monique Morris, Tawny Reynolds, Juan Rodriguez, Patty Seldon, Terri Turk, Lisa Vera

Tools:

Equipment: griddles, stereo, speakers, microphone

Food and drink: pancake batter, sausages, coffee, milk, juice, maple syrup

Materials: cups, napkins, plates, silverware, tables, chairs

Event Budget Sheet: Fund-Raiser

When an event involves money, a budget sheet is helpful for organizing where and how you spend your money. The following budget sheet tracks the money spent to put on a pancake breakfast and the money earned from the ticket sales. (See also page 230.)

Pancake-Breakfast Budget Sheet

Expense		Estimated Cost	Actual Cost
Advertising			
	Fliers/posters/tickets	$40	$37.50
	Social media	Free	Free
	Announcements	Free	Free
Venue			
	Community Terrace	Free	Free
Equipment			
	Griddles	Free	Free
	Microphone/stereo	Free	Free
Materials			
	Chairs/tables	Free	Free
	Plates/cups/utensils	$35	$36.16
	Napkins	$10	$8.74
Food/drink			
	Pancake mix	$25	$24.44
	Toppings	$20	$21.02
	Drinks	$25	$22.75
	Other (eggs, oil, etc.)	$15	$14.89
Total expenses		$170 (budget)	$165.50
Ticket sales			
	Adult ($5.00)		42 ($210)
	Kids ($3.00)		27 ($81)
Total ticket sales			$291
Total expenses			$165.50
Total profit			$125.50

Your Turn

Go to thoughtfullearning.com/p460 to download a budget sheet. Create a rough budget for an event you are planning or one you would like to plan.

Event Work Roster: Fund-Raiser

The success of any event depends on the volunteers knowing their assigned jobs and when to do them. The following work roster lists student and parent volunteers, when they need to report to duty, and what their duties are.

The first column names the job and the duties.

The second column gives a start time for each job.

The third column lists the students and adults who signed up for each job.

Pancake-Breakfast Work Roster

Job	Arrive By	Volunteers
Food Set up griddles, warming pans; prepare pancakes, sausage	6:30 a.m.	**Students:** Lon Chan, Tricia King, Monique Morris
		Adults: Lee Chan, Terrence McDonald, Clara Morris, Linda Peters
Beverages Brew coffee, mix punch, keep milk and orange juice on ice	6:30 a.m.	**Students:** Eli Goldberg, Tawny Reynolds, Lisa Vera
		Adults: Donna Goldberg, Ron Vera
Tables Set out place settings; bus tables; clean floors	6:45 a.m.	**Students:** Bendon Davis, Patty Seldon, Terri Turk
		Adults: David Davis
Tickets Set up table, cash box; sell tickets	6:45 a.m.	**Students:** Ashley Archer, Juan Rodriguez
		Adults: Pepe Rodriguez
Runners Odd jobs, getting supplies, assisting	7:00 a.m.	**Students:** Donny Curtis, Raul Jones

Your Turn

Create a work roster for an event you are planning. (Download a template at thoughtfullearning.com/p461.)

Inquire   To Run a Contest

1. **Question** the situation for the contest.
   - **Subject:** What sort of contest is it? What is the focus? What do you want out of it? Will there be a prize? How will you pick the winner?
   - **Purpose:** Why are you running the contest?
   - **Audience:** Who will participate? How will you convince people to take part?

2. **Plan** the contest by completing a planning sheet. (See page 261.)

3. **Research** the contest.
   - **Gather** information and ideas for contests. Compare your idea to similar contests. What worked for others? What didn't work for others? Decide what kind of prize will generate interest.
   - **Arrange** the steps or assignments for running the contest. Establish the contest rules in a logical order.
   - **Publicize** the contest using print or digital resources. Use social-media sites for further publicity.

4. **Create** the contest.
   - **Introduction:** In a short paragraph, introduce the contest as a fun, exciting event.
   - **Rules:** Make the rules clear and easy to follow. Answer the main questions the reader might have.
   - **Notes:** Explain any special rules or considerations that will make an entry acceptable or unacceptable.

5. **Improve** the contest.
   - **Evaluate** the contest.
     Does the contest fulfill its purpose?
     Will the participants enjoy the contest?
     What improvements can be made?
   - **Revise** your contest.
     Add any rules that answer the reader's key questions.
     Delete any rules that make the contest complicated.
   - **Edit**
     Check all print and digital material for spelling and grammar errors.

6 **Present** the contest to your audience.

Competition Rules: Contest

The following competition rules tell how students can enter the student-council school motto contest.

The beginning gives an overview of the contest.

Harrison Student-Council Motto Contest

Promote your school and win a month's worth of free hot lunches in the school motto contest! The Harrison Student Council is seeking a new school motto that shows off our pride. We want to hear from you!

Contest Rules

1. **Who can enter?** Anyone can enter the school motto contest.
2. **What can I win?** The first-place winner will receive a month's worth of free hot lunches and recognition as the creator of the winning motto. Three runners-up will also be recognized for their mottoes.
3. **How do I enter?** First, come up with a short, punchy motto that shows school pride. Then go to the Harrison Student Council Web site, click on the "Motto Contest" button, and fill out the form. Or go to the office and fill out the same form on paper.
4. **How long does the contest run?** The contest runs from Monday, September 27, through Tuesday, October 12.
5. **When will winners be announced and where?** The winner and runners-up will be announced on Monday, October 18, in the morning announcements, on the Web site, and in the school newspaper.
6. **How will entries be judged?** The student-council president, vice president, secretary, and treasurer will review all entries and vote on them, narrowing the field down to four finalists. Then Principal Reynolds will choose a winner.

Note: The student council will not accept any entries that are anonymous or that contain material that is not school appropriate.

The middle part gives specific rules.

A note explains any special rules.

Inquire   To Run a Campaign

1. **Question** the situation for the campaign.
   - **Subject:** Whom or what does the campaign promote? What candidate or cause should it focus on?
   - **Purpose:** Why am I running this campaign? What do I want people to do?
   - **Audience:** Who is my core audience? Who else can I convince? What do these groups need and want? How can I reach them?

2. **Plan** your campaign by completing a planning sheet. (See page 261.)

3. **Research** your campaign.
   - **Gather** information about what the audience needs or wants and how your cause or candidate can provide it.
   - **Focus** on the basic needs of the audience by developing a platform, planks, and a slogan (see page 466).
   - **Organize** others to assist in your campaign, giving them important roles and helping them work together.

4. **Create** your campaign, considering the following components.
   - **Posters:** Provide a clear slogan, an attention-grabbing visual, and details (see pages 418–419). Post online and on paper.
   - **Fliers:** Create slips to distribute at school or local businesses.
   - **Campaign Wear:** Create buttons, bracelets, or T-shirts (see pages 420–421).
   - **Speeches:** Write and deliver a speech for the cause or candidate. (See pages 440–445.)
   - **Personal Touch:** Introduce yourself and your cause or candidate, shake hands, and encourage people to get involved.

5. **Improve** your campaign.
   - **Evaluate** parts.
     Does each part fulfill my goals and objectives?
     Does each part focus on my cause or candidate? Does it convince people? Does it reach its audience? Is it working?
   - **Revise** your campaign to make it more effective.
     Remove parts that aren't needed.
     Rearrange parts that appear out of order.
     Rework parts that don't work well.
     Add new ways of reaching out to the audience.
   - **Perfect** each part, making sure it is polished and impressive.

6. **Present** your campaign, adjusting parts as you go.

Campaign Speech

The following campaign speech was recorded and presented online to support the animals in a local shelter.

Help Take Care of Pets-to-Be

The **beginning** appeals to the audience's emotions.

Do you have a pet at home? Did you once have a pet? Think of your pet's eyes as it looked up at you. Now imagine the hopeful eyes of dogs and cats waiting to become someone's pets. Until they do, the animals at the Dover Humane Society need you. There are many ways you can help them:

The **middle** provides a list of ways to help, from simple to more involved.

1. **Donate food and supplies:** Dog and cat food as well as rawhides, litter, and chew toys cost a little but help a lot.
2. **Donate time:** For just a few hours a week, you can help the trained veterinarians care for the animals at the shelter.
3. **Consider adopting a pet:** The animals in the shelter need good homes and loving owners.
4. **Avoid buying from pet stores:** Instead of increasing demand for dogs from "puppy mills," help a homeless animal.
5. **Report cruelty or neglect:** Make sure that the animals you see daily are being well cared for.

The **ending** calls the reader to act—"Help take care of these pets-to-be."

The dogs and cats at the Dover Humane Society may not be your pets, but they will belong to someone someday. Help take care of these pets-to-be.

Targeting Your Campaign

Remember that a campaign must target real needs in order to work. Consult the needs pyramid developed by Abraham Maslow. What needs does your cause or candidate address?

morality, creativity, problem solving

self-esteem, respect, achievement, confidence

friendship, family, acceptance

health, property, security, employment

air, water, food, clothing, shelter, sleep

Your Turn

Write down the needs you will address. For example, the writer of the speech on page 465 appealed to property, friendship, family, and acceptance.

Planks

In a political campaign, a plank is a statement that addresses a core idea connected to the audience's needs. A set of planks is called a platform.

Your Turn

Write planks for your campaign. Start by listing audience needs on the left. Then, for each need, complete the sentence "We believe that . . ." by stating an idea that meets the need. Here's an example:

Audience Need	Plank of Campaign
Property	We believe that _every pet deserves a loving owner._
Friendship	We believe that _a pet can be a person's best friend._
Family	We believe that _a pet is part of the family._
Acceptance	We believe that _a pet accepts you as you are._

Slogan

Every campaign needs a catchy slogan that will fit on buttons, shirts, and posters—and will stick in people's minds.

Your Turn

Write a slogan beginning with a command word and telling the audience what to do.

Help take care of these pets-to-be!

Publicity

Of course, a campaign is all about getting the word out and convincing people. Here are some of the options for presenting your slogan and the main points (planks) of your campaign.

- **A poster or flier** provides visual persuasion. It features a strong slogan, an engaging visual, and the details about how the audience needs to act. (For sample posters, see pages 314, 389, 419.) Posters should be printed, posted, and also displayed online in places that your audience visits.

- **An event** gathers people together for a cause. (See pages 458–463.) Sample events include rallies, demonstrations, contests, speeches, and debates.

- **A speech** allows you to persuade by performing, using tone of voice, facial expressions, and body language to communicate. (For sample speeches, see pages 441, 444–445, 465.) You can also use multimedia and props to make your point.

- **A debate** takes a speech to the next level. In a debate, you argue for your position and respond against the position of an opponent. Debates help define an issue through argumentation and the exchange of ideas.

- **The "personal touch"** means connecting with the audience one-on-one. Greet the person, smile, shake hands, explain what your campaign is trying to do, and encourage the person to help.

- **Social media** allow you to deliver your message to anyone in the world in a timely fashion. You can use social media to present your ideas in the form of short messages, Web links, or audio and visual media. (For more on social media, see pages 139–154.) The key to good publicity is being social, not pushy. Show off your personality!

Your Turn

List the types of publicity you will use to promote your campaign.

Inquire To Create a Club

1. **Question** the situation for your club.
   - **Subject:** What is the focus? What will members have in common?
   - **Purpose:** What is the purpose of the club? Why will people join? What will they get out of being involved?
   - **Audience:** Who will belong to the club? Who will want to join?

2. **Plan** your club by completing a planning sheet. (See page 261.)

3. **Research** the best way to set up your club.
   - **Learn** as much as you can about the focus of the club and the people who are interested in that focus.
   - **Network** in person or online with others who have this interest.
   - **Study** similar clubs to learn how they are organized, how often they meet, who attends, and how they like the club.
   - **Organize** your club, writing a mission statement, telling who is in charge and how decisions are made, and deciding how people join.
   - **Find** a place to hold meetings and ask possible members when and how often they could meet. For school clubs, find an advisor.

4. **Create** your club.
   - **Invite** people to come to the first meeting.
   - **Hold** a first meeting and explain the purpose of the club. Have people introduce themselves; ask for ideas and input.
   - **Plan** a typical activity for your club. Focus on the topic of interest, and make the activity fun and interactive.
   - **Encourage** everyone to return for the next meeting, giving the time and place.

5. **Improve** your club.
   - **Evaluate** the meetings.
     Do they achieve your goals for the club?
     Do they focus on the topic? Do they fulfill their purpose?
     Do people enjoy them and keep coming back?
   - **Refine** your meetings.
     Remove activities or parts that are off topic or uninteresting.
     Rearrange meeting times and places for members' convenience.
     Rework the club charter as needed.
     Add new activities and invite new members.

6. **Present** your club, writing an article about it.

Club Charter

Official clubs often have charters—documents that spell out the most important features of the club. Here is an example.

An opening statement identifies the purpose of the club.

Live Poets Society Charter

Mission Statement

The Live Poets Society is a student club for anyone interested in writing, reading, and talking about poetry. Our purpose is to

- **encourage** people to write and share poetry.
- **help** poets improve their work by providing helpful feedback.
- **create** a community for poets and poetry lovers.
- **promote** poetry reading and writing in our school and community.

Times, dates, and locations are provided.

Meetings

The Live Poets Society meets every Tuesday after school in Mrs. Schmaling's room, 201, from 3:00 to 4:00 p.m.

Membership requirements are provided.

Membership

The Live Poets Society is open to any student at Brighton School. To join, students only need to show up.

The club structure is outlined.

Leadership

The Live Poets Society has a student leader who is elected each year at the first meeting of the club. The society also has a faculty advisor (Mrs. Schmaling).

Your Turn

Create a charter for a club or an organization you would like to start. Download a charter template from thoughtfullearning.com/p469.

Types of Clubs

Here is an overview of some general types of clubs. If none of these types fits your purpose, create a unique club of your own.

Social

Some clubs are created for the purpose of getting together with people and having fun. For these clubs, the main focus is the people within the club.

Honors

An honors club connects people who are outstanding in some (or many) ways. An honor society is made up of people who excel in academics and involvement.

Interest-Based

Other clubs gather people who share a common interest such as chess, politics, drama, model building, paintball, and so on. The heart of the club is the common interest.

Cause-Based

A cause-based club takes an interest one step further, stating a desire to change a situation. These clubs launch campaigns to help the poor, fight cancer, rally for rights, and so on.

Event-Based

An event-based club is connected to specific periodic activities. A booster club might gather to watch every football game or every debate of their school teams. A supper club meets once a week to share a meal.

Service

Some clubs, such as Circle-K, are set up to encourage members to serve their communities. Club members volunteer to help with community events such as food drives, fairs, farmers markets, and other events.

Your Turn

Pick three types of clubs from above. Then, for each type, name the focus of a club you might form.

How to Do Everything

One of the early titles that we brainstormed for *Inquire* was *How to Do Everything*. That title didn't stick, but it captures the idea of the book. If you can think critically and creatively, if you can collaborate and communicate and problem solve, you can do anything. Inquiry is the process for successfully doing everything from grocery shopping to landing human beings on Mars.

So, what do you want to do? Anything is possible. You have the tools in your hands and in your head. Use them to create the best possible future.

Your Turn

Go out there and find your future. But when you touch down on some distant world, send us an e-mail to tell us you have arrived safely: contact@thoughtfullearning.com. We look forward to hearing from you!

Index